COVER: Fresco from the Portrait of America series by Diego Rivera. In the foreground are Benjamin Franklin and Tom Paine presenting the Rights of Man to the masses. Behind them, to the right, is a Stamp Act demonstration and a tarred and feathered British stamp agent; Sam Adams looks on. Behind him a group of signers of the Declaration of Independence stands in front of Independence Hall. The scene at the center and left is the Boston Massacre, with Crispus Attucks at the head of the colonists.

America's Revolutionary Heritage

Marxist essays edited with an
introduction by George Novack

PATHFINDER PRESS   NEW YORK

Library of Congress Catalog Card Number 76-12292
ISBN cloth 0-87348-464-9; paper 0-87348-465-7
Printed in the United States of America

PATHFINDER PRESS, INC.
410 West Street, New York, N.Y. 10014

Contents

THE SLAVOCRACY

THE SECOND AMERICAN REVOLUTION

THE TRIUMPH OF THE MONOPOLISTS

THE FIRST WAVE OF FEMINISM

Introduction

Two hundred years ago the American colonists waged a War of Independence against British tyranny and economic domination—the first victorious national liberation struggle of modern times. Today, when many Americans are reexamining our revolutionary heritage, the publication of this new edition is especially timely and appropriate.

The essays on various aspects of American history collected in this volume appeared over a span of forty years in the *International Socialist Review* and its predecessors, *The New International* and *Fourth International*.* They were prompted by special occasions or written in response to particular problems. Yet all have been motivated by a comprehensive conception of the rise of American civilization that differs in essentials from the views taught in the schools and universities and accepted as gospel by most scholars and students.

Is There a Pattern in American History?

The most popular nineteenth-century historians of the United States, such as George Bancroft and John Fiske, had no doubts about the significance of our history. They were convinced, along with most of their contemporaries, that the ascendancy of the Yankee republic exhibited, above all, the triumph of the spirit of liberty and the institutions of democracy peculiar to the Anglo-

---

* With the exception of "The Rise and Fall of the Cotton Kingdom," originally written in 1939, which appeared in 1968 in *Studies in Afro-American History,* published by the National Education Department of the Socialist Workers Party.

Saxon genius—achievements that were god-guided and god-given.

The liberal scholars of our own day are far less certain than the older patriotic nationalist historians that any definite or dominant pattern can be discerned in the era extending from the European discovery of the New World to the revelation that capitalist America had a special mission to defend "freedom" against the aggressions of communist totalitarianism.

In *America as a Civilization* Max Lerner, the *New York Post* syndicated columnist who teaches at Brandeis University, lists twenty efforts by other authors to capture the uniqueness of the American experience. One picks out the lack of a feudal past, another the refusal to accept authority, a third the multiplicity of ethnic groups, and so on. None of their answers satisfy him. What comes forth when he seeks an explanation of his own?

Let another authority, Daniel Bell, former *Fortune* editor and now professor of sociology at Harvard, tell us. In a review reprinted in *The End of Ideology* he points out that Lerner's treatment of American civilization lacks any coherence or unifying vision. Bell writes: "In the end, like a mountain climber unable to gain a foothold on the slippery rock face, he suddenly lets go, and says: 'There is no single talisman to the secret of American civilization.'"

Bell himself does not intend to remedy the deficiency he accurately spots in Lerner. Instead he agrees that it is fruitless to try to find any underlying organizing principle in the development of our nation. "To ask, What is the Secret of America? is to pose a metaphysical question whose purpose is either ideological or mythopoeic."

According to him, scholars can determine why and how certain particular "configurations of character and institutions have emerged in the United States." That is all. They cannot go beyond that point. There is no explanation available for the general course of American history.

This is like saying: it is possible to chart the lifeline of a specific corporation, like General Motors, but not the fundamental tendency toward the dominance of monopolies in our economy or the role such a tendency plays in the development of American and world capitalism in our century. Such a patchwork procedure deprives historical knowledge of any internal causation, regular sequence, and consistency.

In 1963 Oscar Handlin published *The Americans: A New*

History of the People of the United States. In its last section the Harvard professor asked what was the sum and substance of his review of 355 years of American life. He concluded that experts like himself can only tell what happened but cannot explain it. Let us listen to his musings:

> . . . at the typing machine, a man wonders: meaning? How fond his predecessors were of geometric analogies—progress, a straight line up; decay, a straight line down; a spiral upward; a wavy, wavy cycle. How fond they were of purpose—the hand of God, the Over-soul, the evolutionary first cause, the dialectic of the class struggle. Perhaps.
>
> It is not his task to subject the complex drama the words tap out to any such enfolding figures. If he can explain *how*, let others believe each their own *why*. There is meaning enough in the story itself.

Such a purely descriptive way of writing history is as unsatisfying and unscientific as its agnostic conclusion. All genuine science, including the science of history, seeks to find out not only the how but the why, the causes of what happened. Empiricism, pragmatism, positivism can rest content with a surface description of the course of development. But a straight narration of events is only the first step in scientific inquiry about the historical process, not its end or major purpose. The next stage is to ascertain why, under the given circumstances, things turned out as they did and not otherwise.

A scientific method ought to distinguish the mainstream of progress from the minor eddies and crosscurrents in the flux of American events. This may not have been what its participants or its chief protagonists thought it was at the time they helped make that history. They may well have been mistaken about the real nature and direction of their collective efforts, however much of the truth they grasped. But a historical method which probes the dynamics of the whole process should be able to disclose the essential unity of the constituent stages which resulted in its present state and will shape the next one.

However, the wisdom of Brandeis, Columbia, and Harvard as conveyed by these learned liberals coincides in a common skepticism that admits no master key to unlock the secrets of our development as a nation.

Is the situation really so hopeless? These Marxist essays on American history attempt to show that meaningful insights into the motive forces of our national life—its main line of march and eventual outcome—are much more possible than these skeptics make out. It is possible to make sense out of the overall course of American history and assess its fundamental meaning. The mysteries that so baffle the liberal schools of historians and sociologists can be deciphered with the aid of a correct method of investigation: the theory of historical materialism which guided the production of these articles.

American History in World History

American history has first of all to be approached as part of something much greater than itself. It is both a subordinate segment and a continuing product of world history. In the evolution of its social organization, humanity has ascended by successive steps from savagery through barbarism to civilization. Civilization itself, which originated in the Middle East, is less than ten thousand years old. During that time humanity has gone through various forms of society ranging from slavery to modern capitalism. Having reached its peak, this final embodiment of class society is cracking up and beginning to be supplanted by the rudiments of a higher order, the world system of socialism.

This, in brief, has been the main route of the human race as it has climbed from animality to the atomic age. Where do the American people fit into this world-historical procession, what place does our national history occupy in this evolutionary order?

From this universal standpoint the history of humanity in North America breaks into two major divisions marked by qualitatively different types of social structure. Humanity has lived in the Eastern Hemisphere for over a million years; the Americas have been inhabited for only about thirty thousand years. The first comers migrated from Siberia over the Bering Strait, which was then connected with the Alaskan mainland. Their descendants thereafter fanned out slowly, down to the tip of South America and over to the Atlantic Coast. This epoch of tribal life, when the Indians had exclusive possession of the Americas, evolved apart from the Old World. By their own efforts the aborigines attained the heights of the Mayan, Toltec, Aztec, and Inca cultures. However, despite many remarkable achievements, they did not pass beyond the Stone Age or quite reach the threshold of a well-defined class society, whatever aristocratic features they possessed.

Civilization, private property, and other institutions and

customs of a highly advanced class-divided system were first brought to America through the West Europeans who landed here from the sixteenth century on. Modern American history opens at this juncture. The coming of the white invaders marked a decisive sociological turn because they brought something basically novel with them. Along with many things belonging to the more ancient past, they imported a particular mode of civilized life and culture, the highest then attained. This was the capitalist type of social relation. Primitive collectivism was succeeded by the bourgeois individualism which has been gathering strength in North America for the past five hundred years.

American and World Capitalism

The self-contained, purely internal evolution of America was ended once it was drawn into the mainstream of civilization. Thenceforth the key to American history is to be found in the impact and influence of events in the maritime countries of Western Europe upon this hemisphere, in the interactions and relations of the Old World and the New. The settlement of North America was occasioned by the unsettlement of Europe, which was undergoing what was the most profound social transformation before the anticapitalist upheavals of our own century. This was the overcoming of feudalism by the forces of the bourgeois order.

The economic processes which brought about this revolution began in the field of exchange and subsequently passed over into the domain of production. The creation and extension of a world market based upon an international division of labor for the first time supplied the impetus and incentives for an unprecedented growth of commerce along capitalist lines. The leading discoverers, explorers, and settlers of Spanish, Portuguese, French, Italian, Dutch, and English origin sailed across the Atlantic for very material, even transparently mercenary, motives. They aimed to grab wealth by opening new trade routes; plundering the natives of precious metals; selling and exploiting slave and indentured labor; growing cheap crops of staples like sugar, tobacco, and indigo for the world market; and planting colonies to produce other articles of value for the European economy (furs, hides, lumber, fish, etc.). The coastal colonies were outposts of business enterprise, branches of the budding, bustling commercial capitalism which flourished under monarchical regimes as in

France, or under republican auspices as in Holland and Cromwellian England.

This fact holds the chief clue to American history after 1492. Its quintessence consists in the introduction, establishment, and expansion of capitalist relations on American soil. The three million Europeans and Africans who inhabited the colonies at the time of the First Revolution had come for a variety of reasons: the Blacks as slaves, the white indentured servants under direct economic compulsion, the Puritans and others for religious motives, and many of the pioneer immigrants to improve their living conditions and prospects. Irrespective of their motivations or compulsions, they all had to fit into a social structure increasingly shaped by private property, profiteering, and a network of bourgeois institutions.

The ordinary citizen has a quite different picture of America's rise to eminence. The popular image of our national greatness is patterned after Horatio Alger's success stories. Sturdy pioneers, rugged individualists on the frontier, shook off foreign influences, giving birth to an unalloyed American spirit, going forward to conquer a continent and making the most spectacular progress of all time. This oversimplified version has bits of fact in it. But it leaves out the most important of all the factors which directed and determined the course of American civilization.

That factor is the special relation the North Americans have had with the development of the rest of the world capitalist system. This is, indeed, the prime peculiarity of our national history.

The history of the American people has above all recorded the formation and the transformation through successive stages of its bourgeois society, not simply within the changing national boundaries but on the world arena. This distinguishes our history from that of all the great nations of Europe and Asia. England, France, Russia, Germany, Japan, and China all had long precapitalist pasts and sturdy feudal institutions which have powerfully marked their social evolution to this day. Unlike them, North American civilization has from its beginnings been raised upon the commercial, financial, industrial and property relations characteristic of the bourgeois way of life and labor.

Since capitalism is international by its very nature, it is impossible to understand the central developments in any period of American history since the end of the sixteenth century without considering its connections with what was happening in the whole of the capitalist system at that juncture. This is the central thesis of the article entitled: "Historians and the Belated Rise of American Imperialism."

The New World was opened up by the Old as part of its leap from feudalism to capitalism, and the North American colonies were the transatlantic offspring of the European money-makers. As the Scottish historian Edmund Wright has written in his study of colonial America entitled *Fabric of Freedom:* "The colonies had been founded expressly for profit, either for those who settled the land, for the proprietor to whom a charter was granted, or for the company under whose direction the whole venture was risked." (p. 34.)

The main paths of colonial history from the first overseas expeditions to the last musket fired at Yorktown were marked out by the impulses and requirements emanating from the capitalist world market headquartered in Western Europe. Independence did not remove the dependence of the American economy upon Europe. This was not fully overcome until the war of 1914-18, when the relations between the Old World and the New underwent a sharp reversal.

The Uprooting of Precapitalist Forces

While capitalist conditions, both international and national, have been paramount, other, older kinds of social formations have also participated in the making of American history. But their roles were not decisive in shaping its main direction and destination. None of the precapitalist forces could maintain predominance on this continent. All were subordinated by the operations of bourgeois society and finally subjugated and eliminated by its agents.

The three most important powers based on precapitalist forms of labor were the Indian tribes, the semifeudal proprietors, and the slaveholding planters. All contributed to the building of the bourgeois order in its formative stages: the Indians through the fur trade; the landed proprietors by importing capital, labor, tools, and provisions into the new settlements; the planters through the crops they grew and the wilderness areas their forced laborers cleared and cultivated. But, after performing useful services, they were themselves cleared away as they became obstacles to the further expansion of bourgeois property, production, and power.

The fate of the Indians, pushed back and slaughtered over four centuries, is well known. As the articles on the destruction of Indian tribalism aim to prove, this war to the knife was not simply a racial conflict between white and red as it is usually depicted. It was a clash between two antagonistic and irreconcilable types of socioeconomic organization: one rooted in Stone Age hunting, food gathering, and gardening, marked by collective customs; the other based upon private property and the profiteering individualism of an aggressive bourgeoisie, from rich merchants to small farmers.

The next group to collide with the native bourgeois forces was the landed proprietors and the crown retinue, which administered the colonies largely for the benefit of the ten thousand merchants, manufacturers, and landlords ruling Britain. These semifeudal and foreign oppressors and exploiters were driven out by the War of Independence. This First American Revolution culminated in a partial and temporary victory for the northern moneyed interests, which had to share supreme power in the young republic with the southern planters.

Then the rise of the Cotton Kingdom imparted an ironic twist to our national development. This agricultural anachronism based on slave labor was the product of two interlinked innovations: the invention of the cotton gin, and the industrial revolution of the steam engine and the factory. The insatiable demands of England and New England's textile manufacturers for cotton lifted the southern slaveholders to the heights. They dominated this country for decades, just as the monopolists do today.

In order to dislodge these rivals from sovereignty and consummate their conquest of power, the northern industrial interests had to wait until the further development of American and world capitalism created a regroupment of social forces strong and resolute enough to overwhelm the slaveholders. This was brought into being by the middle of the nineteenth century. If the first phase of the industrial revolution (centered in England) exalted the cotton planters, its second phase (centered in the United States) led to their downfall, dispossession, and destruction at the hands of the newly enriched captains of industry and their allies, the small farmers of the Northwest, the insurgent slaves, and the urban wageworkers.

The Civil War was the Second American Revolution, or more precisely the concluding stage of the bourgeois-democratic revolution in this country. This irrepressible conflict between the slaveowners and the northern industrialists was the last of the death grapples for supremacy between the precapitalist and the procapitalist elements, which cleared the ground for the fullest and freest expansion of capitalist enterprise. Viewed in this light, the first 350 years of American history provided a battleground from which the masters of capital emerged in secure possession of the major sources of wealth and means of power. When more primitive and less productive systems of labor stood in the way of oncoming capitalism, they were ultimately overcome and eradicated, no matter how powerful they appeared at any given time, no matter how hard they fought to survive or what alliances they had. The Indians were wiped out; the British overlords and their feudal dependents were expelled; the insurrectionary slaveholders were "gone with the wind" of the Civil War.

The Supremacy of Big Business

American history demonstrates that the capitalists of the United States have not been averse to all revolutions but only to those which bring them no benefit. In past centuries they got rid of whatever antagonists blocked their advancement and rulership by the most forceful means.

Having crushed the Confederacy on the battlefield, abolished four billion dollars' worth of property in slaves, and shattered the political hegemony of the planters, the northern captains of industry and finance proceeded to fortify their economic, political, and cultural control. From the end of Reconstruction to the First World War, they made the most of their unexampled opportunities. The Robber Barons feasted at what Vernon Parrington called "The Great Barbecue" as the trusts came to dominate the economy. The reconstituted two-party system served big business well. So did the Supreme Court, which ruled in 1886 that the Fourteenth Amendment to the Constitution protected corporate as well as civil rights. (In practice, it shielded the first much better than the second.)

Time and again the hosts of the Populist and Progressive crusades endeavored to resist the piracies of the plutocrats and reverse the concentration of power in their hands. Like the fabled Irish warriors, "they went forth to battle but always fell." Although the antimonopolist reformers did succeed in gaining some minor concessions, they proved incapable of dislodging big money from its dominion. The futility of their efforts to curb the monopolists was best exemplified by what happened in the oil industry. In 1909 the federal government ordered the Standard Oil octopus severed into a number of parts. But as soon as it was dismembered, it was recombined behind the scenes by the Rockefeller banking interests.

Nowadays the oil magnates exert greater influence on national and international affairs than ever before. They have demonstrated their unchecked power by manufacturing a worldwide energy crisis, which succeeded in boosting profits in the oil industry to record heights. Professor Robert Engler, in his study *The Politics of Oil,* maintains that the oil industry in its dependence on huge financial benefits from the government, its privileged tax position, and its influence on domestic and foreign politics "virtually has organized a government within a government—an entity with tremendous power and insufficient responsibility." Together with the "military-industrial complex" the oil magnates function as prime decision-makers on the commanding heights of the United States.

Capitalist competition, resulting in the take-over of smaller enterprises by larger concerns, fosters the inevitable growth of monopoly and the increasing concentration of the ownership and power of the American ruling class, which with each passing year becomes smaller, more entrenched, more wealthy, and more dominant in the economy and the state apparatus. This has been well documented by Morton Mintz and Jerry Cohen in *America, Inc.* (New York: Dell, 1971): "In 1968 the one hundred largest corporations had a greater share of manufacturing assets than the two hundred largest had in 1950, and the two hundred largest in 1968 controlled a share equal to that held by the thousand largest in 1941." (p. 61.) In 1969, they also report, the top two hundred manufacturing corporations controlled two-thirds of all assets held by corporate manufacturers. This gigantic concentration of power is further consolidated through the control exercised by banks at the pinnacle of the economic pyramid.

Guidelines for Analyzing America's Evolution

No set of summery assertions can encompass the diversity, deviations, and complexities of five hundred years in the life of a colossal nation like the United States. Nevertheless, the principal landmarks and turning points in the road traveled by the

American people can be mapped. The essential can be separated from the incidental, the durable from the episodic and ephemeral, the preponderant from the less effective factors in the making of events.

The following propositions can be useful guidelines for analyzing American history to date; they can also serve as guideposts to the next stage of our national progress.

1. From the standpoint of universal human development, American history is divided into two opposing parts. These are the thirty thousand years of preclass social life based upon Indian tribal collectivism, and the five hundred years of class society ushered in by the Europeans.

2. American civilization is above all the product of the growth of the bourgeois system both on an international and on a national scale.

3. The process of building capitalism on this continent has passed through three main phases, each bound up with a corresponding stage of world economic development from commercial through industrial to monopolist capitalism. The colonial period from 1492 to 1789 witnessed the origin and formation of its social structure and political superstructure; the decades between the beginning of the Republic and the end of the Civil War saw the strengthening of industrial capitalism and its victory over the slave power; the century since has seen the supremacy of big business and high finance.

4. All the precapitalist forms and forces—the Indians, the landed proprietors, and the slaveholders—were caught up, swept along, and ultimately submerged by the omnipotent trend toward the construction and consolidation of the most highly developed of all national capitalisms.

5. The struggles of these hostile social formations supplied the main internal driving forces for forward movement in the first two stages of American civilization. The contests for supremacy between the precapitalist and procapitalist forces culminated in two great social and political revolutions, which represented the high points in the activity of the bourgeois-democratic elements in our national life.

6. In the past, capitalism has made immense contributions to human advancement and brought many benefits to the American people. But American civilization is not preordained to remain encased indefinitely within the bourgeois framework in which it has taken shape and operated up to now. The historical function

of capitalism has been to prepare the preconditions and the forces for its own replacement by a new and superior way of living and working together.

7. Contemporary capitalism has become the source and sustainer of the most malignant evils at home and abroad. The deepening world crisis of imperialism, the consequences of Washington's foreign policies and the menace of nuclear warfare, coupled with the incapacity of U.S. capitalism to provide adequate solutions to the problems of poverty, inflation, unemployment, discrimination, and other scourges, have prepared the ground for a resurgence of social struggles in this country.

8. Since the Republican-Democratic compromise of 1876 restored white supremacy in the South, the development of the United States has been marked by three major processes. These are the conversion of industrial into monopolist and imperialist capitalism, the growth of organized labor, and the awakening of the Black masses. The most important social struggles of this period have been the contest between the plutocrats and plebeians, which ended in defeat for the reformism of the middle class Progressives; the conflict between the big employers and wageworkers, which culminated in the industrial union organizing drive of the 1930s; and the rise of the Black liberation struggle, which initiated a new wave of radicalization in the United States.

9. The demands of the American people for a better life and a secure future can be realized only through changes of greater magnitude than those achieved by the War of Independence and the Civil War. Like the crown rulers and the Cotton Kings before them, the monopolists will have to be deposed and expropriated by the revolutionary action of the insurgent masses.

10. The specific features of capitalist oppression in the U.S. have made it clear that the third American revolution will have a combined character. It will be a revolution by the oppressed nationalities for self-determination together with a working-class revolution to take power, which will open the road to the destruction of capitalist exploitation, alienation, oppression, racism, and sexism—and the construction of socialism, the first truly human social order.

George Novack
January 1976

THE NATIVE AMERICANS

The Conquest of the Indians

George Novack (1949)

The capitalist rulers of the United States rose to power through a series of violent struggles against precapitalist social forces. The first of these upheavals took place at the dawn of modern American history with the invasion of the Western Hemisphere by the nations of Western Europe and the conquest of the aboriginal inhabitants. The uprooting of the Indians played a significant part in clearing the way for bourgeois supremacy on this continent.

However, the pages of the most learned historians contain little recognition and less understanding of this connection between the overthrow of Indian tribalism and the development of bourgeois society in America. As a rule, they regard the ousting and obliteration of the natives simply as an incident in the spread of the white settlers over the continent. They may condemn the treatment of the Indians as a lamentable blot on the historical record, but they do not see that it has any important bearing upon the formation of the United States.

This conventional view of Indian-white relations is shared by conservative and liberal writers alike. In their classic liberal interpretation of *The Rise of American Civilization,* Charles and Mary Beard, for example, utterly fail to grasp the social significance of the wars against the Indians, making only scanty, disconnected references to them.

President Conant of Harvard supplied an instructive illustration of how far the Indian conquest has faded from the consciousness of bourgeois thinkers during a speech at the New York Herald Tribune Forum in October 1948: "In the first place, this nation, unlike most others, has not evolved from a state founded on a military conquest. As a consequence we have nowhere in our tradition the idea of an aristocracy descended from the conquerors and entitled to rule by right of birth. On the contrary, we have developed our greatness in a period in which a fluid society overran a rich and empty continent. . . ." Conant's speech summoned American educators to demonstrate in theoretical questions what American capitalism must prove in practice—the superiority of bourgeois ideas and methods over the "alien importations" of the "philosophy based on the writings of Marx, Engels, and Lenin." The Harvard president insisted that "not words, but facts" must be the weapons to convince the youth and defeat Marxism. The passage we have cited will hardly promote that purpose, for it contains two serious misstatements of fact about early American history.

In the first place, contrary to Conant's assertion, the bourgeois structure of this nation did "evolve from a state founded on a military conquest." It was the conquest of the Indian tribes, not to speak of wars against the Spanish, Dutch, and French, that gave England and her colonists mastery of North America.

Secondly, although North America in colonial times was far more thinly populated than Europe or Asia, it was scarcely "empty" of inhabitants. In order to occupy and overrun the continent, the pioneers first had to "empty" the land of its original possessors. The founders of Harvard could tell its president many tales of the difficulties involved in this task.

What are the reasons for this extraordinary blind spot in bourgeois historians and those who, like Conant, push to the extreme their preconceptions of our national origins?

There is, first of all, the weight of tradition. Historians continue to treat the Indians with the same disdain and lack of comprehension that their forefathers manifested in practice. The pioneers looked upon the Indians as little more than obnoxious obstacles in the path of their advancement who had to be cleared away by any means and at all costs. The English colonists rid their settlements of Indians as ruthlessly as they cleared the lands of trees and wild animals. In fact, they placed the Indian "varmints" and "serpents" on the same level as wild beasts. In early New England bounties were paid for Indian scalps as today they are awarded for the tails of predatory animals.

The contemporary professors do not know how to fit the Indians, and the facts of their dispossession and disappearance, into their schemes of interpretation any more than the pioneers were able to absorb them into bourgeois society. The government's final solution of the Indian problem has been to segregate the survivors in reservations, an American equivalent of the European concentration camps and the African compounds. The historians dispose of the Indians by also setting them off to one side, in a special category completely detached from the main course of American historical development.

Indeed, because of their unconscious and narrow class outlook, the bourgeois historians, on the whole, are hardly aware that the fate of the Indians presents any problem. They assume that private property must be the normal foundation of any "good" society. And so the annihilation of Indian collectivism by the white conquerers for the sake of private property seems so much in the nature of things as to require no explanation.

But there is more involved than inertia or indifference. Freud has explained individual lapses of memory by an unconscious wish to hide from whatever is shameful, fearful, socially unacceptable. Where a social lapse of memory occurs, a similar mechanism and similar motives for suppression are often at work, especially where representatives of ruling classes engage in systematic forgetfulness. That is the case here. The abominable treatment of the Indians is extremely unpleasant to contemplate, and equally unpleasant to explain.

At the bottom of their censorship lies the bourgeois attitude toward the communal character of Indian life. The bourgeois mind finds communism in any form so contrary to its values, so abhorrent and abnormal, that it recoils from its manifestations and instinctively strives to bury recollections of their existence. In any event, the run-of-the-mill historian feels little impulse to examine and explain primitive communism, although it was the cradle of humanity and, in particular, formed a starting point of modern American history.

Even contemporary writers sympathetic to the Indians, such as Oliver LaFarge, go out of their way to deny that the basic institutions of the Indians can be termed "communistic" even while offering evidence to the contrary. "The source of life, the land and its products, they [the Indians] owned in common," writes LaFarge in *As Long as the Grass Shall Grow.* (p. 25.) "Loose talkers have called this Communism. It is not." Here is a striking example of how deep anticommunist prejudice runs.

Class calculation reinforces this tendency toward suppression. An understanding of the customs of the Indians and the reasons for their extinction may raise doubts about the immortality of private property and the standards of bourgeois life. Such knowledge spread among an enlightened people may be dangerous to the pervasive ideas of the ruling class. Does it not indicate that, at least so far as the past is concerned, communism is not quite so alien to American soil as it is pictured by the witch-hunters?

Thus the expunging of the real facts about the Indians from historical memory today is no more accidental than was their physical elimination yesterday. Both have their ultimate source in the promotion of the material interests of the owners of private property and the champions of free enterprise.

Modern American society did not originate on unencumbered soil in the pure and painless way pictured by Conant. It arose from the disintegration and ruin of two ancient societies: European feudalism and primitive American communism. Its birth was attended by two violent social conflicts. One was the struggle between the feudal order and the rising forces of capitalism in the Old World. The other was the collision between Indian tribalism and European civilization, which resulted in the breakup of the Indian way of life as a prelude to the establishment of the bourgeois regime in North America.

The historians center their attention on the first process, and it is easy to understand why. Modern American society is the offspring of European civilization; its foundations rest upon a whole series of "alien importations" from across the Atlantic.

The contributions of the Indians in the making of modern America were not on the same scale and belonged to a different order. But this is no warrant for counting them as a negligible factor in the peculiar evolution of the American nation. For several centuries American events were conditioned by the struggle against the Indian tribes. And the European civilization transplanted to the New World grew at the direct expense of Indian life. Let us see why this was so.

In the Indian and the European, ancient society and modern civilization confronted each other and engaged in an unequal test of strength. Over thousands of years the Indians had worked out ways and means of living admirably suited to the North American wilderness. The North American Indians were organized in hundreds of thinly dispersed tribes, numbering from a few score to a few thousand people, bound together by ties of blood kinship. Each of these tiny tribes constituted a self-sufficient economic unit. They were far more directly and firmly attached to their natural habitats than to one another. The dispersed bands had little unity of action or power of resistance against enemies like the white man. They were easily pitted against one another since, despite an identity of social structure and institutions, few of them had any traditions of cooperation.

The sparseness and separation of the Indian population resulted from their method of producing the necessities of life. Although there was considerable diversity of conditions from tribe to tribe and from region to region, their basic economic features were remarkably uniform. Except along the seashores, most of the North American tribes lived mainly by hunting wild animals such as deer and buffalo. Fishing, fowling, berry-picking, and farming were important but accessory sources of subsistence. Every type of social organization has laws of population and population growth corresponding to its mode of production. It has been estimated that three square miles of hunting ground were required to sustain each Indian. This imposed narrow limits on the size of the Indian population. Each tribe had to occupy sizable areas to support its members. The Iroquois sometimes traveled hundreds of miles on their hunting expeditions.

The segmentation of the Indians into hundreds of petty tribal units and their slow but persistent expansion over the entire Western world had arisen from the inability of a foraging and hunting economy to sustain many people on a given area. This was likewise the main cause for the warfare between neighboring tribes and for the Indians' unyielding defense of their hunting and fishing grounds against invaders. Heckewelder reports that the Indians cut off the noses and ears of any individual found on their territory and sent him back to inform his chief that on the next occasion they would scalp him. (*The Evolution of Property,* by Paul Lafargue, p. 37.)

The only way to overcome the restrictions inherent in a hunting economy was through the development of stock raising or agriculture, a shift from food *collecting* to food *producing*. But unlike the Asians and Europeans, the Indians of North America domesticated no animals except the dog and the turkey. They had no horses, cattle, pigs, or sheep.

The Indians (that is, the Indian women, who did the work) proved to be outstanding agriculturists. They domesticated over forty useful plants, among them maize, tobacco, potatoes, tomatoes, peanuts, beans, and others that then and later had considerable economic importance. Agriculture based on maize production gave birth to the various grades of village Indians and made possible the more concentrated populations and brilliant achievements of the Mayan and Aztec cultures.

But Indian progress in agriculture became stymied by insurmountable technological barriers. The Indians derived their meat and clothing from wild game, not from tamed and tended animals. They did not invent the wheel or the axle; they did not know of iron. Their implements were mostly made of stone, wood, bone, and fiber. Without draft animals and iron, it was impossible to develop the plow or even an efficient and durable hoe.

Without these technological aids, agriculture could not advance to the point where it could yield enough food and grain to support extensive and constantly increasing bodies of people. According to recent investigations, it was the extinction of the forests and the exhaustion of the available corn-bearing lands cultivated by the crudest stick methods that eventually caused the collapse of Mayan culture. (See *The Ancient Maya,* by Sylvanus G. Morley, 1946.)

The whites, however, bore with them all the means for advanced agriculture accumulated since the invention of the animal-drawn plow. These improved implements and methods of cultivation were the stepping-stones by which Europe had approached capitalism. But along with superior tools and techniques of production the Europeans brought their correspondingly different property forms and relations.

Although the Indians possessed personal property, they were unfamiliar with private property in the means of production, or even in the distribution of the means of subsistence. They carried on their principal activities—hunting, fishing, cultivating, homemaking, and warfare—in a collective manner. The product of their labors was more or less equally shared among all members of the tribe.

Above all, the North American Indians knew no such thing as private property in land, which is the basis of all other kinds of private ownership in the means of production. When the whites arrived, there was not one acre from the Atlantic to the Pacific that belonged to a private person, that could be alienated from the community or assigned to anyone outside the tribe. The very idea that ancestral lands from which they drew their sustenance could be taken from the people, become an article of commerce, and be bought and sold was inconceivable, fantastic, and abhorrent to the Indian. Even when Indians were given money or goods for a title to their lands, they could not believe that this transaction involved the right to deprive them of their use forever.

"The earth is like fire and water that cannot be sold," said the Omahas. The Shawnee chief Tecumseh, who sought to combine all the Indians from Canada to Florida against the encroachment of the whites upon their hunting grounds, exclaimed: "Sell land! As well sell air and water. The Great Spirit gave them in common to all."

But the "Great Spirit" animating and dominating the whites had an entirely different revelation. The intruders looked upon the new-found lands and their occupants through the eyes of a civilization founded on opposite premises. To them it was natural to convert everything into private property and thereby exclude the rest of humanity from its use and enjoyment. The conquerors maintained that whatever existed in the New World, or came out of it, was to be vested either in an individual or a power separate and distinct from the community or towering above it, like the monarchy, the state, or the church. They did not exempt human beings from this process. The invaders seized not only the land but its inhabitants, and sought, wherever they could, to convert the Indians into their private possessions as chattel slaves.

Those who were driven across the Atlantic by religious and political persecution were a minority. The majority were motivated primarily by the lust for aggrandizement and the greed for personal gain. It was these material motives, more powerful than wind or wave, that propelled the first Europeans overseas and then inevitably brought them into collision with the aboriginal inhabitants.

The conquerors came as robbers and enslavers; they stayed as colonizers and traders. America had belonged to the Indian tribes both by hereditary right and by life-and-death need to maintain themselves and perpetuate their kind upon the tribal territories. The Europeans needed land not simply for hunting, trapping, and fishing, but for extensive agriculture, for lumbering, for settlements and trading centers, for commerce and manufacture —for private exploitation on an expanding scale.

Thus, regardless of their wishes, the Indians and Europeans were sharply counterposed to each other by virtue of their contradictory economic needs and aims. The Indians could maintain their economy, with its primitive communistic institutions and customs, its crude division of labor between the sexes, and its tribal ties of blood kinship, only by keeping the white man at bay. The newcomers could plant their settlements and expand their economic activities only by pressing upon the Indian tribes and snatching their territories. This antagonism, flowing from their diametrically opposed systems of production, governed the dealings between red and white from their first contacts.

The means by which the natives were enslaved, dispossessed, and exterminated cannot be set forth here in detail. The pattern of robbery, violence, debauchery, and trickery was fixed by the Spaniards as early as the landings of Columbus. In their lust for gold, Columbus and his men depopulated Hispaniola. Through overwork, abuse, starvation, despair, and disease, the original population of the island dwindled from 300,000 in 1492 to an actual count of 60,000 in 1508. Only 500 survived by 1548.

The same story was repeated on the mainland of North America time and again during the next four hundred years by the Dutch, the English, the French, and the Americans. The Indian wars in New England demonstrated how ruthless and irreconcilable was the conflict between the opposing social forces. While the first colonists in Massachusetts were busy securing a foothold, Indian neighbors established friendly and helpful ties with them. They gave the Pilgrims food in time of distress, taught them how to cultivate maize and tobacco and how to cope with the forest and its wildlife.

But the divines who enjoined the Puritans not to covet their neighbors' wives taught otherwise about the Indian hunting grounds. These religious and political leaders insisted that all land not actually occupied and cultivated belonged, not to the Indians, but to the Massachusetts Bay Colony, which they controlled. Roger Williams was tried and banished from Massachusetts in 1635 because he declared that "the Natives are the true owners" of the land. His heretical views on the land question were condemned as no less dangerous than his unorthodox religious opinions.

The New England colonists annexed the tribal lands by waging wars of extermination against the natives over the next eighty years, beginning with the Pequot War in the Connecticut Valley in 1643 and concluding with the expulsion of the Abenakis from the Maine and New Hampshire coasts in 1722. The fiercest of these conflicts, King Philip's War (1675-78), was directly provoked by the struggle over the land. The increase in white population in the Connecticut Valley from 22,500 in 1640 to 52,000 in 1675 whetted the land hunger of the settlers at the same time that it threatened to engulf the Indian hunting grounds.

Their defeats brought death or enslavement to the Indians, expulsion from the tribal territories, and distribution of their land to the whites. The rich corporation of Harvard University today derives income from landed property originally seized from these Indians "by military conquest." Shouldn't its president show more respect for the historical origins of his own state and for the deeds of his Pilgrim ancestors?

The same predatory policy was duplicated in the other colonies—and no less vigorously prosecuted after they secured independence. An itinerant preacher, Peter Cartwright, testifies in his autobiography concerning the conquest of Kentucky: "Kentucky was claimed by no particular tribe of Indians, but was regarded as a common hunting ground by the various tribes, east, west, north and south. It abounded in various valuable game, such as buffalo, elk, bear, deer, turkeys and many other smaller game, and hence the Indians struggled hard to keep the white people from taking possession of it. Many hard and bloody battles were fought, and thousands killed on both sides; and rightly it was named the 'land of blood.' But finally the Indians were overpowered, and the white man obtained a peaceful and quiet possession of it."

This combat to the death continued until the last frontier was settled and the choicest lands seized. "The roster of massacres of Indian men, women and children extends from the Great Swamp Massacre of 1696 in Rhode Island, through the killing of the friendly Christian Indians at Wyoming, Pennsylvania, when the republic was young, on through the friendly Arivaipas of Arizona, the winter camp of the Colorado Cheyennes, to the final dreadful spectacle of Wounded Knee in the year 1890," writes Oliver LaFarge. That is how America was taken from the Indians.

Before the white conquerors eradicated Indian society, the Indians passed through an intermediate stage in which their customary relations were considerably altered. The acquisition of horses and firearms from the Europeans opened up the prairies to the Indians in the interior by enabling them to range far more widely and effectively in hunting buffalo and deer. But the ensuing changes in the lives of the Plains tribes were accomplished by their independent efforts without direct intervention by the whites and within the framework of their ancient institutions.

The fur trade with the whites had quite different and damaging effects upon Indian life. The fur trade early became one of the most profitable and far-flung branches of commerce between North America and Europe. The fur factors, hunters, and trappers served as agents of the rich merchants and big chartered monopolies dominating the business and acted as advance scouts of capitalist civilization.

The Indians were first drawn into the orbit of capitalist commerce largely through extension of the fur trade. In the course of time the fur-trading tribes embraced all the North American Indians except those in the extreme South and Southwest. The growing interchange of products between them and the traders upset the relatively stable Indian existence.

At first this exchange of goods lifted the living standards and increased the wealth and population of the Indians. An iron ax was better than a stone hatchet; a rifle better than a bow and arrow. But, as the fur trade expanded, its evil consequences more and more asserted themselves. The call for ever-larger quantities of furs and skins by the wealthy classes here and abroad led to the rapid destruction of fur-bearing animals, which reproduced too slowly to meet this demand.

Indians without contact with western civilization were careful not to slaughter more animals than were needed for personal consumption. But once they trapped and hunted for the market, other incentives came into play. These drove the tribes whose hunting and fishing grounds approached exhaustion into bitter competition with adjoining tribes for control of the available supply.

The new conditions produced bloody clashes between competing tribes as well as with the white men who sought possession of the hunting grounds for their own reasons. In trade and war, occupations which are not always easily distinguishable, the role of firearms proved decisive. The Indians could not manufacture or repair firearms or make powder. They had to bargain with the whites for these and the other indispensable means of production and destruction upon which their lives and livelihoods came to depend.

This placed the Indians at the mercy of bearers of the more advanced culture—who showed them little mercy. Consequently the Indians became the victims not only of civilized diseases and such civilized vices as alcoholism and prostitution, but also of the good things acquired from the Europeans. And through the fur trade they were sucked into a vortex of commercial rivalry, intertribal and international wars that carried them toward destruction.

Various Indian tribes sought to defend themselves and their hunting grounds from relentless encroachment of the colonists by confederation, or by allying themselves with one great power against another. They leagued with the French against the British, the British against the French, the Spanish against the British, and the king against the Patriots. Later some southern tribes were to attach themselves to the Confederacy against the Union.

Although the Indians fought with unexampled courage and tenacity, neither heroic sacrifices nor unequal and unstable alliances could save them. They lacked the numbers, the organization, and above all the productive capacity for carrying on sustained warfare. They had to limit themselves largely to border raids and scalping expeditions and were often laid low by hunger in winter and scarcity of weapons and ammunition. Neither singly nor in combination could the natives do more than delay the onward march of their white adversaries. Their history is essentially a record of one long retreat across the continent under the onslaught of the conquerors.

The French had more harmonious relations with the Indians than the English, primarily because of differences in their economic aims and activities. Except for the Quebec *habitants,* the French were mainly engaged in hunting and trading; they did not covet the Indian lands but sought to maintain favorable trade relations with the tribes. It is recorded that for two centuries, from 1690 to 1870, there were only sporadic acts of hostility between the natives and agents of the Hudson Bay Company, which monopolized the Indian trade in Canada. The reason? "In no case, did the French intruders ask, as did the English colonists, for deeds of territory." (*Narrative and Critical History of America,* ed. by Justin Winsor, Vol. I, p. 285.)

Behind the English hunters and traders swarmed the solid ranks of colonizers, farmers, planters, speculators, and landlords who wanted the Indian hunting grounds for their own property.

This contrast was emphasized by Duquesne when he tried to win the Iroquois from their friendship with Britain. The

Frenchman told them: "Are you ignorant of the difference between the king of England and the king of France? Go see the forts our king has established and you will see that you can still hunt under their very walls. They have been placed for your advantage in places which you frequent. The English, on the contrary, are no sooner in possession of a place than the game is driven away. The forest falls before them as they advance and the soil is laid bare, so that you can scarce find the wherewithal to erect shelter for the night."

The incompatibility of the hunting economy with advancing agriculture also became a major source of division between the American colonists and the English government. King George's proclamation of 1763 forbade royal governors to grant land or titles beyond the Alleghenies or private persons to buy land from the Indians. This Quebec Act, designed to monopolize the fur trade for the English and contain colonial settlement on the coastal side of the Allegheny Mountains, imparted a powerful stimulant to colonial revolt.

The height of the onslaught against the Indians was attained when the capitalists took complete command of the government. The three decades following the Civil War have been correctly called by the historian Bancroft "the history of aboriginal extermination." The Civil War generals turned from battle against the slaveholders to consummate the conquest of the Indians in the West. General Halleck urged that the Apaches "be hunted and exterminated," and General Sheridan uttered his notorious remark, "There are no good Indians but dead Indians." The attitude toward the Indians was bluntly expressed by the commissioner of Indian Affairs in his report to Congress in 1870: "When treating with savage men as with savage beasts, no question of national honor can arise. Whether to fight, to run away, or to employ a ruse, is only a question of expediency."

Capitalist civilization could not stop halfway at reconstructing Indian life and subordinating it to its needs. With the expansion of settlement, the colonists kept pushing the Indians westward, hemming in their living space, violating agreements with them, taking over more and more of their territories. The late nineteenth century witnessed the final mopping-up operations by which the Indians were deprived of their lives, their lands, and their independence. The few hundred thousand survivors were then imprisoned in reservations under government guard.

Victimization of the Indians did not cease even after they had been reduced to an impotent remnant on the reservations. Lands which had not been seized by force were thereafter stolen by fraud. Through the land allotment system the Bureau of Indian Affairs generously gave a small piece of the tribal lands to each Indian, declared the remainder "surplus," and sold or allotted it to the whites. Thus the last of the communal lands, with some exceptions, were broken up and absorbed into the system of private property and free enterprise.

The insuperable opposition between the two social systems was equally evident on the side of the Indians in their determination to preserve their established ways. There was no lack of attempts, for example, to enslave the natives. But they defended their freedom as fiercely as their lands. The Indians could not suffer servitude. Such a condition was repugnant to their habits, feelings, and productive activities. They resisted to the death any reversal in their status and occupations, sickened in captivity, refused to reproduce, and died off. They could not be broken on the wheel of slave agriculture.

It has always been a difficult and protracted job to reshape human material molded by one social system into the labor conditions of another, especially when this involves degradation in status. Moreover, as the experience of the Spaniards testifies, it is easier to transform cultivators of the soil into slaves than to subjugate hunting people.

The same attachment to their roving hunting life which induced the Indians to resist enslavement led them to reject and withstand assimilation while so many other groups were being mixed in the great American melting pot. The Indian tribe was indissolubly united with its home territory. The areas which provided food, clothing, and shelter formed the center and circumference of their actions, emotions, and thoughts. Their religious ideas and ceremonies were bound up with the places associated with their ancestors. To sever the Indians from these lands was to shatter the foundation of their lives.

The Indians either had to remain aloof from white civilization or else remake themselves from top to bottom in the image of their enemy. The latter course involved forfeiting their cherished traditions and traits and converting themselves and their children into human beings of a strange and different type. This leap across the ages could be taken by scattered individuals but not by whole tribal communities.

Even where they attempted to absorb it bit by bit, white

civilization did not permit the Indians to avoid corruption or extinction. The Indians found that they could not borrow part of the alien culture without swallowing the rest, the evil with the good; they could not modify their communal culture with the attributes of civilization and preserve its foundations intact. The most conclusive proof was given by the fate of the Cherokees, one of the "five civilized tribes." The Cherokees, who inhabited the southern Alleghenies and were one of the largest tribes in the United States, went the furthest in acquiring the ways of the white man. In the early decades of the nineteenth century, the Cherokees transformed themselves into flourishing and skillful stock-raisers, farmers, traders, and even slaveowners. They amassed considerable wealth, created an alphabet, and formed a government modeled upon that of the United States.

However, they took these steps without discarding communal ownership of the lands, which had been guaranteed to them forever in 1798 by the federal government. Thus the Cherokee nation stood out like an irritating foreign body within southern society. The southern whites were resolved to bring the Cherokees under the sway of private property in land and the centralized state power. Under their pressure federal troops forced the Cherokees from their homes and deported them en masse. Their lands were distributed by lottery to the whites.

Even after the Cherokees resettled on the Indian Territory in Oklahoma, they could not keep undisturbed possession of their lands and customs. The Bureau of Indian Affairs inflicted the vicious land allotment system upon them, whereby the tribal territories were cut into individual lots and placed upon the free market. The government changed the mode of inheritance along with the system of landholding by decreeing that property should henceforth descend through the father instead of the mother.

This capped the process of despoiling the tribe of its lands and its rights and overthrowing the basic ancestral institutions of the community. Private property, patrilineal inheritance, and the centralized oppressive state displaced communal property, the matriarchal family, and tribal democracy. The Bureau of American Ethnology reported in 1883 that the Cherokees "felt that they were, as a nation, being slowly but surely compressed within the contracting coils of the giant anaconda of civilization; yet they held to the vain hope that a spirit of justice and mercy would be born of their helpless condition which would finally prevail in their favor."

Their hope was vain. "The giant anaconda of civilization" crushed its prey and swallowed it. By such food has American capitalism grown to its present strength and stature.

The Destruction of Indian Democracy

George Novack (1949)

The previous essay refuted the contention that capitalist America was not based on conquest, by setting forth the real historical facts about the wars of extirpation against the Indians. From that false premise about the virgin birth of bourgeois society the capitalist apologists draw an equally false conclusion. For example, in his anti-Marxist polemic at the New York Herald Tribune Forum in October 1948, Conant declared that "we have nowhere in our tradition the idea of an aristocracy descended from the conquerors and entitled to rule by right of birth." This assertion is no better grounded in historical fact, and is indeed the opposite of the truth, as we propose to show.

So far as the relations between the Indians and the whites are concerned, the subjugation of the natives initiated the distinctions between conquerors and conquered along the racial lines which have survived to this day. From the landing of the Spanish conquistadores, through the crushing of the last insurgents among the Plains Indians by federal troops, up to the present government policy of "enlightened guardianship," the American whites have maintained a hostile attitude toward the Indians. They have taken for granted that a white person is better than an Indian; that the Indian has no rights the overlord is bound to respect; and that the white man is entitled by right of birth to the red man's submission and humiliation.

The bearers of capitalism introduced on North American soil the cleavages and conflicts between master and slave, exploiter and exploited, idler and toiler, rich and poor that have flourished ever since. Alongside the degradation and suppression of the Indians by the whites, there developed profound antagonisms between diverse sections of the new society.

38

Since the planting of the first colonies, white America has never been without privileged possessing classes at its head. In colonial days the masses were dominated by aristocrats of birth and money; after the War of Independence, by northern capitalists and southern slaveholders; since the Civil War, by millionaires and billionaires. These ruling minorities have all elevated themselves above the common people—not to speak of outcasts like foreign immigrants, Negroes, Latin Americans, and Orientals—and subordinated to their narrow class interests whatever democratic institutions the people have acquired.

This darker side of the social transformation wrought by the impact of European civilization upon ancient America is usually passed by in silence, or at least slurred over without explanation, by bourgeois historians. Yet the emergence of class stratifications formed one of the essential lines of demarcation between Indian collectivism and white society.

Conant's own mind has been warped by these unspoken traditions and betrays their influence, although in refined forms. The disdain of the Anglo-Saxon conqueror can be discerned in his dismissal of the existence and struggles of the Indians. What is this but an unconscious—and thereby all the more meaningful— admission of that racial arrogance and antipathy which induces white scholars to disparage the real role of the colored races in American history? This comes from that white-supremacist prejudice which for centuries has been directed not only against the Indians but against the black and yellow peoples as well.

Bourgeois scholars distort and deny the truly democratic nature of Indian institutions and of the whole net of social relations stemming from primitive communism just as they suppress the motives for the destruction of this system. Both cast discredit on the bourgeois past.

Despite their backwardness in other respects, far more genuine democracy prevailed among the Indians than among their successors. Village and camp were administered by elected councils of elders. The tribes discussed and decided all important issues in common. Military leaders and sachems were chosen for outstanding talents and deeds, not for their wealth and birth. Even where chieftainship was hereditary, the chiefs could not exercise arbitrary authority or command obedience without consent of the community. Military service was voluntary. The Indians knew no such coercive institutions of modern civilization as police, jails, courts, taxes, or standing armies.

The equalitarianism and primitive humanism of Indian relations surpassed the proudest claims of bourgeois society. Mutual assistance was the watchword of the community. The tribe cared for all the aged, infirm, sick, and young. Hospitality was a sacred obligation, and the Indian was considerably more generous toward the needy and the stranger than the "superior" bourgeois. So paramount was this law of hospitality that even an enemy who came without threats had to be given food and shelter.

William Bartram, the naturalist, noted in 1791 that the Creeks had a common granary made up of voluntary contributions "to which every citizen has the right of free and equal access when his own private stores are consumed, to serve as a surplus to fly to for succor, to assist neighboring towns whose crops may have failed, accommodate strangers and travelers, afford provisions or supplies when they go forth on hostile expeditions, etc. . . ."

In his description of *The Indians of the United States,* Clark Wissler, dean of the scientific staff of the American Museum of Natural History and an outstanding authority on Indian life, writes that the Indian "was not really a communist, but he was liberal with food. So long as he had food, he was expected to share it." (p. 225.) (The bourgeois scientist cannot refrain from trying to convert the Indian into a philanthropic "liberal," whereas the habit of sharing possessions with others was an integral aspect of their primitive communist mode of life.)

Anyone in the tribe, for example, could borrow without permission the belongings of another—and return them without thanks. There were no debtors or creditors where private property and money were absent. William Penn wrote: "Give them a fine gun, coat or any other thing, it may pass twenty hands before it sticks. . . . Wealth circulateth like the blood, all parts partake, and . . . none shall want what another hath."

How this tribal solidarity was broken up by civilization can be seen from the following petition by the Mohegan Indians to the Connecticut State Assembly in 1789:

Yes, the Times have turned everything Upside down. . . . In Times past our Fore-Fathers lived in Peace, Love and great harmony, and had everything in Great plenty. . . . They had no Contention about their lands, it lay in Common to them all, and they had but one large dish and they Could all eat together in Peace and Love—But alas, it is not so now, all our Fishing, Hunting and Fowling is entirely gone. And we have now begun to Work on our Land, Keep Cattle, Horses and Hogs And we Build

Houses and fence in Lots, And now we plainly See that one Dish and one Fire will not do any longer for us—Some few are Stronger than others and they will keep off the poor, weake, the halt and the Blind, and will take the Dish to themselves . . . poor Widows and Orphans must be pushed to one side and there they must Set a Crying, Starving and die.

This pathetic petition concludes with a plea "That our Dish of Suckuttush may be equally divided amongst us," if it had to be divided.

To this day the traditions of communal equality are so ingrained among Indians uncontaminated by civilization that they put capitalist society to shame. Recently when oil was found on lands allotted to Jicarilla Indians in northern New Mexico, the individual owners could have legally insisted upon taking the entire income for themselves. This would have meant riches for a few and nothing for the others. However, after deliberation in council, all the Indians made over their mineral rights to the tribe so that whatever was gained should be applied to the good of the whole people. How remote are these "backward" Apaches from the standards of bourgeois "morality."

The Indians found incomprehensible many traits of the whites: their disregard of pledges considered inviolate by the natives; their fondness for indoor life; their intolerance of other people's ways; their lust for material possessions and money. As primitive hunters and warriors, the Indians were accustomed to slay not only wild game but rivals who interfered with their essential activities; they scalped enemies, tortured and burned captives. These customs were justified and sanctified by their religious beliefs. But they could not understand the duplicity of Christians who preached peace and goodwill and yet waged relentless war upon them.

The Indian was repelled by the inhumanity displayed by members of the same white community toward each other, the heartless egoism which flowed from class society and bourgeois anarchy. There was greater equality in work and play, in distribution and enjoyment of goods, in social intercourse and status among the Indians than among the whites. Every member of the tribe shared alike in good times or in bad, in feast or in famine, in war as in peace; no one went hungry while a few had more than enough to eat. "They think it strange that some should possess more than others, and that those who have the most should be more highly esteemed than those who have the least." (*The Evolution of Property,* by Paul Lafargue, p. 35.)

This spirit of equality extended to women and children, and even to those war captives adopted into the tribe. Women not only stood on an equal footing, but sometimes exercised superior authority. The Indian elders rarely abused or whipped their children. There was no servant class—and therefore no masters.

The forms of society which displaced Indian tribalism surpassed it in a great many respects—but, we repeat, they were never more equalitarian. The American natives lacked many things known to the whites, but they did not suffer from a ruling aristocracy of birth or wealth. The institution of aristocracy in general is bound up with the growth of property and the concentration of wealth in private hands—and these were indeed "alien importations" of white civilization.

The contrast between the contending cultures was most sharply expressed in their attitudes toward the acquisition of private wealth. The passion for property was absent among the Indians. On the other hand, the quest for riches was the most powerful driving force of the new society, the principal source of its evils and the most conspicuous trait of its outstanding representatives.

The precious metals were the quintessence of wealth, prestige, and power in Europe and the Holy Grail of the pioneer explorers in the age of discovery. In a letter written to Ferdinand and Isabella from Jamaica in 1503, Columbus rhapsodized: "Gold is a wonderful thing! Whoever owns it is lord of all he wants. With gold it is even possible to open for souls a way to paradise!"

Imagine his astonishment when the Haitians, who used the metal for ornament but not for money, freely handed over gold to the Spaniards in exchange for trinkets. This served only to inflame their greed. After stripping the natives of the gold they possessed, Columbus and his men drove them to forced labor for more. But the Caribbeans did not yield their liberty as readily as their gold.

"These chattel slaves were worked to death. So terrible was their life that they were driven to mass suicide, to mass infanticide, to mass abstinence from sexual life in order that children should not be born into horror. Lethal epidemics followed upon the will to die. The murders and desolations exceeded those of the most pitiless tyrants of earlier history; nor have they been surpassed since." (*Indians of the Americas*, by John Collier, p. 57.)

The Aztec chief Tauhtile thought that "the Spaniards were

troubled with a disease of the heart, for which gold was the specific remedy." This disease was in fact the normal mode of behavior of the white invaders. As the subsequent conquests of Mexico and Peru demonstrated, nothing sufficed to quench their thirst for the precious metals.

Although Sir Walter Raleigh and other English colonizers hoped to emulate Cortez and the Pizarros, they found no ancient civilizations on the North Atlantic coasts to plunder. Their conquest of the Indians, although inspired by similar sordid motives, was conducted along somewhat different lines. The traders cheated and debauched the natives; the settlers seized their hunting grounds and massacred the tribes; the governments incited one band of Indians against another while destroying the rights and freedom of all. This despoiling of the Indians by the whites dominates the entire historical record, from the first settlements in Virginia to the recent attempt by the Montana Power and Light Company to deprive the Flathead Indians of their territorial rights.

Belonging as they did to incompatible levels of social existence, both the Indians and whites found it impossible to reach any mutual understanding for any length of time. The Indians, baffled by the behavior of these strange creatures from another world, could not fathom their motives. Not only the Aztecs but the North American tribes had to pass through many cruel experiences before they realized how implacable were the aggressions of the whites—and then it was too late. They may be excused for their lack of comprehension. But the same cannot be said of bourgeois historians of our own day who still fail to understand them after the fact.

The founders of the capitalist regime in North America had a double mission to perform. One was to subdue or eliminate whatever precapitalist social forms existed or sprang up on the continent. The other was to construct the material requirements for bourgeois civilization. The destructive and creative aspects of this process went hand in hand. The extirpation of the Indian tribes was needed to clear the ground for the foundations of the projected new society.

The overthrow of the Indians had contradictory effects upon the subsequent development of American life. The installation of private property in land and the widening exchange of agricultural products at home and in the world market provided the economic basis and incentives for the rapid growth of colonization, agriculture, commerce, craftsmanship, cities, and accumulation of wealth. These conditions fashioned and fostered the virile native forces which prepared and carried through the second great upheaval in American history, the colonists' revolt against England.

The rise of the English colonies in North America and their successful strivings for unhampered development form one of the most celebrated chapters in modern history. But an all-sided review of the process must note that a price was paid for these achievements, especially in the sphere of social relations.

The Struggle for the Land

George Novack (1949)

A correct conception of the place occupied in American history by Indian society throws much-needed light upon another fundamental question of this country's social evolution—the struggle for possession of the land. That struggle begins with the wresting of the tribal hunting grounds from the Indians and the transmission of this land to new owners belonging to a different type of social organization who needed it for new economic activities—agriculture, trade, mining, ranching, industry, etc.

At various stages along the route, this struggle has involved the principal state and clerical powers of Western Eι rope as well as the various classes transplanted to American soil. Our land has changed hands several times since the sixteenth century, passing not only from country to country but also from class to class and from person to person. Questions concerning the use, distribution, and ownership of the land have played crucial roles in every great American upheaval: in the wars against the Indians, in the fight against British domination (the abolition of crown lands and other royal restrictions, abolition of entail and primogeniture, confiscation and sale of Loyalist estates), and in the Civil War (the Homestead Act, the land question in the southern states).

The outcome of all this has been to disperse the land among various categories of individual owners, and at the same time to concentrate the best situated and most productive areas in the hands of a wealthy minority. At no time since the overthrow of Indian tribalism by the bearers of landed private property has the American earth belonged to the inhabitants thereof, even when it formally belonged to the government. For each of these governments, controlled by the propertied classes, served as no

45

more than a temporary custodian before turning title to the land over to private owners.

The unexpressed assumption of all except the most radical representatives of bourgeois thought on this problem (such as Henry George) is that the land along with the other means of production shall forever be used and abused by private proprietors, and any redistribution will take place within the framework of private ownership.

It cannot be denied that they have what the jurists call a prima facie case, since that has been the main trend for over four hundred years and appears to be the unshakable state of affairs today. The moneyed men with their banks, insurance companies, and corporations continue to gather the best part of the land into their hands and reap its benefits. At the same forum where Conant spoke about the blessings of democratic capitalism, cries of alarm were raised by other speakers over the mismanagement and waste of our national resources owing to capitalist anarchy and greed.

What will be the ultimate conclusion of the contest which began with the dispossession of the Indian? Will the American people permit the small fraction of wealthy proprietors to engross the land and its wealth, to ravage the national resources, and exclude the majority of the population from rational management and enjoyment of the land?

It would be an illusion to think that the struggle over the land, which has already passed through so many changes, will stop at its present point and at the limits imposed by the interests of the rich. In fact, the fight against their monopoly and misuse of the land is bound to flare up again as it has during every great social crisis.

In his autobiography, Oscar Ameringer tells an interesting anecdote in this connection about an Oklahoma cattleman who had firmly opposed socialist ideas until he was ruined by the Depression. In 1932 he approached Ameringer and declared: "What we got to have is this here revolution you used to preach about."

"You mean divide up and start all over again?" asked Ameringer.

"No, not divide up," exclaimed the cattleman angrily, "but own our land and cattle and things in common like the Indians use to do before the government robbed them of everything by giving them title deeds."

"That's better," Ameringer acknowledged, "provided we add railroads, banks, packing plants and a great many other things to those you mentioned."

The impact of the oncoming social crises will undoubtedly call forth similar responses from considerable sections of farmers who today appear eternally wedded to "free enterprise."

The actual cultivators of the soil—small farmers, indentured servants, tenants, or slaves—never reconciled themselves in the past to the exploitation of labor on the land, to landlordism or absentee ownership. The embattled farmers carried through the fight for independence and democracy against British-backed feudalism during the First American Revolution. Their vanguard in Kansas who challenged the slave power were the forerunners of the farmers who filled the Union armies in the Civil War. The agrarian Populists conducted stubborn struggles against the tyranny of the plutocrats in the last part of the nineteenth century. These memorable precedents prefigure how the toilers on the land, whether small owners, sharecroppers, or wageworkers, are bound to assert their presence and power as the oppressions—and depressions—of monopoly capitalism drive them to seek a new road.

Whatever phases the struggle for the land will go through as class antagonisms become more pronounced, the method of its final solution has already been indicated by Marx:

> From the point of view of a higher economic form of society, the private ownership of the globe on the part of some individuals will appear quite as absurd as the private ownership of one man by another. Even a whole society, a nation, or even all societies together, are not the *owners* of the globe. They are only its *possessors,* its users, and they have to hand it down to the coming generations in an improved condition, like the good fathers of families. (*Capital*, Vol. III.)

Just as the private ownership of one human being by another had to be abolished in this country, so the socialist revolution of our time will have to abolish private ownership of the land.

The destruction of primitive communism based on common land ownership among the Indian tribes was indispensable to the development of American capitalism. The rapid growth of unalloyed bourgeois relations in the United States was made possible by the thoroughness with which the bourgeois forces swept aside all precapitalist institutions, beginning with those of the Indian.

Now this historical cycle is coming to a close and a new one is opening up. The main direction of American society since the crushing of the Indian has been away from primitive collectivism toward private property in more and more developed capitalist forms. In the worldwide reversal of social trends now under way, the main line of progress is away from private property and toward collectivism in socialist forms.

When the American people, under the leadership of the industrial workers, succeed in their task of converting capitalist landed property into public property, they will in effect revive on a far higher level and in more mature forms the common ownership of the soil and the collective use of the means of production that we meet on the very threshold of modern American history.

Thus the struggle for the land in America is reproducing, at its own pace and in its own peculiar ways, the basic pattern of development being traced out by civilized society as a whole. This pattern, too, has been explained and foreseen by the founders of Marxism. Engels wrote in *Anti-Dühring:*

All civilized peoples begin with the common ownership of the land. With all peoples who have passed a certain primitive stage, in the course of the development of agriculture this common ownership becomes a fetter on production. It is abolished, negated, and after a longer or shorter series of intermediate stages is transformed into private property.

But at a higher stage of agricultural development, brought about by private property in land itself, private property in turn becomes a fetter on production as is the case today, both with small and large landownership. The demand that it also should be negated, that it should once again be transformed into common property necessarily arises. But this demand does not mean the restoration of the old original common ownership, but the institution of a far higher and more developed form of possession in common which, far from being a hindrance to production, on the contrary for the first time frees production from all fetters and gives it the possibility of making full use of modern chemical discoveries and mechanical inventions.

Champions of capitalism such as Conant imagine that, thanks to its unique features and exceptional capacities, the United States is set apart from the rest of the capitalist world. All its peculiarities and powers, however, will not suffice in the future, any more than they have in the past, to enable the bourgeoisie in this country to escape the operation of the laws of the class struggle. These laws, which formerly worked in their favor, are now more and more turning against their regime. Although American capitalism may follow paths marked out by the special conditions of its own historical development, these lead toward the same ultimate destination as its counterparts: the graveyard where obsolete social systems are buried.

The transition from ancient Indian collectivism to the various forms of production rooted in private property also casts considerable light upon the means by which the forces of bourgeois society arrived at their present eminence in America.

In their catalog of crimes against humanity, the spokesmen for capitalism include the expropriation of property without "just compensation," the use of violence to overturn established regimes, and the resort to extralegal measures. They also recognize as the crime of crimes the extermination of entire populations, for which the term "genocide" has been coined. These self-professed humanitarians ascribe such aims above all to "Marxist" and "Communist" devils. In contrast they hold up the angelic respect for property rights, love of peace, regard for law and order, preference for gradual change by democratic consent, and other virtues presumably inculcated by American "free enterprise."

This is a handy set of principles to justify the capitalist regime while defaming its opponents. But all these principles have little application to the conduct of the bourgeoisie in American history.

Historians fired by zeal to indict the opponents of capitalism for these offenses should first direct their attention to the ancestors of contemporary American capitalism. No class in American history invaded the property rights of others more ruthlessly, employed violence so readily, and benefited so extensively by revolutionary actions as has the American bourgeoisie on its road to power.

The precursors of the monopolists acquired their property by expropriating the Indians, the British crown along with its Loyalist lackeys, and the slaveholders, not to mention their continued bankrupting of the small farmers and self-employed workers. They effected these dispossessions of other people's property not simply by peaceful, legal, or democratic means, but in extremely violent, high-handed, and militaristic ways. Whatever they could not get by bargaining or money, they took by force.

The conquest of the Indians, as we have seen, takes its place in this series of events as the earliest and crassest case of the rapacity, ferocity, and duplicity with which the bourgeois forces smashed the impediments on the way to their objectives. They themselves committed the supreme crime they falsely attribute to the aims of revolutionary socialists. The extermination of the Indian was the outstanding example of genocide in modern American history—and it was the first rung in the ladder by which the bourgeoisie climbed to the top.

The transmission of the continent into their hands was not accomplished by peaceful agreements. It is common knowledge that virtually every treaty made with the Indians for over four hundred years was broken by the architects of the American nation. By brute force, by the most perfidious deeds, by wars of extermination, they settled the question of who was to own and occupy the continent and to rule it. The treatment of the Indians exemplifies to what lengths the owners of private property can—and will—go in promoting their material interests.

The methods by which the white invaders disposed of the Indian problem had far-reaching results. The Indians' ancient society was shattered and eradicated, and powerful masters were placed over them and over North America. The main social substance of that sweeping change consisted in the conversion and division of tribal property in land, owned in common and cooperatively used, into private property. This continent passed from the loose network of tribal communities into the hands of kings, landed proprietors, planters, merchants, capitalists, small farmers, and town dwellers who directed and composed the new society.

The conflict between the Indian and the white is usually represented as essentially racial in character. It is true that their mutual antagonism manifested itself and was carried on by both sides under the guise of racial hatred. But their war to the death was at bottom a *social* struggle, a battle for supremacy between incompatible systems of production, forms of property, and ways of life. Like all profound social struggles, the scramble for the sources of wealth was at its root. In this case, the chief prize was individual ownership and "free" disposition of the land and its products.

These material stakes account for the tenacity of the conflict, which persisted through four centuries, and for the implacable hostility displayed by white settlers of all nationalities toward the Indians of all tribes. This was also responsible in the last analysis for the impossibility of any harmony or enduring compromise between the two. One or the other had to go under.

That is how the materialist school of Marxism interprets the cruel treatment accorded the Indians and the reasons for their downfall. If this explanation is accepted, prevailing views of early American history must be discarded. School children, and not they alone, are taught nowadays that the first great social change in this country came from the Patriots' fight for independence in the last quarter of the eighteenth century. In the light of the foregoing analysis, this long-standing misconception has to be rejected.

The colonial uprising, for all its importance, was neither the first social transformation in America nor the most fundamental. It was preceded, interwoven with, and followed by the white invasion and penetration which overthrew the Indian tribal network. This process of struggle, undertaken to install the rule of private property and its corresponding institutions in place of communal property and institutions, was an even more radical social upheaval than the contest between the colonists and the mother country.

The struggle of the eighteenth century was waged between forces and institutions which, although rooted in different countries and in different historical backgrounds, nevertheless shared relations of private property at their foundations. The fight against the Indians on the other hand arose from the unbridgeable chasm dividing archaic society from modern civilization, primeval communism from budding capitalism.

The grand course of social evolution on American soil falls into three main stages. It starts with the development of the Stone Age many thousands of years ago. This primitive period reached its peak in the Aztec, Mayan, and Incan cultures, and came to a close with the invasion of the whites at the end of the fifteenth century.

The second great epoch begins with the bringing of civilization by the Europeans. It proceeds through the various phases in the formation and transformation of bourgeois society which have culminated in the national and world supremacy of the American monopolists. The third stage, arising out of the second, had its inception with the birth of large-scale industry and the wage-working class.

What are the relations between these three overlapping epochs which mark off decisive steps in the advancement of American society? It is characteristic of the low theoretical level of bourgeois historians that they do not even broach this question, although it is fundamental in American history. They view capitalism as the sole system of society with solid substance and enduring structure; all others are passing phantoms. Indian tribalism, as we have noted, is to them a forgotten relic; socialism a horrible specter or an impossible fantasy; while civil society in its capitalist forms remains an eternal necessity. Consequently they cannot see or admit that there *are* distinct stages of American history; that these are interlinked in a necessary chain; or that any significant sequence of development can be discerned in the complex social process.

Nevertheless, behind the sequence of social forms which bridged the transition from savagery to civilization on this continent, there is a lawfulness. Although it had endured for thousands of years, the communal organization of the Indian tribes had to give way before the superior forces of private property. When the further development of the productive forces was blocked by the feudalists, tied up with English rule, and later the slaveholders, they too were extinguished by the creators of capitalist power.

The bourgeois thinkers concentrate attention upon that side of American historical development in which precapitalist methods of production and forms of property were displaced by ascending bourgeois relations. They largely ignore other aspects of the same process. It is true that the regimes following Indian tribalism multiplied the powers of production through the practices and passions of private ownership and "free enterprise," improved techniques, widened culture, and opened new vistas to humanity. But these acquisitions had to be paid for by increased inequality and the intensified oppression by the rulers over the ruled. Precious qualities of freedom and fraternity were lost in the shift from primitive collectivism to modern capitalism. As a result of the prevailing class division of society, humanity has remained stunted and defective.

Yet bourgeois thinkers assume that the triumph of capitalism coincides with the highest attainable summit of human existence. History is to be halted while the American people perpetually salute their capitalist commanders in the reviewing stand. How does such an outlook essentially differ from that of the slaveholders who could not adjust themselves to the advent of higher social forms?

In reality, the steps leading to the consolidation of capitalism were only a prelude to the building of a truly civilized life for the American people, and not at all the crowning acts of American civilization. These remain to be taken as the next great stage of our evolution matures—as we move toward socialism.

In the anti-Marxist polemics of bourgeois intellectuals, there is a fatal inconsistency. On one hand, they point to the unlimited potentialities of abundance in the manufacture of automobiles, atom bombs, supersonic planes, and other things—in a phrase, to the dynamic nature of our productive forces. On the other hand, they demand that these productive forces remain forever encased in capitalist ownership. While everything else is subject to improvement, capitalist control of the productive facilities, and the political system which protects it, are to be considered immutable. These alone are exempt from radical reconstruction and so close to perfection that they cannot be surpassed, at least not in any foreseeable future.

Whatever changes there may be, they say, must remain within the boundaries of capitalist relations. The method of social development must be restricted to small doses of change in accordance with the needs of the ruling class.

There is no warrant for such arbitrary assumptions, in American history, in the dynamics of our productive forces, or in the present state or prospects of class relations. The forms of property and methods of production in America have undergone at least three vast transformations in the past. When Indian tribalism, British-born feudalism, and southern slavery collided with the new bourgeois forces of production, they were demolished. How absurd it is for the defenders of capitalism to bank for its salvation upon the very expansion of the productive forces which, increasingly stifled by capitalism, must lead to its downfall.

These students of history stubbornly refuse to learn from the past when the slow, steady evolution of social conditions exploded at critical junctures into tremendous upheavals which overturned the old order. American history is full of such sudden transitions and forward leaps. After the Indian tribes held the continent for thousands of years, invaders burst in from overseas, ousted the natives, and built an entirely different type of society here. Mother England dominated her thirteen colonies for over a century and a half until abruptly, within a decade, a definitive break occurred between the former ruler and the American people. Then, beginning with 1800, the planting power became predominant in national affairs—until the election of Republican President Lincoln in 1860 unleashed the Civil War.

Such reversals of existing conditions, resulting in a radical reconstruction of American society, are not at all restricted to the past. They are inherent in the present situation of American capitalism, which faces the same prospect as Indian tribalism, colonial feudalism, and chattel slavery. It has become obsolete and opposed to progress. The major evils from which humankind suffers are directly attributable to the outworn institution of capitalist private property. The emancipation of the human race from poverty, tyranny, and war is inseparable from the liberation of the means of production from the grip of capitalist ownership and monopolist control.

At the same time the colossal expansion of socialized production under capitalist auspices has given birth to a new mighty social power. This is the industrial working class, which is itself the principal force of production in modern economy. By its ideas, outlook, and actions, labor opens up an unrestricted historical horizon for humanity in the socialist future of the free and equal. The material prerequisites for this new form of production and collective life are taking shape within the capitalist structure itself.

This new social power has already announced itself through the swift insurgence of the CIO in the late thirties when, after operating like uncontrolled despots in basic industry for many decades, the monopolists suddenly were challenged by powerful unions of industrial workers. These organized workers will next be knocking on the doors of political power.

Let us assure both the witch-hunters and the witch doctors of capitalism that the American monopolists will not be overthrown, like the Indians, by foreign forces. They are destined to be dislodged from within, like the feudal landlords, the English crown, and the southern slavocracy. This job will be done by social forces generated under their own system and provoked by their own reactionary rule. Not least among these forces will be the descendants of the red, black, and brown peoples, which were subjugated by the bourgeois property owners on their way to supreme power.

The instinctive dread of this prospect accounts for the malevolence of the monopolists toward the workers and the belligerence of their intellectual defenders toward the socialist-minded vanguard. These banner-bearers of reaction do not dread so much the importation of ideas from abroad, for they welcome fascism and other brands of obscurantism. What they fear is the enlightenment and inspiration Marxism can give American workers and the oppressed nationalities in working out the ways and means of their emancipation. Hence the irreconcilable hostility toward "the philosophy of Marx, Engels and Lenin" expressed in Harvard President Conant's call to ideological battle.

When the pioneers of bourgeois society confronted their precapitalist foes, they had both the power and the historical mission to conquer. Their plutocratic heirs of the twentieth century have neither. In our time the workers are the pioneers and builders of the new world, the bearers of a higher culture. They embody a more efficient method of production and are fully capable of assimilating, mastering and applying all the achievements of science and technology, including the science of social change and the techniques of struggle for political power.

Uprooting all the abominations of class society and cultivating everything worthy in the techniques, knowledge, and culture taken over from capitalism, the builders of the coming society will vindicate the achievements of the past by surpassing them. The "liberty, equality, and fraternity" known in America's infancy, which the bourgeoisie blasphemed and buried, will be regenerated and enjoyed in its finest forms through the socialist revolution of the working people.

It is the capitalist proprietors who are the barbarians in the midst of modern society, resorting in their desperate struggle for survival to the most fiendish weapons and practices. To remove them from the seats of power is the central task of our generation. Humanity cannot resume its upward climb until civilization is rescued from capitalist barbarism.

THE FIRST AMERICAN REVOLUTION

Was the Revolution Necessary?

George Novack (1975)

On March 22, 1765, George III gave his royal assent to the Stamp Act, which had passed both houses of Parliament with no more commotion than "a common Turnpike Bill." The effects of this hateful tax measure on the American colonists and the attempts to enforce it provoked the first large-scale outbursts against the crown.

Ten years later, on March 23, 1775, Patrick Henry stood up and, in answer to those opposed to arming the people, told the Second Virginia Convention that war with Britain was inevitable.

"We have petitioned, we have remonstrated, we have supplicated, we have prostrated ourselves before the throne. . . . Why stand we here idle?" Henry asked. "What is it that gentlemen wish? What would they have? Is life so dear, or peace so sweet, as to be purchased at the price of chains and slavery? Forbid it, Almighty God. I know not what course others may take; but as for me, give me liberty or give me death!"

The motion to take up arms against the king passed by a small majority and the next week a committee, including George Washington, Thomas Jefferson, and Richard Henry Lee, established a plan for a militia in Virginia.

Why did loyal subjects become converted into rebels-in-arms over those ten years?

This question poses a highly debatable issue in history and politics. Have revolutions been produced by lawful causes or is their occurrence an avoidable accident? And how necessary was the First American Revolution?

The concept of historical necessity is in disrepute in contemporary American thought and has been disavowed by such influential English professors as Sir Isaiah Berlin and Karl

Popper. The former categorically asserts, "For historians determinism is not a serious issue."

These liberal theorists dismiss determinism as a pernicious fallacy. Historical inevitability is a relic of dogmatic metaphysics, an aberration of Marxism, that has no validity in social science and should be expunged from historical exposition. They see no necessities at work in the evolution of class societies, and especially not in their own time and place.

Revolutions come about, according to them, not when all the conditions for their occurrence—from the economic to the individual—converge to the breaking point, but because of mistaken judgments by one side or the other. Revolutions are therefore more or less aberrant phenomena and might be averted if greater wisdom were brought to bear on the situation by representatives of the respective antagonists.

Marxists take the contrary view that social phenomena are regulated by their own laws, that the conflict of classes with opposing material interests and aims is the motive force in civilized societies, and that intensification of class antagonisms logically and irresistibly leads toward a revolutionary showdown in the contest for supremacy.

This line of thought originated among the Greeks, notably in the works of Thucydides and Aristotle. In examining the reasons for the Peloponnesian War, Thucydides wrote that "what made war inevitable was the growth of Athenian power and the fear which this caused in Sparta." Two and a half millennia later, Marxism gave a far more deepgoing and rounded formulation to this mode of historical interpretation.

The bicentennial celebration of the Declaration of Independence provides a timely occasion for testing the merits of these two types of historical explanation: the indeterminist and probabilist approach of the positivists and empiricists versus the dialectical determinism of the historical materialists.

The revolution that took place along the coastal area of North America during the last quarter of the eighteenth century introduced a salutary change in the destiny of the American people. Nowadays no one will contest this judgment. There are no Loyalists to be found in the fifty states, as there are in Canada and New Zealand. Today scarcely a single voice will lament that the colonists broke away from British rule. Patriotism, realism, and two centuries of national sovereignty make such a position ridiculously anachronistic.

Despite the unanimous opinion that the revolution was desirable and beneficial, wide disagreement persists on the degree of its objective necessity. This uncertainty goes all the way back to the decade before the Declaration of Independence, when the revolt was ripening behind the backs of its prospective signers.

Tom Paine wrote in *Common Sense* that "it is contrary to nature that a whole continent should be tributary to an island." Nonetheless, England had dominated North America for almost two centuries and was then the strongest imperial power in the world.

Although some colonials believed that their fellow citizens would one day cut loose from England's apron strings, before 1775 they could not see how independence could be achieved, nor did they expect that it would come in their lifetimes.

The decision to proclaim national freedom crystallized quite suddenly in the early months of 1776. It had taken a decade of compromises before the desirability and the immediacy of independence merged in the minds and deeds of the Patriots.

Here we bump into another familiar philosophical, historical, and moral problem: the relation of end to means.

The rebels finally resorted to armed struggle to attain their goals. Did they have to apply violence for that purpose, and was this revolutionary means justified?

Marxists have no difficulty in answering these questions affirmatively. The liberal thinkers since that time have found it as difficult to resolve this dilemma in theory and square it with their principles as the moderates did at the time of the revolt.

Many scholars argue that armed conflict might have been averted if reason and moderation had prevailed in adjudicating the differences. They seek to rearrange the course of history in accord with their preconceptions much as a teacher corrects mistakes in a pupil's paper. Yet they are the ones who have the most to learn from the actual historical process of their own country.

The revolutionary cycle in which the Declaration of Independence falls was launched by the Stamp Act demonstrations in 1765—the first intervention of the plebeian masses as an independent force in the contest against British exactions—and was consummated with the establishment of the Constitution in 1789.

Here was a tenacious twenty-five-year struggle, involving millions on both sides of the Atlantic and the major maritime powers. Was it an event that might as well not have happened? Or was it an *inescapable* stage in the advancement of the American people that had been in the making for decades and had necessary and sufficient causes for its emergence and development?

A scientific historian who wants to explain how something came to be—rather than to explain it away—has to face up to this crucial issue.

To be sure, alternative possibilities are *to a certain subordinate extent* lodged in the unfolding historical process. In connection with an exposition of the causes responsible for the specific course of events, it should be shown why these other paths were shut off and could not be taken by the antagonists at that juncture. But the indispensable task is to account for the main line of development.

It was, for example, not foreordained that independence be proclaimed on the particular date of July 4, 1776. The colonists might have launched into armed revolt as early as 1766 if the British government had tried to force the Stamp Act down their throats instead of repealing it.

Gov. Francis Bernard of Massachusetts said later that after the Stamp Act it was apparent that the "weak patchwork government" in America had no power to prevent colonial independence "one hour after the people have resolved upon it."

But Britain, caught by surprise by the angry reaction of the colonials and barely recovered from the exhausting Seven Years' War, was ill-equipped and undisposed to impose repressive measures three thousand miles away and had to make a concession to the protesters.

What this episode signified was that, while many of the preconditions required for resistance were already present, all the necessary factors had not yet ripened. That would take ten more years of experience on both sides of the Atlantic.

The concrete problem comes down to analyzing the concatenation of causes during the prerevolutionary period from 1765 to 1775 that rendered armed conflict inevitable. The conditions that go into the creation of a revolutionary situation are multiple and complex; they extend from the underlying economic relations to the feelings, ideas, and responses of the individual colonist.

However, these diverse interacting factors have a gradation in importance; they did not all exert the same degree of influence upon the birth, growth, and outcome of the struggle. The most objective, weighty, and decisive determinants were the environing historical circumstances that produced the special alignment of class forces within the colonial social structure.

These generated the sharpening clash of interests between the colonists and the crown, as well as between the differing strata within the provinces, that found political and ideological expression through the Patriot movement.

The range of options for action that appeared open to both sides in the first phase of their confrontation kept narrowing down until they were reduced ten years later to the polar opposition expressed by Patrick Henry: "Liberty or death!"

The most sweeping aversion to this materialist approach comes from those academic American historians who pick out changing ideas, rather than the clash of class interests, as the main cause of the social and political upheaval.

Thus a reviewer of the thirteen volumes of *The British Empire before the American Revolution* by Lawrence Gipson wrote in the *New York Times Book Review* of July 3, 1966: "Yet the American Revolution was above all else an ideological revolution, and it is in ideological terms essentially that its origination is comprehensible. A complex tradition of ideas, fused into a coherent whole largely in the very early years of the 18th century, came into conjunction with a peculiar structure of informal politics in America to create, already by mid-century, a latently revolutionary situation."

Similarly, in *The Ideological Origins of the American Revolution*, the Harvard scholar Bernard Bailyn asserts, "The American Revolution was above all else an ideological, constitutional, political struggle and not primarily a controversy between social groups undertaken to force changes in the organization of the society or the economy."

The priority given to ideological factors in the genesis of the conflict stands the sequence of mutual determination on its head. This is an extremely shallow idealistic approach that takes a big step backward from the interpretations given by Charles and Mary Beard, Curtis Nettels, and other liberal historians of earlier generations. Despite their shortcomings, these historiographers of the Progressive school did recognize the importance of the economic basis of politics and the role of class interests in generating and promoting oppositional developments in the colonies.

Two major considerations speak against the thesis that ideas took precedence in the revolutionizing process.

The call for independence was voiced and supported not at the inception but only at the climax of the prerevolutionary period. And this demand for *political* independence was preceded and prepared by the desire and drive for *economic* independence from the colonial system, especially on the part of the merchants, planters, and land speculators. The Continental Congress opened American ports to all trade with all nations in April 1775, more than a year before it approved national independence.

Let us see how the pattern of determination worked out in the successive social and political crises from 1765 to 1775 that eventuated in armed insurrection and the construction of a parallel governmental-type power in opposition to the British colonial structure.

The close of the French and Indian War in 1763 ushered in the prerevolutionary period. All the major European powers participated in this Seven Years' War, which resembled the world wars of the twentieth century in its consequences. It had tremendous effects upon the combatants, whether they were among the victors or the vanquished.

Most importantly, the war introduced profound changes in the relations between England and her North American colonies. Both were struck by a postwar depression, burdensome debts, heavy taxes, and mass discontent.

England had a national debt of 130 million pounds sterling, which cost the people four and a half million pounds a year in interest. Its ruling classes tried to unload an increasing share of these costs of the war upon the colonists by imposing many new taxes upon their trade, beginning with the Sugar Act of 1764 and the Stamp Act of 1765. These measures were designed not only to raise much-needed revenue, but to aid British merchants and manufacturers at the expense of their overseas rivals.

Beginning with the Proclamation of 1763, which prohibited settlements beyond the sources of the Atlantic seaboard's rivers, the crown tightened its hold upon the desirable Western territories. The king's ministers proposed a British standing army of 10,000 men that colonial taxes would have to support. They instituted stricter enforcement of the customs regulations to stop up the countless leaks in the seaport walls. In 1764 they adopted a Currency Act that outlawed colonial paper money.

This series of enactments proved so burdensome and provocative because they hit the colonists in the midst of a serious economic depression. Jobless, landless, impoverished working people were especially incensed by them.

The Northern merchants who had grown rich during the war, thanks to the British pounds that poured into the colonies and through their smuggling trade with the West Indies, were more independent and aggressive. The cession of Canada to England had removed the fear of the French and Indian attacks that had long menaced New England and New York.

On the other hand, Great Britain no longer had to make concessions to the colonists for assistance against the French and Spanish. London had deferred to the colonial opposition to taxation during the war and closed its eyes to the illegal commerce with the French and Spanish possessions. The definitive settlement of accounts in the military arena with these imperial rivals cleared the way for a direct struggle between Britain and her American subjects.

The revolt did not develop in an uninterrupted and steadily rising curve from the Stamp Act demonstrations of 1765 to the clash at Lexington and Concord in April 1775. It proceeded along a spiraling course, marked by three distinct stages of testing out each other's intentions.

The first crisis was touched off by the onerous Parliamentary measures and crown edicts from 1763 to 1765: the Sugar Act, the Currency Act, the Quartering Act, the Proclamation of 1763, and the new enforcement decrees.

This wave of resistance came to a head with the passage of the Stamp Act, which encountered opposition from every grouping in the colonies that had to buy stamps to affix to legal documents. This arbitrary form of "taxation without representation" brought merchants and planters, lawyers and publishers, farmers, laborers, and frontiersmen into a common fighting front against Britain's exactions.

Differing sections of the resistance movement put forward different programs and favored different methods of struggle, corresponding to their social situations and readiness for military action.

The more conservative merchants, fearing to summon wide masses into combat, relied upon nonimportation agreements. By passive resistance through boycotts of British goods, supplemented by petitions, legalistic arguments, and protests to Parliament, they sought to exert enough economic pressure upon their British counterparts to strike a bargain with London whereby the government would repeal the tax and other unpopular measures in return for professions of loyalty and other concessions on their part.

The more radical anti-British "free trading" merchants, in league with the artisans, shopkeepers, laborers, and farmers suffering from hard times and unemployment, brandished a plebeian fist under the nose of the British tyranny.

They backed up the nonimportation campaign by mass actions. The Sons of Liberty in Boston took the lead. In the summer of 1765, under the leadership of Sam Adams, they hanged the stamp distributor in effigy; fourteen days later they invaded the homes of a customs officer and Lt. Gov. Thomas Hutchinson and seized and burned records pertaining to violation of the Acts of Trade.

The Sons of Liberty ruled Boston as completely as workers on general strike. Hutchinson indignantly complained to the British overlords: "The real authority of the government is at an end; some of the principal ringleaders in the late riots walk the streets with impunity; no officers dare attack them; no attorney-general prosecute them and no judges sit upon them."

Similar demonstrations with popular backing took place in Charleston, Newport, and New York.

This stormy protest movement resulted in the calling of the first intercolonial conference on the initiative of the Massachusetts House of Representatives. Delegates to the Stamp Act Congress from nine colonies met in New York's City Hall, adopted a declaration of rights and grievances, and petitioned the king and Parliament to withdraw the Stamp Act.

This was a preliminary step toward the Declaration of Independence that came from the Continental Congress in Philadelphia a decade later.

The mass protests achieved their immediate aim. Parliament, prodded by British merchants cut off from American trade, repealed the Stamp Act in 1766. The Patriots had scored their first big victory by forcing Parliament to retreat. They also had mobilized, trained, and tested their forces and gained useful experience in the ways and means of struggle.

After the Stamp Act was nullified, the unrest subsided—but for a short time only. In 1767, propelled by the same economic necessities, Chancellor of the Exchequer Charles Townshend pushed a new series of colonial duties through Parliament and suspended the New York Assembly.

While the merchants instituted another nonimportation campaign, the radicals responded with direct action. They seized and terrorized the king's officers, tarred and feathered customs officials and informers, and burned revenue ships.

Boston was once again the center of conflict. In a tumultuous contest set off by the arrival of John Hancock's sloop *Liberty,* the townspeople there pushed to the verge of civil war. But they beat a hasty retreat when two regiments of British regulars landed in October.

The time was not yet ripe for a large-scale armed uprising. This second phase of the struggle was ended by the New York merchants, who broke the boycott and jilted the colonial cause in 1770. This gave a serious setback to the rebels. On the other side, influenced by the returning prosperity of the British merchants, Parliament withdrew the most onerous Townshend duties in 1770.

From 1771 to 1773 there ensued a' pronounced respite in the struggle. The masses became passive and their masters felt at ease. This quiet interlude ended in the last months of 1773.

The final phase was unloosed when Parliament, to save the largest firm in the empire from ruin, gave the East India Company a monopoly of the American tea market. The Boston Tea Party on the night of December 16, 1773, started a chain reaction of events that led to the Declaration of Independence.

This act of defiance was met by the dictatorial "Five Intolerable Acts," which were designed to throttle Massachusetts, the head of the resistance forces.

In a mighty surge of solidarity, the colonies answered the coercion acts by sending delegates to the First Continental Congress in September 1774. This was the first national gathering on an independent revolutionary basis: in effect, a constituent assembly. Implemented from below, this congress marked the establishment of the parallel governmental power that asserted its will to fight with arms in hand at Lexington and Concord in April of the following year.

This brief review of events from the Stamp Act demonstrations of 1765 to the outbreak of armed insurrection ten years later indicates how the liberation movement mounted through successive stages. It did not march straightaway to its goal, as though preprogrammed, but took a zigzag course in which sharp clashes between the contending sides alternated with interludes of calm.

Each of the levels in the development of the conflict was

marked off by a crisis in Anglo-American relations. The initiative taken by one side provoked a vigorous counteroffensive by the other. On one occasion the Patriots, on another the crown, beat a retreat and a compromise was arrived at.

For a decade reconciliation was the aim; the prospect of separation was unthinkable. But the periods of harmony turned out to be temporary truces. Although their antagonisms were held in check, the underlying discontents among the colonials kept simmering below the surface, became reheated, and flared into the open at the next provocation.

In its very irregularity the ripening revolt exhibited an inner rhythm that expressed the dynamics of the national-democratic struggle.

As the tensions finally grew, the pulsebeats of revolt pounded faster and faster. Finally, the antagonisms within the imperial system became so unbearable for both sides that they blew up into armed insurrection at Lexington and Concord.

The principal driving force throughout this process was the insurgent masses headed by the Sons of Liberty. Beginning with the Stamp Act demonstrations of 1765, they came forward at every critical juncture of the struggle as the striking arm of the Patriots.

Along the way the plebeians sometimes found themselves not only in conflict with the British authorities, but in disagreement with the moderate merchants and planters whose representatives held the reins in their hands. The patricians were divided among themselves on whether to organize resistance to the regime or to parley indefinitely with it. The colonial merchants were the pivot on which the conflict swung one way or the other.

The sharpening of the struggle cut the ground from under the compromising merchants and hesitating planters both from the right and from the left.

The British policies that started with intensified economic exploitation and territorial encirclement from 1764 on required increased political repression for enforcement. This led to outright military despotism with Gen. Thomas Gage's occupation and choking of the port of Boston.

London's course from taxation to tyranny upset the old equilibrium and smashed the alliance between the wealthy colonial merchants and planters and their English counterparts that had made possible the previous compromise settlements.

The split between Britain and America became unescapable when the merchant classes on opposite sides of the Atlantic could no longer find common ground. The irate crown would yield no more concessions—even slight ones—to the colonists. The rebels had to be whipped and taught a lasting lesson in submission.

By November 1774 George III declared to Lord North that the New England colonies were "in a state of rebellion" and "blows must decide whether they are to be subject to this country or independent."

By this time the more radical Patriots were equally determined not to submit to British tyranny but to resist, come what may. This the Minutemen did at Lexington and Concord the next April.

This sequence of events demonstrated how outright rebellion logically grows out of the preceding period of compromise—or, more precisely, out of its exhaustion.

For ten years the leaders of both sides adhered to a policy of conciliation. It worked—until the deepening of their differences precluded further compromise. By 1775 the ties between England and America that had weathered so many storms had come apart and the issues between them had to be settled by drastically different means.

This outcome was not the product of deliberate design on the part of the colonists or the crown. The Patriots tried to get redress for their grievances through authorized channels until they were driven by forces beyond their control to do it the hard way. The methods of negotiation were superseded by armed combat once the hope of reform within the empire was blasted.

The stern necessity for revolution became manifest, broke through into the consciousness of its major classes, and became an imperative demand only after ten years of inconclusive confrontations. Even after the Boston Tea Party the radicals were in a minority in the Continental Congress at Philadelphia. Early in 1775 John Adams noted that the congress majority "are fixed against hostilities and rupture, except they become absolutely necessary. And this necessity they do not see."

The battle of Concord and Lexington changed their minds. There two irreconcilable necessities clashed head-on—the reactionary necessity of the British government to reinforce its domination in naked tyrannical form, and the progressive necessity of the American colonists to resist to the end.

The ultimate determinant in the making of a rebellion is the readiness of the masses for action against their oppressors. A letter written by a Maryland clergyman to Lord Dartmouth, Britain's secretary of state for American affairs, on December 20, 1775, gives a firsthand description of the "do-or-die" attitude of the rebels.

"Since the battle of Lexington, I have been twice in eight of the thirteen united colonies, namely, Massachusetts-Bay, Rhode Island, Connecticut, New-York, New-Jersey, Pennsylvania, New-Castle, etc, and Maryland, all which, except New-York, are almost unanimous in the voice of liberty. Indeed none (save a few officers under the crown) are willing to be bound by the British parliament. . . . The congresses and committees have so raised and regulated the militia and minutemen, whom they have raised in almost every county, that they make, in every city and town, the most warlike appearance. . . .

"Where government can produce one thousand on the continent, America, with as much ease and expense, can produce ten thousand in opposition: for men, women and children are against the proceedings of administration throughout the united colonies to a wonderful majority. The women, both old and young, being greatly irritated at the inflexibility of administration, are not only willing their sons and brothers should turn out in the field, but also declare that they will give them up and themselves likewise as a sacrifice before they will bow to Pharaoh's taskmasters; this makes the raising of troops on the continent very easy. Let a person go into any province, city, town, or county, and ask the females, 'Are you willing your sons or brothers should go for soldiers and defend their liberties?' they would severally answer, 'Yes, with all my soul, and if they won't go I won't own them as my sons, or brothers; for I'll help myself if there should be any need of mine; if I can't stand in the ranks, I can help forward with powder, balls, and provisions.' . . . This, my lord, is the language of the American women; your lordship knows it is generally the reverse with the English."

The pastor's advice to make peace with the Americans was brushed aside, since the British government had already decided they were to be reduced "to a proper constitutional state of obedience."

Thus the developments that gave birth to the First American Revolution were no less lawfully caused than the birth of an infant. They conformed to the historical rule that once the economic and political preconditions for a revolution have matured, nothing and no one can stop its outbreak. Like a match rubbed on a rough surface, the frictions between the contending camps flared into open revolt at the point of maximum intensity in their confrontation. This general pattern prefigures how the next American revolution will develop and arrive through all the ebbs and flows of the struggle.

The First American Revolution was fully necessary and justified by its aims and has been amply vindicated by its results. To be sure, it did not dispose of all the major difficulties impeding the American people as they advanced under capitalist auspices. Every revolution is limited by the objective realities of its development.

The failure to uproot slavery, which was reinvigorated under the Cotton Kingdom by the expansion of the textile industry and the introduction of the cotton gin, necessitated a second stage of the bourgeois-democratic revolution to accomplish its unfinished historical tasks. And even the mighty Civil War and Reconstruction did not give equality to the legally emancipated slaves.

Since the Civil War most Americans have believed that revolution in this land has been done with for all time. What further need could there be for colossal upheavals of this kind? Two were enough—and these are safely interred in historical museums along with colonial muskets and the uniforms of the Blue and the Gray.

This comforting outlook has been solidified by the fact that small changes within the confines of the established capitalist order have set the pattern of national political life over the past hundred years. But the bicentennial should remind us that prolonged periods of reformist calm can be succeeded by revolutionary storms.

Many Americans nowadays sense that the political atmosphere is overdue for a change and a different season is on the way.

Indeed, elements of another revolutionary situation are beginning to take shape on American soil. As in the last quarter of the eighteenth century, the march of history has piled up and thrust forward a tangle of problems that clamor for solution. These evils have been produced by the remorseless ·operation of monopoly capitalism, which is no less depraved and outworn than was the rulership of the British monarchy—and is no more capable of eliminating the mess it is responsible for.

The social and political problems of the country are too

deepgoing to be disposed of by reformist palliatives; they require revolutionary measures and methods. The prime objective of the coming American revolution is to emancipate the working people as a whole by uprooting the power, property, and privileges of the profiteers. It also has to end the inequalities suffered by the Blacks, Chicanos, Native Americans, Puerto Ricans, and other oppressed nationalities and give them the right to self-determination.

The social transformation must likewise lift the disabilities inflicted upon such segments of our society as women, prisoners, gays, and the aged. The national home will have to be cleansed of capitalist filth and reconstructed from foundation to rooftop by the creative work of the insurgent masses to make it a fit place to inhabit.

These tasks and objectives are inscribed in the social structure of the United States and prescribed by the dynamics of its class relations. They await fulfillment regardless of the current state of awareness among the American people of their existence and of the necessity to undertake and achieve them. That is the essential and objective social, political, and historical necessity of our day and age.

The tasks ahead are more thoroughgoing and ambitious and will be harder to realize than those in the comparable period of the eighteenth century. The socialist revolutionary movement confronts a far more formidable antagonist in the giant imperialist corporations and their political, military, and police defenders than the Patriots faced in the overseas rulers and their local henchmen.

Jefferson wrote in his *Autobiography* about the inherited wealth of the aristocratic families of his time: "The transmission of this property from generation to generation, in the same name, raised up a distinct set of families, who, being privileged by law in the perpetuation of their wealth, were thus transformed into a Patrician order, distinguished by the splendor and luxury of their establishments. From this order, too, the king habitually selected his counsellors of State; the hope of which distinction devoted the whole corps to the interests and will of the crown."

These specifications fit the Rockefellers, Mellons, Morgans, and other ruling families of our own day who are "of more harm and danger, than benefit, to society" and have to be expropriated as the feudal proprietors were.

As the radicalization of the sixties has spread and the

deepening economic crisis of world capitalism overshadows the mid-seventies, more individuals are thinking about the prospect of fundamental change in the United States than at any time since the 1930s. Many more see this as desirable than understand how necessary and unavoidable such an eventuality is.

The irremediable rottenness of capitalist imperialism and the intransigence of the ruthless plutocrats who control the country along with much of the planet can be depended upon to goad the masses further and further along the road of opposition in the period ahead, regardless of their will or present state of consciousness.

The decade from 1765 to 1775 deserves attention because its political evolution exemplifies how the confrontation of contending forces mounts from a starting point of low intensity and awareness to higher levels of antagonisms and consciousness. In this process the hopes and illusions of a peaceful transition from the intolerable and outworn institutions to a new and better order are gradually shed. The hammer blows of the reactionary adversary willy-nilly bring the masses up against the great decision—whether to go forward at all costs or to lie down and submit to tyranny and stagnation.

Twice before in America's history when its people were forced to cope with this dilemma, they realized what they had to do and resolutely went ahead and did it. That's one important lesson to be derived from "the spirit of '76."

Another has to do with the problem of leadership. The leaders of the First American Revolution were sifted out, selected, and trained in the contests with the British authorities in the streets, courts, and legislative assemblies in the years before the outbreak of armed struggle. They had established firm ties with the masses; the people were ready to follow them.

More farsighted and unyielding figures such as Sam Adams and Patrick Henry grasped the necessity for the break with Britain before the others and prepared the people through propaganda and practical action for that eventuality. They were sure that their countrymen could take on and beat the cohorts of the crown.

Marxism teaches that a socialist revolution of the working masses is the only way capitalism can be overturned and replaced by a superior system. The revolutionary contingents and their leaders must be thoroughly imbued with this realistic conviction.

Those who are not convinced of the necessity as well as the desirability of such a revolution and its appropriate modes of action and organization will not be capable of sustaining the burdens of the harsh struggles required to bring it into being and carry it through to its consummation.

The revolutionary potential of the American people has not been exhausted by the efforts expended in the bourgeois-democratic era of the eighteenth and nineteenth centuries. On the contrary, the workers, with the oppressed minorities and their other allies, have more than enough energy and capacities to fend off the assaults of capitalist reaction and go forward to abolish the misrule of the possessing classes. They can also forge a leadership from their midst that can show them the way to do so.

Organizers of the Revolution

George Novack (1975)

April 19 marked the two hundredth anniversary of the battle of Lexington and Concord, the opening of hostilities between the colonists and the crown that had been fermenting since the Stamp Act demonstrations ten years before.

As a youth living in Somerville, situated along the route between Boston and Lexington, I used to watch from my house the yearly retracing of the ride of Paul Revere. He was the Patriot Express who had been dispatched with William Dawes by the Committee of Safety to alert the countryside about the invasion of British troops sent by General Thomas Gage to destroy the arms stored at Concord for use by the·Continental militia.

As Revere's enactor galloped by on his horse, waving a cocked hat, he was patriotically cheered on by us children.

In that innocent time I did not know what a subversive person Paul Revere really was. We were not told that he belonged to a conspiratorial organization called the Sons and Daughters of Liberty that had been diligently working for years to defend the rights of the Massachusetts colonists and rouse them to resist Britain's coercive measures.

We had been taught that the American Revolution was a glorious event. But it had taken place so long ago that it seemed more like an act of nature than the conscious work of revolutionary-minded individuals. We did not inquire what had driven the people who lived in our neighborhood in the last quarter of the eighteenth century to engage in armed combat against their rulers and how they were brought to that point. My own outlook had to be revolutionized before I understood what the rebels of those days were doing.

The transition from one form of society and political regime to another requires the activity of self-sacrificing, persevering, and gifted men and women who strive to change the world around them under the conditions their century has laid down for them. These pathfinders provide conscious guiding elements in what would otherwise be an unthinking and anarchic process. Their will, courage, initiative, idealism, stamina, and intelligence are indispensable ingredients in the making of a successful challenge to the status quo.

The First American Revolution was made by the common people of the thirteen colonies, whom Tories and moderates alike fearfully derided as "the mobility." Fortunately, they were organized and led by uncommon personalities.

Foremost among them were Sam Adams of Boston, Revere's mentor; and Adams's southern counterpart, Patrick Henry of Virginia. Henry, the lawyer-orator who spoke for the people in the backcountry against the aristocratic tidewater planters, took the lead at two crucial turning points in the prelude to Lexington and Concord.

In May 1765 he instigated the resolutions adopted by the Virginia House of Burgesses that first denied Britain's right to tax the colonists without their representation. He concluded his speech with this warning: "Caesar . . . had his Brutus—Charles the first, his Cromwell—and George the third—may profit by their example. . . . If this be treason, make the most of it."

Ten years later, on March 23, 1775, in a speech urging the immediate formation of an armed militia, Henry declared: "Give me liberty, or give me death!" He was outlawed by the British governor for that act of defiance.

The way for the interventions of these revolutionaries had been prepared by historical and economic changes of international scope that had profoundly altered the relations between the Americans and Great Britain as well as between the upper and lower classes in the colonies following the French and Indian War. These developments gave such a powerful impetus to their disputes that a social and political upheaval had become more and more urgent.

The armed encounter on April 19, 1775, was not spontaneous. The oppositional forces had been well organized, mobilized, and propagandized and had come under experienced, authoritative, and able direction in the prerevolutionary period. Who organized the rebel movement against Britain? Who inspired and sustained the struggle through its upturns and downturns, gave the signal for armed confrontation, and eventually piloted the revolution to victory?

The revolutionary movement was prepared and led by the Patriot party, which had its roots in the conflicts between the crown officials and the colonists and between the upper and lower classes in the provinces over the preceding decades. Out of these contests democratically inclined (Whig) factions and aristocratic (Tory) factions had been formed in almost every colony. In Massachusetts these were known as the Country and Court parties.

The democratic groupings were made up of "free-trading" (smuggling) merchants, lawyers, preachers, artisans, shopkeepers, and laborers in the seaport towns, backed up by yeomen and woodsmen in the backcountry. Their claims for greater rights were originally directed against the royal governors and the oligarchies tied up with them rather than against the king. The experiences gained in these encounters with the royal authorities proved valuable in their subsequent dealings with Parliament and the crown.

As the conflict heated up, the champions of colonial liberties began to develop a keener consciousness of their interests as a people separate from those of the overseas rulers and to feel, think, and act more like independent Americans thar like British subjects. These sentiments of distinctive nationality ripened below the surface until they were fully disclosed with the publication of Tom Paine's *Common Sense* and the proclamation of independence in 1776.

The Patriots were not organized along the lines of either the parliamentary or the workers' parties of the nineteenth and twentieth centuries. They were loose aggregations of diverse social layers, each with its own grievance, arrayed against British tyranny.

The leadership and ranks of the forces in all bourgeois revolutions have invariably had an extremely heterogeneous character. This was as true of the Patriots as of Cromwell's men and the Jacobins. The Patriot cause brought together a left flank of urban toilers, craftsmen, and tradesmen along with small farmers, hired hands, indentured servants, Blacks, and frontiersmen, ranged alongside the mercantile interests, anti-British planters, lawyers, land speculators, and large property owners.

They encompassed the richest men in the colonies, such as the Boston "merchant prince" John Hancock and the slaveholding landowner of Virginia, George Washington, as well as the poorest, like the indigent West Massachusetts farmer Daniel Shays who became a captain in the Continental army.

In the northern seaports the Patriot party was built on an alliance between the radical merchants and the plebeians whom the wealthy gentry called "the rabble." They in turn sought political collaboration with the settlers in the rural areas and on the frontiers. In the South, which had no urban centers except Charleston, the planters held the same place as the merchants up North.

Their variegated social composition gave rise to different tendencies that at times generated acute tensions and deep cleavages among the Patriots. United by the common objective of throwing off the British yoke, the divergent components of the coalition found themselves at odds to one degree or another in all three stages of the revolution: its preparatory period from 1765 to 1775; the War of Independence from 1776 to 1783, when open civil strife erupted in several places, leading in Georgia to the formation of two separate revolutionary regimes; and, finally, during the domestic struggles between the patricians and plebeians from 1783 to 1789 that were climaxed by the suppression of Shays's Rebellion in 1787, the Constitutional Convention, the foundation of the Republic, and the adoption of the Bill of Rights.

The left wing of the Patriots was headed by the Sons and Daughters of Liberty. This was the first popular revolutionary formation in North America—the trans-Atlantic equivalent of the Levellers in England and the Jacobins in the French Revolution.

Carrying forward the traditions of the earlier democratic clubs, the Sons of Liberty made their debut as a formidable fighting force during the agitation around the Stamp Act in 1765 and spread swiftly through the colonies. They operated as autonomous local and provincial bodies, communicating with one another through intercolonial Committees of Correspondence.

In a letter to the Boston Sons of Liberty written April 2, 1766, the New York leaders tried to remedy their looseness by proposing a congress of the Sons of Liberty "to form a general plan to be pursued by the whole." Although warmly greeted, nothing came of the suggestion because they lacked a leadership of their own.

At first the Liberty Boys functioned as secret societies for fear of retaliation by the authorities. But as they became more influential and awesome, they began to conduct their affairs more publicly, usually under the cover of some safe auspices. But they did not become legalized until the outbreak of the revolt against Britain.

The Sons of Liberty were by and large a plebeian movement. Mechanics, artisans, and day laborers constituted the bulk of the membership. This was visible in the mass protest demonstration against the Stamp Act called by the Liberty Boys of New York on November 1, 1765. There were between 400 and 500 seamen and 300 carpenters, as well as a considerable contingent of country folk, in the crowd that forced the local stamp agents to resign.

At the head of these working people were representatives of the educated, prosperous, and professional strata, themselves mostly of lower-class origin. Of eighteen leaders in the New York organization, eleven were merchants and four lawyers.

This hierarchy was equally conspicuous in Boston. There "the lowest classes—servants, negroes, and sailors—were placed under the command of 'a superior set consisting of the Master Masons carpenters of the town'; above them were put the merchants' mob and the Sons of Liberty,—known to the Tories as Adams's 'Mohawks,'— upon whom the more delicate enterprises against Tories and Crown officers devolved; and Mackintosh [Andrew Mackintosh, leader of the South End cudgel boys—GN] was given one hundred and fifty men 'trained as regular as a military Corps' to act as storm troops," writes John C. Miller. (*Sam Adams*, p. 70.)

The Liberty Boys functioned as the shock troops of the rebels both in the towns and in the countryside. In the early part of 1766 the Connecticut association was reported to have 10,000 men under arms and Massachusetts and New Hampshire, 40,000. They vowed not to be enslaved "by any power on earth, without opposing force to force."

The Sons of Liberty undertook bold and aggressive actions to enforce their demands. They did not hesitate to take control of the streets and exercise power in their own right against the constituted authorities. In New York they dared board a British warship, insisted on the surrender of an officer who had uttered derogatory remarks against them, and stood ready to fight the British troops.

"They broke out in rioting in Boston, New York, Philadelphia, and Charleston; they pillaged and razed the offices of stamp agents; they burned stamps in the streets; they assailed the houses of royal officers; in Boston the residence of the lieutenant governor was pried open, his chambers sacked, and his property pitched out into the streets," wrote Charles and Mary Beard.

"In fact, the agitation, contrary to the intent of the merchants and lawyers, got quite beyond the bounds of law and order. As Gouverneur Morris remarked, 'the heads of the mobility grow dangerous to the gentry, and how to keep them down is the question.' Indeed, the conduct of the mechanics and laborers was so lawless that it is difficult to paint a picture of the scene in tones subdued enough for modern Sons and Daughters of the Revolution." (*The Rise of American Civilization,* pp. 212-13.)

Conservative property owners were extremely disquieted by the militancy, the disregard for law and property rights, and above all by the growing independence displayed by these sons of labor. They sought to bridle the plebeian insurgents, curb their "leveling tendencies," and keep their activity more in line with their own limited class aims. This clash between the right and left wings within the Sons of Liberty first flared up in 1766.

In New York, according to Herbert Morais, "the conservatives were led by John Morin Scott and William Livingston, the radicals by Isaac Sears and John Lamb. The issue involved a question not only of tactics—reliance upon petitions and theoretical arguments as against the use of direct action—but also of orientation—the introduction of policies designed to advance the class interests of merchants as opposed to the adoption of measures calculated to better the condition of the rank and file of the people. The struggle resulted in a decisive victory for the radicals. From then, the Sons of Liberty became the voice of the artisan democracy." ("The Sons of Liberty in New York," in *The Era of the American Revolution,* pp. 278-79.)

After the Stamp Act was repealed in 1766, the Sons of Liberty temporarily receded into the background. Thrown forward by the first wave of resistance, they became isolated with its ebb. But they continued their agitation no matter what the fluctuations of the struggle.

Between 1766 and the broad resurgence of the mass movement in 1773 the principal figures and activists among them kept the sparks of rebellion burning by issuing leaflets, staging occasional demonstrations, and organizing protests around the Liberty Poles they erected and safeguarded. They were feared as a menace by the well-to-do merchants and persecuted by the British government as sowers of sedition.

But they were not intimidated and could not be crushed, thanks to popular sympathy and support. Finally, during the Tea Act agitation at the end of 1773, the Liberty Boys surged forward at the head of the aroused masses, calling large meetings and anti-British demonstrations, organizing tea parties to prevent the landing of dutied tea, and enforcing nonimportation agreements by terrorizing noncomplying merchants and crown officials. Their offensive set off a chain reaction that culminated in the Declaration of Independence.

In addition, they began to demand democratic reforms for the masses. When in 1774 the New York merchants formed a Committee of Fifty-One "made up of some of the most prudent and considerate persons in New York," the Sons of Liberty organized in opposition a Committee of Mechanics that "claimed equal rights for the classes hitherto excluded from voting." This embryonic plebeian party put up its own candidates for the Continental Congress but later withdrew them.

The Sons of Liberty intervened at every critical juncture to safeguard the revolutionary movement against its enemies and underminers and against unprincipled compromisers and scuttlers. They strove to accentuate its democratic character. When the news about Concord and Lexington came in April 1775, the New York Liberty Boys armed themselves, detained all the vessels in the harbor, and prevented the dispatch of British troops to Boston.

The partisans of the Sons of Liberty formed the backbone of the Minute Men and the Continental army and became the spearhead of the democratizing forces following the War of Independence. Wherever reactionary forces lifted their heads or showed their hands, the Sons of Liberty who remained true to their banner were to be found at their posts. The revolution could not have been sustained and carried through without their audacious activity and sacrifices. These plebeian leaders of the bourgeois-democratic revolution were the precursors of the socialist revolutionaries of today.

Although New York, as the center of communications between the Northeast and South, occupied the key position in the operations of the Sons of Liberty, the Boston Boys were in the forefront of the struggle. Boston was the Paris, the Petrograd of the First American Revolution.

This bustling seaport was the commercial and financial capital of the thirteen colonies. The up-and-coming, daring, and resourceful Boston merchants traded with the whole world. The Whigs among them were ready to take more risks than their colleagues in New York and Philadelphia in political as well as in commercial enterprises. Just as the Puritan merchants of London stood up against King Charles I, so such radical Boston merchants as John Hancock offered staunch opposition to King George III. Great merchants like him employed hundreds of men who followed their lead in politics as well as in business. They could count on direct support from the shoal of small merchants in the city.

Boston was above all the home of what the aristocrats scorned as "the rabble." The Boston mechanics, tradesmen, seamen, shipyard workers, longshoremen, and fishermen were the most democratic-minded, turbulent, and politically conscious people on this side of the Atlantic. They acquired a sense of their own power early on by taking control of Boston through the medium of the town meeting held at Faneuil Hall, "the Cradle of Liberty." These brawny men became expert in battling the colonial aristocracy for a greater share of political power.

Boston was known throughout the colonies, and from one end of the British empire to the other, as a hotbed of rebellion. The Sons of Liberty, cried the Tories, wanted to "Bostonize," that is, revolutionize, the whole continent. Boston, they claimed, wanted to overturn the social and political order and set up a "wild Republic of mad independents."

While the Patriot leaders in Boston primarily depended upon the combativeness of the laboring elements of the town, they found heavy reserves in the farmers of Massachusetts and the rest of New England. Although slower to move than the city populace, they were stubborn fighters once aroused.

Unlike the southern provinces, New England had no large slave plantations; its yeomen were stout and self-reliant individuals imbued with democratic sentiments. In fact, the upper-class patriots in the middle and southern colonies were very much afraid of the New England militiamen because they spread leveling doctrines by their very attitudes.

These were the class forces available for anti-British action. But they needed an organizer. They found that person in Sam Adams.

Although Washington, Franklin, Jefferson, and even his cousin John Quincy Adams became more celebrated, Sam Adams was the preeminent figure of the First American Revolution. He was so regarded by both sides. Jefferson said he was "truly the *Man of the Revolution.*" Lord North called the American patriots "Sam Adams's crew," and General Gage singled him out from the general amnesty he promised the rebels.

Adams was the first long-term professional revolutionary organizer in America; he devoted his entire adult life to working for the cause of freedom from Britain. As the prime mover of the revolution, Adams was the individual most hated, feared, and execrated by the upholders of the established order.

Like other staunch revolutionary leaders, from Cromwell to Lenin, he was dubbed a "dictator." It was said that he worked to see one man at the head of America, Boston at the head of Massachusetts, and himself dictator of Boston. He had in fact come close to realizing these aims by 1775. But if one man was to be supreme in America, the people preferred Adams to the continued rule of King George III. Whatever power he personally exercised was progressive and democratic whereas the continued sway of the crown was tyrannical and ultrareactionary.

Adams was reputed to be "the Greatest Republican [that is, antimonarchist—GN] in America" and "the most extravagant partisan of democracy" in the Continental Congress. The first characterization was accurate; the second a bit extravagant.

As his views and actions demonstrated and his postwar record confirmed, Sam Adams was not a root-and-branch democrat nor a consistent "leveller." He belonged to one of the first families of Massachusetts and was ranked fifth in his class on Harvard College's aristocratic rating scale. His father was a merchant and a leader of the Country party in the fight against the gentry and the squirearchy.

Sam Adams spoke and acted for the most radical section of the Massachusetts merchant class, which leaned for support upon the smaller shopkeepers, craftsmen, laborers, and farmers in their struggles against England and its servitors. He incarnated the link between them. This bourgeois revolutionist teamed up the diverse rebellious elements among the colonial population and then, placing himself and his associates in the driver's seat, guided them along the road to independence. He directed the revolutionary movement in accord with the needs and interests of the progressive northern bourgeoisie, urging the masses forward or restraining them as it suited the merchants of all grades in their quest for power.

He was a masterful political leader and revolutionary organizer. Proceeding from his local activity to its culmination on a continental scale, his achievements can be summarized in six sentences.

1. He laid out a plan of action in defense of colonial rights that served as a programmatic guide for the most resolute anti-British faction.

2. He welded together a strong democratic, revolutionary organization in Boston based upon collaboration among the oppositional merchants, tradesmen, mechanics, and artisans who dominated that key seaport.

3. He forged a firm alliance between this Boston movement and the country people, first in Massachusetts and then throughout New England, leading them in the fight against the gentry and the royal governors and later against the Parliament and king.

4. Through the Committees of Correspondence he succeeded in creating an intercolonial network that knit together all the Patriot forces and assured their unity of action.

5. He was instrumental in promoting the series of Continental Congresses that cemented the ties between the northern merchants and anti-British southern planters and capped the new state power.

6. In the War of Independence he was among the foremost advocates of its vigorous and uncompromising prosecution and thereby helped pull the struggle for liberation through to victory.

No wonder that in London Adams was considered "the first politician in the world" and without a peer in the business of "forwarding a rebellion." He deserved that reputation. Adams was the most astute, ingenious, and implacable revolutionary politician of his time. His organizational methods and activities will repay careful study by all aspiring revolutionists today.

Sam Adams flung himself wholeheartedly into the revolutionary movement and identified himself totally with it. He permitted himself no diversions from that course. This singlemindedness marked him off from most of his contemporaries, who took up or put down the burdens of revolutionary responsibility as the Patriot cause ascended or sagged. He rose above the vicissitudes of the fortunes of the struggle for liberation and measured up to the height of the tasks imposed by history on his class and generation. He made a profession of politics in the best sense, not to feather his nest or advance his personal ends, but solely to further the aims of the revolution.

He was a brilliant educator of the masses, instructing them in the ideas of the progressive bourgeois school. With tongue and pen he sought to raise their self-respect and to teach them to trust in their own strength and to know their rights, originally as free-born English citizens and later as sons and daughters of revolutionary New England.

He encouraged them to defend their cherished rights against all violators by militant methods and, if necessary, with arms in hand. He roused the people against every injustice on the part of the governing classes, warned them against the dangers threatening their liberties, and mobilized them for resistance on all fronts.

Adams was a tireless propagandist and political journalist, an irreconcilable opponent, and a crafty fighter. He wrote articles expounding oppositional ideas and popularizing Patriot doctrines in half a dozen colonial papers under half a dozen different pen names. As early as 1748, when Adams was only twenty-six years old, he and his friends founded a newspaper called the *Independent Advertiser,* which made life unhappy for the gentry, country squires, and colonial governors who were his favorite targets. "Every dip of his pen," moaned Governor Francis Bernard of Massachusetts, "stung like a horned snake."

He concentrated his energies upon organizing the masses for political action oriented toward the fight for power. Needing a mobile and dependable apparatus for that purpose, he created a powerful local machine by uniting the North and South End gangs of workers, which had formerly fought against each other, into a disciplined and responsive battalion to oppose the British authorities.

They were trained and directed by the Boston Caucus Club, which met in the garret of Thomas Dawes's house. The term "caucus" is supposed to come from the "caulkers" among the North End shipyard workers who followed Adams. This Caucus Club, called the "Grand Cork-Ass" by its enemies, formed an alliance with the Merchants' Club and elected their slate of candidates at the Boston town meeting.

The Caucus Club was the parent of the Boston Sons of Liberty, who were recruited largely "from the wharfingers, artisans and shipyard workers of North Boston." Its political committee, known as the Loyall Nine, was not only a deliberative and policy-making body but also an executive arm. Its members took charge of printing and placarding the notices that summoned the Boston citizens to mass meetings, demonstrations, boycott enforcements, tea parties—and ultimately to armed insurrection. Their work was necessarily conspiratorial since it was illegal and highly seditious.

At high points in the unfolding struggle, Sam Adams's Boys tended to slip out from under control and go beyond the limits he and his associates set for them. But the plebeian ranks did not become an independent power in their own right. They were the main agency set into motion, where needed, against the authorities by the revolutionary bourgeois leaders and did not exceed their designated subordinate role.

After almost twenty years of small-time politicking, Sam Adams was swept toward popularity and power on the wave of radicalism generated by the Stamp Act agitation in 1765. He was elected to the Massachusetts House of Representatives, where he headed the "Faction in perpetual opposition to Government."

This provincial legislature was not only his second platform for agitation after the Boston town meeting, but an important springboard for the capture of power. There he drafted and pushed through the famous resolutions and remonstrances that were circulated throughout the colonies and became not only briefs for the Patriot case but bugle calls to action.

Adams used the parliamentary arena without idolizing it. While he advocated measures of reform, he employed the methods of a revolutionist, combining the parliamentary moves and contests of his faction with the independent action of the masses in order to achieve the maximum striking power.

For example, he immediately threw open the proceedings of the Massachusetts House of Representatives, that hitherto august aristocratic body, to the public. This was done not only to exert mass pressure upon its conservative wing, but to convert the House into a school of political learning where many could catch the fire and emerge ardent Sons of Liberty. During most crucial disputes Adams's "Mohawks" crowded the galleries. They listened to their leaders and did not hesitate to tell the Tories below what would happen to their persons and property if they failed to heed the people's demands.

Such scenes at the State House resembled those of the Paris Commune in 1793-1794 and matched the pressures imposed upon the Convention by the Parisian "sans-culottes." Governor

Bernard complained, referring to the tactics of the Adams faction: "What with inflammatory speeches within doors, and the parades of the mob without [they] entirely triumphed over the little remains of government."

The Boston Liberty Boys launched the resistance to the Stamp Act on August 14, 1765, by attacking the stamp agent Andrew Oliver and two weeks later going on to sack the house of his hated brother-in-law, Lt. Gov. Thomas Hutchinson. Bostonians made August 14 a holiday, rightly boasting that the "Resistance *of that Day* roused the Spirit of America." This intervention of the Boston insurgents did in fact mark the beginning of the popular resistance that culminated in Concord and Lexington a decade later.

The assertion of their independent will abruptly changed the relationship of forces in the city. The Liberty Boys came to "rule the roost" in Boston. The authorities confessed their helplessness. "Aristocrats who had sneered at them· a few months before as 'the scum' and 'rabble' were now compelled to bow and scrape before them lest the mob be turned against their fine houses," writes John C. Miller.

"The sheriff's assistants were Sons of Liberty and would not move against their fellow patriots; justices of the peace were 'great favourers of them' and paraded beside them through the streets; juries were packed with Liberty Boys; and the Boston selectmen stood in such awe of them that they did not dare to attempt repression. Whoever was so foolhardy as to oppose the Sons of Liberty in Boston in 1765 was sure to feel the smart of 'the Iron Rod of the popular Despotism.'"

At that time Boston was the most democratic city on earth. The Tories called it "an absolute democracy" because the masses, and not simply a few fine gentlemen, had a voice and a vote and actually exercised power.

Although by Massachusetts law no one could vote in town meetings without paying a property tax, this stipulation was not adhered to in Boston where, it was said, "anything with the appearance of a man" was freely admitted. Although not more than 1,500 were eligible as voters, three or four thousand Bostonians were often present at the town meetings in Faneuil Hall, mostly "the lowest mechanics." The men of property shunned these democratic assemblies where Sam Adams and his comrades presented their proposals and passed them.

Crown officials shrieked that the town meetings controlled by the Sons of Liberty took up all kinds of impermissible matters and were "a constant source of sedition." They were in fact revolutionary tribunals.

Adams skillfully used other representative bodies as forums for agitation and as organs of protest. He converted the Massachusetts House into a powerful engine of revolutionary propaganda by passing petitions, resolves, and bills of complaint that he published in the press before they could be received and responded to by the king or Parliament. He was more concerned with educating and informing the masses than in parleying with their masters.

Adams turned all his talents to good use. Fond of singing, "he organized singing societies among Boston mechanics at which, Tories complained, more revolutionaries were produced than songbirds, because Adams presided over the meetings and 'embraced such Opportunities to ye inculcating Sedition, 'til it had ripened into Rebellion.'"

He made popular celebrations out of the anniversaries of the Stamp Act protests, the founding of the Sons of Liberty, and the Boston Massacre of 1770 to keep alive the flame of freedom and the memory of British crimes.

Here is a glimpse of Adams as a street-corner agitator the morning after the "Liberty Riot" of June 10, 1768, when a group of "sturdy boys and negroes" attacked the commissioners of the customs to enforce the nonimportation of British goods. He was seen in the South End of Boston "trembling and in great agitation" while he harangued a crowd of listeners to make a bold assault upon the royal government.

"If you are men," he exclaimed, "behave like men; let us take up arms immediately and be free and seize all the king's officers; we shall have thirty thousand men to join us from the country."

However, the time was not yet ripe for overt insurrection. The colonial merchants were split and neither the New England farmers nor the New York Liberty Boys were ready to march. After preaching armed resistance, Adams sized up the situation and then, like a good general, sounded a retreat. He pretended that he was preparing and talking about war against France, not the mother country.

He took as the next starting point for his activity the struggle against the military occupation of Boston. His "boys" made the stay of the redcoats there extremely miserable.

Adams was among the first to take to the field of action and the last to leave it. After a breach between the conservatives and radicals in the Whig ranks, that party declined in the lull following 1770. That was when Adams showed his mettle. Almost all the other Patriot leaders lost heart or retired from battle. Hancock flirted with the Tories. Others went over completely. The Whigs seemed "an expiring faction." But Adams remained firm and inflexible. "All of them except Adams abate of their virulence," testified his bitterest foe, Hutchinson.

There is "no Dishonor to be in a minority in the Cause of Liberty and Virtue," wrote Adams. "Where there is a spark of patriotick Fire," he exclaimed, "we will enkindle it."

That fire leaped higher than ever during the resistance to the East India Tea Act beginning in late 1773. The Liberty Boys summoned the people in the country towns to meet and discuss with them the ways and means to repel British tyranny. At these gatherings of Boston mechanics and farmers Adams "never was in greater glory." Tories observed with dismay that many country people were becoming more and more inclined toward vigorous resistance as they rubbed shoulders with the Boston Sons of Liberty in Faneuil Hall. Out of this upsurge came the Boston Tea Party, where Adams's Mohawks served the British overlords a bitter dish of tea made with salt water.

Adams directed the powerfully expanding movement of resistance through the Committees of Correspondence he had initiated by means of a Circular Letter from the Massachusetts House of Representatives. These committees constituted the backbone of the Patriot forces that were soon to seize power.

"At first," write the Beards, "the king's officers looked on the petty committee of correspondence as an absurd instrument of factional strife but they soon discovered in it the menacing force of a new state. One high Tory, Daniel Leonard, called it 'the foulest, subtlest, and most venomous serpent that ever issued from the egg of sedition.'"

The Committees of Correspondence were one of the American innovations in revolution that were copied by the French revolutionists and still later by the first Communist groups in Europe.

As the anti-British struggle deepened and widened throughout 1774 and 1775, the leaders of these committees began to set up independent bodies apart from the legal town assemblies and provincial legislatures. These committees of action, organized into local, county, and state conventions and basing themselves upon the insurgent masses, proceeded to take over the public powers from below. They roughly but firmly administered justice, levied taxes, policed the Tories, and raised troops for the war. This new political power was crowned and presided over by the Continental Congresses.

It was historically fitting that the battles at Concord and Lexington in April 1775 that precipitated the showdown ensued from the British attempt to seize the Patriots' military stores and capture their principal leaders, Sam Adams and John Hancock.

When Adams heard "the shot heard round the world" on Lexington Common, he exclaimed exultantly to Hancock: "Oh, what a glorious morning is this!" He had full right to be joyous. It was the birth of the liberating revolt he had done so much to herald and promote.

Boston bred many other characteristic leaders of the Patriot cause because the rebellious tendencies of the time flourished most vigorously in this hothouse. Among the figures from various levels among the townspeople associated with the Sons and Daughters of Liberty was Crispus Attucks, the huge ex-slave from Framingham, Massachusetts, part Black, part Indian, part white, a veteran street fighter who led the crowd of sailors and porters against the British "lobsterbacks" and fell in the Boston Massacre as the first martyr of the independence movement.

There was Paul Revere, the versatile silversmith, political engraver, and trustworthy artisan ready to fulfill the most dangerous missions; Andrew Mackintosh, the cobbler, who headed the attacks of the Liberty Boys on the stamp agents and Hutchinson's mansion and subsequently led their forays against Tory merchants and British redcoats; and Mercy Otis Warren, the political polemicist and playwright whose house in Plymouth was an organizing center for the top revolutionaries.

More than any among them, and very likely before anyone else, Sam Adams had been determined to conquer power and concentrate it in revolutionary hands. His relation with his followers exemplified two inseparable aspects of the revolution-ary process: the significance of the individual in history-making and the decisive role of the masses. As the chief pilot of the revolutionary vanguard, Adams made the greatest contribution to undermining and overthrowing the royal authority. Yet, skillfully as he steered the Patriot ship toward its destination, the plebeian crew did the work that brought it to port.

The Sons and Daughters of Liberty gave the most forthright

expression to the democratic aims and egalitarian aspirations of the populace. They launched the struggle against British despotism in 1765; carried it on their shoulders through the vicissitudes of the next ten years; and drove it to the point of armed uprising in April 1775.

Sam Adams could not have achieved his ends without the support he received from his "Mohawks," the Liberty Boys and the Minute Men, who responded to his calls for action. He himself was well aware of this dependence upon the moods and moves of the masses. He is reported to have said: "It is often stated that I am at the head of the revolution, whereas a few of us merely lead the way as the people follow, and we can go no further than we are backed up by them; for, if we attempt to advance any further, we make no progress, and may lose our labor in defeat."

This was the tribute he paid to the rank and file in the promotion of the revolutionary cause. From start to finish they were the real heroes and heroines of the struggle for freedom. As it has been in the past, so will it be in the future.

Tom Paine—Revolutionist

Jean Y. Tussey (1952)

Thomas Paine was born on January 29, 1737. On January 10, 1776, his historic call for the American Revolution, *Common Sense,* was published. Both of these events nowadays receive passing notice. But for those who seek to understand the dynamics of the revolutionary process in America and the role outstanding individuals played in it, Tom Paine deserves a much larger place than the official hero-makers give him.

Most history books, if they mention Paine at all, merely note the undeniable fact that *Common Sense* was an important contribution to the preparation of the public mind for the open revolt against England. Few attempt to explain what went into the making of the man and why he was able to leave his indelible mark on American history.

Tom Paine was born in Thetford, England. His father, a corset maker, was a Quaker; his mother was a conservative Church of England member. So from his earliest childhood Paine's critical approach to religion was stimulated by the differences in his own home.

An only child, he was sent for six or seven years to a local grammar school, which differed from most in that it provided some education in history and science. He left at the age of thirteen to be taught corset making. He ran away to sea after five years, was brought back home by his father before he could actually leave the country, but ran away again, this time to spend a brief period on a privateer.

During the rest of his early life in England he supported himself by working from time to time as a tax collector, a corset maker, and a teacher.

In London in 1757 he attended philosophical lectures at night.

The lecturer was A. Ferguson, author of the *History of Civil Society* (1750), which is quoted favorably by Marx in *Capital.* Marx refers to Ferguson as Adam Smith's predecessor and an economist who had a keen appreciation of the harmful effects of the development of capitalist manufacture on the worker. Ferguson undoubtedly influenced Paine's philosophical and political-economic thinking, as expressed in his later writings. Paine also participated in philosophical debates in a club that met at the White Hart Tavern in Lewes, where he was stationed as a tax inspector, in 1768.

In 1772 he acted as spokesman for tax inspectors seeking an increase in pay. He wrote a tract called *The Case of the Officers of the Excise,* which cited the discrepancy between their nominal salary and their real wages, described the scope and effects of poverty, and urged the government in its own self-interest to raise wages in order to guarantee the honesty and loyalty of its employees by removing temptations.

Subsidized by the contributions of the tax inspectors, Paine published the report and spent some time in London lobbying at Parliament. The net result of his negotiations was no raise for the men, and the spotting of Paine as a troublemaker to be removed at the first opportunity.

While in London, Paine met Benjamin Franklin, who was there on behalf of the colonies. Paine made a favorable impression and later received a letter of recommendation from him to friends in Philadelphia.

When Paine was finally removed from his government job, for being "absent without leave," he settled his financial accounts by selling the property of a small shop he and his wife had maintained, separated from his wife, and left for Philadelphia, where he arrived November 30, 1774, with Franklin's letter of introduction.

By January 1775 he was editor of the *Pennsylvania Magazine* and actively interested in the colonial cause. The issue of independence had not yet been set forth positively by the revolutionary leaders, who still functioned on the basis of demands for reforms.

The first clear-cut call to the masses to break with England and monarchy, to give up the "patchwork" of reform and embark on the revolutionary course of independence, was issued in Paine's *Common Sense,* published in January 1776. With this, Paine took his place as the chief propagandist of the American Revolution.

The pamphlet was written in simple, direct language, devoid of all obscure historical, biblical, and other learned references and allusions so common in the literary style of the day. It was a powerful appeal to every segment of the population to join in a broad united front to win complete freedom from England and embark on a career as an independent nation.

An early biographer called *Common Sense* "this pamphlet, whose effect has never been paralleled in literary history. . . ." This statement may be somewhat exaggerated. Nevertheless, the effect of Paine's great tract has still never been paralleled by anything in the literary history of the United States.

We must recall that when Paine penned *Common Sense* the full program of the Revolution had not as yet been given to the people. The revolutionary war was under way, and the people were in effect fighting for independence, but without realizing it. No one, not even Sam Adams himself, had yet put forward the full revolutionary program; not openly at any rate. The dead weight of past centuries—monarchy, empire, feudal servitude, all the untouchables of bygone days—still clouded the minds of the living.

Into this atmosphere, Thomas Paine flung his remarkable pamphlet, which advocated, at one stroke, independence, republicanism, equalitarian democracy, and intercolonial unity! The Revolution was thenceforth armed with a program, or, to put the matter precisely, the program that was in the minds and private conversations of most radicals became the public property of the Revolution.

Paine's great literary gift sparkles from every page of *Common Sense*. He stirred the workers and farmers of colonial times with his blunt and unceremonious comments, such as this: "In England a King hath little more to do than to make war and give away places [positions]; which, in plain terms, is to empoverish the nation and set it together by the ears. A pretty business indeed for a man to be allowed eight hundred thousand sterling a year for, and worshipped into the bargain! Of more worth is one honest man to society, and in the sight of God, than all the crowned ruffians that ever lived."

In similar blunt terms, he made out the case for completing the Revolution by independence. "Everything that is right or reasonable pleads for separation. The blood of the slain, the weeping voice of nature cries, 'TIS TIME TO PART.'" These words sank into the consciousness of the new nation, and prepared the way for the Declaration of Independence, which followed in six months.

It is an indication of how popular Paine's arguments were that *Common Sense* immediately became a best seller. About a hundred thousand copies were sold within the first six months after its publication. Since there was no copyright law, several pirated editions were also widely sold, and the total distribution of the pamphlet is estimated at at least three hundred thousand— and this at a time when the population was less than three million!

Paine's other major literary contributions to the American Revolution were the *Crisis* papers, issued periodically throughout the war. Aimed at maintaining the morale of the soldiers and the colonial forces, they reported on the events in the war, polemicized against the British and American Tories, appealed to the British people, and exuded revolutionary optimism despite defeats.

It is difficult to measure the effect of any particular document, but the circumstances surrounding the issuance of the first *Crisis* pamphlet give some indication of the basis for the comment of Joel Barlow, a contemporary American poet who served as minister to France under Madison, that "the great American cause owed as much to the pen of Paine as to the sword of Washington."

Morale was at a low ebb when Paine started the *Crisis* series. From August to December 1776 the Americans had suffered defeats, retreats, and desertions. Congress had fled to Baltimore. Washington's freezing soldiers were retreating across New Jersey. Paine, who was accompanying them, gauged the mood and the need correctly, when, without false optimism, he wrote the now famous lines:

These are the times that try men's souls: The summer soldier and the sunshine patriot will, in this crisis, shrink from the service of his country; but he that stands it NOW, deserves the love and thanks of man and woman. Tyranny, like hell, is not easily conquered; yet we have this conclusion with us, that the harder the conflict, the more glorious the triumph.

Washington had the pamphlet read aloud to every army detachment. A few nights later the army made the icy crossing of the Delaware that has been immortalized in painting and story, and won the victory at Trenton that began to turn the tide.

Acknowledgments of the tremendous role played by Paine in mobilizing sentiment for the Revolution have been plentiful from his enemies as well as his friends, and from all the leaders of the colonial struggle as well as historians since. But few give a rounded picture of his activity in the Revolution.

In July 1776 Paine joined the army as volunteer secretary to General Roberdeau, commander of the Flying Camp, an outfit that moved quickly to trouble spots where it was needed. From there Paine went to the army of General Nathanael Greene as volunteer aide-de-camp.

In January 1777 Paine was appointed secretary of a commission to negotiate with the Indians in eastern Pennsylvania. His activities in Pennsylvania and around the Continental Congress continued throughout the war and were by no means limited to legal and official bodies. He served, for example, on the Committee of Inspection, a price control committee formed at a mass meeting in Philadelphia on May 27, 1779, to deal with merchants, innkeepers, and others engaging in war profiteering at the expense of the public. As W.E. Woodward puts it in his biography of Paine: "The committee had no legal standing, but it proposed to accomplish its ends by popular pressure; or by force, if necessary."

In April 1776 he was elected secretary of the Committee on Foreign Affairs, formerly the Committee on Secret Correspondence, but was induced to resign on January 9, 1779, after he had exposed what he considered shady dealings by certain individuals in some of the secret diplomacy involved in securing French aid for the Revolution.

When Philadelphia was about to be attacked by the British in September 1777, Paine was convinced the city could be saved if the citizens were called out, fully informed on the military situation, and mobilized to build barricades and prepare for street fighting. Paine went to General Mifflin, who was then in the city, with his proposal, asking Mifflin, in his own words, "if two or three thousand men could be mustered up whether we might depend on him to command them, for without someone to lead, nothing could be done. He declined that part, not being then very well, but promised what assistance he could. A few hours after this the alarm happened. I went to General Mifflin but he had set off, and nothing was done. I cannot help being of the opinion that the city might have been saved. . . ."

In 1779 Paine's chronic poverty was in a particularly acute

stage, but within six months of his election as clerk of the Pennsylvania Assembly in November, he contributed $500 of his annual salary to head a subscription list for the relief of the army. The funds raised were used to establish the Bank of Pennsylvania to provide for the army's needs.

Paine resigned his post in November 1780 and went on a mission to France, seeking aid for the colonies. He returned in August with 2,500,000 livres, but Paine himself was so broke that he had to borrow ferry passage across the Delaware on his way home.

Upon the conclusion of the war Paine spent most of his time at his home in Bordentown, New Jersey, working on his inventions. A typical product of the spirit of scientific inquiry of his age, he was preoccupied after the Revolution with the development of his idea for an iron bridge to span the Schuylkill River at Philadelphia. He also worked on a planing machine, a new type of crane, an improved carriage wheel, and smokeless candles. He corresponded with Franklin, who encouraged him to continue.

Paine left for France with his model bridge on April 26, 1787. When he returned to America fifteen years later, revolutionary sentiment had so far abated that he was much too radical for his former colleagues. He was now a pariah where he had been a hero. He still had some friends, but persons were publicly discriminated against for holding to his views. Jefferson, however, invited him to stay for a while at the executive mansion, and he did.

An attempt to murder Paine was made at his home in New Rochelle, New York, on Christmas Eve 1804. Though he suspected Christopher Derrick, a local laborer, this revolutionist, who exalted objectivity and abhorred personal vindictiveness, refused to press charges.

In January 1805 Paine went to New York City to live. He and his admirers continued to be victimized for his views. When he went to vote in New Rochelle on election day 1806, the witch-hunters of his time got in their final blow: they charged that the man who had lived for nothing but the American cause and the spreading of its principles to Europe was an alien, and denied him the ballot.

When Paine died on June 8, 1809, after a prolonged illness, at 59 Grove Street, New York City, he had been reduced to almost complete friendlessness; the only attendants at his funeral in New Rochelle were a Quaker watchmaker, friends from France—

Mrs. Bonneville and her two sons—and two Negro pallbearers.

The man's significance and his ideas remain, but they cannot be fully appreciated on the basis of his role in the American Revolution alone. Paine was not a narrow patriot in the modern sense; he was a principled revolutionist first. When he went to France, and then England, after American independence was established, he continued to champion the struggles against the ancient order in those countries as wholeheartedly as he had the American cause. "Where liberty is not, there is my country," he is said to have declaimed at his departure from America.

During his stay in England he was the guest of Edmund Burke and other Whig leaders for a period, while they were trying to court favorable trade relations with America. But their friendship cooled when they found him unsympathetic to their proposals.

Paine arrived in Paris in 1789, when the French Revolution was under way. Lafayette gave Paine the key to the Bastille as a token of esteem for George Washington, symbol of the American Revolution.

When the French Revolution was viciously attacked and the divine right of kings upheld by Burke in his *Reflections,* published in 1790, Paine took up his pen again in defense of revolution, and wrote an answer, Part I of *The Rights of Man.* It was approved by the English Society for Promoting Constitutional Knowledge and other democratic groups, but created a considerable controversy not only in England, but in America as well. Jefferson, Madison, and Randolph commended it, and Jefferson sent it to an American printer.

In July 1791 Paine was a prime mover in the organization of the Republican Society, which aimed at the overthrow of monarchy and establishment of a French republic. At the time, many who were later to become Jacobins were still hesitant about advocating the abolition of monarchy, but the Republican Society placarded Paris with a manifesto written by Paine demanding the abdication of the king and elimination of the office.

In November of the same year, back in London, Paine was guest of honor at the annual dinner of the Revolution Society, formed to commemorate the English Revolution of 1688. There he made a speech toasting "The Revolution of the World"—the first man to raise that slogan, according to some historians. His remarks were noted and added to his dossier by the British government, which was preparing to arrest him for sedition.

Part II of *The Rights of Man* was a continuation of the attack on monarchy and aristocracy, and was dedicated to Lafayette. Its publication early in 1792 evoked a veritable lynch campaign against Paine in England. Burke's supporters instigated public protest meetings, book-burnings of *The Rights of Man,* and the distribution of medallions bearing slogans like "The End of Pain," "The Wrongs of Man," and "We dance; Paine swings." Paine's publisher was arrested for printing seditious literature, and the legal sale of the book was stopped by royal proclamation. Black market sales continued. Paine fought the attack on his writings, distributing free copies of *The Rights* and encouraging his supporters to stand up for his ideas at meetings called to incite feeling against them.

Meanwhile the book was translated into French and widely acclaimed throughout France. In August 1792 the French Assembly conferred the honorary title of Citizen on him, and four departments elected him to represent them in the National Convention. Consequently, when the English issued a warrant for his arrest, he left for France. He was found guilty of high treason in England in his absence.

In France, Paine participated in the Convention with the Girondists. He was selected in October to help draft the constitution, but he incurred popular disfavor when he attempted to save the life of the king by urging banishment instead of death, and was eventually expelled from the Convention in December 1793.

Paine was arrested by order of the Committee of Public Safety in January 1794. Through the machinations of the American representative in France at the time, his old enemy, the arch-conservative Gouverneur Morris, Paine was disclaimed as an American citizen and kept in prison. Only when Morris was finally recalled at the request of the French, and replaced with James Monroe, was Paine released.

He remained in France, living with Monroe while completing *Age of Reason,* an attack on the Bible and organized religion and an exposition of his Deist views. Later, when he was living with the editor and publisher, Nicolas Bonneville, Paine was approached by Bonaparte about the prospect of leading a liberating army in an invasion of England. The project did not materialize, but seven years later, in 1804, Paine wrote a letter "To the People of England on the Invasion of England" in which he still favored the idea, which was again being discussed, "as the intention of the expedition was to give the people of England an opportunity of forming a government for themselves, and thereby bring about peace."

The world revolutionist had considerable difficulty in getting back to America, since Britain ruled the seas and he was a marked man. In March 1801, Jefferson, then president, wrote Paine that a frigate would pick him up. Jefferson was attacked for this in America, and Paine declined the offer to save his friend further difficulties on this score. When the war between England and France ended, so that French ships were no longer liable to attack, Paine sailed for the United States, arriving October 30, 1802.

His active participation in the British and French revolutionary movements was at an end, but he continued to write pamphlets and letters, such as the letter to the English people mentioned above, and a series of "Letters to the Citizens of the United States," attacking the Federalists.

Paine was reviled by his contemporary opponents and misrepresented by later writers who repeated their slanders; and has been inadequately or falsely depicted also by the modern liberals who have claimed to "rehabilitate" him.

Of his contemporaries, the British opponents of American independence would, under ordinary circumstances, be the least important since their bias is clear. But many of Paine's antidemocratic attackers on this side of the Atlantic could find nothing better to base their slanders on than the interested political hack jobs written by professional propagandists of the British crown, and therefore it is necessary to trace such slanders to their source.

Two of the earliest hatchet jobs done on Paine were biographies written by Francis Oldys, A.M. (who was actually George Chalmers, a London government clerk), and James Cheetham, an Englishman who came to America to edit an antidemocratic newspaper. Chalmers's book was published in the heat of the controversy between Burke and Paine over the French Revolution.

But Paine's revolutionary ideas made him the butt of equally vicious attacks in America. John Adams, for example, labeled him "the filthy Tom Paine," an epithet that has been continued through modern times.

The New England Palladium called Paine a "lying, drunken, brutal infidel, who rejoiced in the opportunity of basking and wallowing in the confusion, bloodshed, rapine, and murder in which his soul delights."

A more recent example of how the early slanders affected his reputation is the fact that Paine's name was voted down for the

Hall of Fame, where other Revolutionary leaders are honored. Theodore Roosevelt referred to him as a "filthy little atheist," and as late as 1942 the Fairmont Park Commission of Philadelphia refused to permit the erection of a statue to Paine because of his "reputed religious views."

Paine has not fared so well at the hands of the school of "objective historians" or the liberals either.

Curtis P. Nettels of Cornell University, in *The Roots of American Civilization* (1946), stigmatizes Paine as a "restless English adventurer in radicalism and idealism."

W. E. Woodward, in *Tom Paine: America's Godfather* (1945), finds it necessary to deprive him of lasting significance by stating that "Paine was not a radical within the meaning of that term as it is used today. He was an individualist."

John C. Miller, in *Triumph of Freedom, 1775-1783* (1948), says that Paine reversed his line of criticism of the French government before the revolution in that country, accepting a bribe in the form of an offer to serve as paid propagandist for France in America. (Paine answered that old slander himself.) Miller adds that Paine's irreligion was so bad that Sam Adams had to rebuke him for contributing to the "depravity of the younger generation."

James Truslow Adams, in *Revolutionary New England, 1691-1776* (1941), repeats the condescending characterization of *Common Sense:* "Crude and coarse as it was, it was written in words of power."

Probably the best of the liberal treatments of Paine is that of Charles and Mary Beard in *The Rise of American Civilization,* which, though sketchy, gives some indication of Paine's principled consistency as an outstanding product of his times, as one who played an important part in helping shape revolutionary thinking, and as a courageous fighter whose plebeian insight gave his writing a force that none of the superficial or apologetic defenders of the propertied classes could equal.

Paine was in the vanguard of the progressive bourgeois revolution of his day. Influenced by the classical political economists such as A. Ferguson and Adam Smith, and by the philosophy of natural rights, he was well equipped to attack and refute the apologists for the status quo like Burke.

In *The Rights of Man* and other works, Paine expressed the same logic and concreteness in his approach to labor as on other questions. "Several laws are in existence for regulating and limiting workmen's wages," he wrote. "Why not leave them as free to make their own bargains, as lawmakers are to let their farms and houses?"

Paine opposed monarchy, slavery, poverty, organized religion and the Bible, and the unequal status of women. He was an advocate of universal education, reform of criminal law, pensions for the aged and other social security measures, reduction of armaments, and universal peace. But Paine was no meek pacifist. In writing on his proposal for reduction of armaments, he said that if others should refuse to disarm, he would take up his musket and thank God for giving him the strength to do so. Moreover, his enlistment in the colonial army and his whole life of revolutionary activity belie the picture some historians paint of him as a Quaker pacifist.

The explanation for the popularity of his writings, their broad mass appeal, is undoubtedly to be found in the fact that, of all the American revolutionary leaders and writers, he was one who by his origin, background, and way of life represented the plebeian masses and consequently could give more content to the democratic slogans and ideas of the time.

His popularity with the masses was based on his democratic convictions. Sam Adams, the chief organizer of the First American Revolution, also drew his strength from reliance on the masses. That Paine was in contact with and worked closely with Adams is indicated in the following quotation from a letter to Adams dated January 1, 1803:

> I am obliged to you for your affectionate remembrance of what you style my services in awakening the public mind to a declaration of independence, and supporting it after it was declared. I also, like you, have often looked back on those times, and have thought that if independence had not been declared at the time it was, the public mind could not have been brought up to it afterwards.
>
> It will immediately occur to you, who were so intimately acquainted to the black times of Seventy-six; for though I know, and you my friend also know, they were no other than the natural consequences of the military blunders of that campaign, the country might have viewed them as the natural inability to support its cause against the enemy, and have sunk under the despondency of that misconceived idea. This was the impression against which it was necessary that the country should be strongly animated.

Paine's view of himself and the Revolution was clearly stated in another article. Upon arriving in America, he wrote, "I had no thought of Independence or of arms. The world could not then have persuaded me that I should be either a soldier or an author. If I had any talents for either, they were buried in me, and might ever have continued so, had not the necessity of the times dragged and driven them into action."

But Paine's talents as a soldier and author were based on still another quality: he was a revolutionary thinker, honest, courageous, and prepared to go to the root of things. As he put it: "When precedents fail to assist us, we must return to the first principles of things for information, and think as if we were the first men that thought."

That was Tom Paine, revolutionist.

Mercy Otis Warren—
Mother of the American Revolution

Dianne Feeley (1975)

As Mary Beard showed in her book *Women As a Force in History,* the contributions of women in American history have been either ridiculed or ignored by the textbooks. But in fact women have participated in every movement for social change in U.S. history, beginning with the struggle for American independence. Several years before the Boston Tea Party, women formed anti-tea leagues and effectively boycotted British tea. And during the war, some women took up arms against the king.

Perhaps the most important woman of the American Revolution was Mercy Otis Warren. Although she never left New England and never attended school, Warren was as much the mother of the American Revolution as Samuel Adams, Thomas Jefferson, and Thomas Paine were its fathers. Elizabeth Ellet, in her three-volume work *Women of the American Revolution,* states unequivocally: "The name of Mercy Warren belongs to American history. In influence she exercised, she was perhaps the most remarkable woman who lived at the Revolutionary period."

From the opening battles against British tyranny in the 1760s through the fight for a bill of rights in the Constitution, Mercy Otis Warren fought for a complete realization of the democratic ideal. She was the only figure in the American Revolution to write a history of the struggle, and the only one to stand in opposition to the wars against the Native American peoples. She remained an intellectual leader of the radicals in both the prerevolutionary and postrevolutionary periods.

Born in 1728, Mercy Otis grew up in a republican household in West Barnstable on Cape Cod. Books, journals, and fireside debates were a part of her environment. When her older brother James studied with a clerical uncle in preparation for Harvard,

Mercy, for no additional fee, attended all but his Latin and Greek classes. She read Pope, Dryden, Milton, Shakespeare, and Raleigh's *History of the World.* As a result, she was more knowledgeable about English writers than most Harvard graduates of the period.

James Otis went on to study at Harvard for six years. At the time, Harvard was a hotbed of radical thought. Sam Adams, for instance, in his commencement speech in 1740, had argued for lawful resistance to the Supreme Magistrate if necessary. James brought home from Harvard the radical political philosophies he discovered there.

Intellectual companions from childhood, Mercy and James shared a common political outlook. He introduced her to the radical writings of John Locke, the British empiricist. Locke argued that a government's power ultimately rested in its citizens. Whenever the agreement between the ruler and ruled broke down, the people had a right to replace the government.

Mercy Otis married James Warren, a former classmate of her brother's, when she was twenty-six. (For a New England woman of her time, Mercy married much later than the average. By way of contrast, Abigail Smith Adams—who also had a long engagement—was married at twenty.)

James Warren, like Mercy, came from a family of farmer-merchants and republicans. Upon her marriage, Mercy went to live in Plymouth, about twenty-five miles from her birthplace. The friendship that formed the basis of the Warren marriage was reflected in their lengthy correspondence during the Revolutionary War. In Plymouth she raised five boys, and set down her thoughts in poetry and in her letters. Her writings grew out of daily experiences; the poems were often descriptions of the New England countryside.

Her correspondence with Abigail Adams—which was to continue for over fifty years—dates from this period. Despite the political differences that developed between the two after the Revolution, the women formed a friendship that one biographer has compared to the deep bond of sisterhood between Susan B. Anthony and Elizabeth Cady Stanton.

By 1760, James Otis had resigned his position as the King's Advocate in Boston in order to argue against the imposition of the writs of assistance. These writs permitted customs officers to enter a home or business to search for illegal goods. Bystanders were charged with aiding the officers in carrying out the king's orders. Otis's historic speech against this invasion of civil liberties introduced into American history the slogan "Taxation without representation is tyranny." The early historian Tyler has characterized this moment as the "prologue of the Revolution."

John Adams, who sat in the courtroom taking notes, later wrote: "Otis was a flame of fire. . . . Every man of an immense crowded audience appeared to me to go away as I did, ready to take arms against writs of assistance. Then and there was the first scene of the first act of the opposition to the arbitrary claims of Great Britain. Then and there, the child Independence was born."

From the time of that speech in 1761 until his brutal beating in a Tory tavern almost a decade later, James Otis was the leader of the radicals. His enemies judged him one of the most effective orators of his day. But even more important than his pamphlets or his agitational speeches was the organization he and Sam Adams gathered around them. This team of revolutionaries, which was to provide the political leadership of the American Revolution, included Sam Adams, Dr. Joseph Warren, John Adams, James Warren, and Mercy Otis Warren.

The physical attack on Otis in 1769 removed him from the public arena, although he coauthored a pamphlet with Sam Adams as late as 1771 and chaired the first Boston meeting of the Committee of Correspondence.

Although Mercy Warren did not challenge the custom of the time that a woman should not appear in a public gathering and speak, she did challenge other customs. She participated in the private political discussions within the radical circles, something that Abigail Adams never did.

In the early 1770s the Warren household in Plymouth became a weekend caucus club for revolutionaries. As Mercy Otis Warren wrote, "By the Plymouth fireside were many political plans originated, discussed and digested."

Among these was the idea of setting up a network to maintain communication among the radical centers in the various colonies.

This network took the form of democratically elected bodies that became known as the Committees of Correspondence; by 1772 they were functioning throughout the colonies. When the Revolution came, it was these committees that in fact organized the militia, levied taxes, and became the basis of the new government. Practically all historians, including Mercy herself, assign credit for conceiving the organizational plan to James Warren. But at the very least, the idea was the result of the collaboration that characterized the Warren household.

In 1772 an anonymous play, *The Adulateur, A Tragedy,* appeared in the *Massachusetts Spy.* (As many revolutionaries and most women of the period did, Mercy Otis Warren published all of her plays anonymously.) This play satirized the colonial administration. Although the characters bore the names Rapatio, Hazlerod, and Meagre, everyone in the colony knew them to be Governor Thomas Hutchinson and his relatives. Standing in opposition to these haughty men were the patriots, Brutus (James Otis) and Cassius (Sam Adams). The following year she wrote a sequel to this popular play, entitled *The Defeat.* Rapatio, again a central character, explains how he intends to pay for his household improvements with the colony's taxes.

The plays, based on actual events, were not meant to be performed in Puritan New England, but to be read. Mercy never saw a play in her entire lifetime; her knowledge of the theater came from reading Shakespeare.

As popular exposés of colonial rule, the plays helped to ignite the stubborn spirit of defiance necessary to the revolution. In *A Study of Dissent,* C. Harvey Gardiner attributes the creation of the "climate of opinion that led to the Boston Tea Party" to Warren's plays. They spread rapidly throughout the New England area and their characters' names became widely familiar. Sam Adams, referring to Governor Hutchinson in a letter, found it quite natural to write: "Rapatio is now gone to Middleboro to consult with his Brother Hazlerod."

Mercy wrote a popular account of the Boston Tea Party at the suggestion of John Adams, who thought her partisan writing "has no equal that I know of in this country." The resulting poem, *The Squabble of the Sea Nymphs,* was printed on the front page of the *Boston Gazette.*

All seven of Mercy Otis Warren's plays are primarily political and openly take the side of revolution. She was the first playwright to portray women as revolutionaries. In *The Ladies of Castile,* which was written after the war, the character of Marcia appropriates the treasury of the Catholic Church in order to pay the people's militia.

Warren's partisan writing was often claimed by others, and it is only recently that the ribald plays portraying cursing British soldiers have been finally attributed to her. When another author attempted to take credit for *The Group,* she asked John Adams to state that he knew the play to be hers. This was already after the turn of the century, but in spite of his advanced age Adams made a trip to the Boston library, where he wrote a statement in the flyleaf. Opposite the list of characters he set down the names of the people they represented.

After the Battle of Bunker Hill in 1775 James Warren became president of the Provincial Congress. And when George Washington set up headquarters in Watertown, Massachusetts, James was appointed paymaster-general of the army. He was away from his farm and family for almost the entire length of the war, and Mercy, who was not the excellent farmer that Abigail Adams was, nonetheless had the responsibility of organizing and administering the farm.

Mercy was a frequent visitor to the Watertown headquarters. Women played an important role in camp life by organizing meals, nursing, and procuring supplies, none of which were centrally organized. Some women came to the camp as refugees from British-occupied areas; others—such as Margaret Corbin and Margaret Ludwig—accompanied their husbands to war. These women carried water, washed clothes, nursed, cooked, loaded the guns, and participated in the fighting.

Because of her role as financial head of the household—James Warren's salary did not even cover his own expenses, much less those of the family—Mercy could not stay in camp. Yet she was not as confined to her house as Abigail and Elizabeth Adams were. When the Continental army first occupied Boston, Mercy rode into the city to observe the scene firsthand. The British had been routed: ". . . women, children, soldiers, sailors, governors, councillors, flatterers, statesmen and pimps huddled promiscuously either in fishing boats or Royal barks, whichever offered the first means of escape to the panic-stricken multitude."

She was to use this concrete knowledge in *The Blockheads,* a three-act play which portrays General Gage's soldiers while they are holed up in Boston under the American siege. The dialog is faithful to the soldiers' language, whereas her characters usually spoke a more refined tongue. At one point in the play, a British soldier confesses his plight: "I would rather shit my breeches than go without these forts to ease myself."

The Blockheads was written after the city had been retaken by the British under General Burgoyne and was a spirited polemical reply to the intellectual general's skit *The Blockade of Boston.*

Although there are no surviving copies of the play by "Gentleman Johnny," by all accounts it was written to ridicule the American forces. Mercy joined pens with Burgoyne and evidently bested him in his own chosen medium.

Burgoyne's military success, however, meant an important setback for General Washington's army, stationed at Valley Forge. From the reports Mercy received from Boston she learned that pro-British sympathizers had come out of hiding. Nothing could anger Mercy and her friends more than the American-born who sided with the British. Writing to James Warren in early 1778, she observed:

> Burgoyne's troops supplied with arms, our own army without clothes, without provisions and without tents, many of them deserting to the enemy and others on the border of mutiny. . . . We have two British transports now in the harbor. Another of our people went on board yesterday and returned mightily pleased with the civility and the *presents* they received. What a *weakness!*

At the end of 1779 Mercy published *The Motley Assembly,* a play into which she heaped all of her scorn for the Americans who did not support the revolution. She ridiculed the wealthy Boston merchants who were willing to subordinate the revolution's needs to their own profits.

As the war ended, James Warren was relieved of his duties. Returning home with no thought of running for political office, he found himself once more in the role of citizen-farmer.

The tremendous burden of the war debts was placed precisely on the farmer, which led to spontaneous acts of rebellion. Some of the revolutionary leaders—John Adams, for example—viewed the farmers' uprisings with dismay and denounced such actions as Shays's Rebellion. Mercy and James Warren, on the other hand, did not place themselves in opposition to the distraught farmers. They decried the injustice of the debtors' prisons and they were disgusted by the land speculation that followed the war. Both felt that the Boston merchant class had not paid its financial obligations to the revolution. They even saw one of their own sons, Winslow, sent to debtors' prison, and saw their eldest son, James, return from five years of war crippled and despondent.

Mercy Otis Warren feared the growing influence of the Boston merchant class and saw the army officers' Society of the Cincinnati, a hereditary secret organization, as a possible breeding ground for an American aristocracy, although some of her closest friends, including John and Abigail Adams, did not share her fears.

From the earliest days of her marriage, Mercy Otis Warren had kept in touch with radicals through her correspondence. One of her correspondents was Catherine Sawbridge Macaulay, a British citizen who had supported the American side in the War of Independence. Macaulay, who is credited with being the first woman historian, wrote an eight-volume history of England. It became a republican classic. Her vigorous defense of civil liberties in America, however, was too radical for the Whigs.

Catherine Sawbridge Macaulay was further ostracized for committing a still greater social crime: marrying a younger man. When Mercy Warren received the news of how spiteful the English press had been upon learning that Catherine at forty-seven had married a man of twenty-one, she angrily responded: "Doubtless, that lady's independency of spirit led her to suppose she might associate for the remainder of her life with an inoffensive, obliging youth with the same impunity a gentleman of threescore and ten might marry a damsel of fifteen." When Catherine Sawbridge Macaulay came to the United States in 1785, she and her husband were guests in the Warren household.

For nearly the next twenty years of her life, Mercy Warren's major preoccupation was to be the preparation of her *History of the Rise, Progress and Termination of the American Revolution, interspersed with Biographical and Moral Observations.* But there was still one more political fight ahead.

From the outbreak of Shays's Rebellion in 1786 until the adoption of the Constitution of the United States three years later, Mercy Otis Warren once more undertook to organize in defense of the American Revolution. Along with James Warren and Elbridge Gerry, she opposed a federal constitution that did not guarantee any rights to its citizens. The oppositional pamphlet *Observations on the New Constitution, and on the Federal Conventions* was published in Boston in 1788 by "a Columbian Patriot." Traditionally attributed to Gerry, the pamphlet is now accepted as the work of Mercy Otis Warren.

By the time the Constitution was drafted, the men of property desired a strong central government that could quell local disturbances such as Shays's Rebellion. Protection of property was uppermost in their minds. As Mercy wrote to her English friend, the Anti-Federalists "wish for a union of the States on the free principles of the late Confederation" while the Federalists "are for the consolidation of a strong government on any or on new principles; and are for supporting it by force, at the risk of distorting the fairest features in the political face of America." As Mercy Warren outlined in her pamphlet, the Anti-Federalists objected primarily to the lack of democratic guarantees in the Constitution; there was no provision for the right of freedom of the press, the right of conscience, or the right to a trial by jury. The proposed document did not outline basic civil liberties and would not protect the individual from such measures as the odious writs of assistance.

In addition, she opposed a standing army as "the nursery of vice and the bane of liberty," and noted the lack of well-defined judiciary powers. She did not think that one representative for 30,000 inhabitants provided adequate representation, opposed Congress setting its own salaries, and felt elections should be annual. She called the Electoral College an "aristocratic junta," and opposed broad federal powers of taxation. And finally, she commented that the discussion over ratification itself had been too undemocratically organized for the subsequent decision to be an informed and fair one.

This page of history has been for the most part passed over; as Charles Beard has pointed out, most historians have been pro-Federalist. Beard, on the other hand, reports that in the late 1780s, "the debtors everywhere waged war against the Constitution—of this there is plenty of evidence. . . . The wonder is that they came so near to defeating the Constitution at the polls."

While the Federalists vaguely promised the possibility of constitutional amendments, the Anti-Federalists, including James and Mercy Otis Warren, demanded a bill of rights. As Mercy put it, "The very suggestion that we ought to trust to the precarious hope of amendment and redress, after we have voluntarily fixed the shackles on our own necks, should have awakened us to a double degree of caution."

When Thomas Jefferson worked out the Bill of Rights, the Anti-Federalists agreed to support the Constitution. But although Mercy and James Warren supported the Constitution as amended with the Bill of Rights, they were regarded by some as politically suspect. They found themselves estranged from some of their life-long friends, including John and Abigail Adams, who supported the Federalist position.

Just two years later, one of the Warrens' sons, Winslow, was killed in a frontier battle. Mercy had not wanted him to volunteer, and she could not console herself that his death had been for any just cause. Her opposition to the genocidal wars against the Indians was that of a revolutionary who saw American democracy perverted by the ruthless quest for more land. In her diary, she expressed her feelings of revulsion:

> Their [the government's] poor apologies are lost in the most painful emotions when they recollect their country, involved in an expensive war—the flower of their youth driven into the wilderness to support it— and their sons slaughtered by the hands of savages—of savages stimulated to cruelty and revenge by the equally savage and licentious borderers; and not less irritated by the wanton attempt of Government to exterminate the simple tribes or drive them from their native inheritance to the most distant boundaries of the Continent.

By the time her second son died, in 1791, Mercy Otis Warren had completed the major part of her history. Over the next decade the work lay dormant. She did not originally intend to publish it during her lifetime, but with the inauguration of the Jeffersonian era, she set about finishing it and looking for a printer. It was finally published in 1805.

After the publication of her history, John Adams and Mercy exchanged a series of sixteen letters over her evaluation of him as a revolutionary and as a president. Her judgment of him was severe, although she saw his negotiations with the Dutch during the war as a model of diplomacy. In the end, Elbridge Gerry, a friend of both, worked out a reconciliation, bringing the bitter debate to a close.

Although her work is the only history written by a leading American revolutionist of the period, her history never enjoyed popularity. Two histories had appeared before hers, but hers alone outlined the Anti-Federalist viewpoint. No second edition of these three volumes has ever been published, although she left corrections of the first edition for such an eventuality.

In contrast to the now-popular conception that the American Revolution was supported by a minority, Mercy saw that victory for the Americans was based on the Revolution expressing the needs and desires of the vast majority of Americans. She explained the dual power that existed in prerevolutionary America—the official government appointees, whose authority came from the king, and the growing power of the Continental Congresses and Committees of Safety, whose authority was based on the allegiance of the masses. At each step in the deepening confrontation between the two social forces, the majority came to see its interests as represented in the new order.

For Mercy Otis Warren, the actual military events of the revolution were subordinated to its political history. For that reason she emphasized the importance of public opinion—not only in America itself, but also world opinion. By the end of the war, British prowar sentiment had been eroded by corruption at home, the duration of the unwinnable war, and the discontent in other areas of the British colonies, particularly in Ireland and India. In the David and Goliath fight, at a time when Britain was the strongest military and naval power in the world, the Americans won. The British won the major battles, but lost the ability to conduct the war.

Mercy's radicalism, based on her fundamental assumption of equality and her belief in the human capacity to reason, is also reflected in her acceptance of the French Revolution of 1789. Many American radicals shuddered in horror over this event but she saw it as a logical part of a world process initiated by the American Revolution. For her the terror of the revolution was the result of centuries of feudal oppression. In 1791 she wrote the introduction to the American edition of Catherine Macaulay's attack upon Edmund Burke for his denunciation of the French Revolution.

Although her life spanned nearly a century, from 1728 to 1814, she did not live to see the rise of the American feminist movement. But she saw through the hypocrisy of a society built upon a double standard. She protested the secondary status accorded to women, particularly in the area of education. "It is my opinion that that part of the human species who think Nature . . . has given them the superiority over the other mistake their own happiness when they neglect the culture of reason in their daughters, while they take all possible methods of improving it in their sons."

Speaking of men, she said, "They have the opportunities of gratifying their inquisitive humor to the utmost in the great school of the world, while we are confined to the narrow circle of domestic affairs." She protested against the fact that a woman had no property by symbolically bequeathing to a son the copyright of her book as the only thing she could properly call her own—though, of course, even that did not legally belong to her, but to her husband.

One of her sons remarked that he had read Lord Chesterfield's *Letters to His Son*. First published in 1774, these letters attempt witty and elegant observations on the manners of a man of the world. Mercy replied to her son with praise for Chesterfield's style, but with contempt for his cynicism toward women:

I believe in this age of refinement and philosophy, few men indulge a peculiar asperity, disgust, or raillery at the sex in general, but such as have been unfortunate in their acquaintance, or soured by disappointment. . . . It has been asserted by one of his biographers that he was never known to be successful in any of his gallantries except that which brought Mr. Stanhope into the world. I have ever considered human nature as the same in both sexes.

Like her friend Abigail Adams, Mercy Otis Warren never had the opportunity to attend school. Nonetheless, she became one of the intellectual leaders of the eighteenth century, playing a significant role in the fight for democratic rights—before, during, and after the American Revolution. Her accomplishments are all the more remarkable given that she was also responsible for the upbringing and education of five children and that she lived in an era generally hostile to the literary and political accomplishments of women.

Class Forces in the American Revolution

Harry Frankel (1946)

The American Revolution was directed and its fruits were harvested by a coalition of two classes: the budding northern bourgeoisie and the southern landowning aristocracy. For three-quarters of a century thereafter, the evolution of these two classes and their mutual relations were to determine, to a major degree, the course of American history. Their struggles were to cut the main channels in which events would flow.

These two classes were particular and special types of the landowning and bourgeois classes. They were planted on the shores of a rich and vast continent by an already developed Western European civilization. They had no feudal antecedents in this country. Nor did they find it necessary to recapitulate the European stages in the course of their growth. The hitherto unprecedented conditions created an American social structure with a minimum of excess baggage in the form of feudal rubbish. The dead hand of the past lay lightly on the American brow; a society of exceptional vigor and directness was developed.

The differences between the North and South, which led to the development of differing social structures with dissimilar ruling classes, were accentuated by the natural conditions encountered by the early settlers. The Appalachian range, which for two centuries delimited the field of the colonists, forms an angle with the Atlantic coastline, the intersection of which is in the North. Thus the further south one proceeds, the broader is the alluvial belt so necessary for staple crop cultivation. In the North, where the mountains lie close to the coast, the fall line of the rivers is correspondingly close. Thus the rivers and streams of New England are navigable for only a short distance from their mouths. The New England settlements hugged the coast, and such agricultural produce as was raised in the interior was not too readily floated to market.

The southern states, quite the opposite, possessed a vast agricultural domain within the belt allotted to them by the Atlantic and Appalachian boundaries. Broad rivers, navigable even by ocean-going vessels for a long distance into the interior, were provided by nature as future arteries of commerce. The preconditions for a land of great plantations were ready and waiting.

A cheap labor supply, an easily cultivated crop, and a ready market were all that were required for the establishment of the plantation system. The first was provided partly by indentured servants but primarily by Negro slavery. The planters found the second in tobacco. And in the growing addiction of Europe to the new habit of smoking, the planters found their market.

Thus by the beginning of the eighteenth century a plantation system resting primarily, in fact almost exclusively, on tobacco was dominant throughout Virginia and Maryland. In South Carolina and Georgia, the same system, resting upon rice as the chief staple, was prevalent. Around 1750, indigo was introduced into these two states, and soon ran rice a close second. To the cultivation of rice, tobacco, and indigo, North Carolina added the large-scale export of lumber and naval stores.

The plantations were huge in area, their owners were powerful, and towns were small and unimportant. The political hegemony, under these conditions, fell to the plantation owners. This ruling class was a blood cousin to the landowning classes of all history, and yet it possessed certain peculiarities which were to give it great revolutionary significance in American history. In the first place, it possessed no feudal history. The feudal restrictions on land tenure were slight, only such as the British aristocracy and its American allies could impose from afar. Even these remnants of feudalism were to be swept away by the Revolution.

Secondly, the southern plantation owner was a producer for the world market from the very first. His economic position thus gave to his interests and activities a more cosmopolitan cast than is common in landowning classes. True, he could not rival in this respect the merchant of a busy New England port. And yet, throughout the South, ocean-going vessels tied up at the private docks of planters whose lands lay on the broad rivers, and the news of the world was at their front doors.

A third peculiarity of the southern agricultural ruling class carried the most revolutionary potentialities. While they raised the crops themselves, the planters did not market them. The produce of the South was marketed by British merchants, whose agents and factors were concentrated in the coastal towns.

Here the difference between New England and the South can be clearly seen. In the North, three-fourths of the trade that passed through the ports was handled by American-owned ships and one-fourth by British. In the South, on the other hand, only one-fourth of the trade was carried in American bottoms; the proportion was exactly reversed.

The Planters' Plight

How was it possible that the southern planters allowed themselves to be imprisoned in a cell whose key was held only by the British merchants? The answer is simple: it lay in the limitation of the planters by law to the British market only. And the British merchants drove a hard bargain. The English duties on tobacco were from four to six times its selling price in America at the end of the seventeenth century. By 1760 they had risen as high as fifteen times the value of the tobacco, and although a large part or even all of the duty was remitted when the tobacco was reexported to Europe, the planters had small comfort from this since the benefit of it went to the English merchants and bankers.

The results of this system are fully explained by Jefferson, who, being himself a planter in the Piedmont or upland region of Virginia, was in a position to know:

> Virginia certainly owed two millions sterling to Great Britain at the conclusion of the war. Some have conjectured the debt as high as three millions. . . . This is ascribed to the peculiarities in the tobacco trade. The advantages made by the British merchants on the tobacco consigned to them were so enormous, that they spared no means of increasing those consignments. A powerful engine for this purpose, was the giving good prices and credit, till *they got him more immersed in debt than he could pay,* without selling his lands or slaves. Then they reduced the prices given him for his tobacco, so that let his shipments be ever so great, and his demand of necessaries ever so economical, *they never permitted him to clear off his debt.* These debts had become hereditary from father to son, for many generations, so that the planters were a species of property, annexed to certain mercantile houses in London.

In this paragraph Jefferson reveals more of the springs of revolutionary action in his class than in the whole Declaration of

Independence. "The planters were a species of property annexed to certain mercantile houses in London. . . . They got him more immersed in debt than he could pay. . . . They never permitted him to clear off his debt." The superior position of the British merchant, with his access to Parliament where he could make the laws for the colonies, was utilized to the fullest. The more the planters produced, the deeper in debt they found themselves.

Throughout the first three-quarters of the eighteenth century, the price of tobacco was steadily lowered by the British merchants. The import duties in Britain, to which all tobacco had to go, rose. Even the most prosperous of planters sank into debt. We find Washington, the richest planter in the colonies and highly esteemed for his astuteness in managing the affairs of his plantation, writing to London for extension of credit, and explaining that he was far in arrears because of bad crops for three years. When, after 1763, the revolutionary disturbances began and the British merchants took alarm and began to tighten their credit, the southern planters were put in an almost inextricable position. Is it any wonder that they took the revolutionary road, risking thereon "our lives, our fortunes, and our sacred honor"? Without a sharp turn in the situation, their fortunes and their "sacred honor" were virtually forfeit, and what good is life to a landowning gentleman deprived of these?

Nor was this the only condition under which the planters suffered. Certain royal restrictions on the ready acquisition of western lands were very irksome to them as well as to the smaller farmers of the uplands. As we have seen, the planters were constantly under the imperative necessity of increasing the area of land under cultivation, in order to increase the size of their shipments of tobacco. In addition, the wasteful one-crop cultivation exhausted the soil and made movement westward the chief recourse of the planter. The crown restrictions hung heavily on them.

This was the basis upon which arose the struggle between the crown and its royal governors together with their allies— seaboard planters dependent on the king's favor, agents and factors in the coastal towns—on the one side, and the planters and smaller farmers of the interior on the other. Like debtors in all ages, the planters sought a widening of the credit base and a paper money inflation to ease their situation. The colonial legislatures, for example the House of Burgesses in Virginia, would pass debt-canceling laws and were answered with debt-protecting laws passed by the British Parliament. The provincial governor would exercise the royal veto power to nullify the laws of the legislature, whereupon they promptly retaliated by withdrawing his salary.

As the governor's funds ran out, his attitude was relaxed proportionally, and the legislature would carry a point. No sooner was his salary restored than he revoked the laws and the duel began anew.

It was this that prompted the colonial hatred of the Stamp Act: not so much the hardship of paying it as the fact that the royal governors were to be paid out of its proceeds, thus making them independent of the legislatures.

Thus grew up several generations of planters whose political lines circled around the axis of opposition to the British government. The young scions of families like the Masons, the Pendletons, the Henrys, the Randolphs, the Jeffersons, sent to William and Mary or across the ocean to Oxford or Cambridge, studied avidly the revolutionary doctrines with which the English bourgeoisie had justified *its* revolution. Seizing upon the teachings of Coke in jurisprudence, of Sidney and Locke in politics and government, they applied them readily to their own situation. An intellectual climate of revolt accompanied the material acts of the struggle.

The commercial bourgeoisie, concentrated primarily in the northern states, was situated quite differently. Up until 1763 the British mercantilist theory was laxly applied. Despite minor restrictions on their activities, the preceding century had been a golden age for the merchant class.

If New England was hampered by natural conditions insofar as agriculture was concerned, other natural advantages compensated—and, as later events showed, more than compensated—for the deficiency. The coastline provided abundant natural harbors. On its shores grew a supply of excellent shipbuilding timber which extended almost to the waters' edge. The rivers, though they were not navigable, possessed in return many falls, excellent providers of motive power for machinery. The great Newfoundland Banks furnished endless fisheries, and the whaling grounds of the North Atlantic were close at hand. The prerequisites for a maritime and commercial society were present, and were assisted by the poor agricultural prospects which drove capital to sea.

The impression that agriculture was minor would be erroneous. Nine-tenths of the population of the colonies as a whole were engaged in agriculture, and even in New England a majority pursued that chief occupation. But the conditions of agriculture, the poor soil, the many natural obstacles, were such as to discourage the investment of large amounts of capital in the tilling of land. Holdings were in small parcels, and agriculture was carried on by small farmers.

Large urban centers such as Boston and Newport carried the major political weight, and in them the merchant bourgeoisie held the scepter of power.

This merchant class prospered within the framework of the British system. Under the Navigation Act of 1660, the colonial carrying trade was monopolized by British and colonial shipping. Naturally, the shipbuilding industry boomed, and the conditions for this trade were so favorable that soon vessels could be constructed more cheaply in New England than anywhere in Europe. Oak ships which cost fifty dollars a ton in Europe could be built for thirty-four dollars a ton in America.

Building on the basis of this industry, and on the profitable fisheries, the merchants of New England rapidly constructed a vast carrying trade that encircled the globe. None too particular about how they established their fortunes, the stern Puritan captains built the lucrative trade that was based on molasses, rum, and slaves. When the Seven Years' War broke out and the colonies joined Britain in the effort to drive out the French, the merchants did not, despite their avowals of patriotism, shrink from supplying the enemy with foodstuffs at a heavy profit. Through energy, frugality, and unscrupulousness they built the wealth and power of the merchant class, the forerunner of the modern bourgeoisie.

Thus they prospered under the British system and therefore they acquiesced in it. True, the restrictions on manufactures pinched here and there, but manufactures were a minor interest of the bourgeoisie at that time and it is doubtful that they would have grown much more rapidly than they did had the restrictions been removed. True also, the laws of Parliament protecting credit were aimed at American debtors of the London merchants and bankers. But these laws also operated to provide excellent credit terms for the American merchants. Just as American capital poured into Germany after World War I when it was under close financial supervision by the Allies, so too British capital was freely provided for American merchants when the British creditors knew that their loans were protected by legislation. In addition, the American merchantmen that roamed the world could feel secure in the protection of the Royal Navy.

The year 1763 marked the turning point in the relations of the British ruling class and the Yankee merchants. In that year the British concluded the Treaty of Paris which formalized the surrender of the French and their expulsion from America. Turning from that task, the British ministry prepared to deal with its ally, the colonial mercantile class, soon to become a more formidable rival than the recently defeated foe.

The British had been incensed by the commercial relations of New England with the enemy. In addition, the conclusion of the war left them with the enormously swollen national debt of 147 million pounds, the war having added 70 million pounds to the already huge deficit. And what better place to find the money than in the colonies? In 1764, the measures designed for this purpose were passed by Parliament. The duty on molasses was reduced, but the intention was declared of beginning to collect it, and forces were provided to back this declaration. Import duties and restrictive acts of all sorts were multiplied, and in the resulting flare-up of opposition the merchants were placed side by side with the planters in the struggle against Britain.

It would be incorrect to say that the merchant class had not opposed British rule at all before this time. The antagonism between colony and metropolis had existed from the beginning. The colonists had always looked at the royal governors and other officials, who were sent to America to make their fortunes, as unnecessary leeches. The monopoly of Britain in the American market acted as a sort of tax on the Americans, since prices stood higher than they would have been under freer conditions. These and a host of other petty annoyances had always been resented in the North. But the prosperity of the merchants under the system outweighed the disadvantages and they consented to its continuance. With the destruction of some of the main supporting pillars of the edifice of prosperity, such as the untaxed molasses trade, open and violent opposition began. The merchants extended the hand of friendship to the planters, and in 1765, at the Stamp Act Congress in New York, the alliance was concluded. Lincoln once said that the United States was "formed in fact by the Articles of Association in 1774." He might have, with considerably more accuracy, placed the date nine years earlier, when the coalition between merchant and planter was made.

The Role of the Workers

When the planters and merchants sat down to organize the opposition to Britain, they found an unwelcome guest at the table—and even more noticeably in the streets of all their large cities. The interloper was the group known as the "radicals."

Five cities of prerevolutionary times exceeded eight thousand inhabitants: Philadelphia, Boston, New York, and Newport in the New England and Middle colonies, and Charleston in the South. Others, such as Baltimore and Albany, though not so large, were of considerable size for that day. These cities were the scene of action for another coalition of classes not yet mentioned in this summary. Here were the small shopkeepers, the independent artisans, the mechanics, and the laborers. Sections of the petty bourgeoisie and the forerunners of the modern proletariat went to make up that urban mass so succinctly described by the French as *sans-culottes*.

This section of the population was doubly oppressed. They suffered from the despotism of the British as well as from the exploitation of their home bourgeoisie. With the unerring acuteness that they have always displayed in historical situations of this sort, the masses recognized the former as their main enemy.

Two extracts from letters appearing in the *Pennsylvania Gazette* upon the occasion of the Tea Act of 1773, signed by "A Mechanic" (which the author may or may not have been) will serve to give an idea of the reasoning which governed the attitude of the workers:

They [the British] will send their own Factors and Creatures, establish Houses among us, ship us all other East-India goods, and in order to full freight their ships, take in other kind of goods at under Freight, or (more probably) ship them on their own accounts to their own Factors, and undersell our Merchants, till they monopolize the whole Trade. Thus our Merchants are ruined, Ship Building ceases. They will then sell goods at any exorbitant Price. Our Artificers will be unemployed, and every Tradesman will groan under dire Oppression.

Is it not a gross and daring insult to pilfer the trade from the Americans and lodge it in the hands of the East India Co.? It will first most sensibly affect the Merchants, but it will also very materially affect . . . every Member of the Community.

Organized in the Sons of Liberty and similar bodies, the shopkeepers and workers formed the active arm of the struggle in the cities. They carried out in the streets, at the wharves and customs houses, and at the homes of well-known Tories, the program of the merchants, often without their approval, sometimes against their violent opposition. So energetic and widespread did their activities become that, to give one example, when a mass meeting for workers was called in Philadelphia by the radicals in their struggle with the conservative merchants for control of the movement, it was attended by 1,200 mechanics, artisans, and laborers. A huge meeting for those days, its size can be appreciated when one considers that five percent of the population of Philadelphia was there!

The struggle against the Tea Act of 1773 was the high point of the activity of the masses in the cities, especially in Philadelphia and Boston. Later, when the First Continental Congress formed the Continental Association in the fall of 1774, the first collective action to enforce its nonimportation agreement in Massachusetts was taken by the forty-one blacksmiths of Worcester County. They agreed on November 8 not to work for violators of the agreement and, after December 1, to do no work for persons of known Tory leanings. When General Gage wanted to fortify Boston Neck, he had to send to Nova Scotia for carpenters and bricklayers, so tightly did the Committees of Mechanics in Boston, New York, and Philadelphia close the labor market! This they did despite the hard times. Such unanimity in the struggle, even at the sacrifice of earnings, was displayed by no other class.

The "radical" leaders were drawn primarily from the petty bourgeoisie. Chris Gadsden of Charleston was the southern leader, and his chief lieutenant among the workers was Peter Timothy, printer of the *South Carolina Gazette*. Here the workers had, in the election of October 1768, ventured to enter a slate of six for the lower house of the Assembly, and had elected half of it.

In New York, leadership was in the hands of Isaac Sears and of Macdougall, who led the Committee of Mechanics in opposition to the Committee of Merchants. The struggle was duplicated in Philadelphia, where the forces were mustered by Charles Thomson, Joseph Reed, and Thomas Mifflin. In Boston, the leader of the radicals was the incomparable Sam Adams.

Adams bore the unmistakable stamp of the professional revolutionist. In the words of one of his biographers, "He had no private business after the first years of his manhood." His business was in the rope walks and shipyards, the tavern discussions, and the town meeting. His prematurely white hair and his shaking hands were familiar in all the plebeian places of Boston.

Sam Adams stands out among all of the leaders of the American Revolution, marked by the singularity of his belief in the rule of the popular mass and in the efficacy of the work the people can do in meetings and in the streets. He set himself the task of organizing the population for a break and a struggle with Great Britain. A masterful strategist and an indefatigable organizer and agitator, he was eminently suited to the task. His talents and energy found a rare setting in his uncommon selflessness and modesty. At the First Continental Congress, where the most able men who attended were not without a touch of vanity and self-conceit, Adams stood out like a hammer among trinkets. While others regaled themselves in the pleasures of the great Philadelphia mansions, basking in self-importance in the presence of their rich hosts, accepting the hospitality of those who would support their conciliationist arguments with the bounty of their tables and cellars, Adams worked ceaselessly. In his boardinghouse room, he applied himself to his letter-writing, keeping constant watch on the struggle in Boston, advising, organizing, encouraging tirelessly. His wife wrote him uncomplainingly of the poverty of the household. When Adams had left for the Congress, his friends, by stratagem, supplied him with a new outfit of clothes and some money for the journey. This was the man whom Galloway, his Tory enemy, described so aptly in the oft-quoted sentence: "He eats little, drinks little, sleeps little, thinks much and is most decisive and indefatigable in the pursuit of his objects."

The Adams organizations were distinguished by an excellent working harmony, due in the first place to Adams's ability in working with people of all sorts. He was a master of men—"master of the puppets," the irate governor of Massachusetts called him. He utilized men as they came to him, pushing forward now a fiery orator to give ardor to the cause, and again a rich merchant to lend the appearance of solidity. In all his work, his tact and modesty are outstanding. His ability, energy, and selflessness earned him respect (to the point of veneration) and loyalty among the common people. Among his associates in the national councils of the Revolution, where he and his followers were known as "Adams and his vulgar men," he earned a grudging admiration coupled with a large portion of mistrust.

Bourgeois history has attempted to obscure his name, but nothing can destroy his place as the first organizer of the Revolution prior to the opening of hostilities.

The activities of Adams and the radicals of Boston antedated 1764; hence they were already engaged on the battlefield when the merchants appeared in their shining armor. Adams must have had some of the feelings of young Hotspur when, covered with the blood and grime of battle, he beheld the young, scented dandy before him. But Adams had none of the impetuosity of Shakespeare's warrior, and if he had such feelings he effectually concealed them. He quickly pushed Hancock and John Adams to the fore. For he realized that, as he said himself, the merchants were the main force in a battle in which he was an "auxiliary." Later, when the merchants deserted the struggle in one of their moments of weakness, Adams remarked that they had held out longer than he had expected.

In the struggle with the crown led by the merchant-planter coalition, the merchants were the most fickle side of the partnership. Having passed through a golden age of prosperity such as the planters never had enjoyed in their history, they contended for a *return* to the old system, and the smallest concession of the crown was sufficient to breed conciliationism among them. In addition, fear of their energetic allies in the cities brought them to attempt to restrain the movement or abandon it wholesale. In this situation, it devolved upon the radicals to give to the movement in the cities its continuity and intransigence. More than once Adams was deserted by his timid allies. It is among his most brilliant achievements that at one such time he created the revolutionary Committees of Correspondence, a form of organization which spread like wildfire throughout the country, until, by the time of the Revolution, they formed the basis for a dual power. What a tribute to a master organizer and agitator that he made the fight grow despite the aloofness of the merchants!

Bourgeois historians have attempted to accord to the American Revolution two doubtful privileges to distinguish it from other revolutions. The first of these is that the Revolution was a gentlemanly affair unmarked by the too noticeable or too violent interference of the populace. But the rough facts peep through from beneath the frock coat that the historians have flung over the event. The preliminaries and the struggle itself were marked with violent popular demonstrations, having as their end the intimidation of Tories, the destruction of Tory property, and the enforcement of the campaigns and agreements of the revolutionists. From under the disguise of latter-day historians, our familiar and notorious friend *popular revolution* peeps out.

The second "privilege" of the Revolution has been well summarized by the historian J. Franklin Jameson as follows: "Our revolution was unlike other popular revolutions in having no social results flowing from the political upheaval." This idea is as false as the other, and cannot bear the test of facts. All of the crown restrictions on the ready acquisition of western lands were ended. Primogeniture and entail, feudal remnants, were dealt their death blow by the Revolution and, within fifteen years after the Declaration of Independence, were abolished in every state. These changes, together with the confiscation and breakup of the huge Tory estates, constituted a virtual land revolution, opening the way for the populating of the western lands on the basis of small freeholding. The seaboard planters resisted, but the pressure of the farmers of the interior, swept into the political arena by the revolutionary ferment, was too much for them. Similarly, suffrage rights were greatly extended.

Treachery to the Revolution was widespread among the merchants, and thousands of them went into exile. Thus in New England, New York, and Pennsylvania, new strata were everywhere brought to the surface. This is to be distinguished from the course of events in the South, where the planters in the main stood for the Revolution.

How the Constitution Was Written

Harry Frankel (1946)

In the previous essay we outlined the role of the northern merchants and the southern planters in the struggle of the American colonies for independence. If we follow the coalition to the next great stage of its work, we find it in the unification of the nation under the Constitution. At this stage, however, the lead in the coalition changes hands and the merchants become the more aggressive and dominant element.

The cause of this shift is easily traced. The merchant class stood in need of a strong national government far more urgently than its ally in the coalition. Its need was lodged in the classic motivations that have everywhere caused the bourgeoisie to accomplish the task of national unification. The planters, on the other hand, had a lesser interest in the foundation of a strong central government. In the course of the struggle over the Constitution, the erstwhile allies of the planters, the farmers of the interior, turned against them. The planters themselves were lukewarm on the subject. In the light of these conditions, it is not at all strange that the merchant class, taking advantage of its concentration in urban centers, its capacity for swift action, and its superior organization, was able to leap to the front and take the helm in the coalition.

It would be wrong to imagine, however, that the northern merchants alone and against the opposition of the planters formulated the Constitution and established the Union—in other words, that the coalition was broken. This is the error made by Charles A. Beard in his *Economic Origins of Jeffersonian Democracy.*

Beard, in tracing the origin of the first two great political parties in the U.S., the Federalists and the Anti-Federalists or

Republicans, sets out to prove that they had their roots in an economic antagonism between mercantile and planter-farmer interests. In this he is naturally more correct than his opponents in the dispute. However, in his anxiety to trace the dispute along a single straight line, he commits an error which historians of his school would have us believe is made only by Marxists, who are allegedly prisoners of their dogmatic schematism. In the fight over the Constitution, he places the planting interests, who later led the Anti-Federalists, in the camp of the opponents of the Constitution. He does this to prove a continuous line of opposition between the two classes. In reality, the antagonism was not so simple.

The planters and merchants were, in their relations, like intermeshing gear wheels. Their interests revolved in opposite directions, but nevertheless possessed many points of contact and mutual dependence. Chief among these was a vigilance against the restive population in the cities and on the land. This important political congeniality served to unite them at many crucial times, particularly during the writing and ratification of the Constitution.

Sharp rebellion in Massachusetts and the capture of the Rhode Island state government by the indebted farmers had just served notice on the ruling classes of the precariousness of their position in the face of the rising popular clamor. This notice was served in the South as well as the North; we have Madison's authority to authenticate the stories of rebellion in Virginia. That the planters shared the alarm of the merchants at these storm signals, and that they moved to form a strong central government capable of helping the states to maintain propertied rule, is indubitable. Washington, the largest planter of Virginia, shows in his letters the profound effect these events had upon him.

Add to this a further reason, that the planters would benefit from a union that would enable them by commercial treaties to establish their markets outside the British sphere, and the full motivation for the cooperation of the planters in the imposition of the federal Constitution emerges. Beard himself recognized this in his earlier work, *An Economic Interpretation of the Constitution,* where he wrote that despite their interest in a loose union, the planters favored the Constitution because "there were overbalancing compensations to be secured in a strong federal government."

The two men who were later to head the Anti-Federalist Party, the planter leaders Madison and Jefferson, stood behind the Constitution. Madison, indeed, was the central figure of the Constitutional Convention, the "Father of the Constitution." Jefferson, writing from Paris, approved the substance of the work of the Convention:

> I am not of the party of Federalists, but I am much further from that of the anti-Federalists. I approved from the first of the great mass of what is in the new Constitution. . . .

Jefferson goes on to speak for a bill of rights (later adopted), and a provision denying reeligibility to the president. Beard comments on this letter that Jefferson could have been called "with equal justification" an opponent or a friend of the Constitution! That is how far from the truth his mechanical approach to the dynamic relations of two classes led him.

Even the figures which Beard presents on the composition of the Constitutional Convention, figures which speak so eloquently in his behalf at other times, speak against him here. Of the delegates whose later political opinions are known, twenty-five were to become Federalists and eighteen were to become Anti-Federalists. All of the twenty-five merchant representatives, primarily from the North, voted for the Constitution. Of the eighteen later to become Jeffersonians or Anti-Federalists, twelve favored the Constitution and six opposed it—thus the bulk of the planting representatives worked for the adoption of the new instrument.

The true story stands in this light: the planters lost their allies, the small farmers, when they maintained their coalition with the merchants in the organization of the federal Union; the farmers opened a struggle against the Constitution and established the elements of the new party, and the planters later left the coalition to join the farmers in the struggle against the mercantile class when the latter disclosed its plans in the Hamiltonian system.

We now enter upon one of the most amazing chapters in American history. For the first time in close to three decades the planter-merchant coalition that ruled the country was broken. In a brilliant and vigorous stroke the northern bourgeoisie took independent possession of the state power and, for a turbulent decade, used it like a pile driver to sink the foundations of American capitalism.

How was it possible for the mercantile elements to accomplish this? We have already seen how the planters, having a lesser interest in the adoption of the Constitution, left the lead in this work to the merchants. In the struggle over ratification, which necessitated much intrigue and a political fight on the part of the bourgeoisie, the merchants organized a strong political force in the name of Federalism. This force they used to catapult themselves to leadership in the early government. Their activity and their energy everywhere, their strongly organized, class-conscious forces in the urban centers, gave them the hegemony over the planters.

Hamilton's Program

Alexander Hamilton was a brilliant young lawyer of West Indies birth who had served as a colonel on Washington's staff during the Revolution. From his early childhood he had manifested a mental precocity that revolved around two main axes: a splendid capacity for financial analysis and a strong belief in the rule of the rich, aristocratic, and "well-born." Entering Washington's cabinet as the first secretary of the treasury, he demonstrated his abilities and developed his conceptions in the famous "Hamiltonian system" to such good effect that he was soon the idolized leader of the mercantile elements.

Two letters discovered in 1931 by Professor James O. Wetterean testify to the immediate origin of Hamilton's program. In November 1789, William Bingham, Philadelphia "merchant, capitalist and banker," wrote a long letter to Hamilton in which he recommended virtually all of the essential measures subsequently proposed by the secretary of the treasury. Stephen Higgenson, "mariner, merchant and broker" of Boston, also wrote Hamilton in the same vein, advocating measures similar to those finally proposed by Hamilton. Does this discovery detract from Hamilton's genius? Not at all. For Marxists understand that political leaders do not "invent" the programs they advocate, but draw them from the interests of one or another economic class. Hamilton has won his place in American history by the energy and resoluteness of his appreciation of the bourgeois program, and by the brilliance of his defense of his measures.

Hamilton's system was unified by a single conception: the establishment of the rule of the bourgeoisie. In the first place he proposed a funding of the debt of the central government through the issuance of bonds which would repay in full the claims on the government. In the second place, he proposed a similar funding of the debts incurred by the states during the war and their assumption by the federal government. In order to understand the audacity of these measures, it must be remembered that the paper with which the soldiers had been paid was largely in the hands of speculators, brokers, and merchants, who had bought up the "worthless" stuff at as low as a sixth, a tenth, or a twentieth of its face value. Since the total of state and federal paper outstanding was about $60 million, and since those who held it paid, it has been calculated, no more than $20 million for it, Hamilton's proposals amounted to an outright gift of $40 million. The stupendous size of this grant can be appreciated when it is understood that the total land values in all the thirteen states at that time were only ten times that amount.

What a speculator's orgy! They thronged the galleries of Congress like harpies. Would the measures pass? Of the sixty-four members of the House, twenty-nine, almost half, are known to have been owners of paper. Many were speculators. While the measures were under consideration, two fast-sailing vessels chartered by a member of Congress flew southward, freighted for speculation. Coaches drawn by steaming teams rocked over the bumpy roads of the interior, on the mission of securing, at ridiculous prices, the remainder of the paper in the hands of the uninformed veterans. Is it any wonder that the measures passed?

But speculation was not Hamilton's primary motive. He himself held no paper, and he dissuaded his wife's rich family from securing any for fear that it might compromise him. His interest lay in the furtherance of his central conception: the strengthening of the rule of the bourgeoisie through the new federal government. In those who held the paper he saw a stout prop for the government. In their enrichment, he saw the expanding power of the bourgeoisie.

Among Hamilton's other measures were the establishment of a national bank as the centralized engine of the moneyed power, and measures for the development of industry as outlined in his famous *Report on Manufactures* of December 5, 1791. If we were to summarize his program, we would say that it aimed at the sharp stimulation of capitalism. It was carefully calculated to provide a fluid working capital for the bourgeois class, in the form of the certificates of the funded debt backed by the federal government. The whole structure was to support and repay itself out of taxation of the population. Internal excise taxes such as the Whiskey Tax were to provide the revenue.

Hamilton realized the truth of Jefferson's assertion that the capital thus created was barren, producing, like money on the gaming table, "no accession to itself." Thus he sought the alternate redemption of the capital structure out of the proceeds of manufactures, and worked vigorously for their encouragement. The stimulus was to be manifold. Fluid, well-backed capital was to be provided by the funding and assumption of the debt. A tariff wall would protect the infant industries from British competition. Restrictions on the sale of western lands, in the form of large parcels and high prices, would hold the labor supply in the East and eventually lower its cost. So well did Hamilton realize the urgency of this phase of his program that he could even be seen, in those early days, tramping over the Jersey marshes with his merchant associates contemplating sites for factories.

Hamilton's program met with violent opposition from the farmers and their representatives, many of whom had opposed the adoption of the Constitution. Gradually, as they realized that the coalition was entirely ruptured by the audacious Hamilton, the large planters under the lead of Jefferson, Madison, Monroe, and similar figures went into opposition. A great battle opened that was to shake the nation to its roots during the next decade.

The agricultural interests were quick to realize that the work of the first administration was conducted entirely in behalf of the mercantile interests, and, further, that it would pay for itself out of taxes and higher prices borne by the agricultural population, who constituted 90 percent of the country. Stung to fury, they launched a tenacious offensive under the able guidance of Jefferson. In this they had every advantage. The revolutionary ferment, not yet subsided, was aroused to a wave of leveling radicalism by the stirring news from France. This the Anti-Federalists turned skillfully to their advantage and against the authoritative centralist ideology of the Hamiltonians. Jay's treaty with England in 1794, failing to provide for western farm interests by protecting navigation on the Mississippi, increased the indignation of those elements. The agricultural classes, numbering nine-tenths of the population, led by the planters and their able spokesmen who had been trained by the Revolution, formed an irresistible force in the America of that day.

The bourgeoisie stood on too narrow a base, a fact which Hamilton sensed and which he sought to correct by his feverish efforts in behalf of manufactures. It was not until the middle of the 1840s that manufacturing surpassed commerce in the relative composition of the bourgeoisie. In the meantime the opening of the western lands and the admission of new agricultural states to the union increased the weight of the planters. Already during the decade of the great struggle, two new states were admitted which cast their votes in the Jefferson column in the election of 1800.

The bourgeoisie could do nothing to save itself from the planter-led popular storm. Desperately, they worked at the artificial concoction of a war with France which they could use to crush the opposition. This plot failed. Equally vain was the attempt to bind the breaking barrel with the iron hoops of the Alien and Sedition laws. All failed. They felt the pillars crumble beneath them, and the edifice from which they had hoped to gain so much collapsed.

But if the edifice collapsed, the foundations stood (and stand to this day), so well had Hamilton built. His accomplishments in that remarkable decade are truly great. For an anticipatory decade the American bourgeoisie held independent, unassisted power. The taste of the brilliant fruits of their rule still lay in their mouths when they stormed and destroyed the southern ramparts in the Second American Revolution sixty-five years later.

The chief significance of Hamilton's work lies in the fact that he guaranteed the shaky possibilities for union and placed them on a solid foundation. Even had he failed, American capitalism would not have had to wait three-quarters of a century for its Bismarck as Germany did, for the general trend of conditions favored union. Nevertheless, the issue had by no means been decided in 1790, and Hamilton's drastic measures tipped the scales.

Nor did the Jeffersonians molest the basic foundations laid down from 1789 to 1800. In Beard's words, "They decided that the country could not be ruled without the active support, or at least the acquiescence of the capitalist interests." Jefferson made a conciliatory inaugural address, and Hamilton, speaking of it, said: "In referring to this speech we think it proper to make a public declaration of our approbation of its contents. We view it as virtually a candid retraction of past misapprehensions, and a pledge to the community that the new President will not lend himself to dangerous innovations." Although Jefferson ruled primarily in the interests of the agricultural elements, he guaranteed the public credit, left untouched the National Bank, preserved the navy for the protection of commerce, and strengthened the central government. The years that followed saw a trickle of supporters continually flowing from Federalism to Republicanism, including in their number prominent politicians and some of the richest merchants. Despite the efforts of the diehard elements of the merchant class organized in the Essex Junto, the coalition was partially restored.

From 1800 to 1865, the bourgeois heir waited and fought to come into its own. The heritage it carved and struggled for was exclusive political and economic predominance. If the delay seems long, one should remember the enormous agricultural expansion, with the acquisition of vast western lands and the development of the greatest southern staple of all: cotton. Not out of whimsy did the New England merchants fight, in the early period of expansion, against the acquisition of new western lands. Not for nothing were they known as the "little America" party. If a closer barrier than the Pacific Ocean had been the final boundary of the country on its westward side, the commercial and manufacturing bourgeoisie would have come to power much sooner. The plantation system would have died from lack of nourishment in the form of the new lands it needed constantly, labor and capital would have been held in the East, and the manufacturing empire that Hamilton dreamed of would have advanced by forced marches. But things were otherwise, and the bourgeoisie had to wait.

We have now come to the end of the first revolution in American history. We have traced the coalition that ruled from its establishment through its chief modifications, ruptures, and restorations. We have seen how the planters were primarily responsible for independence and the merchants for union. It was a period in which the class battles were fought entirely in the open. The majority of the population was disenfranchised; the deceptive parliamentary facades of today were only in their infancy; and the movements of the classes were plainly imprinted on the pages of history like footprints in deep snow.

THE SLAVOCRACY

Slavery in Colonial America

George Novack (1939)

History is rich in examples of the revival of institutions appropriate to more primitive civilizations in advanced societies. Humankind is infinitely ingenious in adapting old cultural forms to new uses under the changed conditions of a new social order. Like a thrifty housewife, humanity hesitates to discard familiar acquisitions, however outmoded; it prefers to store them in attics or cellars in the hope of finding a use for them in the future. The history of economics, no less than the history of philosophy, religion, and politics, shows that such expectations are often realized.

The rise of chattel slavery in America is a striking case in point. Slave labor was the characteristic form of labor in ancient society and the economic foundation of the classical Greek and Roman cultures. But long after it had vanished from the centers of European society it was reborn in the New World at the dawn of capitalist civilization, and it continued to flourish in the bosom of the capitalist system for three centuries and a half. This reversion of the infant society of the New World to one of the most antiquated social institutions of the Old World, its longevity, and its tenacity make chattel slavery the most conspicuous instance of combined development in American history.

American society, the child of European capitalism, reproduced not only the features of its parent but also those of its more remote ancestors. Almost every form of social relationship known to humankind sprang up on the soil of the New World, either in a pure form or in a medley of combinations. All the successive stages of civilization preceding the advent of capitalism—primitive communism, barbarism, slavery, feudalism—had a place in the sun until they withered away or were uprooted by the advance of capitalist forces. This varied profusion of social institutions makes the early history of America an extremely instructive textbook for the student of civilization.

Except for self-employed farming, chattel slavery was the earliest, the most widespread, and in the long run also the hardiest of all these precapitalist methods of production in agriculture. Wherever the European settled in America, slavery was sooner or later established. It made its way through the Spanish, Portuguese, Dutch, and French possessions; it became the keystone in the structure of the richest English and French colonies; it constituted the foundation of the southern Cotton Kingdom. In the course of three hundred and fifty years slavery thrust its roots so deeply into North American soil that it required the greatest revolution of the nineteenth century to destroy it.

The history of chattel slavery in North America must be divided into two distinct periods. The first extended from the introduction of slavery into the New World by the Spaniards and Portuguese at the beginning of the sixteenth century, through its development in the West Indies and North American coastal areas, to its decline in the British and French colonies at the end of the eighteenth century. The second period covers the rise, growth, and decay of the Cotton Kingdom in the United States during the first part of the nineteenth century.

These two epochs of chattel slavery were the offspring of two different stages in the development of capitalist society. In general, the history of modern slavery cannot be properly understood unless viewed in connection with the development of capitalism. Based upon one form of enslavement, wage labor, capitalism creates and fosters other forms of servitude. Commercial capitalism produced and profited from the African slave trade and from plantation slavery in the West and East Indies. English industrial capitalism of the early nineteenth century thrived upon Negro slavery in the southern states. Twentieth-century American finance capitalism has supported, among other things, the semislave plantations in Liberia, which grow rubber for Akron tire factories.

In its initial phase North American slavery was a collateral branch of commercial capitalism; in its final stage it was an integral part of industrial capitalism. We shall see that opposite forms of plantation life dominated the slave system during these two periods.

The first question that suggests itself in connection with

chattel slavery is: How did such a historical anomaly come into being? Slavery in the Americas is as old as their discovery. When Columbus set sail for "the Indies" in 1492, chattel slavery was a familiar institution in Spain and Portugal. The Spaniards were accustomed to enslave the peoples they conquered. The Moors, the African Negroes, and the American aborigines were all infidels, subject by divine law to serve Christian masters. Slavery did not, however, constitute the productive basis of Spanish society but existed alongside of it in the crevices of feudal life. Many Spanish vessels engaged in the slave trade and carried Negro slaves in their crews. It is not surprising to find that Columbus likewise had African slaves among his crew on his first voyage of discovery. It is even less surprising that within two years after reaching the West Indies he had seized five hundred of the natives and sent them back to Spain to be sold on the auction block at Seville. Chattel slavery was one of the blessings brought, like syphilis, to the natives of the New World by their white conquerors.

The Spanish adventurers who followed Columbus took possession of the inhabitants of the West Indian islands, Mexico, and Peru, forcing them to labor in the mines and the sugar fields. When the West Indians died off from overwork, starvation, and abuse, and only a miserable few were left, large numbers of Negroes were transported from Spain and the west coast of Africa to replace them.

From 1520 on, Spanish, Portuguese, Italian, Dutch, and English vessels poured Negroes in a never-ending stream into the West Indies. Sanctified by religion and legalized by the crown, the African slave trade became the most profitable of commercial enterprises. A Flemish favorite of Charles V of Spain obtained the exclusive right to import four thousand Negroes annually into the West Indies and sold the patent for 25,000 ducats to some Genoese merchants who established the first regular trade route from Africa to America. In 1562 John Hawkins, an English sea dog who scented the profits of the slave trade, sailed to Guinea with three ships and a hundred men provided by a company of gentlemen in London. In Guinea, he procured at least three hundred Negroes and sold them in Hispaniola (Spanish Santo Domingo). The next year the first Negroes were imported into the English West Indies.

The slave traffic had already been flourishing for over a century when the first group of twenty Negroes was brought to

Jamestown, Virginia, in 1620 by a Dutch vessel. Negro slavery made its way more slowly and gradually in the coastal colonies than in the West Indian islands. There were not more than three hundred Negroes in Virginia thirty years after their introduction. By the close of the seventeenth century, however, Negro slaves began to displace white servants as the main body of the laboring population in Virginia and Maryland. Black slavery was soon transformed from a supplementary source of labor into the fundamental form of agricultural production.

Negroes were imported into South Carolina by way of the West Indies following the discovery in 1694 that the lowlands were suitable for rice cultivation. Thereafter slavery spread as fast and as far throughout the English colonies as conditions permitted. Georgia was the only colony to oppose its introduction. So long as the philanthropic Oglethorpe governed the colony, slavery and rum were prohibited. When Georgia reverted to the crown in 1752 the inhabitants were finally allowed to gratify their desires for black labor and hard liquor.

On the eve of the Revolution there were over half a million Negroes among the three million inhabitants of the colonies. Fewer then forty thousand lived in the North. In five southern colonies the Negroes equalled or outnumbered the whites. The reason was obvious. While ownership of slaves in the North was a badge of aristocracy and wealth, in the South it was the economic basis of society.

The Necessity of Chattel Slavery

Why did Negro slavery strike such deep roots in the New World? Some historians attribute its persistence to physical factors. There is no doubt that favorable natural conditions facilitated its development; the tropical and semitropical regions of the earth have always been the motherlands of chattel slavery. This particular form of production thrives best upon an extremely rich soil which yields abundant crops with comparatively little cultivation by unskilled labor. Warm climates moreover enable the work force to labor without pause from one year to the next and to be sustained with the minimum necessities of life. The smaller the amount of labor required for the maintenance and reproduction of the actual producers, the greater is the surplus value available for appropriation by the agricultural exploiter. Slavery cannot flourish without an inordinately high rate of surplus value since it is the costliest of all forms of labor.

Different natural conditions in the North as well as in the regions adjoining the plantation districts in the South led to the prevalence of quite different forms of agricultural labor. Slavery withered away in these parts, not through the indisposition of the proprietors to employ slave labor, but because the rocky soil and harsh climate prevented the cultivation of staple plantation crops. They were suitable only for raising corn, wheat, and other foodstuffs in which expensive slave labor could not compete with the small self-employed farmer or the hired laborer.

However great a role natural conditions played in the development of slavery, they did not constitute the decisive factors. The main reasons for the growth of slavery were to be found in the specific social and economic problems confronting the colonial planters.

They proposed to grow sugar, tobacco, and rice for commercial export to Europe. The large-scale agricultural operations required for cultivating these crops cannot be carried on by solitary laborers. They demand an associated work force of considerable proportions. How were such forces to be procured in the colonies, where land was plentiful but labor lacking?

The labor problem was the most serious of all problems for the colonial planter. Some form of bondage was necessary to bring workers to the new lands and to keep them working thereafter for their masters. The colonizers grasped at any kind of labor within reach. Negro slavery was not the first nor the only form of servitude in North America; it was preceded by Indian and white slavery.

The sparse native Indian population proved no solution. The English colonists tried to enslave the North American Indians in the same manner as the Spaniards enslaved the natives of the West Indies, Mexico, and Peru. When they discovered that the Indians were either not numerous enough or, like certain African tribes, would not submit to slavery but sickened and died in captivity, they had little further use for them. They proceeded either to slaughter them on the spot or to drive them westward.

At first the landed proprietors relied upon the importation of white bondsmen and bondswomen from the mother country. England and the continent were combed for servants to be sent to America.

Some of these indentured servants came of their own accord, agreeing to serve their masters for a certain term of years, usually four to seven, in return for their passage. Many others, especially German serfs, were sold by their lords to the slave merchants and shipowners. In addition, the overflowing prisons of England were emptied of their inmates, and the convicts were brought to America to be sold into servitude for terms ranging from four to fourteen years.

Cromwell's conquest of Ireland in the middle of the seventeenth century made slaves as well as subjects of the Irish people. Over a hundred thousand men, women, and children were seized by the English troops and shipped to the West Indies, where they were sold into slavery upon the tobacco plantations. In *The Re-Conquest of Ireland* James Connolly quoted the following instance of the methods used:

"Captain John Vernon was employed by the Commissioners for Ireland to England, and contracted in their behalf with Mr. David Sellick and the Leader under his hand to supply them with two hundred and fifty women of the Irish nation, above twelve years and under the age of forty-five, also three hundred men above twelve years and under fifty, to be found in the country within twenty miles of Cork, Youghal and Kinsale, Waterford and Wexford, to transport them into New England." This British firm alone was responsible for shipping over 6,400 girls and boys. . . .

As a result of the insistent demands of the planters for labor, the servant trade took on most of the horrible features of the slave trade. Gangs of kidnappers roamed the streets of English seaports and combed the highways and byways of Britain and Ireland for raw material. In the rapacious search for redemptioners the homes of the poor were invaded. Where promises could not persuade, compulsion was brought into play. Husbands were torn from their wives, fathers from their families, children from their parents. Boys and girls were sold by parents or guardians; unwanted dependents by their relatives; serfs by their lords—and all this human cargo was shipped to America to be sold to the highest bidder.

Thus the bulk of the white working population of the English colonies was composed of indentured servants and criminals who had been cajoled or coerced into emigration and had to pass through years of bondage before they could call themselves free. These people and their children became the hunters, trappers, farmers, artisans, mechanics—and even the planters and merchants—who were later to form the ranks of the revolutionary forces against the mother country.

These white bond servants, however, provided neither a sufficient nor a satisfactory supply of labor. They could not be kept in a permanent condition of enslavement. Unless they were marked or branded, if they ran away they could not readily be distinguished from their free fellows or their masters. As production expanded, it became increasingly urgent to find new, more abundant, and more dependable sources of labor.

The Negro slave trade came to the planters' rescue. Negroes could be purchased at reasonable prices and brought in unlimited numbers from the African coasts. By keeping the Negroes scattered, ignorant, and terrorized, the slaveowners could keep them in perpetual subjection and prevent them from escaping with impunity. The color of their skins became the sign of servitude.

The profits of the slave trade were another potent factor in the extension of Negro slavery. The traffic in slaves became too lucrative an enterprise to remain in private hands. The governments of Spain and England contended with each other for the lion's share of the trade to fill their royal treasuries. The possession of the slave trade was one of the richest prizes at stake in the War of the Spanish Succession. The Treaty of Utrecht which concluded the war in 1713 awarded a monopoly to England. Their majesties organized a company for carrying on the traffic. One quarter of the stock was taken by Philip of Spain; another quarter by Queen Anne of England; and the remaining half was divided among her subjects. Thus the sovereigns of Spain and England became the largest slave merchants in the world.

The slave trade became a cornerstone of Anglo-American commerce. Many fortunes in Old and New England were derived from the traffic. This trade enjoyed the special protection of the crown, whose agents persistently vetoed the efforts of colonial legislatures to abolish or restrict it. It is estimated that from 1713 to 1780 over twenty thousand slaves were carried annually to America by British and American ships. In 1792 there were 132 ships engaged in the slave trade in Liverpool alone.

The economic and political pressures behind the rise of slavery are explained in the following extract from a letter written in 1757 by Peter Fontaine, a Huguenot immigrant in Virginia, to a friend across the Atlantic.

The Negroes are enslaved by the Negroes themselves before they are purchased by the masters of the ships who bring them here. It is to be sure at our choice whether we buy them or not, so this is our crime, folly, or whatever you please to call it. But, our Assembly, foreseeing the ill consequences of importing such numbers amongst us, hath often attempted to lay a duty upon them which would amount to a prohibition, such as ten or twenty pounds a head, but no governor dare pass such a law, having instructions to the contrary from the Board of Trade at home. By this means they are forced upon us, whether we will or not. This plainly shows the African Company hath the advantage of the colonies, and may do as it pleases with the ministry. . . .

To live in Virginia without slaves is morally impossible. Before our troubles, you could not hire a servant or slave for love or money, so that unless robust enough to cut wood, to go to mill, to work at the hoe, &c., you must starve or board in some family where they both fleece and half starve you. There is no set price upon corn, wheat, and provisions, so they take advantage of the necessities of strangers, who are thus obliged to purchase some slaves and land. This of course draws us all into the original sin and curse of the country of purchasing slaves, and this is the reason we have no merchants, traders, or artificers of any sort here but what become planters in a short time.

A common laborer, white or black, if you can be so favored as to hire one, is a shilling sterling or fifteen pence currency per day; a bungling carpenter two shillings or two shillings and sixpence per day; besides diet and lodging. That is, for a lazy fellow to get wood and water, £19.16.3, current per annum; add to this seven or eight pounds more and you have a slave for life.

"It seems probable," said Charles and Mary Beard in *The Rise of American Civilization,* "that at least half of the immigrants into America before the Revolution, certainly outside New England, were either indentured servants or Negro slaves." The original foundations of American society rested not upon free but upon slave and semiservile labor, both white and black.

The Colonial Plantation System

In the colonial period, before the rise of large-scale industry, slavery existed in two different economic forms in the Western world, one representing its past, the other its future. The first was the patriarchal form in which it had flourished from time immemorial. The patriarchal plantations were largely self-sustained, retaining many features of natural economy. Production was divided into two parts, one devoted to the cultivation of such cash crops as tobacco, corn, hemp, etc.; the other to the needs of home consumption.

The plantation system developed along these lines in the

Virginia and Maryland colonies. The average estate was relatively small, employing from five to twenty hands, part of whom were likely to be white redemptioners. Blacks and whites worked together in the fields without insurmountable barriers or deep antagonisms between them. Relations between masters and slaves, with notable exceptions, had a paternal character. The slaveowner was not an absentee landlord who entrusted his estate to the supervision of an overseer and was interested solely in the maximum amount of profit to be gained from his operation. He lived upon his plantation the year round and regarded it as his home. Field hands were often indulgently treated. Negro servants, who replaced white servants in the household as well as in the field, were frequently on intimate and trusted terms with the master and his family, remained in the same family generation after generation, and were regarded as subordinate members of the household.

Such plantations raised their own food, wove their own cloth, built their own houses. Agriculture for domestic use was sometimes supplemented by domestic manufacture. George Washington's estate, for example, contained a weaving establishment. Other planters owned spinning and weaving factories employing not only slaves but white servants on a wage-labor basis.

In South Carolina and Georgia the plantation system developed according to a different pattern. There chattel slavery lost its patriarchal characteristics and became transformed into a purely commercial system of exploitation based upon the production of a single money crop. The typical rice and indigo plantations in the coastal regions were large, employing about thirty slaves who worked under a white taskmaster. The proprietors were either absentee owners living in Charleston, Savannah, or Jamaica, who came to inspect the estates several times a year, or owners who lived only part of the year upon the plantation, owing to the prevalence of malaria in the hot months. The economies of South Carolina and Georgia were so utterly dependent upon slave labor that they became the stronghold of the slave system in the English colonies on the mainland.

Until the rise of the Cotton Kingdom, the capitalist plantation system in the English colonies was perfected on the largest scale in Jamaica. The whole island was converted into one vast plantation devoted to the cultivation of sugar cane and the making of sugar, which was then shipped overseas for sale. The individual plantations, carved in large sections out of the fertile soil, were in many cases owned by absentee landlords resident in England and managed by hired superintendents. They were extremely productive and worked entirely by slave labor. Ulrich B. Phillips, in his introduction to the first volume of *The Documentary History of American Industrial Society,* writes:

> The average unit of industry in the Jamaican sugar fields came to be a plantation with a total of nearly two hundred Negroes, of whom more than half were workers in the field gangs. The laborers were strictly classified and worked in squads under close and energetic supervision to near the maximum of their muscular ability. The routine was thoroughly systematic, and the system as efficient on the whole as could well be, where the directors were so few and the Negroes so many and so little removed from the status of African savagery. The Jamaican units were on the average the largest in all the history of plantation industry.

In Jamaica, the concentration of production upon one commercial staple, combined with the exclusive use of slave labor, gave rise to the same social and economic consequences that were later to prevail in the Cotton Kingdom. The small farmers who had originally populated the island were pushed out and gradually disappeared. The inhabitants came to be divided into two absolutely opposed classes: the planters and their agents on top, and the Negro slaves on the bottom. A sprinkling of merchants and mechanics between them catered to the needs of the plantation owners. The sugar lords were absolute rulers of the island, exploiting it for their exclusive benefit and representing it in Parliament.

Slavery and the Revolution

Except for the far South, slavery was a decaying institution in the English coastal colonies at the time of the Revolution. The decline in the value of tabacco compelled many planters to turn to the raising of other crops, in which slave labor could not profitably compete with free labor. Finding their slaves to be an economic liability, some masters entertained ideas of emancipation. The slave system began to disintegrate, giving way here and there to tenant farming, sharecropping, and even wage labor.

Virginia and Maryland were then among the leading centers of abolition sentiment in the colonies. Some of the wealthiest and most influential planters in the Old Dominion, such as Washington and Jefferson, advocated the abolition of slavery and the restriction of the slave trade. Henry Laurens of South Carolina,

President of the Continental Congress, who owned slaves worth twenty thousand pounds, wrote his son in 1776 that he abhorred slavery and was devising means for manumitting his chattels. But most slaveholders, especially those in Georgia and South Carolina, where rice and hemp could not be grown without slaves, flatly opposed any restrictions upon the trade which would prevent them from buying the labor they needed. They found support among northern merchants who benefitted from the slave traffic.

In the first draft of the Declaration of Independence, Jefferson had inserted an indictment of George III for promoting and protecting the slave trade against colonial protests. But, he tells us, "the clause, reprobating the enslaving of the inhabitants of Africa, was struck out in compliance to South Carolina and Georgia, who had never attempted to restrain the importation of slaves, and who, on the contrary, still wished to continue it. Our Northern bretheren, also, I believe, felt a little tender under those censures; for though their people had very few slaves themselves, yet they had been pretty considerable carriers of them to others."

The Revolutionary War impressed the dangers of slavery upon the minds of the colonists. Aroused by proclamations from royal governors and military commanders promising them freedom, thousands of slaves escaped to the British camps and garrisons, while the slaveowners, fearful of insurrection and concerned about the safety of their property and families, were unable or unwilling to serve in the Continental armies. New England, with a population less numerous than that of Virginia, Carolina, and Georgia, provided more than twice as many troops to the revolutionary forces. The South was easily conquered by the Redcoats, although they had been defeated and expelled from New England at the beginning of the war.

Although the Revolution had been proclaimed and fought in the name of liberty and equality, it brought little immediate alteration in the status of the mass of Negroes who lived in the South. Only the few thousands in the North benefited from the liberating legislation of that period. The state constitution of Massachusetts led the way by abolishing slavery in 1780; Pennsylvania passed an act of gradual emancipation the same year; in the succeeding years other northern states made slavery illegal within their borders. But not for a half century after the Declaration of Independence, in 1826, was slavery legally abolished in New York.

When the delegates to the Constitutional Convention met in secret conclave at Philadelphia to form the Union, the question of the abolition of slavery was not even placed upon the agenda. The discussions concerning slavery revolved around those issues pertaining to the interests of the southern planters and northern capitalists whose representatives composed the convention. The questions in dispute concerned the slave trade, the use of slaves as a basis for taxation and representation, and the protective tariff. In return for the protective tariff granted to the northern capitalists, the delegates from South Carolina and Georgia, whose platform was "No Slave Trade—No Union," were granted a twenty-year extension of the slave trade, a fugitive slave law, and a provision allowing three-fifths of the slaves to be counted as a basis for taxation and political representation.

The slaveholders proved powerful enough to obtain a Constitution that not only protected their peculiar institution but even erected additional legal safeguards around it. General Charles C. Pinckney, delegate to the Constitutional Convention, reported with satisfaction to the South Carolina ratification convention that: "By this settlement, we have secured an unlimited importation of Negroes for twenty years. Nor is it declared when that importation shall be stopped; it may be continued. We have a right to recover our slaves in whatever part of America they may take refuge. In short, considering all circumstances, we have made the best terms for the security of this species of property it was in our power to make. We would have made better if we could; but, on the whole, I do not think them bad."

The Constitution, then, was a slaveholders' document; the United States was founded upon slavery. Some of the founding fathers recognized that slavery was the chief crack in the cornerstone of the new Republic, a crack which in time might widen to a fissure capable of splitting the Union apart. Jefferson prophetically warned the slaveholders that they would one day have to choose between emancipation and their own destruction. But before Jefferson's prophecy was fulfilled, chattel slavery was to flourish more luxuriantly than ever in North America and spread beyond the Mississippi to Texas. It was to make cotton king of the American economy and the cotton barons autocrats of the nation; and it was ultimately to flower in that anachronistic southern culture which proclaimed slavery to be "a perfect good," eternally ordained and sanctified by the laws of God, Justice, History, and Mankind.

The Struggle for
National Supremacy

George Novack (1939)

In 1848 American society was divided into three distinct but interdependent systems of production: the slave plantation system, the wage-labor system of industrial capitalism, and the small family farm. Each of these forms of labor was concentrated in a particular part of the country. The planters and their chattels were rooted in the southern states; the manufacturers and their wageworkers were located for the most part in the Northeast; the largest yet least centralized class, consisting of small farmers, was scattered in varying proportions throughout the land. Its most important segment lived in the inland region along the Great Lakes and in the Ohio and Mississippi valleys.

These three principal branches of national economy supported the three great classes which dominated American political life between the First American Revolution and the Second: the southern planters, the northern bourgeoisie, and the petty proprietors of the town and country. Such subordinate social strata as the proletariat of the North and the poor whites of the South were but slightly and indirectly represented in national affairs. Negroes and Indians, like women, were excluded altogether from participation in politics. Political activity was the prerogative of propertied white males, with power accruing to them in geometric proportion to the amount of property at their command.

The mutual relations among these three major social forces determined the political situation at any given moment. Although the lesser bourgeoisie—i.e., the family farmers in the rural regions together with the shopkeepers and craftsmen of the cities—composed the mass of the population, their political weight did not correspond to their numbers. The leading political roles were taken by representatives of the two ruling minorities, the big planters and the big bourgeoisie, whose mighty economic power and superior social standing compensated for their lack of bulk.

With the adoption of the Constitution in 1789 and the launching of the Republic a new social order had been erected, based upon the equilibrium established among the three classes as the result of their preceding revolutionary struggles. The mercantile and planting aristocracies formed the cornerposts and the petty-bourgeois plebeians formed the pedestal of the new state.

The struggle for hegemony between planter and capitalist was the axis of the political history of the United States between the two revolutions. Their contest, beginning shortly after the birth of the Republic, continued to be the cardinal preoccupation of American statesmen until its climax in the disruption of the Union they had organized together. Whoever does not keep firmly in mind the fact that the gravitational center of American politics during the first seventy-two years of its existence lies precisely in this major conflict runs the risk of losing this guiding thread in the labyrinth of events.

The artisans of the Constitution assumed that the planters and capitalists would share sovereignty in the new nation. This theory of a balance of power was based upon a transitory conjunction of mutual interests. In reality, the Constitution simply defined the terms and provided the arena in which their contest for supremacy was to work itself out. The Constitution did no more than adjust the most pressing points of difference between these two propertied classes; it could not, by its very nature as a compromise agreement, determine which one should rule over the other. The answer to this crucial question could be given only by further struggle between them.

No sooner, therefore, had the machinery of the new government been put into operation than the erstwhile allies found themselves opposed to each other on a number of important issues. Their contest for supremacy was resumed on a broader scale within the framework of the Republic. Seven decades of parliamentary struggle, and ultimately a civil war, were required to determine once and for all whether planter or capitalist was to dominate the United States.

A graph of their struggles would show a series of acute crises, alternating with periods of comparative harmony between them.

Setting aside the storms and stresses within each class, the contest passed through three well-defined stages of development from 1789 to 1860.

In the first period of their relations, during the administrations of Washington and Adams, the commercial capitalists controlled the federal machine. Piloted by Hamilton, the most farsighted of the American statesmen, they succeeded in enacting the most important parts of their program. The national debt was refunded and the state debts assumed; a national bank was chartered and a system of internal imposts and revenue taxes instituted; federal troops sent into Pennsylvania to crush the Whiskey Rebellion established the authority of the central power; a pro-English foreign policy was pursued; the dictatorial Alien and Sedition laws were passed. Around the struggle over these issues the division between the merchant capitalists and the commercial agrarian interests, which is the key to early American political history, crystallized into the Federalist and the Democratic-Republican parties.

The brief reign of the commercial bourgeoisie ended in 1800. With Jefferson's election the planters ascended the throne and became the real rulers of the Republic. For the next sixty years their word was law in the United States. The planters dictated the major domestic and foreign policies of the country, made its wars, annexed new territories, nominated presidents and Supreme Court justices, and staffed the government offices and armed forces with their appointees. But the planters had no monopoly of state power. They governed in grudging or willing collaboration with segments of the northern bourgeoisie and western farmers. From 1800 to 1860 specific combinations of class forces at the top changed many times, but they had one common denominator: the planters exercised their domination through them all. As the senior partner in the government, they had the last word on all questions affecting their vital interests.

If the lines of class interest were so tightly intertwined in many of the most important internal issues that it is sometimes difficult, and always tedious, to disentangle them, the dictatorship of the planters stands out clearly in the sphere of foreign affairs, the touchstone of social supremacy. The main lines of American foreign policy from Jefferson's administration to Lincoln's election were laid down in accordance with the interests of the planters and their allies. The purchase of Louisiana, the War of 1812, the conquest of Florida, the promulgation of the

Monroe Doctrine, the annexation of Texas, the Mexican War, the Gadsden Purchase, the Ostend Manifesto—all these actions were undertaken with an eye to the promotion of the agrarian interests, in most cases against the bitterest opposition of northern merchants, moneyed men, and manufacturers.*

The course of territorial expansion followed the path marked out by the planters. Compare the diametrically different policies of the government in regard to Mexico and England in 1844. Despite the popular war cry of "54-40 or Fight," the representatives of the slave power voluntarily compromised with England over the Oregon boundary dispute, while they maintained an attitude of irreconcilable aggression toward Mexico until they had swallowed up half its lands and were preparing to bite off the rest, simply because cotton could be raised and slavery extended

---

*This was substantially the opinion of Henry Clay. "During the first twelve years of the administration of the Government, Northern counsels . . . prevailed; and out of them sprung the Bank of the United States; the assumption of the State debts; bounties to the fisheries; protection to the domestic manufactures—I allude to the act of 1789; neutrality in the wars with Europe; Jay's treaty; alien and sedition laws; and a *quasi* war with France. I do not say, sir, that those leading and prominent measures which were adopted during the administration of Washington and the elder Adams were carried exclusively by Northern counsels. They could not have been, but were carried mainly by the sway which Northern counsels had obtained in the affairs of the country.

"So, also, with the latter party, for the last fifty years. I do not mean to say that Southern counsels alone have carried the measures which I am about to enumerate. I know they could not exclusively have carried them; but I say they have been carried by their preponderating influence, with cooperation, it is true, and large cooperation, in some instances, from the Northern section of the Union.

"And what are those measures during the fifty years that Southern counsels have preponderated? The embargo and other commercial restrictions of non-intercourse and non-importation; war with Great Britain; the Bank of the United States overthrown; protection; protection to domestic manufactures enlarged and extended (I allude to the passage of the act of 1815 or 1816); the Bank of the United States reestablished; the same bank put down by Southern counsels; Louisiana acquired; Florida bought; Texas annexed; war with Mexico; California and other Territories acquired from Mexico by conquest and purchase; protection superseded and free trade established; Indians removed west of the Missouri; fifteen new states admitted into the Union." (*Speech on the Compromise Resolutions*, delivered in the Senate, February 5-6, 1850.)

on the Mexican acres but not in Oregon. No sooner had the government changed hands than the direction of territorial expansion changed with it. Although they had not hesitated to buy Louisiana in 1803, the slaveholders would certainly not have paid millions of American dollars for Alaska in 1869.

Since neither capitalists nor planters commanded enough power or numbers to rule in their own right, they were compelled to seek supplementary political support among the masses. This meant above all going to the farmers, who constituted the vast majority of the population.

The role of the farmers in nineteenth-century American politics is a magnificent illustration of the axiom that an economically subordinate class cannot be the supreme power in political life. The American farmers lacked the internal cohesion, the integrated economic strength, and the broad political outlook to lead the nation. By far the most numerous segment of the population, they were also the most heterogeneous and dispersed. The settled and prosperous farmers of New York and Pennsylvania were almost as far removed in the social scale from the pioneer squatters and immigrant homesteaders of the West as the wealthy cotton planters were from the Piedmont farmers and poor whites on the mudsill of southern civilization. The farmers were divided geographically, economically, politically. The Appalachians separated the eastern from the western farmers; the Ohio River, the western from the southern farmers. One part of the western cultivators found their chief markets in the industrial East and Europe, another in the slaveholding South. Economic dependence led to political dependence. One section of the farmers attached itself to the Democratic Party of the planters. Others linked themselves with the parties of the northern bourgeoisie, the Whig and later Republican parties. Scattered, absorbed in local concerns, without direct connection or community of interests with each other on a national scale, they could conquer power in a single state but not in the federal government.

The nineteenth century witnessed several abortive attempts by the farmers to assume control of the government. In no case did they come closer to that goal than to obtain a minor share of the state power in coalition with one or the other of the two ruling classes. The peak of their influence before the Civil War was under Jackson's administration. Even then, like the Social Democracy in Germany after the 1914-18 war, the farmers' representatives only participated in managing the affairs of state. They did not rule. The repeated failures of the most progressive farmers to perfect an enduring national party of their own, notably the experiments with the Free Soil and early Republican movements, demonstrated their inability to forge the most elementary instrument for taking power.

Prevented by their social heterogeneity, their geographical division, their economic subservience, and their provincial outlook from following an independent, united, and consistent political course, the representatives of the various sections of the farmers fulfilled the function of mediators between the two opposing camps. They were the arbiters of their disputes and the buffers of their collisions. It was no accident that Henry Clay, "the Great Compromiser," came from Kentucky, or that Stephen Douglas, who attempted to reenact the conciliatory role of Clay in a new and different historical situation and failed so miserably, came from Illinois.

The farmers, and especially the frontier farmers, were natural allies of the planters. The political alliance between the agrarian interests, first consummated under Jefferson, continued to be the backbone of the Democratic Party and the cause of its success. The agrarian democracy acted as a broker between the planters and capitalists, serving the interests of their superiors in order to advance their own. The farmers obtained their own demands only as an adjunct to the planter or capitalist program. And nine times out of ten, such political transactions left the farmers holding the short end of the stick. The frontiersmen together with the planters foisted the War of 1812 upon the young nation in the hope of winning Canada. But while the southerners succeeded in snatching Florida from the feeble hands of Spain, the unfortunate westerners failed in their efforts to wrest Canada from England. The same thing happened in 1844 in regard to Texas and Oregon.

The farmers were to have no better luck in their dealings with the big bourgeoisie later. The Homestead Act, part of the price paid by northern capitalists for the western farmers' support in the armed struggle against the slaveholders, ended in a similar fiasco. While the government bureaus bestowed baronial domains upon the land speculators, railroads, mining and lumbering corporations, and big ranchers, the small homesteader had to sweat for years to possess his quarter section.

After Jefferson's victory in 1800, the merchant aristocracy never recovered its lost leadership. The merchants were forced to cede a portion of their political power to their agrarian opponents for every commercial concession they obtained from their regime. So long as the commercial capitalists remained the dominant section of the bourgeoisie, the capitalists offered no serious challenge to the rule of the planters. The friction between them shook the framework of the Republic twice, but never split or overturned its foundations. During the Era of Good Feeling following the War of 1812, the merchants became reconciled to playing second fiddle in the national orchestra conducted by the slaveholders. When Cotton was crowned king, they not only bowed low before his liege lords at Washington but became their most ardent attorneys in the North.

How passionately these men of property defended slavery—and for what reasons—can be seen from the following outburst on the part of a "New York Merchant of first rank" in 1829 to Reverend Samuel May, a prominent abolitionist.

Mr. May, we are not such fools as not to know that slavery is a great evil, a great wrong. But is was consented to by the founders of our republic. It was provided for in the Constitution of our Union. A great portion of the property of the Southerners is invested under its sanction; and the business of the North as well as the South, has become adjusted to it. There are millions upon millions of dollars due from Southerners to the merchants and mechanics of this city alone, the payment of which would be jeopardized by any rupture between the North and South. We cannot afford, sir, to let you and your associates succeed in your endeavor to overthrow slavery. It is not a matter of principle with us. It is a matter of business necessity. We cannot afford to let you succeed. We mean sir [said he, with increased emphasis], we mean sir, to put you Abolitionists down,—by fair means, if we can, by foul means, if we must. (*William Lloyd Garrison*, by John J. Chapman, p. 32.)

As the northern merchants degenerated into utterly reactionary accomplices of the slaveowners, the sole progressive force within the capitalist ranks was the manufacturers, who were destined to be the beheaders of the slaveholders and their successors as rulers of the Republic. In more or less constant opposition to the planters from the earliest days of the Union, they came into sharp conflict with them in 1819 over the question of the extension of slavery into the territories, in 1832 over the "Tariff of Abominations," and in 1845 over the Mexican War. The first struggle ended in a drawn battle; the last two in crushing defeats for the industrialists. They did not begin to gird themselves and organize their forces for the final showdown until the rise of the Republican Party in the fifties. Before they met in mortal combat, however, the slaveholders were to enjoy a noon hour of absolute mastery over the nation.

The third and final chapter in the struggle for national supremacy between the planters and capitalists was just beginning in 1848. This period had three chief characteristics. It was marked by the ever-tightening autocracy of the slaveholders, accompanied by a steady diminution of their economic weight; by the economic and political ascent of the industrial bourgeoisie and the deepening antagonism between them and the slave power; and by the gradual recession of the conciliatory petty bourgeoisie into the background as the head-on collision between the rival contenders for power approached.

With the growth of the nation since 1789 all three classes had considerably increased their size, wealth, and domain. These quantitative changes were accompanied by even more important qualitative transformations. The planting aristocracy of the Atlantic seaboard, whose fortunes had been founded on tobacco and who had given so many leaders to the Revolution and to the Republic, had become impoverished and decayed, yielding its power and place to the new nobility of King Cotton. The commercial aristocracy of the northern seaports had been shouldered aside by the rising manufacturers, whose demands thundered for recognition in the halls of Congress. The small farmers, no longer packed between the Alleghenies and the Atlantic Ocean, were beginning to build an empire of their own upon a foundation of foodstuffs in the Ohio and Mississippi valleys and along the Great Lakes.

Political relations had changed with these alterations in internal social structure. The planters who had allied themselves with the merchant capitalists to form the Union were now at swords' points with the industrialists and preparing to depart from the Yankee Republic. While the northern merchants of the seaboard cities maintained close ties with the southern slaveholders and still supported the new planter aristocracy as they had upheld the old, the bonds between them were weakening. Instead of being allied against common enemies, the northern merchants more and more stood in the old position of the English merchants as exploiters and oppressors of the planters. The farmers were beginning to split into two parts, the Free Soil farmers of the north central states going over to the camp of the industrialists, while the more backward farmers of the southern and border states, retaining a certain community of interests with the slaveowners, continued to follow in their footsteps.

All these relationships were to crystallize into firm formations in the years between 1848 and 1860, ready to be precipitated in 1861.

The Jackson Period

Harry Frankel (1946)

The Jackson period, extending roughly from the election of Andrew Jackson in 1828 through his two terms and one of Martin Van Buren, his chief lieutenant, gave a unique cast to American political life. In addition to reshaping the political methods and institutions of its own day, it has assumed special significance in the liberal bourgeois tradition. In the annals of capitalist historians the Jackson period has gone down as a revolutionary-democratic era of popular rule. The Bryan "revolt," and the Wilson and Franklin D. Roosevelt administrations, referred expressly to the Jacksonian past. Certain renegades from Marxism, such as Lewis Corey, refer to Jacksonianism for proof of the fundamentally democratic character of American capitalism. But Marxists interpret this period in American history in an entirely different manner.

The year 1800 in American national politics marked the triumph of the planting aristocracy led by Jefferson over its northern merchant rival. Southern plantation economy was at that time based upon the slave cultivation of tobacco, rice, and indigo as the chief staples. The next half century saw a displacement of these crops by a new staple. It is well known that the invention of the cotton gin in 1793 provided the initial impetus to the increase of the cotton crop. The cultivation of upland (or short-fibered) cotton had been limited by the difficulty of separating the fiber and seed. By overcoming this the cotton gin freed cotton from its narrow confines in the seaboard area and started it on its career across the Appalachian range to the furthest reaches of suitable soil in faraway Texas. At the height of cotton cultivation two-thirds of southern slaves were engaged exclusively in its production. Between 1791 and 1860 the cotton crop multiplied a thousandfold. This enthronement of King Cotton made possible the most stupendous social reversion of modern times. For southern cotton was raised on the basis of precapitalist, even prefeudal relations: the system of chattel slavery.

For sixty years the southern planters held national power. It was an abnormality for the slavocracy to dominate in an era of rising capitalism. But norms can serve only as guides for the understanding of history; they cannot be substituted for the more complex living social process. U.S. history has shown that the rule of the slavocracy was no symbol of the absolute retrogression of human society as some in that day thought it to be. Rather it was a temporary retrograde motion produced by a transient conjuncture of circumstances which could not endure. History has likewise shown that Jacksonianism, which arose in the period of planter rule, did not overthrow that rule, but represented rather a transitory phenomenon. Jacksonianism continued slaveholder rule with modified techniques.

Andrew Jackson was a man of iron will who left a personal mark upon the history of the United States. He typified in almost every way the rising western cotton planters. A Tennessee slaveholder of considerable wealth (his "Hermitage" was one of the finest mansions of the West), he was, in his early career during the first decades of the nineteenth century, the most important single human instrument of the planters in their westward expansion. His victories in the Indian Wars, and especially in the War of 1812 (where, at New Orleans, he "beat the men that beat Napoleon"), opened the Southwest to the plantation system.

His early political career disproves the contention of Jackson's adulatory historians that he was a democratic figure. Even one of his most enthusiastic historian-adulators is forced to record that in local Tennessee politics Jackson was of the "landholding aristocracy," and together with his class, "normally acted . . . both against the financial aristocracy and the canebrake democracy." (Arthur M. Schlesinger, Jr., *The Age of Jackson.*)

Andrew Jackson became a link of special configuration in the chain of planter presidents that began with Thomas Jefferson and ended forever with Jefferson Davis. The attitude of this group of presidents towards slavery was in stages modified as cotton fixed the "peculiar institution" on the South. Thomas Jefferson was a passive opponent of slavery. Jackson takes his rightful place in the progression as an active defender of slavery, as the planters traveled the sixty-year road to Jefferson Davis. Where Jefferson was a planter of Old Virginia, and Davis a planter of Mississippi, towards the western reaches of the slave power, Jackson takes his accurate geographical place in the shifting center of plantation gravity as a Tennessee planter.

Marxists always approach the question of the class nature of a state by first determining the character of the economy upon which the political structure rests. In this scientific approach they differ from all varieties of vulgar thinkers for whom states are indeterminate formations, dominated now by "demagogues," then by "the people," and again by "dictators." Nor can any pretended exceptionalism exempt the United States from this method. Despite special American conditions, the history of this country will yield its secrets only to the Marxist key.

The American economy up to 1865 exhibited a dual structure. Hewing in one portion of the country to the classic capitalist line, it took on the atavistic shape of a plantation economy based upon slavery in the other section. The cohabitation of these two systems was made partially and temporarily possible by the segregation of the systems, each to its own geographical region. Political decentralization in the form of state governments provided both the bourgeoisie and the slaveholders a measure of local autonomy. Yet national policies of growing importance were decided by the class controlling the federal government. By examining the decisions on these issues we discover which class was in control of the federal government. Up until the Civil War, the important decisions were almost always in favor of the slaveholders. It is instructive in view of the Jackson myths to examine the stand of the Jacksonian party on each of these issues.

The national bank: At the time of Jackson's election, the Second Bank of the United States was in existence, chartered by the Jeffersonian Democrats to finance the War of 1812. The very chartering of such a bank demonstrates that the planter administrations had been pursuing a course of compromise with the northern capitalist class, for the first bank had been destroyed by the Jefferson-led planters' assault. The renewed apprehensions of the slaveholding class, and especially of its newer and more aggressive western sections, led to a new attack upon the bank. Many local state banking interests participated in this onslaught. Jackson destroyed this centralized engine of bourgeois power.

Western lands: The planters' attitude to western lands was determined by their ever-growing greed for more cotton soil. The small farmers also wanted the territories opened to their penetration. But in the planter attitude and the farmer attitude there was a difference—the difference being slavery. This was to tear them apart in the free-soil controversy of later years. But during the Jackson period they united against the bourgeoisie, which was seeking to restrict land sales in order to restrict the planting power and to keep labor in the East. Jackson's policy here again is most clearly revealed as the planter policy. He did everything within his power to enlarge the land area of the Union, aiming even at the annexation of Texas. Land was the capital of the planter. Jackson sought by every means to augment it, while destroying the capitalist bank.

Indian lands: Four Indian tribes in Georgia, Alabama, Tennessee, and Mississippi held ancestral lands aggregating over 33 million acres—almost the combined areas of Pennsylvania and New Jersey. No longer savages, they had developed modern agricultural forms and orderly governments. The story of these lands is described by the historian William E. Dodd in *The Cotton Kingdom:*

> The planters of Georgia first, and later those of other states, who coveted these lands with a covetousness unimagined by the kingly exploiter of Naboth's vineyard in ancient times, vowed that the Indian should not be allowed to develop settled, civilized communities. Since the planters were represented in Congress and the natives had recourse only to executive protection, the contest was most unequal, and when President Jackson gave the Indians over to the tender mercies of their enemies, there was no help for them. The planters had their way, and the Indian lands were rapidly converted into cotton plantations.

It is only necessary to add that when the bourgeoisie, through the chief justice of the Supreme Court, tried to block the planters from the Indian lands, Jackson paid no heed, saying, "John Marshall has made his decision, now let him enforce it."

Abolitionist literature: The growing northern movement for abolition of chattel slavery attempted to penetrate the South with its literature. The planters demanded that the mails be closed to the abolitionists. Here was a problem for Amos Kendall, postmaster general, chief adviser to Jackson and intellectual leader of the Democratic Party. Kendall solved it with a happy "compromise": abolitionist literature could be mailed in the North, but need not be delivered in the South! Such "compromises" are always acceptable to the ruling class.

Internal improvements: This was a contemporary term for canals, roadways, and so forth to be constructed at federal expense. The bourgeoisie saw in them a profitable transportation network necessary for trade and having the additional value of linking the northern bourgeoisie and the western farmers in an economic bloc. With this in view that inimitable juggler, Henry Clay, made "internal improvements" part of his "American system" along with the manufacturers' tariff. But the planters saw no reason why they should bear part of the burden for a program that was primarily of benefit to their rival. Jackson thereupon set his face against this scheme and used his veto power to check it. This is a most important fact in the analysis of the class base of Jacksonianism. For Jackson here showed that he was prepared *to risk his western farmer base in order to carry out the slaveholders' program.*

Tariff: This was one of the most significant controversies of the Jackson period. The tariff, having a direct bearing on the economic welfare of the capitalist and planter classes, was the most hotly contested of all the issues. In the course of this dispute, the positions of the classes on the tariff had been reversed. The planters, hoping to lay the basis of a home market for their crop, had inaugurated a protective policy with the tariff of 1816. They had been opposed by the chief sector of the bourgeoisie, the major interest of which was shipping, which required low tariff rates. The development of manufactures, fostered in part by the very tariff which it had opposed, caused the bourgeoisie to change its stand. It pressed through Congress the bills of 1824 and 1828, the latter with schedules so highly protective that it became known to the planter and farmer interests as the "tariff of abominations." Coming to understand their true interests, the planters turned against a tariff which served as a tax upon them without providing any economic benefit. The remainder of the story is related in the previously quoted work of the most realistic historian of the South, William E. Dodd:

When, in 1828, the South and the West united to place Jackson in the President's chair, it was definitely understood that the "tariff of abominations" was to be abolished, or greatly reduced. The exigencies of national politics caused Jackson to falter and delay. South Carolina allowed the new President four years to make up his mind. When he was still uncertain in 1832, the state proceeded to nullify the offensive national statute. The President then threatened war; South Carolina thereupon paused; but the outcome was the definite abandonment of the higher tariff policy in favor of the lower rates of the compromise tariff of 1833. Every South Carolinian thought that the planters had once again had their war; and South Carolinians were scattered all over the cotton states.

This was the famous "nullification" controversy, which is often cited to "prove" Jackson's independence of the planters. This struggle, it is true, was responsible for much friction, and was partially responsible for the alienation of the Calhoun-led planters from the Jacksonians. But traced to its end it proves the slaveholder hegemony in the Democratic Party in Jackson's day. For the southern oligarchy was finally awarded the reduced tariff rates which it sought.

It has not been difficult to demonstrate the class base of Jacksonianism. It was the political arm of the slaveholders. This was its decisive character. Remaining to be accounted for are the specific configurations of the Jacksonian regime that distinguish it from earlier and later forms of planter rule. For the Democratic Party of Jackson's day reflected an enormous popular ferment that existed at this time in American national politics. This period became a turning point in the development of the techniques of class rule in the United States.

The Underlying Economic Factors

It must be remembered that the period from 1800 to 1860 was a time of enormous social change, both in the North and in the South. Classes were becoming transformed, new sections were arising within existing classes, the relationship of forces between classes was shifting, and an entirely new class, the modern proletariat, was being born. The Jacksonian regime represented a modification of the undisguised planter rule brought about by the interaction of the four main classes: the planters, the capitalists, the petty bourgeoisie, and the rising proletariat.

Let us first turn to the planters. The impact of cotton on the South caused profound changes. The great engine of change was the demand for land. The wasteful mode of cotton cultivation caused the rapid exhaustion of the soil. Charles A. Beard wrote that what the planters were chiefly marketing was the "pristine fertility" of the land. The plantation system plowed inexorably westward, turning up the land like an enormous and insatiable bulldozer. The five years following the War of 1812 saw a huge westward movement known as "The Great Migration." Several hundreds of thousands of people were shifted to the trans-Allegheny region, leading to the formation of two territories, the admission of three states, the merciless clearing of the Indians to beyond the Mississippi, and, indirectly, the "purchase" of Florida. This movement, and the later "Jacksonian Migration," brought Tennessee, Louisiana, Mississippi, Alabama, Florida, and Arkansas into the Cotton Kingdom. If we compare the cotton production of this new western region with that of the older cotton states of the eastern seaboard—South Carolina, Georgia, Virginia, and North Carolina—we get a graphic picture of the western shift of economic power:

Cotton Crop (in Millions of Pounds)

	1791	1801	1811	1821	1826	1834
Southwest		1	5	60	150.5	297.5
Southeast	2	39	75	117	180	160

With the opening of the new Southwest, the old South on the Atlantic seaboard declined in wealth and importance. The rapid exhaustion of the soil led to the impoverishment of the planters. Historians have described with touching pathos how poverty and indebtedness descended upon Jefferson, Madison, Randolph, Calhoun—all planter-statesmen of the eastern region. Indeed, Old Virginia and her neighbors soon found that the slave was their most profitable product, and looked to the breeding and traffic of slaves for the rehabilitation of the region.

Between the older seaboard plantation aristocracy and the rising western planter class existed a strong antagonism. It expressed itself outwardly in an eastern aristocratic snobbery on the one hand, and a western leveling tendency on the other. In the beginning the dispute was between the western and eastern portions of the seaboard states. The solid aristocratic class of the older region feared to take the newer section into full partnership because of the lack of an organized ruling class in the western regions. The larger proportion of pioneer farmers and smaller planters in the west inspired in the old aristocracy fears for the safety of the slave system. Only as slavery took root in the western counties did the eastern slaveholders relax their grip on the state governments. Frederick J. Turner describes this in his *Rise of the New West:*

It was only as slavery spread into the uplands with the cultivation of cotton, that the lowlands began to concede and to permit an increased power in the legislatures to the sections most nearly assimilated to the seaboard type. South Carolina achieved this end in 1808 by the plan of giving to the seaboard the control of one house, while the interior held the other; but it is to be noted that this concession was not made until slavery had pushed so far up the river courses that the reapportionment preserved the control in the hands of slaveholding counties. A similar course was followed by Virginia.

The new western region was rapidly assimilated into the slave system. By 1850 over half of the slaveowners were living in the trans-Allegheny region. Nor did this apply only to small slaveholders; for by this date more than half of the 1700 great planters (those holding from 100 to 1000 slaves) were in the new region. But the old antagonism between the two regions did not die out. On the contrary, new disputes, feeding upon the old mistrust, soon arose.

We must recall that the policy of the Jeffersonian party had been to take the reins of the national government and draw sections of the northern capitalist class into cooperation with the planters. This policy had been so successful that the bourgeois Federalist Party was virtually dissolved in the Jeffersonian party during the administrations of Jefferson, Madison, Monroe, and the second Adams. The eastern planters grew accustomed in this so-called Era of Good Feeling to secure their rule by means of this alliance at the cost of some concessions to the New England merchant capitalists. However, the fundamental antagonism between the two systems could not forever be repressed. In the North an aggressive manufacturing bourgeoisie was supplanting the merchant class. Paralleling this was the rise of an aggressive cotton slavocracy in the Southwest. Here were the chief contenders in the coming irrepressible conflict.

Scorning the alliance with the old Federalists, unafraid of a pact with the anticapitalist agrarian and urban petty bourgeois radicals, the slaveholders of the Southwest burst angrily on the scene. They demanded the retraction of all important concessions to the capitalist class, a more energetic policy to secure western lands, and the breakup of the old closed caste of officeholders. Led by the planters of the Tennessee Valley, the first western cotton planting region, they demanded the elevation of their idol, Andrew Jackson, to the presidency.

While these class shifts were taking place in the South, a far more fundamental process of change was taking place in the North. The development of manufactures was rapidly placing the industrial capitalist in the forefront in New England and the Middle Atlantic states. The old commercial and shipping interests were receding to second place. Hamilton's prophetic vision of a manufacturing empire was beginning to assume shape.

This growing power of industrial capitalism was a threat to the planting class. The increasing vigor of the capitalists and their ever-increasing demands made it more difficult for the slaveholders to rule "in the old way." Every day brought further proof to the southern aristocracy, and especially to its militant western section, that the reliance of traditional Jeffersonian politicians upon compromising with the northern capitalists must come to an end. Jefferson himself lived to see his system shaken. The slavery dispute in 1820 over the admission of Missouri startled him, as he said, "like a fire bell in the night."

Northern industrial development had yet another aspect. It is a historical axiom that the industrial capitalist brings with him his own gravedigger. An American proletariat was growing with every advance of the factory system. With the growth of the working class came its organization into trade unions and its entry onto the political field. Workers' parties and newspapers rapidly spread through New England, New York, and Pennsylvania. The first trade-union and political battles of the American workers occurred at this time.

One further class development in the first decades of the nineteenth century must claim our attention. The small farmers of the North were economic prisoners as long as they remained bound between the Appalachian range and the Atlantic seaboard. Their release in this period is a factor of prime importance in the relation of class forces. On the broad, fertile lands of Ohio, Indiana, Illinois, and the other new farming regions, the farmers grew into a national power.

It is evident at once that the interests of three developing classes converged antagonistically upon the fourth. The planters, the small farmers, and the proletariat, each for its own reasons, fought the rising bourgeois colossus. To the planters, industrial capitalism was a challenge for control of national economic policies. It endangered their whole system. For the farmers, capitalism was the eastern octopus which sucked from them the proceeds of their crops. They were constantly in debt to the eastern capitalists, who furthermore sought to block them off from the ready acquisition of western lands. The proletariat confronted the bourgeoisie as the direct victim of its merciless exploitation.

The convergence of the three classes was a temporary alignment which was smashed by the struggles preceding the Civil War. The workers and farmers were soon to take their place in the fight against the outmoded planter slavocracy, the chief foe of all social progress. Yet the movement of the Jacksonian period played an important role in American history. For it brought to the scene of national struggles the workers and farmers in their capacity of a mass electorate. Indeed, the broadening of the suffrage was one of the most important political developments of the Jackson period. Sharp struggles by the growing worker and farmer masses, culminating in one state (Rhode Island) in armed rebellion, won the vote for the free male population.

These social and political changes wrought a fundamental change in the conditions of political life. The character of the ruling-class political parties was modified to cope with the new conditions. The parties lost their previous candor and disguised themselves in order to gain the same class ends by different methods, in the face of the broadened and suspicious electorate.

While the aristocratic monopoly of politics was being smashed, the aristocratic hold of state power was preserved. "Jacksonian democracy" represented the beginnings of modern concealed class rule. The planters first learned the chief lesson of modern parliamentary "democracy" which the bourgeoisie was to learn and express so well years later: "Men can forego the husk of a title who possess the fat ears of power."

The Jacksonian technique, while basically an enforced accommodation, naturally brought to the fore politicians of the modern, demagogic type. The rising western cotton section of the planting class, the spearhead of Jacksonianism, had been educated by the politics of their locality for their national role. In the western region, small farmers were more numerous, leveling tendencies stronger, and political life more turbulent than on the eastern seaboard. The initial coterie surrounding Jackson—William B. Lewis, John H. Eaton, Felix Grundy, William T. Barry, and James K. Polk—are good examples of politicians who learned the fine art of speaking in the name of the many while ruling in the interest of the few.

The original home of this political art was in the northern wing of the planters' Democratic Party—an auxiliary in enemy territory. It fought the bourgeoisie through sections of the urban petty-bourgeois and proletarian masses, who were mobilized by means of democratic and even anticapitalist slogans. The planting class, resting on unorganized, unrepresented, almost unmentioned slave labor, could afford to countenance reforms which struck against the northern bourgeoisie. The ten-hour day for workers, extension of the vote to the proletariat, attacks upon the factory system, and other such agitations typical of the Jackson period represented no direct economic threat to the planters. During the Jackson period the planters put on their best democratic garb . . . in the North. But during that very same time, barbarous slave legislation multiplied on the statute books in the South. The concessions in the North were part of the slaveholder system of maintaining national power. John Randolph, the erratic phrasemaker of the planter bloc in Congress, gave clear expression to this strategy. "Northern gentlemen," he taunted, "think to govern us by our black slaves, but let me tell them, we intend to govern them by their white slaves!"

In order to govern the bourgeoisie "by their white slaves," the planters, from Jefferson's day on, built a northern party machine of a type familiar to this day in the Democratic Party. Politicians of the modern type began to make their appearance. Aaron Burr had been Jefferson's chief lieutenant on the northern field. Martin Van Buren, operating through the Albany Regency and Tammany Hall, was Jackson's man Friday. Each was awarded the vice-presidency. Van Buren exemplified the increasing importance of the northern auxiliary when he succeeded Jackson in the presidency.

The Jackson and Van Buren groupings, joined by a clamorous farmer element led by such men as Senator Thomas Hart Benton and Colonel Richard M. Johnson, formed a national grouping in the Democratic Party which conducted politics by carefully watching the movement of the popular masses. Their activity, well-adjusted to the new currents which the old-time politicians could scarcely comprehend, much less navigate, raised behind them a sweeping national mass movement. Here the great achievement of Jacksonianism emerges. It inaugurated in national politics that pattern which has endured to the present: *the rule of an exploiting class concealed behind the appeal to the "common man."*

The foregoing analysis, while simplified and schematic, indicates the essential elements of the Jackson period. Bourgeois historians like to see in Jacksonianism a basic transfer of power to the "people." This is false, for while the period was one of unquestionable popular ferment, the hold of the slaveowners upon the state power was not broken.

Three Conceptions
of Jacksonianism

Harry Frankel (1947)

In the previous article a class analysis of "Jacksonian democracy" was presented. An attempt was made to demonstrate that Jacksonianism represented the continuation of the rule of the southern slaveholding class in national politics, with modifications traceable to a specific relation of class forces. Among the specific circumstances were: the divisions among the planters, the growth in the specific weight of the small-farming petty bourgeoisie and the industrial proletariat, and the eruption of these two classes onto the political scene in the form of a clamorous mass electorate. These were circumstances which *modified* the technique of slaveholding rule, but did not *overthrow* it.

This Marxist view is counterposed to the views of bourgeois historians, who see the Jackson period as a time of popular revolution. We shall here consider the theories of two particular schools of American historians. The first is the famous "frontier" school, which views Jacksonianism as a democratic effect of the frontier upon national politics. The second and more recent school considers Jacksonianism to be an expression of the rule of farmers and workers in Washington. The best-known exponent of this view is Charles A. Beard, and it is endorsed by most of the modern liberal historians.

Turner's Theory of Frontier Democracy

Let us turn first to the frontier theory. In 1893 Frederick Jackson Turner read to a gathering of the American Historical Association a paper entitled, *The Significance of the Frontier in American History*. The main ideas of this essay were later expanded by Turner into a series of articles and books dealing with various phases of the frontier and its fancied effects on the national development of the United States. What was his theory? "The existence of an area of free land," he wrote, "its continuous recession, and the advance of American settlement westward, explain American development." Or, as he stated in another article, for two hundred years "westward expansion was the most important single process in American history." And what was the effect of the frontier? "This at least is clear: American democracy is fundamentally the outcome of the experiences of the American people in dealing with the West." That the western land areas were decisive in American history, and that their chief result was "democracy"—this is the heart of Turner's thesis. Turner's writings deal mainly with the Jackson period. It was at that time that the West "came into its own, conquered national power, and had its greatest effect in the furtherance of 'democracy.'"

The Turner school thus starts with a geographical abstraction: the frontier. History is presumed to be based primarily upon a conflict, not of class but of sectional interests. This conception has sunk deep roots in American academic thought. It is common to refer to the Civil War as a conflict between the North and the South instead of more precisely designating it as a clash between slaveholding and bourgeois economy. Even bias and prejudice are often given sectional labels. Historians boast that their work is free, not only of class prejudice, but of "sectional bias." For writers of American history, this terminology has become a substitute for thinking. Partly, this has been the result of the inadequate theoretical equipment of the historians, and partly too it has stemmed from a reluctance to adopt Marxist terminology. Thus "section" has become a cowardly, confused pseudonym for *class* in the language of American historical writing.

There is a certain plausibility in this sectional approach. It resides in the fact that in early United States history economic classes were largely concentrated in geographical regions. "South" thus meant the planters, "North" the bourgeoisie, and "West" the small farmers. In this manner many historians were able to give class analyses in sectional terminology. But to substitute an imperfect concept for a more precise one cannot fail to bring eventual theoretical disaster.

This is the fate of the Turner school, which carried the sectional approach to its furthest limits by elevating one section to omnipotence. The "frontier" is a geographical abstraction based upon a shifting region. Its significance can only be appreciated when analyzed in class terms. A specific frontier at a specific time has a class structure differing from that of the same frontier at another time, or another section of the frontier at the same time. The Illinois farmer had more in common with the Massachusetts or Vermont farmer than with his fellow "frontiersman," the planter further south. If he didn't know this, the Civil War taught it to him, and should have taught it to the historian as well.

By understanding this outstanding flaw in the sectional method, its nonclass approach, we come to grips with the inherent weakness of the frontier school. A study of the frontier and of the chief class which inhabited it, the small farmers, is sufficient to convince a Marxist that this section could never take independent control of the state power. The agrarian petty bourgeoisie, geographically and economically diffused, holding no key position in the national economy, plays an impotent role when it attempts to take an independent course. F. L. Paxson, the chief disciple of the Turner method, in a series of lectures entitled *When the West Is Gone*, unintentionally makes this plain. He points out that every frontier "revolt" up until Bryan and the Populists was a success. Why then was the last wave a failure? "Something had happened," he says, "to break the course of normal American thought and action."

What Paxson fails to grasp is that in every previous movement, the farmers had served as an *auxiliary to a predominant social class*. The farmers fought in 1776 for the planters and the capitalists against England, in Jefferson's and Jackson's time for the planter against the capitalist, and in the Civil War for the capitalist against the planter. In Bryan's day they were allied with no predominant social class; alone, the farmers could not, nor can they ever, take over state power.

Let us consider Turner's thesis from still another aspect. The existence of the vast western lands, in his view, gave birth to democratic institutions in the United States. There is no denying a certain element of truth in this. To a degree which has been greatly exaggerated, the eastern masses drew independence from the western farming opportunities. To a degree, the large class of western farmers helped break down open aristocratic rule. Yet there is another side to the coin which American sectionalist historians have sedulously avoided revealing. And this is—the far greater significance of the western lands for the plantation oligarchy. For that class the existence of a western reserve was economically decisive, because without room to expand the Cotton Kingdom was doomed. The vast land reserves facilitated more than any other single factor the growth of the plantation system after 1800. Considered in this light, the open West made possible the barbaric atavism of an expanding chattel slave system in the nineteenth century! Shall we disregard the armies of slaves thus created, as the Jacksonian "democrats" of that day did? Those who talk of the exemplary democracy of the Jackson period do just that.

So much for the special aspects of the Turner frontier school. To its more general conceptions, which it shares with other liberal historical theories, we shall return later. Let us consider now the more recent trend of thought concerning the Jackson period among modern historians.

A Workers' and Farmers' Government?

The impact of Marxism has visibly affected historical thought in every country of the globe. In the United States, where class struggles have been conducted in such open and undisguised forms, this impact could not fail to produce important results. Thus for over forty years there has flourished a school of historians whose chief occupation has been to borrow for their own use some of the tenets of Marxism while always denying their debt, reserving, as a matter of fact, envenomed shafts for the consistent and avowed Marxists. Charles A. Beard is the most prominent representative of this group; Vernon L. Parrington, Arthur M. Schlesinger, Sr. and Jr., and Louis Hacker are other prominent figures.

The approach of the Beard-type historians to the Jackson period begins with a modification of the Turner school. The "frontier," they realize, is not so omnipotent as its proponents believe. Rather they turn to a class analysis. Arthur M. Schlesinger, Jr., in *The Age of Jackson,* points this out: "It seems clear now that more can be understood about Jacksonian democracy if it is regarded as a problem not of sections, but of classes." This is a promising beginning, but in the end he completes the circle and returns to the traditional conceptions. For Jacksonianism is viewed by these historians, too, as a popular revolution crowned by the rule of the masses.

We need hardly go further than the chapter heading in Charles and Mary Beard's *The Rise of American Civilization* which characterizes Jacksonianism as "A Triumphant Farmer-Labor Party." Subsequent references in this book speak of "the labor and agrarian democracy," and so forth. Arthur M. Schlesinger, Jr., constructed his entire above-mentioned book around this idea, that the Jackson government was a worker-farmer conquest. Thus, common to both the Beard and Turner theories is the illusory notion of the revolutionary transfer of state power in the Jackson period to the popular masses. To these misconceptions must be counterposed the Marxist understanding of the first sixty years of the nineteenth century as a period of uninterrupted, if at times modified, hegemony of the slavocracy in national affairs.

If the conception that under Jackson the popular masses seized power were true, it would represent an important social revolution in the United States. (If revolutions were as simple in reality as they are in the minds of these people, the task of revolutionists would be light indeed.) We must ask, why did the slaveholder South yield so readily to being dispossessed from political power, for which it was to fight tooth and claw thirty years later? If these impetuous historians were to stop and ponder this question before venturing to speak so rashly of "revolution," they could find but one reply in accord with historical fact: that the Jacksonian Democratic Party in power did not lay its hands on a single prerogative or institution of the planting class. On the contrary, it protected, strengthened, and aided that class, while conducting an offensive to weaken the bourgeois enemy of the planters in the North.

But the historian may protest that the workers and farmers got a hearing in Washington from the Jackson administrations. What about the protection of the land interests of the farmers? The ten hour laws? The mechanic's lien laws? The progress made, especially by the workers, is beyond dispute. First of all, however, it must be understood that such concessions did not directly endanger the planting class, and, for that reason, the slaveholders could countenance reforms which gained for them national electoral support. Let us recall how John Randolph, planter spokesman in Congress, challenged the bourgeoisie: "Northern gentlemen think to govern us by our black slaves, but let me tell them, we intend to govern them by their white slaves."

Not one of our "enlightened" historians thinks to suggest that the gains of labor in this period might have resulted primarily from the increasing power and the independent activity and pressure of the workers' organizations. The period just preceding Jackson and during his administrations saw a huge growth of the trade unions and political movements of the workers. Unions were organized in many trades of the growing industrial system. Workers' parties were organized in a number of states, and workers' newspapers mushroomed. A spreading strike movement in the industrial areas, despite the vicious court rulings on "conspiracy" charges, testified to the militancy of the movement. Could not such a movement be expected to wring gains from the bourgeoisie independently of Jackson?

A very instructive case is related by the socialist historian Gustavus Myers in his *History of Tammany Hall.* Tammany was the Jackson arm in New York City. In 1829 a Workingmen's Party was organized, inspired chiefly by Robert Dale Owen, son of the famous utopian socialist. It propagated the typical labor program of that day: opposition to the "feudal land monopoly" and to capitalist banks, in favor of a system of free education, and so forth. In the first election in which the new party put a ticket in the field, it polled 6,000 votes against 11,000 for the established Tammany machine, and elected Ebenezer Ford to the Assembly. Tammany fought the Workingmen's Party bitterly with every weapon in its well-stocked arsenal. As part of its campaign it sponsored a piece of reform legislation designed to win the workers back to Tammany. This was the origin of the Mechanic's Lien Law in New York State, which has come down to us as a gift of the Jacksonians.

The early workers' parties were eventually assimilated into the Democratic Party, and their independent struggle was subordinated to national Jacksonian politics. Schlesinger describes this process with a gleeful air. To those for whom sycophancy is the ideal policy for the labor movement, it was a step forward. After all, what can the workers accomplish as an independent force? They should be happy to attach themselves to any Jackson (or Roosevelt) who might throw them an occasional favor.

Marxists have an altogether different conception of the role of the labor movement, and we are bound to criticize an alliance which was a severe setback to it. For the workers to abandon the construction of independent organizations in order to submerge themselves in the Democratic Party was to break the line of organizational continuity so indispensable for the eventual construction of a national labor movement of power and independence. To those who point to the "reforms" achieved in this period, we reply that at bottom they were the result of the show of power by the workers. An independent policy, designed to take advantage of the division between the planters and the capitalists, would have secured far bigger and more lasting gains. Of course, our criticism here is not of the weak and inexperienced labor movement of that day, but of those "liberal" historians and modern sycophants who would erect this policy of subservience into an ideal standard for the working class.

The miseducation of the workers by their leaders in the Jackson period left a deep scar on the labor movement. The workers, instead of being in the forefront of the abolitionist movement, their rightful place, were in the planter-controlled Democratic Party. Whoever touched the foul slavocracy was defiled by it. The antiabolitionist and chauvinist poison that later surfaced among the workers stemmed from this period of miseducation. Northern Jacksonian "democracy" must bear the blame for this.

Who Were the Jacksonian Reformers?

Our enlightened historians bring forward another "proof" of the democracy of Jacksonianism. All the democratic reformers, they tell us, all the "radical" opponents of "privilege" and "monopoly," were in the Democratic Party. The radical ferment of the period was expressed through Jacksonianism. That is their argument. And it is true that much of the agrarian radicalism, petty-bourgeois reformism, and proletarian discontent found its expression in the Jacksonian party. But here again we must proceed with care, and sift out the kernel of truth from the husk of phrases.

The planting class since Jefferson's day had worked out an elaborate ideology with which to justify its rule and its struggle against the capitalist class. Men like Jefferson, John Taylor, John C. Calhoun, and certain Jacksonian leaders demonstrate this. Their conception of an ideal society was a basically agricultural economy which they could dominate with ease. An extensive polemical literature was developed against bourgeois ideology, placing the "producing classes" on one side of a struggle against the "nonproducing classes." (It would of course be a mistake to suppose that the planters saw themselves for what they really were: the most parasitic class of the nation.) By an ideological sleight-of-hand, based on an absolute disregard of the slaves who were the actual producers, the planters converted themselves into the primary producing class of the South and the nation! Violent declamations against the capitalist thief who steals from the producer the fruit of his toil conjured up visions of the planter and his family in their immaculate white clothes, picking cotton all day in the hot sun, month in and month out, only to be robbed of the fruit of their toil by northern parasites. So spoke the worst thief of all, the slaveholder. And he saw nothing false in his fantastic ideology, so accustomed was he to think of the labor of his slaves as unquestionably "his own," as though he had performed it himself.

The democratic agitation of the northern Jacksonians followed these same lines. It pointed out many valuable truths about the capitalist class, and without doubt it had certain progressive results. But it suffered from an unpardonable defect—that of defending the slave economy. This defect gave it a generally reactionary cast in the national sphere. The apologist-historians protest that slavery was concentrated in the South, and the democratic agitation in the North had to fight the main enemy. They point to a certain type of abolitionist whose misleading role it was to make the sins of slavery an excuse for the sins of capitalism. Here too there is a certain grain of truth. Yet what of the southern Jacksonians? Did they expose and combat slavery? On the contrary, they helped to tighten the noose around black labor's neck. The question should not be posed sectionally to begin with, for Jacksonianism was a national movement. Had it been truly democratic, it would have condemned both slave and capitalist exploitation, and fought first of all against the slave system.

The abolition question, as a matter of fact, is the touchstone of Jacksonianism. It seems difficult to understand how a national movement committed to forthright democratic agitation could have avoided the issue of slavery, or even stood altogether on the reactionary side. Difficult to comprehend, that is, if one does not grasp the fact of slaveholder hegemony in the Democratic Party. It is amazing how many different types of reformers made up the northern wing of the Democratic Party. It was a reform association with one law: you must leave the issue of human slavery strictly alone! Abolitionism was, as Schlesinger (Jr.) mentions in passing, the "untouchable" of the Democratic Party. In *The Age of Jackson* he writes:

The Jacksonians in the thirties were bitterly critical of Abolitionists. The outcry against slavery, they felt, distracted attention from the vital economic question of Bank and currency while at the same time it menaced the Southern alliance so necessary for the success of the reform program [!!]. A good deal of Jacksonian energy, indeed, was expended in showing how the abolition movement was a conservative plot. . . . Ely Moore [a union leader who became a Democratic congressman] spoke for much of labor in his charge that the Whigs planned to destroy the power of the Northern working classes by freeing the Negro "to compete with the Northern white man in the labor market." . . . From reformers like Fanny Wright and Albert Brisbane to party leaders like Jackson and Van Buren, the liberal movement united in denouncing the Abolitionists.

Here, from the mouth of a modern apologist, we have a fair sample of the Alice-in-Wonderland reasoning of the Jacksonian "radicals." An alliance with slaveholders is made to "reform" society, and it must not be endangered by chatter against human slavery!

A democrat who took his democracy seriously, and extended it to the slaves, had no place in the "Democratic" Party. There is an instructive case. William Leggett, one of the ablest journalists of the New York Tammany organization, in 1835 attacked an order issued by Amos Kendall, Jackson's postmaster general (and incidentally radical-in-chief of the Democratic Party!) which barred abolitionist literature from free national circulation through the mails. In return Leggett was promptly excommunicated from the party and ruthlessly cast aside. He was pursued to the grave for his heresy, and afterwards Tammany Hall had the ironical temerity to honor his memory with a bust in the same room in which he had been read out of the party.

The issue of slavery was the key to the real nature of Jacksonianism, as it was to become the key to all parties, issues, and politicians. The uncompromising defense of slavery by Jacksonian "democrats" marks the movement as a planter-dominated upsurge. The custom of historians to ignore this, or to give it only passing reference without halting or modifying their paeans to "Jacksonian democracy," brings them close to dishonesty. They cannot sidestep the issue by pointing to numerous Jacksonians of the North who later became free soil advocates. That belongs to a later period, when the worker and farmer pawns of the slavocracy were torn away by the developments preceding the Civil War. Support of slavery stamps Jacksonianism with an indelible mark.

As a last defense against the conception of Jacksonianism as a planter power, the historians of the Turner and Beard schools point to the fact that the majority of large planters were for a time supporters of Whig policies against Jackson. Here too there is a germ of truth, but again it must be separated from the false interpretation placed upon it.

In our previous article we discussed the role of the large planters, particularly of the eastern region. They had grown accustomed to ruling through an alliance with and concessions to the northern capitalists. When conditions make it difficult or impossible for a class to continue in its previous path, a conservative section of that class tends always to stand in the way of the necessary turn. The Whig planters wanted to continue to rule "in the old way." William E. Dodd, the sharp-eyed historian of the South, has perceived the nature of this split in the planting class; he writes in *The Cotton Kingdom:*

Still there were differences . . . . The larger planters and justices of the older counties everywhere tended to follow Clay, while the smaller planters, the rising business men, liked the rougher Jackson way. Besides, Jackson could carry the West, and the votes of the West were necessary to any aggressive national policy. *But these differences were the differences of older and younger groups, not the differences of social irreconcilables.* Consequently, though each party twitted the other on occasion with being disloyal to slavery, in any great crisis they were almost certain to unite, for whatever happened, the planters felt that they must control the cotton kingdom. [Our emphasis]

Marxists see the Jackson era as a period of continued planter rule, modified in its external aspects by changing class alignments, and attaching to itself a pseudodemocratic movement of petty-bourgeois reformers who drew behind them large urban and agrarian masses. Although Jackson fought the capitalists, he fought them as a representative of the slaveowning class. There cannot be a "return to Jacksonian democracy" any more than there can be a return to slavery.

What of the "modern significance" of Jacksonianism, of which the liberals speak so glibly? Jackson and his party did represent a new departure, a new tradition in American politics. They represented the adaptation of the ruling class to the mass movements of workers and farmers. Every essential element of modern party usage stems from Jackson's time. Extended suffrage, party nominating conventions, publication of the popular vote, choice of presidential electors by popular vote, elective judiciary, and so forth, first began to predominate in his period. Likewise the spoils system in national politics, corrupt political machines, wardheeling politicians, candidates without principles, and demagogic campaigns. Jackson's managers in the campaign of 1828 cleverly concealed his stand on every important issue in national affairs, stressing only his rough western virtues. Little did they realize that they were making a stick to break their own backs. Twelve years later the Whigs had the same brilliant idea, aud put into the field a candidate, Harrison, who could outdrink, outfight, and out-log cabin Jackson's party, and he carried the country. Thus was developed the modern mode of class rule concealed behind the appeal to the common people. In a way it was a political "revolution"—in methods.

Utterly false is the attempt to find a modern significance for Jacksonianism in the phrases and slogans of that movement without regard to its class foundation. Such an attempt leaves the modern liberal with nothing to build on except . . . phrases. But phrases are as powerless against capitalism now as they were powerless against slavery then. Only the movements of social classes have the power to change society. If Jacksonianism has any modern significance it is this: only by allying themselves with an economically predominant class on the road to power can the urban and agrarian petty-bourgeois masses break the capitalist chains that bind them. That modern class, which is the gravedigger of capitalism, is the proletariat. Marxists will work to build the power of this class and to gain for it allies from other classes. We leave empty-headed liberals to celebrate the reactionary subservience of the popular movement to the slaveholding class a century ago, as they celebrated the subservience of the popular movement to Roosevelt's capitalist demagogy more recently.

The Rise and Fall of the Cotton Kingdom

George Novack (1939)

The Civil War, the crucible of the Second American Revolution, was precipitated by the secession of the southern planters. Therefore, the first question to be answered is: What drove the slaveholders of the Confederate States to quit the Union they had helped to establish and govern from its beginning?

The causes and circumstances of this momentous decision were complex and cumulative. But the underlying motives for the action of the southern "lords of the lash" can be traced back to the dynamics of the development of their "peculiar institution": the chattel slave mode of production.

This type of economy was a historical anachronism not only in the nineteenth century but even in the seventeenth when it was introduced into the Americas. Slavery had largely disappeared from Western Europe by that time. And yet, paradoxically, slave labor experienced a large-scale revival in the New World because of the economic needs of the aggressively expanding and far more advanced bourgeois civilization of the Old World.

In its initial stage American slavery was a collateral branch of commercial capitalism. Negro servitude was implanted in the colonies of the Western hemisphere to produce sugar, tobacco, rice, indigo, hemp, and other staples for the world market. Slaves themselves were one of the most lucrative of commodities in the international trade of the time.

In its ultimate stage chattel slavery in the South became an integral part of early nineteenth century industrial capitalism. Its predominant cash crop, cotton, was also the principal export of the United States, a source of considerable enrichment of the North and the chief raw material of British industry.

This Cotton Kingdom had a meteoric rise—and a sudden fatal

crash. Its downfall was the outcome of the interaction of two opposing economic processes. The slave economy was undergoing serious and critical structural changes just when the far more powerful and progressive industrial capitalism of the North and the small freehold farming of the Northwest were moving ahead with tremendous strides.

The frictions between these antagonistic forces generated such insoluble conflicts that the heads of the aging and declining slave system felt obliged to take the desperate step of disunion that brought on the Civil War and their own destruction as a class.

This essay will chart the economic evolution of the Cotton Kingdom from its emergence at the turn of the nineteenth century up to the departure of the slave power from the union.

The Birth of the Cotton Kingdom

The Cotton Kingdom was the first-born child in the United States of the industrial revolution. The South, cotton, and black slavery are so closely associated that it is difficult to realize that black slavery existed for almost two hundred years in the colonies before a cotton crop of any noticeable value was raised in the South. It is recorded that in 1784 eight bags of cotton, shipped to England from the South, were seized at the Custom House as fraudulently entered, "cotton not being a production of the U.S." As late as 1790 the total export of cotton from the U.S. amounted to only eighty-one bags.

Although the cotton plant could grow throughout the South, it was not commercially cultivated because of the excessive labor required to separate the seed from the fiber. The invention of the cotton gin, which enabled one person to clean more cotton in a day than ten could clean by hand in a month, gave an impetus to cotton cultivation which transformed the economy of the slave states. The cotton gin multiplied the productive capacity in the cotton fields a hundredfold, enabling the planters to increase their output from 18 to 93 million pounds from 1801 to 1810.

Cotton, being far more profitable to the planter than any other crop ever raised in the South, quickly supplanted tobacco, rice, and indigo as the chief southern staple. Slavery itself, which originally rested upon the cultivation of these products, came to be supported by bales of cotton.

This economic revolution in southern agriculture was the offshoot of the mightier industrial revolution in England. At the beginning of the nineteenth century steam and the new toolmaking machinery were rapidly transforming English manufacture into large-scale industry. In the center of this process stood the textile mills. The introduction of the spinning jenny and the loom together with subsequent mechanical improvements had the same effect upon cotton manufacture as the invention of the cotton gin in the 1790s had upon cotton cultivation. Jointly they multiplied the productive powers of the workers in both branches of economy to unprecedented dimensions.

This double revolution in the methods of production gave birth to corresponding social changes on both sides of the Atlantic. In England, the gentlemen whom Cobbett addressed as "Seigneurs of the Twist, Sovereigns of the Spinning Jenny, great Yeomen of the Yarn" emerged, together with the modern proletariat, from the womb of the factory system to engage in bitter struggle with the landed aristocracy. In the U.S. the expansion of cotton culture produced new agricultural magnates who not only superseded the old plantation aristocracy of Virginia as the rulers of southern society, but subsequently also became the political masters of America.

At the same time slavery, which had been loosening its hold upon the American economy, was tightly saddled upon the South. Although the upper-class opponents of slavery could find no way of eradicating the institution, they had hoped that, with the extinction of the slave trade in 1808 and the inevitable increase in the poor white laboring population, slavery would die as natural an economic death in the South as in the North. The expansion of cotton culture blasted the expectations of such antislaveryites. The new machinery pumped fresh blood into the constricting arteries of the slave system in the U.S., and, in the process, transformed many of its characteristics.

Capitalist production completely destroys the intimate connection between agriculture and manufacture which existed in the slave economy of classical and colonial times and in the feudal economy of the Middle Ages. This division of production takes place not only within each capitalist country according to the degree of its development, but on an international scale. Out of the worldwide division of labor created by the extension of capitalist production there develop whole nations devoted to either agriculture or industry and vast regions concentrating upon the cultivation of a single staple. The agricultural countries,

confined to the raising of raw materials and foodstuffs required
by the industrial nations, become the economic tributaries of the
latter. This separation of agriculture from industry was pursued
as a conscious policy by the British bourgeoisie in relation to the
American colonies before the Revolution and was one of the
principal causes of the revolt.

But the American economy did not lose its colonial character
when the people won their national independence from Great
Britain. Until the Civil War, the U.S. remained a predominantly
agricultural nation, exporting raw materials and foodstuffs to the
more advanced industrial powers across the Atlantic. The cotton
crop became the leading factor in the American economy before
the Civil War because textile manufacture was the most
important branch of English industry, which in this period
meant also capitalist economy. The two branches of production,
agricultural and industrial, American and English, stemmed
from a single trunk and grew together.

While the English textile mills had a monopoly of the world
market in cotton goods, the southern planters enjoyed a
monopoly over the supply of raw cotton. Three-quarters of the
southern cotton crop was exported to Europe in 1860, constituting
over one-half of all American exports and four-fifths of England's
imports of raw cotton. Wage slavery in the mills plus chattel
slavery on the American plantations was the magic formula that
put fabulous profits into the pockets of English textile magnates,
enabled Britain's cotton goods to conquer the world market, and
extended their reach into such hitherto untouched territories as
India and Africa.

Thus the British manufacturers, who prided themselves after
1833 upon the abolition of chattel slavery within their dominions,
were the chief beneficiaries of American slavery. Moreover, the
most brutal features of the "peculiar institution" of the South
were the peculiar product of English industrial capitalism.

As production came to be more and more concentrated upon the
cotton crop in response to the ever-increasing demands of the
textile industry, the southern plantations discarded their patriarchal features and became transformed into an exclusively
commercial system on the model of the Jamaican sugar estates.
The natural economy that had grown up around the plantations
was shattered by the impact of the new cotton culture, giving way
to the one-sided development characteristic of capitalist economy.
Everything on the cotton plantations was subordinated and

sacrificed to the raising of that one staple. Household industries were given up; the means of subsistence for the work force and the draft animals were often bought for cash; production was carried on simply and solely for the world market. Having forfeited the last traces of economic independence, the cotton plantations became an integral part of the *industrial* capitalist system, just as the earlier sugar and tobacco growers belonged to the mercantile system.

Where cotton was king, the whole economy fell under its sovereign sway. The price of land and the price of slaves were regulated by the price of cotton. A prime field hand was generally calculated to be worth the price of ten thousand pounds of cotton. If cotton was bringing twelve cents a pound, an able-bodied black was worth twelve hundred dollars on the slave market.

The planter, an absolute monarch on his own plantation, was a helpless subject when he came upon the market with his bales of cotton. There he had no more independent power than a marionette whose strings were attached to the hands of the textile manufacturers. How the planters danced to the tune of the world market, played through the pipes of the cotton manufacturers, can be seen in the following letter from Colonel John B. Lamar to his brother-in-law, dated February 9, 1845. Lamar was then managing his family plantations in Georgia. "Cotton is dull—prices have receded a little and the whole world of planters, buyers, etc. are on tip-toe for the news by the steamer which left Liverpool on the 4th of February. My prayers are fervent for advises of a ha'penny advance & large scale, great demand for cotton goods, spinners prosperous, corn plenty & all that sort of parlance, so interesting to us poor toads under a harrow, yclept planters of cotton."

The planters were equally at the mercy of the market when they came to buy their supplies or to borrow money. Under these conditions the mind of the cotton planter was as completely dominated by capitalist ideas as the price of his products was controlled by the capitalist market. Whether the planter was a resident producer or an absentee operator who hired an overseer to manage his estates, he regarded himself as a businessman who invested capital in land, slaves, and other means of production and expected an ample rate of return upon his investment. The cotton plantation was operated as a large-scale commercial enterprise and its accounts were reckoned in terms of annual profit and loss. The planters prided themselves on being the custodians of their own special way of life; they were actually subjected to capitalist conditions, connections, and concepts almost as strongly as the merchant who bought the cotton or the manufacturer who had it spun and woven into cloth.

The slave economy of the South had a peculiarly *combined* character. It was fundamentally an archaic precapitalist mode of production which had become impregnated with the substance and spirit of bourgeois civilization by its subordination to the system of industrial capitalism.

The Form of Agriculture and the Form of Labor

Black slavery was originally established in North America because of the absence of an adequate labor supply, after experiments with Indian and white servitude had failed. This same cause was operative on the frontier wherever the lack of labor was keenly felt. The early settlers in the Indiana Territory, mostly from Virginia, Kentucky, and other slave states, vainly petitioned Congress in 1802 and again in 1806 to allow slavery there on the ground that they were in great need of labor and were accustomed to secure it from slaves.

But there were other reasons in addition to the lack of labor and the force of tradition that kept the planter using slave rather than wage labor, even after European immigration began to deposit a surplus working population in the states. The growing of cotton, rice, tobacco, and sugar, the staples produced by slave labor, was carried on as a large-scale agricultural enterprise, involving heavy investments of capital, extensive tracts of land, and large gangs of laborers. The extensive agriculture of the past inevitably presupposed or gave birth to class divisions. Slave-owners and slaves, feudal lords and serfs, capitalist growers and wage earners are productive relations common to such large-scale agriculture.

Small-scale farming on the other hand does not necessarily involve sharp social differences between the individuals engaged in production. This could be seen in any section of the country populated by small farmers who cultivated their own land. The farm family usually performed all the necessary labor. For the extra labor needed at certain seasons and on special occasions, they would either call upon friends and neighbors or else draw upon the hired hands floating around the vicinity. Propertyless workers who hired themselves out for wages by the day, week, month, or year quickly appeared in all settled farming communities, later constituting a shifting stream of labor which flowed back and forth between town and country.

On the frontiers there were no sizable permanent bodies of employers and employees so long as any able-bodied person could easily possess enough land to become a self-employed farmer. Nor in most farming sections were there any hard and fast distinctions between the farmers and hired hands. As a rule, they worked side by side in the fields; ate at the same table; lived in the same house; and regarded each other as social equals. The hands were "help," not slaves. Manual labor, which was looked upon as degrading by the slaveholder, was regarded as the most worthy of occupations by the freehold farmer. Before the rise of the industrial workers, this sturdy class of plebeian citizens formed the backbone of the democratic forces in the United States.

Free labor differs from slave labor in two essential respects. In the first place, the free laborer has the right to sell his or her own labor power upon the market. Their persons are their own property. In the second place, they sell their labor power only for a definite, limited period.

Chattel slaves, on the other hand, cannot sell themselves for they belong to another. They are bought and sold in the market like any other kind of merchandise, and not only they but their offspring belong to the owner for life. From the standpoint of the laborer, it makes all the difference in the world whether he or she is enslaved or free. But the capitalist is indifferent to the form of labor he employs. His aim is to obtain the maximum amount of profit from it. So long as slave labor can produce more surplus than other forms of labor, well and good. When it cannot, the planter-capitalist will turn to a different system of labor in which the prospects of profit seem surer. It is all one with him.

When slaves became an economic liability to the Virginia planters, they were inclined to grant them formal freedom. On the cotton plantations of the South today most planting corporations have changed over from the semiservile system of sharecropping that succeeded chattel slavery to day labor, because the latter is more profitable under present mechanized conditions of production.

Chattel slavery, therefore, remained the prevailing form of plantation labor under the regime of King Cotton because the proprietors found that it was more profitable to invest their capital in black slaves, provide them with the necessary means of production and subsistence, and consume their capacities for labor during their active lives than to use wage labor or to adopt the sharecropping system. In extenuation of slavery, blunt John Adams declared to the Continental Congress: "It is of no consequence by what name you call your people, whether by that of freeman or slave. In some countries the laboring poor men are *called* freemen, in others they are called slaves, but the difference is imaginary only. What matters it whether a landlord employing ten laborers on his farm gives them annually as much as will buy the necessaries of life or gives them these necessaries at short hand?"

It mattered in one extremely important respect to the southern planter. So long as his labor could be steadily at work on the plantation the year round, it was cheaper to keep slaves than to use hired labor. From this standpoint cotton was an ideal crop for the slaveowner. With the exception of sugar cane, no other crop afforded such constant employment for unskilled labor. Plowing, planting, weeding, picking, ginning followed one another in regular sequence from one year's end to the next. There was no season when the experienced and capable planter could not find some productive work for his slaves on a cotton plantation.

The planters had other reasons for keeping the yoke of chattel slavery firmly fastened upon the blacks' shoulders. They feared that the emancipated black would join the procession of emigrants to the frontier and leave them without an adequate supply of labor. Many northern manufacturers who shared the same fear with respect to their own wage slaves not only opposed the opening of the western territories to settlers but attempted to impose legal restrictions upon such mobility to keep a plentiful supply of cheap labor at their command.

In a powerful polemic against the abolitionists in 1837, Chancellor Harper of South Carolina summed up the economic arguments of the planters for slavery:

The first and most obvious effect [of emancipation] would be to put an end to the cultivation of the one great southern staple. And this would be equally the result if we suppose the emancipated Negroes to be in no way distinguished from the free laborers of other countries, and that their labor would be equally effective. In that case, they would soon cease to be laborers for hire, but would scatter themselves over our unbounded territory to become independent landowners themselves.

The cultivation of the soil on an extensive scale can only be carried on

where there are slaves, or in countries superabounding in free labor. No
such operations are carried on in any portion of our country where there
are not slaves. Such are carried on in England, where there is an
overflowing population, and an intense competition for employment. . . .
Here, about the same quantity of laborers is required at every season, and
the planter suffers no inconvenience from retaining his laborers
throughout the year. (*Memoir on Slavery*, pp. 4-5.)

Free white labor might be more productive but it was less
reliable than slave labor. "Imagine," Harper goes on to remark,
"an extensive rice and cotton plantation cultivated by free
laborers, who might perhaps *strike* for an increase in wages, at a
season when the neglect of a few days would insure the
destruction of the whole crop; even if it were possible to procure
laborers at all, what planter would venture to carry on his
operations under such circumstances?"

Well might the corporation-farmers and shipper-growers of
California, Colorado, Ohio, and New Jersey, who today have so
much difficulty in suppressing untimely strikes by their workers,
envy their predecessors and sigh for the days of chattel slavery
when strikes were forbidden under penalty of death!

That the possibility of strikes was a factor militating against
the use of wage labor is confirmed by the following incident,
recounted by Charles Lyell, the famous geologist, from a
conversation with "an intelligent Louisianian" in 1846:

The sugar and cotton crop is easily lost, if not taken in at once when
ripe; the canes being damaged by a slight frost, and the cotton requiring
to be picked dry as soon as mature, and being ruined by rain. Very lately
a planter, five miles below New Orleans, having resolved to dispense with
slave labor, hired one hundred Irish and German immigrants at very
high wages. In the middle of the harvest they all struck for double pay.
No others were to be had, and it was impossible to purchase slaves in a
few days. In that short time he lost produce to the value of ten thousand
dollars. (*Second Visit to the United States.* Quoted from *Documentary
History of American Industrial Society*, Vol. II, p. 183.)

"I need hardly say," Harper remarked, "that these staples
cannot be produced to any extent where the proprietor of the soil
cultivates it with his own hands. He can do little more than
produce the necessary food for himself and his family." (*De Bow's
Review*, Vol. X, No. 47, January 1851, p. 588.) Slaves were
indispensable for the creation of the surplus product which
enriched the slaveowners.

Slavery was an absolute necessity in the frontier regions where few whites would work for others when they could so easily manage to get a living by themselves. The reason for this was well formulated by the anonymous author of two articles on "Slave-Labor and the Conditions of Its Extinction" in the English *Economist* of October 10-17, 1857.

Compulsory labor has one salient advantage and one only—that the capitalist can collect, group, and organize it at pleasure even in the centre of the most thinly populated district, and far from any labor market. It thus supplies to the American planter, directly and easily, the solution of the question which so puzzles our theorists on colonization—how to bring labor in a new country into sufficient dependence on capital. . . ."Buy your labor," they say, "not from the laborer himself, but from the owner of the laborer," and then for a fixed sum you can organize it, even in the depths of the wilderness, much as you please. And this is one economical advantage of slavery, that it carries a large scale system of cultivation out of reach of labor markets, and enables you to cultivate large areas of the richest land, and to get the largest net profits out of it, without reference to any condition but that of easy and cheap transport for the products.

The Expansion of the Cotton Empire

Owing to the restricted area within which tobacco, rice, and sugar could be raised and the comparatively limited markets for these crops, the southern plantations had grown rather slowly before the nineteenth century. With the coming of King Cotton the plantation system entered upon an era of rapid expansion. The rich calcareous loam so suitable to cotton cultivation girdled the foothills of the Appalachians all the way from Virginia to the Gulf states and thence west across the Mississippi bottomlands into eastern Texas. This enormous "black belt," combined with the apparently infinite elasticity of the market, freed the cotton planters from the narrow boundaries that hemmed in their predecessors and gave a steady impetus to the extension of the Cotton Kingdom.

The rapid exhaustion of the soil, caused by the improvident methods of cultivation pursued by the slaveowners, was one of the chief centrifugal forces in the outward drive of the plantation system. In their eagerness to extract the last penny of profit as quickly as possible from their agricultural operations, the plantation owners exhausted the natural powers of their land as recklessly as some among them exhausted the energies of their slaves. By failing to diversify their crops or provide for proper drainage, they robbed the soil of its fertility and allowed it to deteriorate, undermining the natural foundations of their own wealth. The resultant impoverishment of the land compelled the planter either to clear new lands adjoining his own, and thus add more acreage to his estate, or else to change location and move southwestward in search of cheap virgin soil.

Pillage of the land was a characteristic feature of the commercial plantation system in all stages of its development. The tobacco planters had plundered the soil no less prodigally than did the cotton growers. A graphic description of the decay of an entire region in Virginia from this cause is given by a black observer named Charles Ball, who was one of a band of slaves driven through the region by a slave trader in 1805.

It had originally been highly fertile and productive, and had it been properly treated, would doubtless have continued to yield abundant and prolific crops; but the gentlemen who became the early proprietors of this fine region, supplied themselves with slaves from Africa, cleared large plantations of many thousands of acres—cultivated tobacco—and became suddenly wealthy, built spacious homes and numerous churches . . . but regardless of their true interest, they valued their lands less than their slaves; exhausted the kindly soil, by unremitting crops of tobacco, declined in their circumstances and finally grew poor upon the very fields that had formerly made their possessors rich; abandoned one portion after another, as not worth planting any longer; and, pinched by necessity at last sold their slaves to Georgian planters, to procure a subsistence; and when all was gone, took refuge in the wilds of Kentucky; again to act the same melancholy drama; leaving their native land to desolation and poverty. (*Narrative of the Life & Adventures of Charles Ball, a Black Man*. Quoted from *Documentary History of American Industrial Society*, Vol. II, p. 62.)

In the course of two and a half centuries, similar cycles were enacted in the sugar islands of the West Indies. An island thrown open for settlement would at first be inhabited by free proprietors, cultivating their own land. A period of general prosperity and rough equality would prevail among the white colonists. Gradually, however, as production came to be concentrated in estates of larger and larger size, gangs of slaves would crowd out the small farmers. In a short time the rapacious planters would begin to exhaust the soil. With the diminishing fertility of the land and the increasing expensiveness of slave labor, the costs of production would rise. At this stage the supply of products from the new islands, occupied by immigrants from the old, would be thrown upon the market, and the competition would bring slow ruin to the old planters.

Thus the Windward Islands first supplied almost all the then limited consumption of sugar and coffee in Europe; Jamaica rose on their decay, and went through precisely the same stages of existence; San Domingo in turn greatly eclipsed Jamaica, but was overwhelmed by the great Negro insurrection, and never reached the period of decline. Lastly the Spanish colonies of Cuba and Porto Rico, after centuries of comparative neglect, started all at once to the front rank of the exporting islands, while the British planters with the aid of their accumulated capital, were struggling against encroaching decay. (Introduction by Ulrich Phillips to *Documentary History of American Industrial Society,* Vol. I, p. 92.)

The plantation system of the Cotton Kingdom ran through the same process of development on a grander scale and at a more rapid rate. As the land in the old plantation regions deteriorated and the call for cotton increased in the early decades of the century, the cotton planters pushed their way in successive waves of immigration from the seaboard states into the rich alluvial lands of Alabama and Mississippi, driving the small farmers, hunters, trappers, and Indians before them, trampling them underfoot or thrusting them aside into the piedmont or onto the sandy soils unfit for cotton. Jefferson's purchase of Louisiana placed at the planters' disposal an extraordinarily fertile and extensive area, already dedicated to slavery. Quickly taking possession of the lower part of the Louisiana Territory and expelling the Indian tribes beyond the Red River, the slaveholders soon overflowed into the neighboring state of Texas, then under Mexico's jurisdiction.

Although slavery was legally forbidden in Mexico, the planters evaded this prohibition by special exemptions and contracts binding blacks to serve ninety-nine year "apprenticeships." This was, however, not enough. The planters then conspired, like the Hawaiian sugar growers fifty years later, to rebel against the established government; set up an independent republic of their own; and agitated for its annexation to the United States. The Mexican War of 1845 set a seal upon the incorporation of Texas into the Union, just as the Spanish War of 1898 led to the annexation of Hawaii.

The center of the Cotton Kingdom kept shifting, the proportion of slaves to the white population decreasing in the older states while increasing in the states farther south and west. In 1821 two-thirds of the cotton crop was raised on the Atlantic seaboard. With the westward trek of cotton culture the proportion was reversed. Pioneering South Carolina produced 28 percent of the total crop in 1821, 15 percent in 1834, 12 percent in 1850, and only 6.6 percent in 1860. In that year 77.5 percent of the staple was produced west of the Appalachians; the plantations of Texas and Arkansas then accounted for larger crops than the state which had begun the cultivation of cotton seventy years before.

The Cotton Kingdom reached the peak of its power and glory around the middle of the nineteenth century. In 1850 the cotton country covered about 400,000 square miles, stretching from South Carolina on the east to San Antonio, Texas, on the west. It extended in breadth from two hundred miles at its extremities in the Carolinas and Texas to six or seven hundred miles in its center in the Mississippi Valley. The rich virgin soil in this territory produced abundant crops of the most various kinds with a relatively small expenditure of labor. It was cross-hatched by many navigable rivers that made transportation and communication easy and inexpensive for the planters.

The cotton planters were the economic, political, and social potentates of the American nation. Cotton was the most important crop not only in the South but in the national economy, constituting over one-half of the total exports for the U.S. in 1850. The entire economy of the southern states was adapted and subordinated to the needs of the cotton cultivators. The development of the non-cotton-raising regions was sacrificed to the nobles of the Cotton Kingdom. The cotton country consumed most of the produce of the slave breeders and tobacco planters; the whiskey distillers, corn and rye growers of Virginia, Kentucky, and North Carolina; the cattle raisers, pork packers, mule and horse owners and drovers from Kentucky, Tennessee, and the Northwest; and especially the grain growers of the northwestern states.

A good portion of the commerce, manufacturing, and banking of the North depended upon the Cotton Kingdom. The merchants and shippers of New York, Boston, Philadelphia, and Baltimore, the mill owners and textile workers of New England, the financial houses of the North subsisted upon one or another branch of the cotton trade. Thousands of individuals who took no direct part in cotton production had money invested or derived revenues from the slave system or some collateral branch of it.

The cotton nobility came to form the First Order in the federal government and its armed forces. They controlled the president, the cabinet, both houses of Congress, the Supreme Court, the foreign service, and they dictated the major policies made in Washington. The social prestige and influence of the slaveowners were enhanced by intermarriage between the leading families of the North and South, just as their political power was multiplied and fortified by the alliance between the southern and northern wings of the Democratic Party.

Since southern cotton was the foremost staple of international commerce and the basis of England's great textile industry, the spokesmen for the cotton magnates came to view the whole of industrial civilization as revolving around their peculiar system of labor and dependent upon the latter's produce for its existence and prosperity. Monarchs of all they surveyed in the South, sovereign in the U.S., and principal producers for world trade, it was small wonder that the leading slaveholders exclaimed: "Cotton is King!"

Confidence in the prospects of their peculiar system was greatly enhanced at a most critical juncture by their ability to withstand the impact of the depression of 1857, the most severe economic crisis of the nineteenth century. Thanks to its narrow agricultural basis, the Cotton Kingdom escaped the full fury of the blast. The steady demand for cotton in the world market buoyed up the South while falling prices for almost all other commodities dragged down the rest of the country.

At the same time the South was too closely connected with the national economy not to suffer from the effects of the crisis. The planters felt the panic in the contraction of credit which caused the failure of several important southern banks and the suspension of others, making it difficult for them to secure their usual financial accommodations and forcing them to throw quantities of cotton onto the market in order to meet their obligations. This enforced liquidation depressed both the price of cotton and the spirits of the planters. Such a reminder of their dependence upon northern capital further enraged the cotton growers and threw fresh fuel upon the fires of secession sentiment.

This was only a minor irritant, however, compared to the losses sustained by the Yankees. In general, the slaveholders congratulated themselves on their good fortune. Just as they were accustomed to boast of the superior safety of slave over free labor, so now they exulted in the superior stability of their agricultural society over the industrial North.

The Maturing Crisis in the Slave System

At first glance it would seem that the southerners had ample reason for their self-satisfaction. The production of cotton had doubled during the 1850s and reached a record of five million bales in 1860. Despite a drop to eight cents in 1851-1852, the average price per pound for the decade was between ten and eleven cents, a profitable level of production.

But this superficial appearance of prosperity during the fifties was as deceptive as the hectic flush on the cheeks of the consumptive. At bottom, all was far from well within the Cotton Kingdom. The slave system was the victim of a wasting and incurable disease that was ravaging it from within at the same time that its rivals were endeavoring to choke it from without.

The germs of this disease were latent in the very constitution of the slave system and had bred periodic disorders within it. To understand the nature of this disease and the reasons why it acquired a malignant form toward the end of the fifties, it will be necessary to expose the roots of the slave economy and the laws that governed its growth.

It has been previously pointed out that while the slave economy retained its antique form, it had acquired a highly bourgeoisified character through its affiliations with industrial capitalism. As a subordinate part of world capitalism, the slave economy suffered from all the evils of that system, shared its vicissitudes, and added its civilized vices of calculated overwork and uncalculated overproduction to its own.

The primary condition for the growth and well-being of the Cotton Kingdom was the continual extension of its market. Here the South suffered not only from the backwardness of its own system of production but from the anarchy of the world economy. Any slackening in the cotton industry had immediate repercussions in the economic life of the South, which was wholly at the mercy of the cotton market. On this score, however, the big planters had small reason for complaint. Cotton consumption continued to soar steadily until the Civil War, despite the periodic interruption of overproduction crises. The cotton crop doubled with every decade from 1800 to 1840, trebled from 1840 to 1860.

Five million bales were produced and sold in 1859-60, compared with one million bales in 1830-31.

The main causes of the impending crisis in the South were, therefore, not to be found outside the Cotton Kingdom but within it. For, in addition to the evils contracted from its association with industrial capitalism, the slave system was subject to far more serious maladies, which grew out of the contradictions inherent in its own method of production. What was the nature of these contradictions and how did they affect the development of southern society?

The cultivation of the staple crops produced by slave labor was mainly carried on as large-scale agricultural operations, requiring heavy investments of capital, extensive tracts of rich soil, and large gangs of unskilled labor. Each of these three fundamental factors in the slave economy, capital, land, and labor, possessed an intrinsically contradictory character. These contradictions constituted the motive forces that drove the slave system forward at the same time that they imposed limitations upon its growth. The antagonism between these productive forces and the social relations that encased them gave birth to chronic troubles within the Cotton Kingdom. Little as many of its inhabitants suspected their presence, the constant pressures exerted by the actions and counteractions of these antagonistic forces upon southern society were as much a part of their environment as the pressure of the atmosphere.

Competition was no less important a motive force of production within the Cotton Kingdom than outside it. Under the spur of competition the planter, like the cotton manufacturer, was driven to extend his scale of operations. This entailed the investment of ever larger sums of money in slaves and land, the principal means of production, just as the manufacturer was forced to install more and better machinery in textile mills to produce more cheaply and thus steal a march on his competitors. Thus the fixed capital of the planters tended to grow faster than the rest of their capital and to form a constantly greater portion of their total wealth.

The agricultural users of slave labor were under far more intense pressure than the industrial employers of free labor to extend the scale of their operations. The factory owner could sweat more surplus value out of his hands either by prolonging the working day or by increasing the intensity of their labor. The peculiar conditions of forced labor prevented the slaveholders from doing this to any great degree. The ordinary field hands would not fulfill more than the daily task allotted them by custom; they could not be driven beyond a certain fixed point without passive but no less effective resistance on their part. Indeed, it required the unceasing vigilance of the taskmaster, combined with the severest forms of punishment and cruelest means of torture, to ensure the slaves' completion of their stint.

The slaves were not only unwilling but also uneducated workers. The technique of labor upon the plantations could not be improved except within the narrowest limits, owing to the enforced ignorance of the captives and their handling of draft animals and implements. The planters had no other way of acquiring greater profits from their operations than through the amplification of their units of production.

The unremitting pressure upon the planters to reconvert their surplus capital into additional means of production in order to extend their scale of operations as cotton prices tended to fall gave rise to a chronic internal crisis within the Cotton Kingdom, which threatened to become fatal. It was a common saying in the South that the slaveowner grew more cotton to get more money to buy more slaves to raise more cotton, and so on, in a never-ending spiral. This nemesis that harried the planter arose from the very nature of his productive system. He could not escape it so long as he remained wedded to chattel slavery as an appendix to capitalist industrialism.

It was precisely during the periods of greatest prosperity for the planters that this process of the transformation of profits into fixed capital, that is, into slaves and land, took place at the fastest rate and on the greatest scale. This had important economic consequences. The general increase in the productivity of labor resulting from the continual extension of production led to overproduction crises, which from time to time depressed the prices of cotton below the level of profitable cultivation, especially in the older cotton-growing regions. The opening of new lands to cultivation in the Southwest at the end of the twenties, for example, caused considerable distress among the South Carolina and Georgia cotton raisers.

Another consequence of the remorseless extension of production was the tendency of the planter to fall into debt. At the beginning of each crop year, the average planter found himself with little liquid capital on hand. In order to maintain his family and carry on production until the shipping and sale of his next crop, he had to borrow money. He was in an even more difficult predicament if he borrowed money to buy more slaves and land. In both cases, the planter fell into the clutches of the merchants, bankers, factors, or slave traders who advanced him credit.

Moreover, the rich planters, like other agricultural aristocrats of baronial stature, were notoriously improvident and extravagant in the management of their affairs. Many left the task of supervising their estates to hired overseers or managers while they disported with their families in the southern cities, Europe, or northern watering places. As they sank deeper and deeper into debt, they again extended their operations with similar results. The only end to this vicious circle was bankruptcy and ruin.

Along with this expansion in the area of production, the means of production became concentrated in fewer hands. The big planters, able to command the capital and credit required by large-scale production and satisfied with a lower rate of return, bought or chased out the smaller farmers who had originally cleared the land and reduced it to cultivation. The petty producers, ground to dust by competitive struggle, were trampled underfoot, pushed aside onto poorer soils, or else driven forward into the unsettled territories toward the West.

This phenomenon, observable in all stages and centers of the slave economy, reached its peak in the South in the decade preceding the Civil War. In Alabama in 1850 "the great mass of the slaves belonged to a comparatively small number of men. As a matter of fact, less than 30,000 persons, that is to say less than seven percent of the white population of Alabama, owned the 335,000 slaves in the state. The average holding of slaves was therefore between eleven and twelve. Three-fourths of all slaves were owned by less than 10,000 men. The land holdings of these men were in proportion to their holdings of slaves. Their plantations frequently included thousands of acres, and from the big plantations came the bulk of the cotton crop." *(The Lower South in American History,* by William Garrett Brown, p. 34.)

The census of 1860 put the white population of the slave states at 8,099,760 and the slaves themselves at 3,953,580. The slaves were owned by only 384,000 whites, of whom 107,957 owned more than 10; 10,781 owned 50 or more; and 1,733 owned 100 or more. More than two-thirds of the white population had no direct interest in slavery, and but a small segment of the remainder gained much wealth from the system.

The concentration of wealth, as revealed by ownership of

slaves, was confirmed by statistics of the annual incomes of the uppermost crust. Around 1850, says Dodd, a thousand families received $50 million a year, while the remaining 666,000 families received only about $60 million, "a concentration of wealth and income hardly surpassed in the most advanced stage of an industrialized society." Together with this monopoly of the means of production and this concentration of wealth went a monopoly of social prestige and political authority in the hands of the rich slaveholders.

Owing to its superficial, rapacious, and improvident methods of cultivation, the slave plantation system required a steady supply of new, cheap, and fertile semitropical soil. In their triumphant progress the cotton planters laid waste the land like an invading army. "Even in Texas, before it had been ten years under cotton cultivation," reported Olmsted, "the spectacle that was so familiar in the older slave states was frequently seen by the traveler—an abandoned plantation of 'worn-out' fields with its little village of dwellings, now a home only for wolves and vultures."

The planters began to fear that cotton culture would shortly reach its natural limits. They could no more abide such a prospect with equanimity than a healthy person can face old age and death. The immediate economic consequence of this fact was an enhancement in the value of good cotton fields in the settlements. This still further increased the cotton growers' costs of production. By making the acquisition of new property and the retention of the old increasingly difficult for the poorer cultivators, it also accelerated the tendency toward the accumulation of the land in the hands of the wealthier planter-capitalists, and intensified the pressure from the middle ranks of southern society for the seizure of fresh territories.

A convergence of economic factors, the deterioration of the land, the ousting of the smaller cultivators, the necessity for keeping capital and slaves at work, urged the southerners forward. Strenuous but ineffective efforts were made to carry cotton culture into Missouri, Kansas, and other states where natural conditions were less favorable than in the southern regions

Hemmed in on the north and to the west, the planters could proceed in only one direction—toward the tropics. "The Conquering Republic" had broken through its territorial limits in the past by means of an aggressive foreign policy. Accordingly, even before they had digested the domains taken from Mexico at the end of the forties, the land-hungry slaveholders sought to stretch the boundaries of their slave empire. But their efforts to procure fresh fields were to prove far less successful in the fifties than in the forties.

A third source of difficulty for the slave system was contributed by its special form of labor. While factory operators in the North found a virtually inexhaustible reservoir of labor in emigration from Europe, the plantation owners had access to no such ample external source of supply. The importation of slaves had been forbidden since 1808 and, although smuggling continued, it was costly, dangerous, and added only a few thousand raw hands a year, compared with hundreds of thousands of free white immigrants.

The slaveholders, therefore, had to rely upon the "natural increase" in the slave population for their additional labor. Black women were urged or forced into becoming prolific breeders. Howell Cobb's overseer informed him that his Negroes increased "like rabbits." It was common for the slave population on a plantation to double in less than a dozen years. Part of the profits of the big slaveowners was derived from this propagation, just as part of the middle western farmer's profit came from the increase in the value of land. "Unearned increment" has been a most important part of the crop in all stages of the expansion of American agriculture.

The suppression of the African slave trade spurred the practice of raising slaves for the market to feverish levels. This vile profession was the ripe fruit of the slave plantation system in the Cotton Kingdom. In other countries and in less civilized ages the custom of breeding beings for sale was rare or unknown. Slaves were obtained either by conquest or by the importation of captives previously enslaved by others. The older plantation aristocracy added this crowning refinement to the southern slave system. The Virginia, Maryland, North Carolina, and Kentucky plantations, which had become ill-adapted to cotton cultivation, were turned into stock farms for raising blacks for sale to the cotton planters farther south. The breeding of "cotton niggers" was a far more lucrative business for decadent and impoverished slaveholders than the breeding of oxen, horses, and mules. At a time when horses were selling at a hundred dollars each, prime field hands brought from one to two thousand dollars on the auction block; young blacks were estimated to be worth ten dollars a pound; and every newborn child added a hundred dollars to its owner's wealth.

Where human beings were placed in the same category as stock animals, it is hardly necessary to dwell upon the consequences. The most revolting practices outlawed by civilized society became an accepted and sanctified part of the social system in the South. Where the slaveowner had a direct monetary interest in promoting the number of births among his slaves, whatever means tended to that result met with his acquiescence. Female slaves were publicly advertised as excellent breeders and fetched higher prices on that account.

Every decent sentiment and human relation was violated by the slave traffic. Married couples were sold separately by their owners and forced to take new mates in order to augment the slaveholder's wealth. Children were sold to strangers who carried them hundreds of miles from their homes and parents into the Carolina swamps or the wild regions of the frontier. Is it any wonder that slaves sought to escape or revolted periodically, or that fears of their uprising haunted and tormented their possessors?

The most sinister figures in this bestial business were the slave traders who moved between slave breeder and cotton planter. Although little attention has been paid to their activities, these dealers in human beings were powerful personages in the life of the South. The trader in blacks held the fate of many a planter in his hand. He was the best customer of the black-raising planter and his last resort in time of need. He was also often the master of those cultivators who bought slaves from him on credit.

Even though the slaves multiplied fast, the supply kept falling short of the demand, especially during boom periods. The growing demand for cotton combined with the restriction upon the foreign slave trade kept forcing up the price of slaves. A prime field hand, who in 1808 was worth $150, cost between two and three thousand in the boom years just before the Civil War.

The irrepressible tendency of the price of slaves to rise under this economic pressure was aggravated by the fact that slaves were the main repositories for investment and speculation in the South. "The universal disposition is to purchase," remarked the South's foremost economist, J.D.B. De Bow, in January 1861. "It is the first use for savings, and the Negro purchased is the last possession parted with."

The slave market occupied the same place in the southern

economy as the stock market under contemporary capitalism. Southern moneyed gentry invested their surplus funds in slaves as the modern investor puts them into stocks and bonds. The speculation in slaves tended to force up the price of slave property artificially, augmenting the costs of production for the planters.

This tendency reached its peak in 1859-60. Despite the warning of conservative southerners, investors plunged into speculation far beyond their depths. "Men are borrowing money at exorbitant prices. . . . the old rule of pricing a negro by the price of cotton per pound . . . does not seem to be regarded. Negroes are 25 percent higher now with cotton at ten and a half cents than they were two or three years ago, when it was worth fifteen and sixteen cents. Men are demented on the subject. A reverse will surely come." So warned the *Federal Union* of Milledgeville, Georgia, on January 17, 1860. In fact, the speculative bubble had approached its limit when the war cut across the maturing crisis.

The planters were persistently plagued by the inefficiency of slave labor and its extremely primitive technological level. In a detailed analysis of the southern system one of the editors of the *Southern Cultivator* frankly admitted that "the amount of labor used on an ordinary southern plantation is greater per productive acre than the amount of labor used in the most perfectly cultivated portions of Europe." Olmsted calculated that the average day laborer in the North did from three to four times as much work in the field per day as the slave hand. Indeed, chattel slavery was the most expensive form of labor in the world.

It was also among the most backward. The one "modern" agricultural implement used on the typical cotton plantation was the plow. The value of the farm tools on the standard plantation of a thousand acres and a hundred slaves was well under five hundred dollars. This was half the cost of a single field hand. The conditions of forced labor kept the plantation system tied down to this low technological level.

While all these economic factors harassed the planters individually, they found collective expression in the constantly rising costs of production. The cotton growers suffered from competition amongst themselves on the one hand and from the monopolies of the northern capitalists on the other. Their position as producers was quite different from their situation as consumers. They had to sell their products on an open market ruled by free competition, while they had to buy commodities on a protected national market controlled by slave breeders, manufacturers, merchants, and railroad and ship owners.

The plight of the poorer and less efficient planters in this respect was worsened rather than lightened during boom periods. Despite fair prices for cotton, the rising costs of production made it harder for them to derive an annual profit from their operations. And behind the increased prices of land and slaves lurked ominous signs of decay.

The accumulated wealth incorporated in slaves and land was distributed in an extremely one-sided manner. The upper tier of the planting class was being enriched by this doubling of southern wealth; the lower orders were being impoverished by it. The principal means of production were being placed beyond the reach of the lesser cotton growers at the same time that the prices of the things they had to purchase became more expensive. Slaves, land, superintendents' wages, clothes, food, mules, manufactures, freights, commissions, interest, and other essential items of production were rising in price faster than the price of cotton. The growers were caught in a steadily tightening vise. And the poorer the planter, the tighter was the squeeze.

How to get more land, cheaper slaves, cheaper means of subsistence in general, how to lower the costs of production and thereby arrest the falling rate of profit—these were the prime economic concerns that obsessed the cotton cultivators.

The system of chattel slavery in the South had entered the same stage of development that the system of wage labor was later to undergo in the United States. After a prolonged period of widespread prosperity, the planters entered upon a period of prosperity for the fortunate few and impoverishment for the many. This was true not only for the whole of southern society but also for its upper classes. Competitive slavery was giving birth to a monopolist slavery in which the great bulk of the means of production and wealth were gathered into the hands of the plantation magnates—the Hairstons, Cobbs, Aikens, and Davises. The "Sixty Families" who rule contemporary America had their predecessors in these seigneurs of the slaveowning South, who held most of the slaves and the best land, received three-fourths of the returns on export trade, and enjoyed a monopoly of political power, social prestige, and the good things of life.

The oppression and exploitation emanating from this small ruling group weighed upon the rest of southern society, intensifying their restlessness and discontent. This found expression in loud demands for expansionism from the less favored planters, in burning resentment among poorer whites and small farmers, and in more runaways and incipient revolts among the millions of black slaves. This growing dissidence forced the ruling group toward a radical solution of their problems.

The crisis developing in the slave states was therefore more serious than the passing crisis that ravaged the free states in 1857-58. The latter, although acute, originated in an infantile disease that was soon thrown off and from which the North emerged healthier and stronger than ever. The impending crisis in the South, however, was a crisis of decay, not of growth. It was an expression of the deepest contradictions within the slave states. While the wage-labor system was still in the prime of youth both on a national and on a world scale, southern chattel slavery was approaching its death agony, and no power on earth could prevent the former from expansion or save the latter from eventual extinction.

The planters did not remain passive in the face of these problems. They were in the main an enterprising breed, accustomed to conquer the obstacles in their line of march. In the years immediately preceding the Civil War they set about to remedy their economic weaknesses, bolster the foundations of the slave system, and prevent the internal crisis from deepening. If they did not solve the problems that beset them, the cause of their failure lay not in their lack of energy but in economic conditions and political forces which proved in the end to be mightier than their own resources.

The cotton cultivators combatted the mounting costs of production in accordance with the means at their command. The richer planters extended their properties, seeking to offset decreasing profit by augmenting its mass. Large plantations, which could be operated more efficiently and produce more cheaply, became the rule throughout the Cotton Kingdom. This trend toward concentration, which took place at a faster rate in the newer cotton states than in the old, acquired a furious momentum during the fifties.

The inevitable results of this process were pictured by Cassius C. Clay, Jr., in *De Bow's Review* for December 1855:

> I can show you, with sorrow, in the older portions of Alabama, and in my native county of Madison, the sad memorials of the artless and exhausting culture of cotton. Our small planters, after taking the cream

off their lands, unable to restore them by rest, manures, or otherwise, are going further west and south, in search of other virgin lands, which they may and will despoil and impoverish in like manner. Our wealthier planters, with greater means and no more skill, are buying out their poorer neighbors, extending their plantations, and adding to their slave force. The wealthy few, who are able to live on smaller profits, and to give their blasted fields some rest, are thus pushing off the many, who are merely independent.

Of the twenty millions of dollars annually realized from the sales of the cotton crop of Alabama, nearly all not expended in supporting the producers is reinvested in land and Negroes. Thus the white population had decreased, and the slave increased, almost *pari passu* in several counties of our state. In 1825, Madison county cast about 3000 votes; now she cannot cast exceeding 2300. In traversing that county one will discover numerous farm-houses, once the abode of industrious and intelligent freemen, now occupied by slaves, or tenantless, deserted, and dilapidated; he will observe fields, once fertile, now unfenced, abandoned, and covered with those evil harbingers—fox-tail and broom-sedge; and he will find "one only master grasps the whole domain" that once furnished happy homes for a dozen white families. Indeed, a country in its infancy, where fifty years ago scarce a forest tree had been felled by the axe of the pioneer, is already exhibiting the painful signs of senility and decay apparent in Virginia and the Carolinas; the freshness of its agricultural glory is gone; the vigor of its youth is extinct; and the spirit of desolation sits a brooding over it.

Signs of decadence similar to these in the very heart of the cotton belt could be observed in a more or less advanced stage throughout the entire South.

While the slave system promoted the growth of large estates, at the same time it set limits to the size of individual plantations. Slave labor, being unwilling labor, required the closest supervision. Moreover, the slaves, possessing but one means of transportation, their two legs, had to be able to walk to and from the fields without too much loss of time. The optimum size for the most profitable working of a plantation was found to be an estate of about two thousand acres. It was better to multiply the units of production than to increase their area indefinitely. Accordingly, the wealthiest planters owned and operated several plantations, often widely separated from each other. The Hairston family, for example, which held 1700 slaves, had plantations in Virginia, Alabama, and Mississippi. This diffusion of their properties through the South, freeing these magnates from local and state prejudices, enabled them to formulate a pan-southern policy and later set up a Confederacy in conformity with their interests.

The big planters built up their estates at the expense of the small proprietors, who were degraded in the social scale. A process of polarization was at work among the cotton growers. While the main mass of the means of production and wealth was falling into the hands of the gentry, petty producers were being crushed in the competitive struggle, forced to sell out and move to the frontier for a fresh start.

The swift concentration of wealth in the hands of an ever diminishing number of planter-plutocrats resulted in a more rigid stratification of southern society. The formerly fluid frontier settlements began to set into fixed castes. It became harder for a poor white to become a substantial small farmer, for a small producer to become a slaveowner, for the small slaveowner to grow into a large planter. The fierce competitive struggle made it increasingly difficult for the little men to keep their heads above water; it thrust them into a debtor's servitude to merchants, bankers, slave traders, and factors, or it ruined them completely. During the fifties there occurred a sharp decline in the number of small farms, a tremendous increase of indebtedness, and a general shutting down of economic opportunities among the southern middle classes. In the midst of this devastating crisis, the first families of the South continued to prosper.

These conditions could not fail to arouse bitter resentment against the cotton aristocrats among the less favored whites. Hinton Helper's *The Impending Crisis of the South: How to Meet It* (1857) was in essence nothing but a bill of particulars drawn up by an angry advocate for the oppressed southern middle classes in their case against the "lords of the lash." The sharpening antagonism between the large planters and the small farmers was one of the significant symptoms of the developing crisis in the South.

The economic stagnation within the Cotton Kingdom combined with urgent political considerations to speed up the southern campaign for the extension of slavery into the territories and for the conquest of new lands. In order to maintain their balance of power within the federal government, the slaveholders strove to make slave states out of Kansas and Nebraska. Political considerations played a no less important part in the drive toward the tropics. The emancipation of the slaves in the English and Mexican dominions, coupled with the expansion of the free states in the Union, threatened the slave states with encirclement by a ring of free territory. Slavery was being penned within a narrowing area, threatening it with slow suffocation.

Throughout the fifties the slaveholders made abortive attempts to break through this encirclement by going further to the West and further to the South. Strenuous efforts to carry cotton culture into Missouri, Kansas, and other states where natural conditions were less favorable than in the South, met with failure. As the *New Orleans Bee* pointed out at the height of the conflict over "Bloody Kansas": "Slavery will go where it will pay. No slaveholder for the sake of an abstraction will amuse himself by earning five percent in Kansas on the labor of his chattels, when with absolutely less toil it will give him fifteen percent on the cotton and rice fields of Louisiana." The incorporation of New Mexico and California into the Union held out little hope of relief, owing to their remoteness and the high costs of transportation, and especially after the Californians barred slavery.

The southerners hoped to appease their craving for rich land in the tropics. Adventurous agents instigated insurrections in Cuba and the countries of Central America with the design of duplicating their Texas coup and setting up new outposts of the slave empire. These unofficial expeditions were in some cases supported and supplemented by official intrigue and action. The Ostend Manifesto of 1854, signed by three proslavery American ministers to Europe, including Buchanan, who was to become president two years later, proclaimed with brutal frankness the determination of the southern slavemasters to take Cuba from Spain. There was considerable talk in slaveholding circles of adding the valley of the Amazon to their possessions. North America was becoming too small for the most ambitious of the slaveholders.

But all these dreams of empire could not be carried into execution because of opposition from the free states. The slaveholders no longer had enough political weight to unite a coalition behind them of sufficient strength to inveigle the nation into another foreign war. Thus the conquest of new lands was at the same time necessary and impossible for the planters. Their representatives wrestled with this dilemma in the sphere of foreign policy throughout the fifties without finding any satisfactory conclusion. In the end there seemed only one means open to obtain a free hand for the execution of their plans of imperial conquest. That was to cut loose from their bondage to the free states in the Union.

The way to acquire additional slave labor and lower the high price of slaves was to remove the restrictions upon the foreign slave trade. The law forbidding the slave trade was, in effect, a protection of the American-grown slave commodity against the foreign product. The prohibition of slave importation seemed as odious and oppressive to the cotton planters in need of labor as the protective tariff upon cotton fabrics.

The uninterrupted rise in the price of slaves led to extensive agitation for the reopening of the African slave trade. Proposals to this effect were debated and approved at the commercial conventions held in the southern capitals during the late fifties. In 1859 prominent secessionists organized the African Labor Supply Association to promote the movement for the legalization of the slave trade. Its advocates argued that the renewal of the traffic would cheapen the cost of slaves and enable the slaveholders to compete with the free farmers from the East and Europe in settling beyond the Mississippi and controlling it politically. They likewise saw in this repeal an opportunity for binding the discontented poor white farmers of the South more firmly to the slave system by making slaves available to them.

But this clever scheme for the cheap mass distribution of slaves, like kindred utopian proposals for the mass distribution of property under industrial capitalism, never advanced beyond the stage of conversation for impregnable economic reasons. The proposal to renew the foreign slave trade conflicted with the vested interests of both the slave breeders and the large slaveowners. The first were opposed to having their monopoly broken or the price of their product lowered; the latter were opposed to having the value of their property in human beings depressed.

Although this agitation proved fruitless, the insistent demand for slaves gave an impetus to the illegal trade which had been carried on surreptitiously—and even flagrantly—since 1808. It has been estimated that 270,000 slaves were smuggled into the country between 1808 and the Civil War. The traffic more than doubled from 1857 on. The number of successful ventures can be estimated from the fact that twenty vessels were seized as slavers even by a friendly federal government in the last nine months of 1859. Southern juries usually refused to convict arrested slave traders, and the federal authorities were lenient so long as the friends of the slave power controlled the government. The Republican assumption of power not only meant sterner prosecution for the illegal slave traders, but also snuffed out any hope of removing the constitutional prohibitions on the trade.

Secession seemed to hold out the promise of a definitive solution of this problem. Here, too, the slaveholders were deluded. Opposition from the slave breeders prevented even the Confederacy from legalizing the importation of slaves.

A few planters turned toward the employment of white day laborers. Cheap white labor here and there supplemented the more expensive slave labor, especially in such dangerous and unproductive work as ditchdigging and draining in malarial swamps where planters hesitated to risk the lives of their valuable field hands. "If an Irishman died," it was said, "it merely increased the Kingdom of Heaven; if a slave were killed there was $1,500 gone!"

But environing social circumstances prevented free white labor from replacing black slavery to any extent. The poor whites refused to work side by side on an equal footing with the slaves, and Irish and German immigrants shunned the slave states like plague spots. If wage labor was more productive, it was far less dependable. Hired hands were liable to strike and demand higher wages in the midst of a harvest, to get drunk and not appear for work, or to quit the plantation if working conditions were unsatisfactory. Thus slavery tended to perpetuate itself and ward off the encroachments of alternative forms of labor.

Along with their campaign to reopen the slave trade, the slaveholders' representatives in Congress launched a drive to lower the tariff rates. Toward the end of the 1850s they succeeded in forcing down the rates to their lowest levels since 1807. But this reduction in rates brought them little relief.

During the forties and fifties progressive planters and ambitious southern capitalists also made energetic efforts to diversify their economy and catch up with their northern rivals in the spheres of transportation and industry. Conventions for the promotion of commerce, for the improvement of agriculture, and for the building of railroads were held in leading southern cities. An all-southern commercial convention met annually after 1852 to discuss such problems connected with the economic advancement of the South as the establishment of direct steamship lines to Europe, a Pacific railroad, the encouragement of southern manufactures, and the improvement of waterways.

These commercial conventions were the nuclei of the future Confederacy. The most prominent secessionist leaders, De Bow,

Yancey, Ruffin, and their associates, were the promoters and keynote speakers at these meetings. Here the seeds of secessionism were sown and nurtured. Here the interests of the slave system could be discussed in common without regard for the claims of other parts of the country. Here southern economists and politicians came forward with their schemes to strengthen and save the ailing South.

The physicians who congregated at the bedside of the slave economy had no lack of prescriptions for restoring their patient's health. They were in general agreement that railroads were the indispensable foundation of economic progress. Every southern metropolis dreamed of becoming a rail center. Mobile aimed to get a share of the shipping that floated down the Mississippi to New Orleans, just as Norfolk hoped to divert toward itself part of New York's commerce. Even the complacent merchants of New Orleans were compelled by its rivals' threats to its supremacy to enter the railroad construction race in which the whole country participated from 1849 on.

The southern cities had a joint interest in snatching the trade of the Upper Mississippi Valley from the North. Plans for linking the Ohio Valley with the South had been broached as early as 1836 at a railroad convention in Knoxville headed by the great southern statesman Hayne. Most of these grandiose projects remained on paper; others proceeded very slowly. During the forties the South built mainly short local lines. Railroad construction spurted forward with the congressional land grant to the Illinois Central in 1850. The rate of construction in the South during that decade was greater than in the rest of the country, though this was because the section had fallen so far behind in the preceding decade. From 1850 to 1860 its total trackage jumped from two to ten thousand miles, over a third of the total in the nation.

The main lines connecting the slave states with the Middle West were not completed, however, until after the decade ended, when the trunk lines from the Northeast had already reached into the West as far as Chicago and Saint Louis. The South could not keep abreast of the North in the rail race. The most important results of the railroad building during the fifties were the unification of the scattered slave states, the extension of their area, and greater centralization of their economy. The embryonic Confederacy was given an iron framework.

Parallel projects for steamship lines between the southern ports and Europe materialized in few cases. Those established either failed or handled only a small volume of the coastal and transatlantic shipping. These remained, as before, in the hands of northern shipmasters.

Despite the urgent appeals of forward-looking southern economists to lessen their dependence upon the North by diversifying their one-crop economy, the development of industry proceeded at a snail's pace in the Cotton Kingdom. The slave economy interposed formidable barriers in its way. The necessity for sinking enormous sums of money annually into slaves and land devoured the surplus capital of the planter; northern and English capital found more attractive investments elsewhere.

Textile manufacturing was the natural first step toward industrializing the South. "The planters know that their production of cotton is at a sacrifice which looks to ruinous consequences because the substance of their land is annually wasting away," remarked the farsighted De Bow. "The remedy which we now insist upon is for the planter to resolve that the cotton mills shall be brought to the cotton fields; that they have been paying toll to the English mill long enough." By fabricating their own textiles the southern capitalists, according to De Bow's reckoning, would not only provide employment for their poor whites but would buttress their world monopoly of cotton cultivation with a similar monopoly of manufacture and selling of cotton goods.

But when ambitious entrepreneurs did set up textile factories, they encountered all sorts of troubles. There was an absence of experienced and reliable factory hands. Slave labor could not serve as a basis for factory production, while, at the same time, it prevented the growth of a class of white wageworkers. Slavery also discouraged immigration. White workers not only suffered from the competition of slave labor but felt keenly the social stigma attached to their occupations in the South and the absence of an atmosphere of social freedom and political equality. Attempts to import skilled female operatives from New England failed. Not even higher wages would induce them to stay in the slave states.

A weak textile industry could not stand up against competition from New and Old England. The infant industry required tender nursing and state subsidy in order to thrive. As it was, the flood of cotton goods from outside sources stifled southern cotton manufacturing in its cradle.

As a result, although the material prerequisites for textile manufacturing were at hand, the industry made slow progress in the prewar South. During the forties and fifties only a few of the cotton mills established in various parts of the South prospered. The majority went under. That the slave economy alone held back the expansion of the textile industry to considerable dimensions was manifested by the leap forward taken by the industry after Reconstruction.

The efforts to implant industry in the slave states failed to meet with consistent encouragement from their rulers. So long as prosperity haloed the head of King Cotton, most of the planters were satisfied and were little disposed to worry about industrial enterprise. Some recognized, too, that the factory was the Trojan horse which would introduce a mortal enemy inside their citadel. No sooner had textile manufacturers set up their machinery than they began to demand a protective tariff in concert with their colleagues above the Mason-Dixon line. On his visit to the United States, Charles Lyell reported that at Columbus, Georgia, "the water-power at the rapids has been recently applied to some newly-erected cotton-mills, and already an anti–free trade party is beginning to be formed."

The planters could hardly be expected to nurse the abominable high-tariff viper in their bosom. The proposals to industrialize the South meant a radical break with all they held dear, a surrender in principle to their northern antagonist. The cotton lords were far from confessing their bankruptcy. On the contrary, in season and out, they proclaimed their confidence in the omnipotence of the Cotton Kingdom and their undying fealty to its king.

The slaveholders listened more attentively to suggestions which did not involve the undermining of their established institutions or entail the abandonment of their cherished practices. Not the least popular was a plan for joining the newly settled regions of the Mississippi Valley and the Pacific Coast into an indissoluble economic union with the South. Circumstances at first seemed to favor the consummation of such a commercial alliance. The southern and middle western states were already connected by numerous close ties. The South was considerably nearer to the Pacific than the North. The grand waterway of the Mississippi was the natural outlet for products and people of the Mississippi and Ohio valleys. These states had originally been colonized by emigrants from the slave states. The planters consumed many of the products of midwestern agriculture. The largely Democratic farming population there had long been political helpmates of the planters against the Whig businessmen of the North.

One key to the success of this project lay in the building of railroads linking these regions with the commercial centers of the South. The Illinois Central Railroad was planned as the first link of a grand trunk line which, together with the Mobile and Ohio, would join the Great Lakes to the Gulf. Shortly afterwards, New Orleans capitalists projected the New Orleans, Jackson, and Great Northern route, which was to extend up from New Orleans to the North and compete with the road from Ohio to Mobile.

In comparison with the North, these lines crawled toward their destinations. The New Orleans road was not connected until January 1860; the Mobile and Ohio not until April 1861—too late to stave off the Civil War, but just in time to help the South wage it more effectively.

The railroad to the Pacific was not even begun. Although everyone South and North acknowledged that a line to the Pacific Coast was necessary and inevitable, and that private capital could not sustain the enterprise without government aid, no congressional majority could agree upon the route, the eastern terminus, or the amount of federal subsidy. Each specific bill for an all-southern route was killed in Congress; the deadlock continued until after the Civil War. Although a strip of land was purchased from Mexico especially with a view to constructing a southern road, the proposition got no further toward realization than an appropriation enabling the secretary of war to survey as many routes as he thought proper.

The main currents of economic development in the Upper Mississippi Valley and on the Pacific Coast were running against such a union with the South. The new railroad network, the telegraph, and canals were diverting the trade of the grain kingdom from the mouth of the Mississippi to the northern ports. Trade was irresistibly attracted from the agricultural West to the industrial North by better shipping and financing facilities, by the enormous extension of eastern markets, and by their proximity to Europe. The influx of eastern and European immigrants, detesting slavery and all its works and profiting little from it, broke the old social and political ties between West and South. Though the westerners strove to retain both, the eastern markets became more important than the southern. The beginnings of industry in the Middle West forged another link

between the West and the Northeast. The Far West was likewise
bound to the East by a similar labor system, by the telegraph and
merchant marine, and by its gold mines.

Economic union with the Middle West and the Pacific Coast
was supposed to be the first step in a larger southern scheme for
the formation of an international commercial empire constituted
by industrial England, the cotton states, and the food-raising
West. The slave states were to form the keystone of this
magnificent edifice. This plan was outlined in 1856 by David
Christy in his book *Cotton is King!*

"Slavery attains its importance to the nation and to the world
by standing as an agency, intermediate between the grain-
growing states and our foreign commerce," he wrote. "As the
distillers of the West transformed their surplus grain into
whiskey, that it might bear transport, so slavery takes the
products of the North and metamorphoses them into cotton, that
they may bear export." In this way, there "was a tripartite
alliance formed, by which the western farmer, the southern
planter, and the English manufacturer have become united in a
common bond of interest, the whole giving their support to the
doctrine of free trade."

According to this scheme, the North was to be deprived of its
industries and converted into an agricultural province of the
South. Ironically, the role of the intermediary between the
western farmers and industrial Europe which the proponents of
this bold plan assigned to the South was actually assumed by the
manufacturers and merchants of the North. It was not the North
but the South that was transformed into an agricultural
appendage and excluded from the benefits of midwestern trade.

The intelligent experiments of southern agronomists in
diversifying southern economy met with scanty success. A few ill-
fated attempts at tea and silk raising in South Carolina, and in
more scientific agriculture by Edmund Ruffin of Virginia and
others, constituted spasmodic efforts along these lines. The
improvement of southern agriculture was retarded by the same
general causes that hobbled the development of industry: the
inefficiency and expensiveness of slave labor, the cultural and
social backwardness of the South, and the lack of capital and of
any incentive for its employment in other fields of agriculture.

The difficulties of the slaveholders were multiplied and
aggravated by the very means they took to overcome them. The
extension of cotton production resulted in so great a concentra-

tion of capital that thousands upon thousands of small proprietors were ruined and the antagonism between the plantation plutocracy and the rest of the whites increased. Their struggle for new lands led to conflict with the North and with neighboring nations. The agitation for the reopening of the foreign slave trade divided the slave states rather than united them. The tariff reductions widened the breach with the northern industrialists without cheapening their costs of production to an appreciable degree. To cap it all, the costs of production continued to rise. Twist and turn as they might, the slaveholders could not disentangle themselves from these intolerable contradictions.

The planters were tormented not only by the infirmities and backwardness of their peculiar system of production but by the humiliating dependence upon the North which flowed from it. This dependence was virtually complete. The southern states depended upon Northern capital for the credit required to carry on production and for the capital to build railroads or establish manufactures. They depended upon northern merchants for the export of commodities to Europe and for the importation of goods from Europe. They depended upon northern mills for the making of their cotton into cloth. They depended upon the North for most of the necessities used upon the plantations and for every luxury known to the towns. They depended upon northern shipyards for their ships and upon northern mines and iron works for their railroad supplies and machinery. They were even dependent upon the North for their culture, education, and entertainment. The slave states were, in effect, virtually a northern colony.

The southerners' resentment against this dependence burst forth continually. An Alabama journalist complained in 1851:

At present, the North fattens and grows rich upon the South. . . . Our slaves are clothed with Northern manufactured goods, have Northern hats and shoes, work with Northern hoes, ploughs, and other implements, are chastised with a Northern-made instrument, are working for Northern more than Southern profit. The slaveholder dresses in Northern goods, rides in a Northern saddle . . . patronizes Northern newspapers, drinks Northern liquors, reads Northern books, spends his money at Northern watering places. . . . In Northern vessels his products are carried to market, his cotton is ginned with Northern gins, his sugar is crushed and preserved by Northern machinery; his rivers are navigated by Northern steamboats, his mails are carried in Northern stages, his negroes are fed with Northern bacon, beef, flour and corn; his land is cleared with a Northern axe, and a Yankee clock sits upon his mantelpiece; his floor is swept with a Northern broom, and is covered with a Northern carpet; and his wife dresses herself in a Northern looking-glass; . . . his son is educated at a Northern college, his daughter receives the finishing polish at a Northern seminary; his doctor graduates at a Northern medical college, his schools are supplied with Northern teachers, and he is furnished with Northern inventions and notions.

Northern capital, said Hinton Helper, ruled the southern whites from the cradle to the grave.

In one way or another we are more or less subservient to the North every day of our lives. In infancy we are swaddled in Northern muslin; in childhood we are humored with Northern gewgaws; in youth we are instructed out of Northern books; at the age of maturity we sow our "wild oats" on Northern soil; in middle life we exhaust our wealth, our energies and talents in the dishonorable vocation of entailing our dependence on our children and on our children's children and, to the neglect of our own interests and the interests of those around us, in giving aid and succor to every department of Northern power; in the decline of life we remedy our infirmities with Northern canes; in old age we are drugged with Northern physic; and finally, when we die, our inanimate bodies, shrouded in Northern cambric, are stretched upon the bier, borne to the grave in a Northern carriage, entombed with a Northern spade, and memorized with a Northern slab.

One southern newspaper declared that the "Lord North" of 1851 was a greater oppressor than the Lord North of the British ministry who turned a deaf ear to the petitions of the American colonials in 1775. Southern statisticians calculated that the South paid fifty million dollars in annual taxation to the federal government, of which only one-fifth was returned in the form of federal expenditures, and that the total tribute paid yearly by the South to the North amounted to between one and two hundred million.

The following analysis of the annual circulation of capital in the South, based upon figures presented by Dodd, shows what was happening to the proceeds of the plantations.

Although New Orleans was one of the greatest exporting cities in the country, the amount of money on deposit in her banks was insignificant. Less than a third of the returns of cotton which annually left her docks ever found place in her financial institutions. On the other hand, New York and Philadelphia always had on deposit more money than the total value of her exports. What was true of New Orleans was true of the cotton belt as a whole. Though the cotton, rice and sugar of the South sold for $119,400,000 in 1850, the total bank deposits of the region amounted to only some $20,000,000. Ten years later, when the value of the crops had increased to more than $200,000,000, less than $30,000,000 was deposited in the banks of the cotton and sugar belt.

The yearly earnings of the South flowed in two different directions. One stream ran back into slaves and land; the other eventually made its way into the reservoirs of northern and English capital in the shape of tariffs, freights, commissions, and other forms of profit. In either case, the southern masses received little of this wealth derived from their joint exploitation by the slave magnates of the South and the capitalist overlords of the North.

Mutual relations between the slave and free states were further embittered by the constantly increasing superiority of the northern economy over the southern. The North far outstripped the South not only in industry but in agriculture. Those who shouted "Cotton is King!" could not be totally oblivious of the fact recorded in the 1850 census, that the combined value of all the southern staples—cotton, tobacco, rice, hemp, and sugar— scarcely equaled the value of the hay crop alone in the North. By 1860 the North possessed three times as many miles of railroad as the South.

While the slaveholders held on to political hegemony, their relative economic strength was fast declining in favor of their northern rivals. This was one reason why Hinton Helper's statistical demonstration of the backwardness of the slave states in *The Impending Crisis* touched so sensitive a nerve and drew such howls of rage from the slaveholders.

The Secessionist Movement

What was to be done in the face of these facts?—thinking planters asked themselves. Economic reforms were patently insufficient to give more than temporary relief. The mechanism of the slave economy continued to grind out its terrifying social products. The failure of the slave states to transform their one-sided economic life was manifest, as the South fell farther and farther behind the North in all fields of economic activity. As the constricting crisis coiled more tightly around them, the planters began to rely to a greater degree upon political measures for the protection and promotion of their welfare.

During the fifties the slave power employed all the agencies and resources of the federal government as weapons in their struggle for supremacy. Command of the national apparatus had become an absolute necessity for the economically enfeebled planters. Yet, just when they needed it, they felt that control slipping from their grasp. The old forms of political action, confined within the framework of the Union, were inadequate to cope with the consequences of the crisis. To wage a successful struggle against their enemies, bolder and more direct forms of action were called for by the changed conditions.

The growing power of the free states made it increasingly hard for the slaveholders to obtain full satisfaction of their demands. With the rise of the Republicans, their old allies in the North became more and more unamenable and restless under their dictates. Such aggressive political measures as the Kansas-Nebraska Act and the Dred Scott decision had served to divide their own forces and solidify the resistance of their opponents. The slaveholders were consequently driven in upon themselves and forced to rely upon their own independent strength. After 1857 more and more southerners saw the only way out of their impasse in considerably more radical measures. The more advanced spokesmen for slaveholding interests began to advocate a boycott of northern goods and commercial nonintercourse —the nineteenth-century version of imperialist "sanctions." These suggestions for economic independence were only a prelude to more serious moves toward political independence. Economic warfare was the harbinger of armed civil war.

From all sides the hopes and needs of the southern upper classes converged toward the single solution of secession. South Carolina was the hotbed of the secession movement because there the processes of economic decay had reached the most acute stage. But all over the South hard-pinched agriculturalists clamored for relief. They saw the author of their ills not in their own system of production, but in the free states to the North which drained away their wealth and obstructed every effort to better their situation. To get rid of Yankee oppression and exploitation became the obsession of militant southerners.

Thus the deepening crisis revived and fortified the secession movement which represented the slaveholders' ultimate hope of salvation. The secessionist leaders formulated the demands of the ruling whites and assembled a unified program for southern autonomy. They generalized the particular grievances of the various sections of the agricultural population into a comprehensive philosophy, knit them into a political program, and gave their separate impulses a common goal, direction, and mass force.

The secessionist movement was therefore the perfected political expression of the deepening crisis within the chattel slave system. The successful surmounting of episodic crises in the past by the slave power had kept the secessionist movement from coming to fruition. Now the time was ripening for its consummation. The social and political conditions which had up to then enabled the planters to overcome their difficulties within the Republic were fast disappearing. After decades of dazzling progress, the Cotton Kingdom had passed the peak of its power and was slipping down from its formerly unassailable eminence. The secessionist movement represented the last desperate effort on the part of the slaveholders to counteract the operation of the immanent laws of the slave economy and to arrest their decline.

By the surgical operation of separation from the Union the planters hoped to rid themselves at one stroke of all the ills from which they suffered. The secessionists argued that national independence of the slave states would forever guarantee the existence of their peculiar institution; would enable the slaveholders to throw off their Yankee parasites; would open the door for free expansion toward the tropics; would ensure free trade with the rest of the world; and would draw the Northwest to the South while crushing the North and leaving it prostrate.

These were in great measure fanciful visions. The roots of the evils from which the planters suffered were too deeply embedded in the constitution of the slave system to be cured by secession. Even if southern independence were achieved—which was by no means guaranteed—the life of slavery could not be indefinitely prolonged.

The slave economy was under sentence of death. So expensive a method of production could not stand up much longer in the capitalist world. The abolition of chattel slavery within the British and French empires prefigured the economic future of southern agriculture. If the Civil War had not forcibly extirpated slavery, the southern planters would in time have been compelled to give it up and change over to other, less costly forms of agricultural labor.

Nor would political autonomy have conferred any fundamental economic independence upon the South. In the Union or out of it, so long as slave agriculture remained the basis of its existence, the South was predestined to remain an economic colony of more advanced powers. At this time two great powers were contending for control of the South: northern industrial capital on the one hand and English capitalism on the other. The southern planters had no independent orbit. They had to choose whether they should become satellites of the American or of the English bourgeoisie. In the final analysis, therefore, the struggle around secession was a gambit in the broader struggle between American and British industrial capital for economic supremacy over the agricultural South.

Representatives of northern capital were aware of Great Britain's stake in secession. That was one potent reason for their obdurate opposition to southern independence and their distrust of England. This was clearly evidenced in the belligerent attitudes and actions of Lincoln's secretary of state, Seward, towards England. To monopolize the exploitation of the South, this fertile field must not fall into the hands of their chief competitor.

When Lincoln was elected president in 1860 and the balance of power in the federal government shifted heavily to the advantage of the antislave forces, the representatives of the slave oligarchy could not abide the loss of their national sovereignty. After they had failed to bluff, bulldoze, or blackmail their rivals, they had no recourse but to leave the Union and establish an independent regime under their unimpeded control. But this turned out to be simply an alternative road to ruin.

Southern slavery, which entered the world as an offspring of European capitalism, was slain and buried as a victim of American industrial capitalism. It was the last of the antiquated forms of production to meet this fate at the hands of the all-conquering Yankee bourgeoisie. After annihilating the slave power, the masters of capitalism no longer had to contend with any formidable precapitalist forces within the United States. From then on, their domestic opponents have been the human elements of their own system of production itself.

Foremost among them today is the wageworking class and in particular—ironically enough—its Afro-American contingent. In the century following the Emancipation Proclamation, this segment of the labor force passed from chattel slavery through sharecropping to wage slavery. It is destined to be the vanguard of the next American revolution.

Homage to John Brown

George Novack (1938)

John Brown was a revolutionary terrorist. But there was nothing alien or exotic about him; he was a genuine product of the American soil. The roots of his family tree on both sides reached back among the first English settlers of Connecticut. The generations of Browns were pious Protestant pioneers, tough and upstanding, and singularly consistent in their ideas, characters, and ways of life. John Brown was the third fighter for freedom of that name in his family, and was himself the parent of a fourth. His grandfather died in service as a captain in the Revolutionary War. His father was an active abolitionist, a stationmaster and conductor on the Underground Railway.

From his birth in 1800, the pattern of John Brown's first fifty years reproduced the life of his father. His father had married three times and had sixteen children; John Brown married twice and had twenty children, every living soul among them pledged to hate and fight black bondage. Like his father, John was "very quick on the move," shifting around ten times in the northeastern states before his call to Kansas. He was successively—but not very successfully—a shepherd, tanner, farmer, surveyor, cattle expert, real estate speculator, and wool merchant. In his restlessness, his constant change of occupation and residence, John Brown was a typical middle-class American citizen of his time.

How did this ordinary farmer and businessman, this pious patriarch, become transformed into a border chieftain and a revolutionary terrorist? John had inherited his family's love of liberty and his father's abolitionism. At an early age he had sworn eternal war against slavery. His barn at Richmond, Pennsylvania, where in 1825 he set up a tannery, the first of his commercial enterprises, was a station on the Underground

Railway. Ten years later he was discussing plans for the establishment of a Negro school. "If once the Christians in the Free States would set to work in earnest in teaching the blacks," he wrote his brother, "the people of the slaveholding States would find themselves constitutionally driven to set about the work of emancipation immediately."

As the slave power tightened its grip upon the government, John Brown's views on emancipation changed radically. "A firm believer in the divine authenticity of the Bible," he drew his inspiration and guidance from the Old Testament rather than the New. He lost sympathy with the abolitionists of the Garrison school, who advocated the Christ-like doctrine of nonresistance to force. He identified himself with the shepherd Gideon who led his band against the Midianites and slew them with his own hand.

A project for carrying the war into the enemy's camp had long been germinating in John Brown's mind. By establishing a stronghold in the mountains bordering southern territory from which his men could raid the plantations, he planned to free the slaves and run them to Canada. On a tour of Europe in 1851 he inspected fortifications with an eye to future use; he carefully studied military tactics, especially guerrilla warfare in mountainous territory. Notebooks on his reading still exist.

However, his first assaults upon the slave power were to be made not from the mountains of Maryland and West Virginia, but on the plains of Kansas. In the spring of 1855 his four eldest sons had emigrated to Kansas to settle there and help win the territory for the Free Soil Party. In May, John Brown, Jr., sent the following urgent appeal to his father:

While the interest of despotism has secured to its cause hundreds and thousands of the meanest and most desperate of men, armed to the teeth . . . thoroughly organized . . . under pay from Slave-holders,—the friends of freedom are *not one fourth* of them *half armed,* and as to *Military Organization* among them it *no where exists in the territory* . . . [with the result] that the people here exhibit the most abject and cowardly spirit. . . . We propose . . . that the anti-slavery portion of the inhabitants should *immediately, thoroughly* arm, and *organize themselves* in *military companies.* In order to effect this, some persons must begin and lead in the matter. Here are 5 men of us who are not only anxious to fully prepare, but are thoroughly determined to fight. We can see no other way to meet the case. "It is no longer a question of negro slavery, but it is the enslavement of ourselves." We want you to get for us these arms. We need them more than we do bread. . . .

Having already resolved to join his children in Kansas, John Brown needed no second summons. In the next few months he collected considerable supplies of arms and sums of money from various sympathetic sources, including several cases of guns belonging to the state of Ohio which were "spirited away" for his use. In August he set out for Kansas from Chicago in a one-horse wagon loaded with guns and ammunition.

Upon arriving in Osawatomie, Kansas, John Brown became the captain of the local militia company and led it in the bloodless "Wakarusa War." Then he plunged into the thick of the struggle for the possession of the territory that gave it the name of "Bleeding Kansas." In retaliation for the sacking of Lawrence by the Border Ruffians, Brown's men, including four of his sons, slaughtered five proslavery sympathizers in a night raid near Pottawatomie Creek. Brown took full responsibility for these killings; he fought according to the scriptural injunction: "An eye for an eye, a tooth for a tooth."

Reprisals on one side bred reprisals on the other. The settlement at Osawatomie was pillaged and burned, Brown's son Frederick killed, his forces beaten and scattered. Thereafter John Brown and his band were outlaws, living on the run, giving the slip to government troops, launching sudden raids upon the proslavery forces. Brown became a power in Kansas. His name equaled "an army with banners" in the eyes of the militant Free Soil colonists. The whisper of his presence sufficed to break up proslavery gatherings. He continued his guerrilla warfare throughout 1856 until Kansas was pacified by the federal troops.

His experiences in Kansas completed the transformation of John Brown into a revolutionist. "John Brown is a natural production, born on the soil of Kansas, out of the germinating heats the great contest on the soil of that territory engendered," wrote J.S. Pike, the Washington correspondent of the *New York Tribune,* after the Harper's Ferry raid. "Before the day of Kansas outrages and oppression no such person as Osawatomie Brown existed. No such person could have existed. He was born of rapine and cruelty and murder. . . . Kansas deeds, Kansas experiences, Kansas discipline created John Brown as entirely and completely as the French Revolution created Napoleon Bonaparte. He is as much the fruit of Kansas as Washington was the fruit of our own Revolution."

Between 1856 and 1858, Brown shuttled back and forth between Kansas and the East seeking support for the struggle against the

Border Ruffians. He received supplies, arms, and moral encouragement from many noted abolitionists, such as Gerrit Smith, the New York philanthropist, and numerous members of the Massachusetts State Kansas Committee—T.W. Higginson, Theodore Parker, etc. But there was no place for John Brown in the condition of armed neutrality that reigned in Kansas after 1856.

No longer needed in Kansas, John Brown reverted to his long-cherished scheme of mountain warfare. To prepare for his enterprise he called a convention of his followers and free Negroes at Chatham in Canada and outlined his plans to them. One of the members of the convention reported that, after invoking the example of Spartacus, Toussaint L'Ouverture, and other historical heroes who had fled with their followers into the mountains and there defied and defeated the expeditions of their adversaries, Brown said that "upon the first intimation of a plan formed for the liberation of the slaves, they would immediately rise all over the Southern States. He supposed they would come into the mountains to join him . . . and that we should be able to establish ourselves in the fastnesses, and if any hostile action (as would be) were taken against us, either by the militia of the separate states or by the armies of the United States, we purposed to defeat first the militia, and next, if it was possible, the troops of the United States, and then organize the freed blacks under the provisional constitution, which would carve out for the locality of its jurisdiction all that mountainous region in which the blacks were to be established and in which they were to be taught the useful and mechanical arts, and to be instructed in all the business of life. . . . The Negroes were to constitute the soldiers."

The revolutionary spirit of the constitution adopted by the convention for this projected Free State can be judged from this preamble:

Whereas, Slavery, throughout its entire existence in the United States is none other than a most barbarous, unprovoked, and unjustifiable War of one portion of its citizens upon another portion; the only conditions of which are perpetual imprisonment, and hopeless servitude or absolute extermination; in utter disregard and violation of the eternal and self-evident truths set forth in our Declaration of Independence: *Therefore*, we citizens of the United States, and the oppressed people, who, by a recent decision of the Supreme Court are declared to have no rights which the White Man is bound to respect; together with all other people degraded by the laws thereof, do, for the time being, ordain and establish for ourselves the following provisional Constitution and ordinances, the better to protect our persons, property, lives, and liberties; and to govern our actions.

John Brown was elected commander in chief under this constitution.

For all its daring, Brown's scheme was hopeless from every point of view and predestined to fail. Its principal flaws were pointed out beforehand by Hugh Forbes, one of his critical adherents. In the first place, "no preparatory notice having been given to the slaves . . . the invitation to rise might, unless they were already in a state of agitation, meet with no response, or a feeble one." Second, even if successful, such a sally "would at most be a mere local explosion . . . and would assuredly be suppressed." Finally, John Brown's dream of a northern convention of his New England partisans which would restore tranquillity and overthrow the proslavery administration was "a settled fallacy. Brown's New England friends would not have the courage to show themselves so long as the issue was doubtful." Forbes's predictions were fulfilled to the letter.

Convinced that "God had created him to be the deliverer of slaves the same as Moses had delivered the children of Israel," Brown overrode these objections and proceeded to mobilize his forces. Before he could put his plan into operation, however, he was compelled to return to Kansas for the last time, where, under the nom de guerre of Shubel Morgan, he led a raid upon some plantations across the Missouri border, killing a planter and setting eleven slaves at liberty. Both the governor of Kansas and the president of the United States offered rewards for his arrest. With a price of $3,000 on his head, John Brown fled to Canada with the freedmen.

Early in the summer of 1859 a farm was rented about five miles from Harper's Ferry. There John Brown collected his men and prepared for his coup. On the night of October 16 they descended upon the town, took possession of the United States armories, imprisoned a number of the inhabitants, and persuaded a few slaves to join them. By noon, militia companies arrived from nearby Charlestown and blocked his only road to escape. The next night a company of United States marines commanded by Colonel Robert E. Lee appeared and at dawn, when Brown refused to surrender, stormed the enginehouse in which Brown, his surviving men, and his prisoners were barricaded. Fighting with matchless coolness and courage over the body of his dying son, he was overpowered and arrested.

Ten men had been killed or mortally wounded, among them two of Brown's own sons, and eleven captured in the assault.

The reporter of the *New York Herald* covering Brown's trial describes the scene during his cross-examination: "In the midst of enemies, whose home he had invaded; wounded, a prisoner, surrounded by a small army of officials, and a more desperate army of angry men; with the gallows staring him full in the face, he lay on the floor, and, in reply to every question, gave answers that betokened the spirit that animated him." John Brown steadfastly insisted that a single purpose was behind all his actions: to free the Negroes, "the greatest service a man can render to God." A bystander interrogated: "Do you consider yourself an instrument in the hands of Providence?"—"I do."— "Upon what principle do you justify your acts?"—"Upon the golden rule. I pity the poor in bondage that have none to help them; that is why I am here; not to gratify my personal animosity, revenge, or vindictive spirit. It is my sympathy with the oppressed and the wronged, that are as good as you and as precious in the sight of God."

Convicted of "treason to the Commonwealth" and "conspiring with slaves to commit treason and murder," John Brown was promptly sentenced to death by the State of Virginia.

During his stay in prison John Brown rose to the most heroic heights. His dignified bearing and his kindliness won his jailers, his captors, and his judges. His letters from the prison where he awaited execution were imbued with the same resolute determination and calm, conscious acceptance of his sacrifice in the cause of freedom as the letters of Bartolomeo Vanzetti, his fellow revolutionist. To friends who contemplated his rescue, he answered, "I am worth infinitely more to die than to live." To another he wrote, "I do not feel conscious of guilt in taking up arms; and had it been in behalf of the rich and powerful, the intelligent, the great—as men count greatness—of those who form enactments to suit themselves and corrupt others, or some of their friends, that I interfered, suffered, sacrificed and fell, it would have been doing very well. . . . These light afflictions which endure for a moment, shall work out for me *a far more exceeding and eternal weight of glory.* . . . God will surely attend to his own cause in the best possible way and time, and he will not forget the work of his own hands."

On December 2, 1859, a month after his sentence, fifteen

hundred soldiers escorted John Brown to the scaffold in the shadow of the Blue Ridge Mountains which had for so many years held out to him the promise of freedom for the slaves. With a single blow of the sheriff's hatchet he "hung between heaven and earth," the first American executed for treason. The silence was shattered by the speech of the commander in charge. "So perish all such enemies of Virginia! All such enemies of the Union! All such foes of the human race!"

The compromisers who attempted to fasten slavery forever upon the American people against their will, and the representatives of the slaveholders who prompted them, were, in the last analysis, responsible for the raid upon Harper's Ferry. Little needs to be added to the following historical judgment, written in the midst of the events by the same journalist whose characterization of John Brown we have already quoted:

Let those . . . who have reproaches to heap upon the authors of the Harper's Ferry bloody tumult and general Southern fright, go back to the true cause of it all. Let them not blame blind and inevitable instruments in the work, nor falsely malign those who are in nowise implicated, directly or indirectly; but let them patiently investigate the true source whence this demonstration arose, and then bestow their curses and anathemas accordingly. It is childish and absurd for Governor Wise to seize and sit astride the wounded panting body of Old Brown, and think he has got the villain who set this mischief on foot. By no means. The head conspirators against the peace of Virginia are ex-President Franklin Pierce and Senator Douglas. These are the parties he should apprehend, confine, and try for causing this insurrection. Next to them he should seize upon Senators Mason and Hunter of Virginia, as accessories. Let him follow up by apprehending every supporter of the Nebraska Bill, and when he shall have brought them all to condign punishment, he will have discharged his duty, but not till then. . . .

Old Brown is simply a spark of a great fire kindled by short-sighted mortals. . . . There is no just responsibility resting anywhere, no just attribution of causes anywhere, for this violent attempt that does not fall directly upon the South itself. It has deliberately challenged and wantonly provoked the elements that have concentred and exploded.

John Brown expected the shock of his assault to electrify the slaves and frighten the slaveholders into freeing their chattels. His experiment in emancipation ended in complete catastrophe. Instead of weakening slavery, his raid temporarily fortified the proslavery forces by consolidating their ranks and stiffening their resistance.

John Brown was misled by the apparent effectiveness of his

terrorist activities in Kansas. He did not understand that there his raids and reprisals were an integral part of the open struggle of the Free Soil settlers against the invasion of the slaveholders' Hessians, and were accessory and subordinate factors in deciding that protracted contest. That violence alone was impotent to determine its outcome was demonstrated by the failure of the Border Ruffians to impose slavery upon the territory.

John Brown's attempt to impose emancipation upon the South by an exclusive reliance upon terrorist methods met with equal failure. Other ways and means were necessary to release, amplify, and direct the revolutionary forces capable of overthrowing the slave power and abolishing slavery.

Yet John Brown's raid was not wholly counterproductive in its effects. His blow against slavery reverberated throughout the land and inspired those who were to follow him. The news of his bold deed sounded to people on both sides like a fire bell in the night, arousing the nation and setting its nerves on edge. Through John Brown the coming Civil War entered into the nerves of the people many months before it was exhibited in their ideas and actions.

On one hand, the South took alarm. The "acts of the assassin" confirmed their fears of slave insurrection provoked by the northern abolitionists and "Black Republicans." Brown's personal connections with many prominent abolitionists were undeniable, and their disclaimers of connivance and disapprobation of his actions did not make them any less guilty in the slaveowners' eyes, only more cowardly and hypocritical. The slaveholders were convinced that their enemies were now taking the offensive in a direct armed attack upon their lives, their homes, their property. "The conviction became common in the South," says Frederic Bancroft, the biographer of Seward, "that John Brown differed from the majority of the northerners merely in the boldness and desperateness of his methods."

The majority of official opinion in the North condemned John Brown's "criminal enterprise" and justified his execution. Big Unionist meetings exploited the incident for the benefit of the Democratic Party. The *Richmond Enquirer* of October 25, 1859, noted with satisfaction that the conservative proslavery press of the North "evinces a determination to make the moral of the Harper's invasion an effective weapon to rally all men not fanatics against the party whose leaders have been implicated directly with the midnight murder of Virginia citizens and the destruction of government property." The Republican leaders, a little less directly but no less decisively, hastened to denounce the deed and throw holy water over the execution. Said Lincoln: "We cannot object to the execution," and Seward echoed, "It was necessary and just."

But at the same time many thousands rallied to John Brown's side, hailing him as a martyr in the cause of emancipation. The radical abolitionists spoke up most boldly in his behalf and most correctly assayed the significance of his life and death. At John Brown's funeral service, Wendell Phillips spoke these words: "Marvellous old man! . . . He has abolished slavery in Virginia. . . . True, the slave is still there. So, when the tempest uproots a pine on your hills, it looks green for months—a year or two. Still, it is timber, not a tree. John Brown has loosened the roots of the slave system; it only breathes—it does not live—hereafter." Longfellow wrote in his diary on the day of the hanging: "This will be a great day in our history; the date of a new Revolution—quite as much needed as the old one. Even now as I write, they are leading old John Brown to execution in Virginia for attempting to rescue slaves! This is sowing the wind to reap the whirlwind, which will come soon."

Finally, Frank P. Stearns, a Boston merchant who had contributed generously to Brown's Kansas campaign, declared before the Senatorial Investigating Committee: "I should have disapproved of it [the raid] if I had known of it; but I have since changed my opinion; I believe John Brown to be the representative man of the century, as Washington was of the last—the Harper's Ferry affair and the capacity shown by the Italians for self-government, the great events of this age. One will free Europe and the other America."

On his way to the scaffold John Brown handed his last testament to a friend: "I John Brown am now quite *certain* that the crimes of this *guilty land:* will never be purged *away;* but with blood. I had *as I now think: vainly* flattered myself that without *very much* bloodshed: it might be done." His prophetic previsions were soon to be realized.

A year and a half after his execution, John Brown's revolutionary spirit was resurrected in the Massachusetts volunteers who marched through the streets of Boston, singing the battle hymn that four of them had just improvised: "John Brown's Body." Their movements were open and legal; John Brown's actions had been hidden and treasonable. Yet the marching men proudly acknowledged their communion with him as they left to take up the war in Virginia.

There the recent defenders of the Union had become disrupters of the Union; the punishers of treason themselves traitors; the hangmen of rebels themselves in open rebellion. John Brown's captor, Robert E. Lee, had already joined the Confederate army he was to command. Ex-Governor Wise, who had authorized Brown's hanging, was conspiring, like him, to seize Harper's Ferry arsenal, and, as a crowning irony, exhort his neighbors at Richmond to emulate John Brown. "Take a lesson from John Brown, manufacture your blades from old iron, even though it be the ties of your cart-wheels."

Thus the opposing forces in the historical process that John Brown called God, each in their own way paid homage to the father of the Second American Revolution.

Martin R. Delany—
Pioneer Black Nationalist

Derrick Morrison (1972)

I propose, sir, an army of blacks, commanded entirely by black officers, except such whites as may volunteer to serve; this army to penetrate through the heart of the South, and make conquests, with the banner of Emancipation unfurled, proclaiming freedom as they go, sustaining and protecting it by arming the emancipated, taking them as fresh troops, and leaving a few veterans among the new freedmen, when occasion requires, keeping this banner unfurled until every slave is free, according to the letter of your proclamation. I would also take from those already in the service all that are competent for commission officers, and establish at once in the South a camp of instructions. By this we could have in about three months an army of forty thousand blacks in motion, the presence of which anywhere would itself be a power irresistible. You should have an army of blacks, President Lincoln, commanded entirely by blacks, the weight of which is required to give confidence to the slaves, and retain them to the Union, stop foreign intervention, and speedily bring the war to a close.

So went Martin Robison Delany's account of his meeting with President Abraham Lincoln on the morning of February 8, 1865.

Lincoln gave approval to Delany's proposal, and had the secretary of war, Edwin M. Stanton, commission him the first Black major in the United States army.

However, Delany's plan for a Black army never really had a chance to unfold. Sixty days after the meeting with Lincoln, Robert E. Lee, the Confederate general, surrendered at a courthouse in Appomattox, Virginia, and the war was over.

Delany conceived the plan for a Black liberation army as early as October 1861, when he expressed it to Asa Mahan, the first

231

president of Oberlin College. When he finally got Lincoln's ear he knew that there were close to 200,000 Black troops in the Union army, a great number of whom had been recruited by Delany and other Black abolitionists. He also knew that these Black soldiers were targets of much abuse. They received unequal pay and equipment, were officered by whites, and sometimes had to fend off attacks from white fellow soldiers in the midst of battle with the Confederate enemy. For these and many other reasons, the Blacks—slave and free—were not always enthusiastic about the Union army. These difficulties and the desire to bring the Civil War to an end are what prompted Lincoln's acceptance of Delany's plan.

This plan for the independent military organization of the Blacks was most characteristic of the thought and actions of Martin Delany. Of all the Black abolitionists of that period—of whom there were many, contrary to some histories—he stands out as the precursor of many of the currents and tendencies that make up today's Black nationalist movement.

Delany represented an attempt by pre-Civil War Blacks to work out their nationality not only as Americans—of which Frederick Douglass was the supreme expression—but as Africans. Delany consistently agitated in the Black community for an awareness of its African heritage—as an abolitionist leader in Pittsburgh in the 1830s and 1840s, as a Black emigrationist (or separatist) in Chatham, Ontario, during the last half of the 1850s, or as Major M.R. Delany, subassistant commissioner of the Freedmen's Bureau in Charleston and the Sea Islands of South Carolina.

His treatment at the hands of American historians is very instructive as to how the Black past has been distorted, twisted, and in many cases declared nonexistent.

American capitalist society has always granted the right of Black people to be counted as Americans (that's in the Constitution), but never the right to *be* Americans. However, this is but one aspect of the Black nationality. Black people are also Africans. This is the half that America's capitalist rulers have never tolerated, have never countenanced.

As an expression of this proscription, bourgeois historians have concocted a mythical conflict between the American and African expressions of the Black nationality. That is, Black people embarking upon the road to the "melting pot" were taught to emulate and imitate everything American—arbitrarily defined as

European—and to shed every thread of any African identity. The Black past was presented in a whitewashed version featuring such types as Dr. George Washington Carver and Booker T. Washington.

The suppression of Black history went hand in hand with the lack of any powerful and extensive upsurge of the Black masses. To be sure, there was the post-World War I Black radicalization that achieved its highest expression in Marcus Garvey's Universal Negro Improvement Association, and there was the mobilization sparked by the growth of the Congress of Industrial Organizations in the 1930s and 40s.

But these two movements were either snuffed out or domesticated by a combination of (1) the power and financial strength of American imperialism (e.g., the American capitalist class responded to the depression of the 1930s with the "New Deal," whereas its less prosperous German counterpart resorted to fascism), and (2) the Stalinization of the American Communist Party, which kept the labor upsurge inside the bounds of the capitalist Democratic and Republican parties. These two factors interacted, reinforcing one another.

The Black upsurge that would force the most extensive reexamination of Black history had to await the aftermath of World War II. Fed by the decisive weakening of the West European imperialist powers, the overturning of capitalist property relations in Eastern Europe, China, North Korea, and North Vietnam, and the outburst of national liberation struggles in Africa, Asia, and Latin America, it is this Black radicalization that we are experiencing today. The new Black militancy stimulates and is stimulated by a radicalization of youth, workers, and oppressed nationalities on a world scale.

Both aspects of the Black nationality are receiving powerful expression today, forcing a reworking, reshaping, and in most cases junking, of all previous analyses of the Black condition, and precipitating the long and arduous task of restoring the real Black past.

One of the figures fast becoming the object of such restoration is Delany. The beginning—not the end, but just the beginning—of a real appreciation of this Black giant is Victor Ullman's *Martin R. Delany: The Beginnings of Black Nationalism*. It is the most definitive book to date on Delany. (Boston: Beacon Press, 1971.)

This book will not only serve to help establish some proper perspective on the maliciously falsified accounts of Black history served up by bourgeois historians, but also on the paraphrases of those accounts that appear in some of the radical press.

An example of such a job is provided in the January 1972 issue of *Political Affairs,* the monthly journal of the Communist Party. Here Henry Winston, national chairman of the CP, authors an article entitled, "From the Anti-Slavery to the Anti-Monopoly Strategy." What Winston tries to establish is that the "antimonopoly" strategy developed by the CP and more or less accepted by Martin Luther King, Jr., in his last days has as its predecessor the pre–Civil War antislavery strategy of the Black abolitionist, Frederick Douglass.

Winston's attempt to make this tenuous connection is but a new variant of the Communist Party's attack on Black nationalism, a new twist in their effort to counterpose the African and American expressions of the Black nationality.

Winston asserts: "Like King, Douglass matured in struggle against sectarian, separatist and accommodationist tendencies within the movement of his time. For example, throughout the crucial decade of the 1850s, he resisted the separatist alternative of emigrationism which would have weakened the anti-slavery front. Douglass saw that emigrationism, a forerunner of Pan Africanism, objectively meant accommodation to the slave power."

However, even a superficial glance would show the gulf separating Douglass from King. True, both fought against the oppression of Black people, but Douglass was a radical and King a liberal. Whereas Douglass advocated self-defense, King was a pacifist who equated the defensive actions of the oppressed with the violence of the oppressor. The militancy of Douglass's speeches and writings was more akin to Malcolm X, not the religiously steeped "I have a dream" rhetoric of King. More important, Douglass never, under any circumstances, countenanced working in the political parties of the slavemaster, the Whig and Democratic parties. King, however, counseled reliance upon the Democratic Party, a party of U.S. imperialism.

It should be noted here that the criteria for this political assessment of the two leaders are anchored in two different historical periods. In Douglass's day, there was an irrepressible and irreconcilable conflict rending the U.S. ruling classes. On the one side was the Northern industrial bourgeoisie, and on the other was the Southern slavocracy.

Slavery represented an anachronistic social system; nonetheless, it had been a necessary stimulant in the initial accumulation of capital. The Whig and Democratic parties were the political representatives of this initial stage. The Republican Party, which emerged in the 1850s, represented the next stage where the bourgeoisie cut all links to the slavocracy. For this reason, it was correct for Douglass and other abolitionists to ally themselves with this party.

However, the Democratic and Republican parties of King's time—and the present—have no differences of substance between them. Each is an organ for the political rule of U.S. imperialism. The major contradiction today is between capital on one side and labor and the oppressed national minorities on the other, manifested in the struggles of the workers, of women, and of Blacks, Chicanos, Puerto Ricans, and other oppressed nationalities. For the oppressed and exploited to make headway they must break with the two capitalist parties and forge new ones based upon labor and the oppressed nationalities.

Thus the antislavery strategy of Douglass bears no resemblance to the "antimonopoly" strategy of the CP. While the former rejected the political parties defending chattel slavery, the latter is predicated upon collaborating with and supporting the Democratic Party, one of the parties—if you please—of monopoly capital. The CP has been supporting the Democrats ever since 1936, an application of Stalin's Popular Front policy of allying the Soviet Union with "lesser evil" imperialist states.

Because the Black nationalist upsurge today threatens the adherence of Black people to the Democratic Party by sowing sentiment for an independent Black party, Winston labors in vain to employ Douglass—by way of King—to dampen and derail that sentiment, and to offer a defense of the bankrupt policies of the CP. Douglass was a revolutionist against slavery, although he was not a nationalist, i.e., for setting up an independent Black identity. But Douglass possessed many of the militant attributes that Winston attacks nationalism for. He was unequivocal and resolute in his opposition to slavery, subordinating the struggle neither to ruling-class institutions nor to ruling-class prejudices. The first conscious expressions of nationalism, of which Delany was the most prominent spokesman, took the form of separatism, of advocating that Blacks emigrate from the United States to set up a separate state.

Douglass sharply differed with Delany, not from the right as is the case with Winston, but from the left, as this review will show. But first, let us unveil Delany.

Delany was born of a free mother and slave father in

Charleston, West Virginia (then part of Virginia) on May 6, 1812. The town had less than 1,000 whites, slaves, and free Blacks at the time. Pati, his mother, was known as an "uppity Negress," and because she was discovered teaching Martin and her four other children to read and write—a serious breach of Virginia law—the family fled to Chambersburg, Pennsylvania, in 1818. Five years later his father, Samuel, bought his freedom and joined them.

Pennsylvania, in 1780, was the first state to abolish African chattel slavery, albeit gradually, and thus allowed the growth of "free" Black (or, in the term in use at that time, "colored") communities. Black people lived in ghettos then as they do now.

Delany arrived in Pittsburgh in the fall of 1831. The first extensive Black awakening was under way. A year earlier, on September 30, the first national Black convention had met in Philadelphia with thirty-eight delegates. This was the beginning of a series of national Black conventions held over the next three decades. A second such affair was held in June of 1831, followed by a convention of the "Colored Citizens of Pittsburgh" on September 1.

These first shoots of the independent organization of Black people in 1830-31 arose out of the awareness that slavery was not going to wither away. Rather than weakening after the First American Revolution, Black slavery had been given a new lease on life with the invention of the cotton gin, an important factor enabling the Southern slaveholders to become the prime suppliers of cotton to the British textile industry. The prosperity of the South fueled the growth of finance and commerce in the North, making more remote than ever the thought of abolishing slavery.

As a solution to the contradiction of having free Blacks walking around among slaves, the American Society for Colonizing the Free People of Color in the United States was formed. This organization, which came to be known as the American Colonization Society, aimed at ridding the country of free Blacks, not slaves. It was covertly backed and financed by the slaveholders and the federal government itself. With their aid, the society purchased what has become known as Liberia. By 1860 the society had transferred 15,000 Blacks to this area, which had been nominally an independent country since 1847.

With the expansion of the society during the 1820s, the free Blacks began to organize in opposition. Regional and statewide gatherings led to the first national Black meeting in 1830. These independent expressions of the Blacks played a direct role in the organization of the abolitionist movement—a fact clearly established in Ullman's book.

The positions held by Blacks helped educate and harden the antislavery attitudes of William Lloyd Garrison and other abolitionists. For instance, many whites who started out on the road to the abolitionist movement thought the Colonization Society was acting in the interests of the Blacks by sending them to West Africa, since they obviously couldn't enjoy the benefits of citizenship in this country. And the chance to do missionary work in Africa ingratiated many Christian churches.

Only when the free Blacks met and aired their opposition to the Colonization Society, exposing its complicity with the slaveholders and affirming their right to be American citizens and enjoy the fruits of the blood and toil of their forefathers and mothers, did abolitionists like Garrison become irrevocable opponents of this scheme.

Three months after the first national Black convention, Garrison brought out *The Liberator*. Two years later he, along with other white and a few Black abolitionists, organized the American Anti-Slavery Society.

Indispensable to this ferment in the North were two other forms of independent activity by the Blacks. One of them was the slave rebellions, the biggest of which was led by Nat Turner in Virginia in 1831. The other was the continued stream of escaping slaves; their flight northward compelled the organization of the Underground Railway, which became the biggest single center of abolitionist activity.

These two kinds of slave resistance heightened the objective contradiction between the expansion of the capitalist North and the slaveholding South, and made impossible any peaceful coexistence between the two regions.

One of the nerve centers of the Black awakening was Pittsburgh. There were 435 free Blacks and eight slaves in the city according to the 1830 census. Delany came, thirsting for more education and looking to help better the lot of his people. He attended school at the local African Methodist Episcopal church. (At that time Blacks were barred from the city's schools, although they paid taxes to support them. To cope with the educational needs of its youth, the Black community met in 1832 in the AME church to form the African Education Society.) While attending school, Delany was active in the organization of various Black youth groups.

In 1833 he began a medical apprenticeship under the guidance of a radical white doctor, there being no trained Black physicians. In three years' time, at the age of twenty-four, he became a "cupper, leecher, and bleeder," and set himself up in practice. This provided a source of income which allowed him to study and do community work.

In the course of his activities in the community, and as one of the cogs in the Underground Railway, Delany began publishing a newspaper, *The Mystery,* in 1843. The idea originated at a statewide convention of Blacks in Pittsburgh two years earlier, but because of the gap between word and deed characteristic of such conventions, Delany initiated the project alone.

Whereas previous Black publications had been able to stay above water only for very short periods, the life of *The Mystery* stretched over four years. The paper declared itself "free" and "independent," and dedicated to the "moral elevation of the Africo-American and African race, civilly, politically, and religiously." Delany wrote about the Black past as well as contemporary affairs, and combatted all of the notions then being palmed off as science about the alleged inferiority of Black people.

Ullman found only two copies of *The Mystery.* But articles from the paper were frequently reprinted in Garrison's *Liberator* and in the *Pennsylvania Freeman,* a local abolitionist newspaper. Even the Pittsburgh bourgeois press reproduced articles from *The Mystery.* Reprints also appeared elsewhere inasmuch as the paper had circulation agents in eight states and one territory.

To keep it afloat, prominent Blacks in Pittsburgh organized a publishing committee to take care of the business end. This enabled Delany to concentrate solely on writing and editing. The committee held fund-raising affairs in which the Black community and antislavery whites participated.

Delany's stature as a Black abolitionist writer and editor is what prompted Frederick Douglass to broach to him the project of the *North Star.* Douglass, in 1847, was already an internationally known abolitionist leader.

Born in February of 1817, Douglass had been a slave until his escape from Maryland in 1838. He had joined the ranks of the abolitionists and become a powerful and effective platform speaker. While he was in England in 1845-47, British abolitionists raised enough money to enable him to purchase his freedom. The British abolitionists also promised him a printing press and seed money for a newspaper. However, when Douglass came back to the states, Garrison discouraged the idea and urged him to develop his powers of oratory. Douglass assented, and he and Garrison went on a speaking tour in August 1847.

The two spoke on the same platform with Delany in Pittsburgh. It was here that Douglass probably resurrected the idea of a newspaper, since a month later a Pittsburgh paper carried a notice advertising the forthcoming *North Star*. Douglass broke with Garrison over the matter, moving from Boston to Rochester to begin the new publication.

Delany and Douglass were the founders and coeditors of the *North Star*. The first issue appeared December 3, 1847.

This opened a new episode in Delany's life. It took him out of Pittsburgh and placed him on the national scene, where things were quite different. As he traveled the country speaking and getting subscriptions for the paper, he became much more aware of the schisms, splits, and feuds prevailing in the abolitionist movement.

He saw public sentiment polarized as abolitionist speakers were mobbed, stoned, and sometimes killed. Coupled with the financial hardships suffered by his family at the time, this led Delany into a state of discouragement. He left the *North Star* some time in 1849, returning to Pittsburgh in September.

While rethinking matters, he kept up a modicum of activity. With the help of some friends he attended one term at Harvard Medical School in the winter of 1850. The furor engendered by his attendance prevented a second term, which was all he needed in order to graduate.

The Emigrationist Idea

But acutely sensing the need for new directions and ideas, Delany, while on business in New York City the following winter, sat down and wrote an impressive work. It was entitled, *The Condition, Elevation, Emigration and Destiny of the Colored People of the United States, Politically Considered.*

This work signaled the first elaboration of the emigrationist idea, the first break by a prominent abolitionist with the assumption that the destiny of Black people could be worked out within the United States.

Delany declared that the 4.5 million Black people, slave and free, were a "nation within a nation," as the "Poles in Russia, the Hungarians in Austria, the Welsh, Irish, and Scotch in the

British dominions." After running down the plight of Black people and the shortcomings of the abolitionist movement, he concluded:

> The claims of no people, according to established policy and usage, are respected by any nation, until they are presented in a national capacity. . . . We must make an issue, create an event, and establish a national position for ourselves; and never may expect to be respected as men and women, until we have undertaken, some fearless, bold, and adventurous deeds of daring—contending against every odds—regardless of every consequence.

He called for the establishment of a Black nation on the east coast of Africa. In setting forth his emigrationist or separatist scheme, he clearly distinguished and counterposed it to the American Colonization Society and its dependency, the Republic of Liberia.

His separatist ideas had been in gestation for over a decade, achieving ever greater expression with the erosion of the position of the free Blacks. For example, in 1839, after a state constitutional convention met to legally disfranchise Pennsylvania's 40,000 Blacks, Delany went south to Texas to investigate emigration possibilities.

This convention occurred after a judge ruled that a Black who was barred from the polls could not vote since Blacks were not citizens in other states. The convention brought Pennsylvania into line. The judicial decision sent shock waves through the Black people of the state, causing them to ask, if the Northern states could be influenced by the slaveholders to deny them suffrage, then at what point would it stop? Might not slavery be restored?

These were the questions swirling in Delany's mind when he went to Texas, then a territory. But finding conditions wanting, he came back and helped organize a statewide convention of Blacks in 1841 to protest the measure. Contrary to previous conventions, no white observers or participants were allowed.

Another experience that helped give birth to the book *Condition and Elevation* was Delany's attendance at a "North American Convention of Colored Men" held in Toronto in 1851. He was impressed with the organized and capable air of the Blacks in attendance. Although fugitive slaves or the children of fugitive slaves, they were landowners, farmers, skilled tradesmen, and college students. They voted and served in the Canadian militia.

In other words, they were all the things that the free Blacks in the northern states of the U.S. could only desire to be.

Many of the Canadian Blacks lived in the refugee towns of Chatham, Malden, Amherstburg, and Sandwich just across the Detroit River. In order to help settle newly-arrived fugitives, they organized the Refugee Home Society and were publishing their own newspaper, *Voice of the Fugitive*. Delany later moved to Chatham to conduct his separatist activities.

Potent factors undergirding emigrationist sentiment were the Fugitive Slave Act of 1850, the Kansas-Nebraska Act of 1854, and the 1857 Dred Scott decision of the U.S. Supreme Court. The first legitimized activities of slave-catchers in the North, making it possible for any Black to be apprehended as a runaway. The second opened the western territories to the penetration of slavery. And the third, which upheld the constitutionality of the 1850 act, declared that a slave had no legal rights.

Ullman writes that under the impact of these measures the Black population reached 50 or 60,000 in Canada's province of Ontario, signifying a migration of more than 20,000, the bulk coming from the North, not the South.

Running contrary to these events, however, and proving more decisive in the long run, was the spiraling dissatisfaction of the northern industrial bourgeoisie with the stranglehold exercised by the slaveowners on national life. The Liberty Party and the Free Soil Party dimly reflected this sentiment in the 1840s—dimly not because of program but because these parties were small.

The sentiment grew bolder when disenchanted elements broke from the Whig and Democratic parties to form the Republican Party in 1854. Many Free Soil and Liberty activists flocked to its banner. Its election to power touched off the Civil War, the Second American Revolution, in 1860.

Ullman does not go into this process at any length, but it is important to study it in order to make sense of the conflicts and debates rending the abolitionists. Because Douglass and others— some Black but mostly white—drew sustenance from this political differentiation, they were fiercely opposed to the emigrationist designs of Delany, as well as to Garrison's rejection of participation in the electoral arena.

The divergences between Delany and Douglass found expression in the last three national Black conventions held during the decade before the Civil War. Those who held fast to the position of continuing to organize against slavery from the North met with Douglass in July of 1853 in Rochester. They felt the destiny of Black people could be worked out satisfactorily in the United States.

The emigrationist Blacks met the following year in August in Cleveland. They met again in the same city two years later. An interesting feature of the first emigrationist convention was the seating of twenty-nine fully accredited and voting women delegates, including Kate Delany. Delany and Douglass, when they were attending Black conventions together, had always fought for the inclusion of Black women. Both were staunch supporters of the women's rights movement of that day.

The Rochester convention netted the largest number of delegates to any Black convention—114. The Cleveland meeting in 1854 seated 106. In contrast to the one in Rochester, the Cleveland gathering succeeded in setting up an ongoing apparatus, appointing a nine-member national board of commissioners with Delany as president. Emigration sites considered were Central America, Haiti, and Africa. Canada was ruled out because Delany thought it would one day be annexed by the United States.

To operate more effectively, Delany moved to Chatham in February of 1856. A number of Black Canadians were attracted to the second emigrationist convention in Cleveland; one of the results was the establishment of the Chatham *Provincial Freeman,* a Black weekly edited by Mary Ann Shadd Cary and published by Israel D. Shadd, as the organ of the emigrationist movement.

The third convention, held in Chatham in 1858, appointed Delany to undertake a mission to Africa. By this time, Haiti and Central America had been written off—because of lack of natural resources in the case of the former, and domination by the United States government in the case of the latter.

Lack of funds and other problems reduced Delany's projected "Niger Valley Exploring Party" from five to two. Delany and Robert Campbell, a Black chemist of West Indian origin residing in Philadelphia, set sail for West Africa in May 1859. There they traveled for several months among the Yoruba, Egba, and Ijebu peoples in what is today southwest Nigeria. In April 1860 they sailed to England.

Both wrote accounts of the trip. In Delany's "Official Report of The Niger Valley Exploring Party," he deplored European colonization of Africa and coined the slogan, later to be raised by

Marcus Garvey, "Africa for the Africans." His account and Campbell's—"A Pilgrimage to My Motherland: An Account of a Journey Among the Egbas and Yorubas of Central Africa, in 1859-60"—have been put together in a recent book (1971), *Search for a Place: Black Separatism and Africa, 1860*. It has been published as an Ann Arbor paperback and is another sign of the renewed interest in Delany. His "Official Report" shows that Delany's plan for setting up a Black state was imbued with the thinking of that time. It envisaged a small group of able-bodied and skilled Black settlers, not the masses of Blacks, colonizing the designated area, and using the labor supplied by the indigenous peoples to cultivate cotton. Through agreements struck in England, the settlers would then begin to supply the British textile industry. Out of this commerce, a powerful Black state would arise, thus undermining and eventually severing England's dependence on the South, a consequence of which would be the collapse of the slavocracy. Delany calculated that cotton could more cheaply be produced and marketed from West Africa than the South. To this end, treaties were signed with the West African chiefs at Abeokuta, in what is now Nigeria.

As a first step in securing British backing, the African Aid Society was organized during his stay of several months in London, with Lord Alfred Churchill as its chairman. The purpose of the society was to raise funds and materials for the emigration of the first group of African-Americans to Abeokuta.

There were historical precedents for Delany's scheme—witness such former colonial settlements as the United States, Canada, the rest of the Americas, and Australia. But history was not willing to wait on the task of convincing the British textile interests to endorse it.

Delany arrived back in Chatham in December 1860. Four months later civil war broke out in the United States, and seven months more found Delany in the thick of activity in the North, his emigrationist work shelved.

Upon his arrival, though, a great demand arose to hear an account of his travels, especially from Blacks in the North. Anguished and beset with constant racist propaganda professing Africa to be a haven for the savage and the "heathen," they wanted to hear an account from a pro-African Black. Delany combined talks on his travels with lectures on previous African civilizations.

As a result of a number of requests for speaking engagements in the East, Delany moved to Brooklyn some time in 1861. In November he accepted an invitation to join the New York-based African Civilization Society. Originally created in 1858 by Black abolitionists who opted for emigration, but under the tutelage of the American Colonization Society, the group had now broken all its ties with the Colonization Society. Its aim was still emigration, but its activity now dealt with taking advantage of the Civil War to better the lot of Black people in the U.S.

Ullman does a good job of exposing Abraham Lincoln's colonization schemes during the first years of the war. Despite Lincoln's attempt to tie his plans in with those of the emigrationists, Ullman clearly distinguishes between separatist plans originated by the oppressed, and apartheid plans originated by the oppressor.

Lincoln's actions during these years induced deep demoralization in the ranks of the non-emigrationist Black abolitionists. And many Blacks in the North began to see emigration as a more attractive possibility after the early victories chalked up on the battlefield by Confederate armies.

But when, following these defeats, Lincoln took the only recourse left to him—that of freeing the slaves in the rebellious states, through the Emancipation Proclamation—their attitude changed overnight.

After recounting this episode, the recruitment of Blacks into the Union army, and Delany's commission as a major, Ullman gives an extensive account of the role Delany played throughout Reconstruction in South Carolina. He was probably one of the few abolitionists to play so direct a part in a Reconstruction government. He first spent three years as an army major and an official of the Freedmen's Bureau.

Ullman describes the great hunger for land manifested by South Carolina Blacks, the subsequent retreat by the federal government on this question, and the reduction of the Blacks to rural laborers and finally to sharecroppers. On the Sea Islands, Delany and the Black troops under his command tried to defend and extend the initial seizures of the land. Failing that, they organized the Black laborers to get a just wage and equitable conditions from the returning owners.

Upon leaving the military in 1868, Delany also left South Carolina—only to return in 1870 to immerse himself in Republican Party politics. One powerful factor attracting him back was the existence of 400,000 Blacks in the state—a figure almost equal to the Black population dispersed throughout the northern states. In South Carolina the Blacks were in the majority; the whites numbered only 300,000.

He was one of the small number of Blacks who not only opposed but actively organized against the corruption that racked the Republican Party as northern capital gained access to the South. An Independent Republican ticket in 1874 featured Delany for lieutenant governor and Judge John T. Green, a South Carolina white, for governor. Out of 149,000 votes cast, Green lost by only 11,585 votes, Delany by 15,985.

In the elections of 1876, which marked the end of Reconstruction, Delany supported the Democratic Party, the party of the former slaveholders. His move was prompted by an attempt to combat the corruption of the Republican Party, and to reach a modus vivendi with the leaders of the Democratic Party. He failed in both endeavors and lived to regret it.

The dilemma he faced reflected the expanding power of the northern bourgeoisie, which prevented the emergence of independent Black political organization. The South of 1876 was not the Santo Domingo of 1799, where, taking advantage of the length of the French Revolution and their geographical position, the Blacks had constructed their own army, which they used to retake the island and thwart the reenslavement plans of Napoleon; out of the struggle was born Haiti in 1804.

Delany died on January 24, 1885, at the age of seventy-two. Ullman's book stands as a monument to this Black hero, and the first in-depth account of the pre–Civil War Black radicalization, whose independent thrust has only been surpassed by the present Black awakening.

THE SECOND AMERICAN REVOLUTION

The Civil War—Its
Place in History

George Novack (1961)

The historical significance of the American Civil War has to be appraised from two standpoints: one national, the other international. What place does this immense conflict occupy in the development of American society? And what is its place in the world history of the nineteenth century?

The most penetrating liberal historians, headed by Charles Beard, have correctly designated this event as the Second American Revolution. But they have failed to explain clearly and fully its essential connection with the first.

The Civil War had deep historical roots. It was the inevitable product of two interlacing processes. One was the degeneration of the First American Revolution, which unfolded by slow stages until it culminated in open counterrevolution. The other was the rise of capitalist industrialism with its contradictory effects upon American social development. The interaction of these two fundamental factors, the first rooted in national soil and the second stemming from world conditions, constituted the principal driving force in American history between the close of the first revolutionary struggle and the outbreak of the second.

It is impossible to understand the necessity for a Second American Revolution without grasping the dynamics of these two interpenetrating processes out of which it emerged. The First American Revolution took place in the last quarter of the eighteenth century. The second unfolded in the middle of the nineteenth century. Separated by an interval of almost seventy-five years, these two revolutions are customarily regarded as totally different and completely disconnected events. This view is superficial and false. In reality the First American Revolution and the Civil War form two parts of an indivisible whole. They comprised distinct yet interlinked stages in the development of the bourgeois-democratic revolution in the United States.

The bourgeois-national revolutionary movement in North America had five main tasks to fulfill. These were: (1) to free the American people from foreign domination; (2) to consolidate the separate colonies or states into one nation; (3) to set up a democratic republic; (4) to place state power in the hands of the bourgeoisie; and (5) most important of all, to rid American society of its precapitalist encumbrances (Indian tribalism, feudalism, slavery) in order to permit the full and free expansion of capitalist forces of production and exchange. These five tasks were all bound together, the solution of one preparing the conditions for the solution of the rest.

The First Revolution solved the first three of these tasks. The Patriots' struggles liberated thirteen colonies from British rule; the ensuing class contention for power (1783-1788) led to the creation of a federal union; the new nation set up a democratic republic. It went quite otherwise with the last two. Although the Revolution cleansed the colonies of much feudal rubbish and cleared the ground for the swift growth of American capitalism and American nationhood, it failed to place the scepter firmly in the hands of the big bourgeoisie or to effect a thoroughgoing reorganization of American society on a bourgeois basis.

These deficiencies of the first bourgeois revolution were not immediately evident and took time to manifest themselves in full force. At first the Revolution seemed entirely successful and its outcome satisfactory to the northern capitalists. They had attained the paramount position in the new republic, which they governed together with the southern planters with whom they had waged the war, written the Constitution, and formed the Union.

But the merchants, financiers, and manufacturers proved incapable of maintaining their hegemony. After a brief though important period in supreme authority during Washington and Adams's administrations, their direct political representatives were compelled to turn over national leadership to the plantation aristocracy. The bourgeois conquest of political power had turned out to be premature. This was confirmed when the mercantile capitalists subsequently failed to recover the supremacy they relinquished in 1800 to the slavocracy and had to rest content with second rank.

This displacement of the big bourgeoisie of the North by the southern planters provided positive proof of the shortcomings of the eighteenth-century revolutionary upheaval. But this *political* reversal was rendered possible by the underlying *social* relations and their channels of development. Why was the northern bourgeoisie unable to hold the predominant position it had won? Precisely because the fifth and most fundamental task of the revolution—the liquidation of all precapitalist social forces—had not been completely carried out. Thus mercantile capitalist rule fell victim to the economic backwardness of American society. The First Revolution unfolded in a colonial country with a relatively low level of economic development based on agriculture. The contradiction between the extremely advanced political regime in the United States after the revolution and its still immature economy was the primary cause of the political weakness and the downfall of the big bourgeoisie.

The social structure of the United States at the end of the eighteenth century was a composite of slave and free labor, of precapitalist and capitalist forms of production. To complete the reconstruction of society along bourgeois lines, it would have been necessary to break up the soil in which slavery was rooted. This proved impossible under the prevailing conditions. The slave interests were sufficiently powerful at the time of the Revolution to prevent any tampering with the institution in its southern strongholds and even to obtain constitutional warrant for its perpetuation. The opponents of slavery could do no more than restrict its scope by providing for the abolition of the foreign slave trade at the end of twenty years, for emancipation in certain northern states where slavery was of slight economic importance, and for its prohibition within the unsettled northwestern territories.

Chattel slavery was becoming so unprofitable and burdensome a form of production to many planters toward the close of the eighteenth century that opponents of slavery consoled themselves by looking forward to its withering away in the South as in the North. The problems it presented would thereby have been automatically resolved by a gradual transition from slave to free labor. These expectations were nullified by the rise of King Cotton. This economic revolution in southern agriculture imparted such virility to the moribund slave system that its economic masters and political servants not only wrested command of the national government from the Federalist bourgeoisie with the accession of Jefferson to the presidency in 1800, but managed to maintain their sovereignty unimpaired for the next sixty years.

The struggle for supremacy between the proslavery forces centered in the South and the free labor forces headed by the northern bourgeoisie was the decisive factor in the political life of the United States in the period bounded by the two revolutions. From 1800 on, the big bourgeoisie kept ceding political ground to the planters. Supreme political power inevitably gravitated into the hands of the economically predominant cotton nobility. The capitalists could not regain their lost leadership until the economic development of the country had produced a new combination of social forces strong enough to outweigh the slavocracy and its allies and then to overthrow it.

Thanks to the achievements of the Revolution and to exceptionally favorable international economic circumstances, the United States took tremendous steps forward during the first half of the nineteenth century. The productive forces of the nation, agricultural and industrial, slave and free, grew by leaps and bounds. The gains accumulated as a result of the Revolution and the ensuing economic progress were distributed, under pressure from the people, in the shape of numerous small, gradual, democratic reforms. This part of the planter-bourgeois regime was a comparatively pacific period in domestic politics. The chief disputes which arose among the governing classes (including those issues directly pertaining to slavery) were settled by compromise.

Around 1850 a radical reversal of these processes set in. The rise of large-scale industry in the North and the expansion of small farming in the Northwest upset the economic equilibrium upon which the planters' power had rested and led to a new correlation of social forces. Goaded by the prospect of losing supreme power and by the economic decline and social disintegration of the slave system, the planting interests absolutely opposed themselves to progressive tendencies in all fields of national life. Their despotism became increasingly intolerable. Not only the Negro chattels but the entire American people were being made the victims of the arrogant, unrestrainable slaveowners. To check this growing reaction and to assure continued progress in the nation, it was imperative to break the grip of the slave power.

The most eligible candidate for leadership in the fight against the southern planters was the second-born of the bourgeoisie, the manufacturing class. This section of the capitalists had long been striving to regain the position of political supremacy in the U.S. which its elder brother, the merchant aristocracy, had lost in

1800. The smoldering struggle between the planters and industrialists, which flared up periodically, had been smothered by compromise in 1820, 1832, and 1850. With the organization of the Republican Party in the fifties, the industrialists launched their final struggle for the conquest of supreme power.

Two methods for delivering the people from their bondage to the slave power were proposed by representatives of different social strata in the North. The spokesmen for the ascending industrial capitalists hoped to depose the planters by class compromise and by peaceful constitutional means after the precedent set by the English industrialists in the West Indies. The political agents of the British manufacturers had come to terms with the landed aristocracy at home, as well as with the West Indian planters, and in 1833 instituted compensated emancipation of the slaves in the English colonies by parliamentary enactment.

The American way of abolishing slavery, however, was to differ from the English. Nor did it follow the course of political and social reform envisaged by the conservative Republicans. It took the revolutionary trail pointed out by the radical abolitionists. These pioneers of the Second Revolution, reflecting the views of the plebeian democracy (small farmers and wageworkers in the North, and the chattel slaves in the South) advocated root-and-branch extermination of the slave power.

Very few Americans considered so radical a program desirable or feasible during the fifties. But the alarming aggressions of the slaveholding reaction and the sharpening of the social crisis swiftly transformed the general outlook. In its early stages the slave system rested upon the political foundations laid down by the First American Revolution. But the democratic institutions had become unbearable fetters upon its activities, which the slavocracy yearned to cast aside.

Southern secessionism, the frankest expression of these reactionary tendencies, aimed at nothing less than a total reversal of the aims and achievements of the Revolution. Its program explicitly called for an unconditional denial of its democratic and equalitarian principles, the destruction of the Union, and the shackling of the nation's productive forces to the anachronistic slave system. Secession implicitly entailed the abandonment of representative republican government and even threatened the loss of national independence to the imperialist vultures of France and England, who were hostile to the Union.

The victory of the Republican Party in the presidential elections of 1860 and the ensuing departure of the slave states brought to a head the struggle between the southern planters and northern bourgeoisie, the proslavery and antislavery camps, the counterrevolution and the revolution. The secessionist coup d'etat revived all the problems of the bourgeois-democratic revolution, including those which had presumably been forever settled.

At this critical point three main perspectives opened before the American people. A victory for the Confederacy could have effaced the remnants of the Revolution and fastened the hated dictatorial rule of the slaveholders over all America. Another ineffectual compromise between the contending camps would have permitted the struggle to drag along and exhaust the people. A victory for the revolutionary forces would clear the way for a full and final disposal of the unfinished business of the bourgeois-democratic revolution. The developments of the Civil War soon excluded any middle course or ground for compromise, leaving open only the two extreme variants.

The favorable alternative triumphed. The bourgeois Republicans, who had taken power on a program of restricting the slave power, found that they could hold it against the assaults of the Confederacy only by resorting to increasingly revolutionary measures leading to the overthrow and abolition of the slave power. *In order to conserve the conquests of the First American Revolution, it was found necessary to extend them through another.* A supplementary upheaval of social-economic relations was required to support the political overturn in 1860.

In the course of this Second Revolution, the most radical representatives of industrial capital and their plebeian allies completed the tasks initiated by their predecessors in the first. Placing themselves at the head of the antislavery forces, the Radicals took complete control of the federal government and concentrated its apparatus in their hands. They defeated the armies of the Confederacy on the battlefields of the Civil War; shattered the political and economic power of the slave oligarchy; consolidated the bourgeois dictatorship set up during the war; and remodeled the Republic into conformity with their own class aims and interests.

This Second American Revolution not only installed a new governing class in office but, by abolishing chattel slavery, scrapped the principal form of property and labor in the South. The great political and social problem which had agitated the

United States ever since the birth of the republic—how to dispose of the slave power and its "peculiar institution"—was definitively settled.

The Second Revolution also concluded the progressive political role of the American bourgeoisie. After it helped annihilate the slave power and slavery, its political usefulness was utterly exhausted. Like the plantation aristocracy before it, the new ruling capitalist oligarchy rapidly transformed itself into a thoroughly reactionary force, until it came to constitute the main obstacle to social progress not only within the United States but throughout the world.

Revolution in the Old World and the New

Just as American historians have ignored the organic affiliation between the First American Revolution and the Second, so they usually overlook the affinity between the revolutionary movements in the United States and Europe during the mid-nineteenth century. Yet the upheaval in the New World cannot be completely and correctly understood unless its connections with the revolutionary processes then going on in the Old World are made clear.

At every stage of its development, American history has been a product of the interaction between international and inner forces. Western Europe, which dominated the New World during its discovery and colonization, continued to determine the main lines of social and economic development in America decades after the United States achieved political independence.

The Second American Revolution was not simply necessitated by unsolved problems rising from the first one. It was no less the outgrowth of the whole course of historical evolution in the Western world since 1789, and more particularly since the world-shaking political events of 1848 in Europe. These developments posed new problems before the American people. They also provided ways and means for solving the old problems along with the new.

Between the close of the First American Revolution in 1789 and the beginning of the Second Revolution in 1861 a far greater revolution took place in the Western world. This revolution occurred in the field of production. The introduction of power-driven machinery transformed the technological basis of production, gave birth to the factory system, and made possible large-scale industry. The capitalist method of production for the first time stood upon its own feet and began to assert its mastery in the decisive spheres of economic life. The age of industrial capitalism had succeeded the age of commercial capitalism.

The rise of industrial capitalism, which began toward the end of the eighteenth century and lasted until the beginning of the twentieth, was a turbulent epoch in world history. With furious zeal the emissaries of capitalism attacked and destroyed the remnants of feudal and barbarian civilizations and erected a new world on their ruins. The extension of the exchange of products gave capital, labor, and culture an unprecedented mobility. Capital ranged throughout the globe, seeking openings for trade and investment; millions of people were redistributed from the Old World to the New in the greatest mass migrations in history; culture became more cosmopolitan. Science and invention quickened the pace of capitalist industry.

The Second American Revolution occurred during the height of this development. From 1852 to 1872 industrial capitalism experienced its most impetuous growth. The unprecedented volume of world trade during this period indicates the extraordinary tempo of economic expansion. After rising from $1.75 billion in 1830 to $3.6 billion in 1850, the volume of world trade leaped forward to $9.4 billion in 1870—an increase of well over two and a half times. This rate of increase has never been surpassed by world capitalism. It was during this century of industrial revolution that the modern capitalist world took shape.

The epoch of the most rapid expansion of capitalism, from 1847 to 1871, was likewise a period of wars and revolutions, in three consecutive phases. The crisis of 1847 produced the first mighty wave of uprisings. These were cut short by a series of victories for reaction and by the economic revival following the California gold strike of 1849.

After a prolonged period of prosperity, the world crisis of 1857 gave rise to a second sequence of wars and revolutions. This began with the first Italian War for Independence and was followed in rapid succession by the American Civil War of 1861, the Polish Insurrection of 1863, Napoleon III's Mexican adventure, and the campaign against Denmark in 1864 which opened the series of Prussian wars led by Bismarck. This revolutionary impulse was felt as far away as Japan where, through the Meiji Restoration, the rulers partially adapted their economy and regime to the demands of the new industrial system.

The final period lasted from 1866 to 1871. Initiated by the crisis of 1866, it witnessed the republican uprising in Spain that toppled Queen Isabella from the throne, and the culmination of Bismarck's campaign of expansion, beginning with the attack upon Austria in 1866 and ending triumphantly in the unification of Germany after the victory over France in 1871.

The civil war in France, following Bismarck's defeat of Napoleon III, was the historical high water mark of this epoch. The Paris Commune was the first time in history that the proletariat seized power. With the crushing of the Communards and the restoration of bourgeois order in the Third Republic, the revolutionary tide receded for the rest of the century.

Thus for almost twenty-five years the entire Western world was a fiery furnace of war and revolution. These were the most turbulent years humanity had experienced since the Napoleonic Wars or was to know until the First World War. Within this furnace were forged not only the imperialist powers of modern Europe, which were to rule the earth until 1914, but the nation destined to outstrip them as the mightiest of world powers: the capitalist United States of North America.

The Second American Revolution must be viewed within this world-historical setting. Our Civil War was neither an isolated nor a purely national phenomenon. *It was one of the most important links in the chain of conflicts that issued directly out of the world economic crisis of 1857 and constituted the great bourgeois-democratic revolutionary movement of the mid-nineteenth century.* While the revolutions of 1848 and 1871 in France were the chief events in the first and final stages of that movement, the revolution that started in 1861 in the United States was the central event in its second chapter. This was the most important revolutionary struggle of the nineteenth century, as well as the most successful.

The Results

The development of the bourgeois-democratic revolutionary movements of the mid-nineteenth century proceeded at different tempos, assumed different forms, and had different results in the various countries. From Ireland to Austria, the uprisings of 1848 in Europe uniformly ended in disaster and the restoration of the old order—with superficial changes at the top. At the same time these frustrated assaults made possible numerous reforms in the ensuing decades and prepared the way for further advances by the progressive forces.

The revolutionary movements of the second and third wave were more successful in attaining their objectives. The triumph of the Union in the United States was of far greater historical importance than the failure of the Polish Insurrection in 1863. The conquest of national unification and independence by the German and Italian peoples was more significant than the fact that it was achieved under monarchical auspices.

Even where the revolutionary struggles failed to reach fruition, they engendered valuable reforms (extension of the franchise in England, national autonomy for the Swiss cantons, limited constitutional liberties in Hungary, etc.). By 1871 the bourgeoisie had secured liberal constitutional governments in most of the leading countries of Western Europe, with the exception of Germany, Russia, and Austria-Hungary. These nations had to pay their long overdue debts to history in double and triple measure when the next all-European revolutionary tide rose during 1917-18.

Except for the United States, social reforms were largely restricted to the removal of the vestiges of feudalism, which hampered capitalist development. Thus the revolution of 1848 led to the abolition of serfdom in Hungary; in 1863 Alexander II decreed the emancipation of the serfs within Russia's dominions. In the U.S. alone did a really revolutionary transformation of social relations take place.

Here the problems of the bourgeois revolution were solved with maximum success. Here the magnates of industrial capital became the sole rulers of the Republic by destroying the slavocracy and slavery. Elsewhere, as in Germany and Italy, the bourgeoisie faltered for lack of revolutionary energy, fell short of its goals, and remained the servant of the old upper class, which retained the reins of government in its hands.

The American bourgeoisie was able to fulfill its historical mission so brilliantly because of the exceptional character of American social development. Their drive for power was based upon the great achievements of the First Revolution. The American people had already attained national independence, gotten rid of the altar and the throne, and enjoyed the blessings of republican democracy. These advantages gave the American bourgeoisie a head start that made it easier to outdistance the Europeans.

Moreover, the economic power, political independence, and social weight of the capitalists in the United States considerably surpassed that of their German and Italian compeers. The American masters of capital were no political novices. They had taken almost a century to prepare themselves for this final showdown; they had once held supreme power and felt it was theirs by right. They had already created their own parliamentary institutions and taken legal possession of the state apparatus before the battle was joined. They entered the arena with their own party and program.

The role of the bourgeois Republicans as defenders of the Union and its democratic institutions enabled them to rally around their banner the progressive forces within the nation and throughout the civilized world. The North could count on support from the Negroes in the South, whose sympathy weakened the Confederacy even where the Union leaders feared to encourage their initiatives. They succeeded in winning over the mass of small farmers to their side, while the slaveholders failed to draw their sympathizers among the governments of Western Europe into the conflict. The importance of these alliances can be estimated when it is remembered that the rebel colonists were enabled to defeat their British overlords through the military intervention and financial aid of France, Spain, and Holland.

The economic strength of the northern capitalists was no less superior to that of their adversary. The boom preceding the crisis of 1857 poured streams of wealth into the coffers of the northern industrialists and financiers and placed large resources of capital and credit at their disposal. The Unionists had an extensive and solid industrial and agricultural base beneath their feet. The Confederacy, on the contrary, had neither an adequate industrial foundation (they exhausted their energies trying to improvise one under stress of the Civil War), nor quantities of liquid capital at their command, nor easy access to the resources of the world market. The war, which depleted the assets of the Confederacy, crippled its slave economy, and cut off its great saleable crop from the market, only lent an impetus to the expansion of industry and agriculture and the accumulation of capital within the loyal states.

Finally, the clear-cut and irreconcilable antagonism between the slavocracy and the industrialists on the one hand, and the immaturity of the proletariat on the other, enabled the radical bourgeoisie to carry through the struggle against its class enemy to the end. At every stage of its struggle with the princes and Junkers on its right, the German bourgeoisie had to reckon with a distrustful working class on its left. Except for a brief explosion in the middle of 1863, the industrial workers in the United States did not assert themselves as a powerful independent factor.

The revolution was led by the Radical Republicans, the most resolute representatives of the bourgeoisie. The Radicals were the last of the great line of bourgeois revolutionists. Thrusting aside the conciliators of every stripe and crushing all opposition from the left, they annihilated their class enemy, stripped the slaveholders of all economic and political power, and proceeded to transform the United States into a model bourgeois-democratic nation, purged of the last vestiges of precapitalist conditions.

After the Civil War and Reconstruction, the capitalist magnates who enjoyed economic and political mastery saw no need for further fundamental changes in American society. And it was true that the time for revolutionary transformations within the framework of capitalism had ended. That did not mean, however, as the upholders of that system taught, that all possibility of revolution had forever been banished from the United States.

This most successful of bourgeois revolutions had still left important things undone. For instance, it carried out agrarian reform in a highly inequitable manner. The Homestead Act of 1862 gave the small white farmer free access to the territories in the West claimed by the federal government and awarded huge tracts of the best land to the railroad corporations.

But the Negro cultivators of the soil, who had contributed so much to victory over the planters, were shabbily treated. Although the Republicans emancipated the slaves, they refused to give them the material means for economic independence ("forty acres and a mule") or to guarantee their social equality and their democratic rights. In the disputed presidential election of 1876, to ensure their continued sovereignty in Washington, the Republican leaders sealed an agreement with the southern white supremacists which erased the last of the equality and democracy the Negroes had won for themselves during Reconstruction.

The failure of the bourgeois regime to solve the Negro problem has plagued our country to this day. It appears that this job, left unfinished by the nineteenth-century revolution, will require a struggle of comparable magnitude before it is performed.

American democracy was defended and extended by the coalition of class forces that fought and won the Civil War. But at its best this democracy has remained restricted. At no time since have the masses of American people exercised decisive control over the national government. Whether Republicans or Democrats held the White House and Congress, the plutocrats have ruled the country and determined its major policies in war or peace.

This formal political democracy is still further abridged by the industrial autocracy of the big capitalists who own and operate the national economy for their private profit. The workers who produce the wealth of the United States have no control over its distribution.

By 1960 the monopolists held the same position in American life that the slaveholders occupied in 1860. They are an obsolete social force, the major brake upon national progress, the fiercest enemies of democracy. Instead of leading progressive movements in the interests of the people, they have become the organizers of counterrevolution and the allies of reaction throughout the world.

Their course is slowly but surely creating the preconditions for a mass resistance to their rule which will culminate in a third American revolution. This new movement of emancipation, based upon the workers, will have a socialist program and aims and be directed against capitalist reaction. But its organizers and leaders can learn much from the Radicals of the Civil War years who met the challenge of the slaveholders' counterrevolution head on, crushed their resistance on the field of battle, confiscated billions of dollars' worth of their property, and totally uprooted their outmoded social system. They showed by example how to deal with a tyrannical ruling class that refuses to retire peacefully when the time has come for it to go.

The Emancipation Proclamation

George Novack (1963)

Lincoln's Emancipation Proclamation went into effect a century ago on January 1, 1863. The freedom heralded by that decree is far from won; slavery was buried but Jim Crow is very much alive.

Despite this excessive gradualism, the Emancipation Proclamation stands as a monumental landmark in the advancement of liberty, not only for the Negro people but for all Americans. Even though Lincoln resisted Senator Sumner's plea to issue the proclamation on the Fourth of July, this charter of freedom ranks with the Declaration of Independence in our revolutionary heritage.

However, the vast discrepancy between the promise held out by the 1863 pronouncement and the performance of the possessors of power in the past hundred years presents problems for historians as well as for the political defenders of the existing order. What caused this failure and where should the responsibility for the perpetuation of Negro inequality be placed?

The Civil War ushered in the Second American Revolution. This was the most momentous event in the entire nineteenth century, for out of it came the capitalist colossus of our own day. The Emancipation Proclamation was the greatest event in that conflict. Its significance—and shortcomings—cannot be understood except in the context of the Civil War and the divergent interests and aims of the social forces on the winning side.

The Civil War erupted as the climax to a prolonged contest for command over the country between the northern businessmen and the southern planters. Ever since the Missouri Compromise of 1820, the moving force in American history and the pivot of its political affairs had been the now muffled, now acute struggle for supremacy between the beneficiaries of slave labor and the upholders of free soil and free labor. Just as the rulership of big business is central to the problems of our generation, so throughout the first half of the nineteenth century the major social issue before the American people was: What is to be done about the slave power?

In the decades before the Civil War the cotton nobility became dominant not only in the South but over the nation. Its representatives and accomplices controlled the White House, the Senate, the Supreme Court, the armed forces; they charted the main lines of foreign and domestic policy.

This sovereignty of the slaveholders was first seriously challenged by the Republican Party, organized in 1854. It was a coalition composed of the rising industrialists, the small farmers of the Northwest, the urban middle classes, and part of the wageworkers—all the elements opposed to the slave power.

When Lincoln was elected president in 1860, the long-established balance of power in national politics was profoundly upset. Until that point the slaveholders could count on a pliant and even servile administration to do their bidding at Washington. The Republican assumption of command meant that the authority and resources of the federal government had slipped from their grasp and were being taken over by their foremost rivals, the northern manufacturers and their associates.

Because of the grave difficulties besetting their antiquated system of production, the southern planters and slave dealers could ill afford to lose possession of the heights of power they had so long and so profitably occupied. Like other ruling classes on the skids, they placed defense of their privileges ahead of the democratic decision of the electorate. Up to 1860 the wealthier and more conservative planters had rejected the arguments of the southern "fire-eaters" that departure from the Union was the cure for their ills. Now they swallowed the desperate remedy of secession, formed the Confederacy, and fired on Fort Sumter.

The immediate cause of the Civil War was therefore political: the shift of supremacy from the cotton barons to the industrial bourgeoisie and their allies. The secessionist coup d'etat confronted Lincoln's government with the choice of resubmission to the dictates of the slavocracy or taking the field of battle to clinch by bloody warfare its constitutional triumph in the 1860 elections. The loyal states mobilized to beat down the defiance of the "lords of the lash."

The statesmen on both sides brought forward legalistic and constitutional arguments. But these covered up a far deeper issue. Behind the embattled governments and armies were two antagonistic forms of property and production. The Confederacy was conceived in chattel slavery, property in human beings; the Union rested upon wage labor and freehold farming. The planters had plunged into secession in order to safeguard their "peculiar institution" at all hazards; the fate of the slave system hung on the outcome of the Civil War.

The founders of the Confederacy were far more cognizant of this fundamental feature of the conflict than were their northern adversaries. In a grandiloquent speech in defense of the Confederate Constitution on March 16, 1861, Alexander Stephens, vice-president of the Confederacy, declared:

> The new Constitution has put to rest forever all the agitating questions relating to our peculiar institution—African slavery as it exists among us—the proper status of the Negro in our form of civilization. This was the immediate cause of the late rupture and the present revolution. Jefferson, in his forecast, had anticipated this, as "the rock upon which the Old Union would split.". . . The prevailing ideas entertained by him and most of the leading statesmen at the time of the formation of the Old Constitution were, that the enslavement of the African was in violation of the laws of nature; that it was wrong in principle, socially, morally, and politically. . . . These ideas, however, were fundamentally wrong. They rested upon the assumption of the equality of races. This was an error. . . .
>
> Our new government is founded upon exactly the opposite ideas; its foundations are laid, its cornerstone rests upon, the great truth that the Negro is not equal to the white man; that Slavery, subordination to the superior race, is his natural and normal condition. [Applause.] This, our new Government, is the first in the history of the world, based upon this great physical, philosophical, and moral truth.

Stephens was all wrong in his assertion that the Confederate Constitution had "put to rest forever" agitation about slavery. The very act of secession had given the most crucial importance and extreme urgency to the issue. The United States could not be reunited until slavery itself had been put to rest forever.

But in the opening stages of the Civil War the Republican high command did not view or approach the situation in this light. In the immense upheaval convulsing the country they believed it possible and desirable to leave standing the underlying cause of it all! They had held this position from the birth of the

Republican organization, which was not designed to be a party of social revolution but of political reform.

The manufacturing and business interests at its head sought protective tariffs, transcontinental rail lines, lucrative government contracts, favorable immigration and banking policies; the representatives of the small farmers and middle classes in its ranks wanted homesteads, better transportation facilities, educational grants, etc. The Republican leaders were resolved to wrest political predominance from the planters, bridle the aggressive ambitions of the slave power on the foreign field, and fence in their domain. But they were willing to leave slavery alone if the southern cotton magnates would accommodate themselves to the changed relationship of forces. Again and again they declared: We have no intention of disturbing or destroying slavery and are ready to give firm guarantees of its continuance wherever it legally exists.

Just as the upper crust among the planters had resisted secessionism in the 1850s, so the most influential Republicans indignantly and sincerely repudiated abolitionism as subversive of the established order and the devilish fomenter of slave insurrection. Seward, Lincoln, and others approved the hanging of John Brown. It took the bourgeois heads of the North several more years to come abreast of the requirements of their revolution than it did their slaveholding counterparts in the South to recognize and act upon the imperatives of their counterrevolution.

The Republican leadership followed this course of conciliation with slavery for over a year after the Civil War broke out. In his inaugural address Lincoln reassured the slaveholders in these words: "I have no purpose, directly or indirectly, to interfere with the institution of slavery in the states where it exists; I believe I have no lawful right to do so and I have no inclination to do so." As late as July 26, 1861, after the rout at Bull Run, the Senate, by a vote of thirty to five, resolved that the war "was not being prosecuted for the purpose of overthrowing or interfering with the rights and established institutions" of the seceding states.

Since the slaveholders would not accept second rank in a northern-dominated Union, and the Republican coalition would not forfeit its legally acquired supremacy, decision could only be rendered by an armed fight to the death—and this portended the death of slavery.

The abolitionists and other consistent opponents of the slave power saw this clearly and urged Lincoln to conduct the war in a revolutionary manner by freeing the slaves. On November 7, 1861, Marx and Engels wrote from London in a dispatch to *Die Presse* of Vienna: "The present struggle between the South and North is, therefore, nothing but a struggle between two social systems, between the system of slavery and the system of free labor. The struggle has broken out because the two systems can no longer live peacefully side by side on the North American continent. It can only be ended by the victory of one system or the other."

If, as Secretary of State Seward later remarked, "the Emancipation Proclamation was uttered in the first gun fired at Fort Sumter," he and his colleagues took a long time to get the message. For the Republican directorate the question of slavery was subordinate to the preservation of the Union under their own hegemony, and so they started to wage a hesitating, purely military campaign against the rebels, which was highly ineffective. Even after losing hope of compromise with the secessionists, they feared to antagonize the upper classes in the border states by tampering with their accumulated wealth and labor supply.

The government feared to arm the free Negroes and enroll them in the Union forces. It was even more indisposed to encourage the slaves to rise up against their masters, sabotage production, and escape from the plantations. In 1861 Lincoln overruled General Fremont's order freeing the slaves of all Missourians supporting the Confederacy, and as late as May 1862 he voided General Hunter's action emancipating slaves in Georgia, Florida, and South Carolina.

The administration's refusal to strike blows at slavery provoked angry protests throughout the North and chilled the enthusiasm of foreign friends for the Union cause. Almost from the day that armed conflict began, the Republican regime was subjected to a tremendous tug-of-war between the conservative faction led by Secretary of State Seward, which wanted to maintain the status quo, and the Radicals headed by Secretary of the Treasury Chase, Senator Sumner, and Representative Thaddeus Stevens, who pressed for political and military action aimed at crushing the Confederacy and demolishing the slave power. To Stevens, "the vile ingredient called conservatism" appeared "worse than secessionism."

Lincoln vacillated between these opposing tendencies. As a private person, he detested slavery. As a moderate Republican, he proposed to solve the problem by gradual and compensated emancipation followed by colonization abroad of the former chattels. He offered this scheme to the border states, whose officials rejected it.

The Radical and abolitionist leaders deeply distrusted the president for his caution and compromise on this all-important issue. Frederick Douglass denounced "the slow-coach at Washington." Wendell Phillips, speaking at a Republican rally in Boston, was applauded when he accused Lincoln of treason and urged his impeachment for nullifying General Hunter's proclamation.

The emancipationists were not all of one breed. The bourgeois Radicals in high posts like Chase, Stanton, and Wade insisted on ruthless measures to combat the slavocracy in order to clear the field for the unhampered expansion of industrial capitalism. Their upper-class motivation was to emerge more clearly during Reconstruction. The abolitionist agitators like Douglass and Phillips were bent on destroying the slave power in order to get justice and equality for the Negroes and fulfill the democratic ideals of the Republic.

During the first half of 1862 the antislavery forces conducted a relentless campaign to compel the president to change his course. The difficulties in handling the large numbers of slaves who ran away and sought refuge behind the Union lines and in the army camps, the need for more men and money to carry on the war, and the desire to placate European liberal opinion made the old conciliatory policy less and less tenable. The mounting impatience of the most energetic supporters of the administration with its temporizing attitude toward the rebels was expressed in the open letter that the editor of the *New York Tribune,* Horace Greeley, known as the Tom Paine of the Radicals, addressed to Lincoln on August 20, 1862. Headed "The Prayer of Twenty Millions," it demanded that the president liberate the slaves in both the secessionist and border states at once and turn to the Negroes for aid against the South.

To this Lincoln replied: "My paramount object in this struggle is to save the Union, and is not either to save or destroy slavery. If I could save the Union without freeing any slave, I would do it; and if I could save it by freeing all the slaves I would do it; and if I could save it by freeing some and leaving others alone, I would also do that."

Despite the restraint in this restatement of his guiding line, Lincoln had reached the point where he could no longer withstand the fierce pressure of emancipationist sentiment. He was losing popularity in the North and risking the leadership of his own party. The powerful Congressional Committee on the Conduct of the War, controlled by the Radicals, was insisting that the military deadlock could not be broken without the suppression of slavery.

Lincoln had made up his mind to take action by June 13, 1862, when he informed Seward and Welles that the Union would be subdued if he did not free the slaves. The legal basis for this exercise in executive power had been laid by the Confiscation Act passed by Congress on July 6, 1862, for the unshackling of slaves belonging to the secessionists. On September 23, after Lee had been driven back at Antietam, Lincoln made a preliminary public announcement of emancipation. A hundred days later his definitive proclamation was issued.

Few nowadays have read the Emancipation Proclamation. Compared with the fiery Declaration of Independence it is a pallid document. According to Professor Richard Hofstadter, "it has all the moral grandeur of a bill of lading." Lincoln did not present the edict as an affirmation of democratic principle but as "a fit and necessary war-measure." It did not outlaw slavery as such or free any slaves. It applied only to areas over which the federal government exercised no control and specifically exempted all regions under federal military occupation. In the scornful words of British Lord Russell: "It does no more than profess to emancipate slaves where the United States authorities cannot make emancipation a reality, and emancipates no one where the decree can be carried into effect." In the text Lincoln took care to enjoin orderly behavior upon the Negroes and "recommend to them that, in all cases when allowed, they labor faithfully for reasonable wages."

But these defects of the document turned out to be far less significant than its issuance. Governor Andrew of Massachusetts rightly observed that the Emancipation Proclamation was "a poor document but a mighty act." It signalized the decisive turning point when the Civil War was transfigured into a social revolution against the last major precapitalist formation in the United States. The further course of the conflict was powered by the irresistible dynamism of its attack upon the structure of slavery. The proclamation gave official sanction to the Negroes' efforts to free themselves; it opened the Union armies to them. From that time on every advance of the Union troops into the South became a step toward full emancipation. The sentence of death which the Emancipation Proclamation in effect passed upon the slave power was carried out in the subsequent stages of the Second American Revolution.

Referring to the problem of slavery, Lincoln truthfully remarked that circumstances controlled him more than he controlled circumstances. The Republican switch from the path of reform to the highroad of revolution, from the expectation of negotiating a deal with the deposed slaveholders to their extirpation, from the shielding of slavery to its suppression, is a remarkable example of how the exigencies of a life-and-death struggle can transform people, policies, and parties. The necessities of waging a war to the hilt against the Confederacy compelled the Republicans to depart from the restricted perspectives of their original platform and enforce the far-reaching antislavery measures which they previously had opposed. The ascending revolution propelled the people of the North to ideas and positions advocated until then only by a tiny, isolated minority. The abolitionists, who had made emancipation their war cry long before secession, anticipated the march of events and the needs of national progress far better than the "realistic" and opportunistic professional bourgeois politicians.

In retrospect, it can be seen how emancipation advanced step by step as the Civil War developed, overcoming one obstacle after another. The Republicans abolished slavery in the District of Columbia in April 1862; they fulfilled their campaign pledge to forbid slavery forever in the territories the following June; Lincoln opened the floodgates with his Emancipation Proclamation on January 1, 1863. When the Radical machine went into high gear, it put over the most revolutionary solution, confiscating slave property without compensation and enacting the Thirteenth Amendment. Thus a mighty revolutionary shakeup revolutionizes the mentality and politics of its participants and leaders.

Today Kennedy occupies the same White House tenanted by Lincoln a century ago. The president has condemned the Fidelistas because they did not confine their actions to the pronouncements of their original national-democratic, humanistic platform, but went on to take socialist measures. He refuses to see that in order to realize their democratic objectives and carry out their pledges to the poor, the honest and courageous Cuban revolutionaries had to go far beyond their initial intentions.

The leaders of the Cuban Revolution had good precedent for this in North American history. They acted no differently than the heads of the Second American Revolution, who discovered that they could not preserve the Union, defend democracy, and clear the way for national progress without dispossessing the counterrevolutionary slaveholders. The Republicans who started out as reformers became converted by force of circumstance (and much to their surprise) into bourgeois-democratic revolutionists. The Fidelistas, who began as bourgeois-democratic rebels, ended up as socialist revolutionists. The Cubans of the 1960s took up where the American revolutionists of the 1860s left off; the Castro regime which Kennedy is so intent on destroying has uprooted racial discrimination in Cuba.

This is well worth noting on the centenary of the Emancipation Proclamation. Instead of blaming Castro for transgressing the limited aims of the July 26 Movement in its infancy, Kennedy's propagandists—including historians like Arthur Schlesinger, Jr.—might better direct attention to the following questions closer to home: Why didn't the president's predecessors of Civil War days succeed in eliminating racial oppression? Why must Negroes still be fighting today to acquire the status of full citizenship?

Enlightenment on these points can be obtained through understanding the motives and aims of the ruling capitalist class in its progressive and reactionary phases of development. It took four years of civil war and twelve years of military occupation of the South before the northern statesmen felt securely entrenched at the summits of power. So long as they feared a political comeback by their traditional adversary, the Republican bourgeoisie had to make substantial concessions to keep the allegiance of the farmers and Negroes.

At each turn of events from 1861 to 1876 their conduct was primarily shaped not by consideration for the needs of the common people, and still less for the claims of the four million Negroes, but by the shifting requirements of their drive for unchallenged supremacy. After the Confederacy had surrendered and the slaves were freed, the problem of remolding the Cotton Kingdom came to the fore. Was the South to be democratized by transferring control to the emancipated blacks and the poorer whites—or would a new oligarchy take the place of the subjugated slavocracy?

This issue was fought out during the Reconstruction period. In the first years after 1865 two contending programs were put forward for handling the South. Lincoln's successor, President Andrew Johnson, sought to restore order as quickly as possible and keep the Negroes subjected by enforcing the Black Codes, denying them the vote, and restricting changes in social relations to the minimum. The Radicals, backed by the abolitionists and the Negroes, set out to complete the demolition of the planting aristocracy.

To forestall any resurgence of the unregenerate rebels, the aggressive agents of northern business and banking found it expedient to give the Negroes the vote and sustain by military force the reconstructed state governments established and administered by opponents of the old order. These introduced many worthwhile innovations in education, taxation, the criminal codes, and other domains.

As in all modern revolutions in backward areas, agrarian reform was the most burning need of southern society. Here the Republican administration defaulted. In some places the ex-slaves seized the plantations, worked them for their own account, and defended them arms in hand. Generally, they expected that a generous federal government would give them "forty acres and a mule." They waited in vain.

"Confiscation is mere naked justice to the former slave," declared Wendell Phillips. "Who brought the land into cultivation? Whose sweat and toil are mixed with it forever? Who cleared the forests? Who made the roads? Whose hands raised those houses? Whose wages are invested in those warehouses and towns? Of course, the Negro's. . . . Why should he not have a share of his inheritance?"

But the representatives of the rich in Washington refused to hand over this rightful inheritance by providing the masses of freedmen with the material means for economic independence: land, livestock, seeds, cheap credit, and other essentials for raising crops. Consequently, the four million landless, helpless agrarian laborers fell back into servitude in new forms to the merchants, moneylenders, and landowners. In a few years this economic dependence led to the loss of their civil rights and political power as well.

In the showdown the Republican bourgeoisie had abolished four billion dollars' worth of property in slaves, since that kind of investment was unsuited to their own mode of exploitation. They were happy to transfer title to the western territories that had been seized by the federal government to homesteaders and to railroad, mining, and lumbering corporations because this brought profit to their enterprises. But it was pushing social revolution too far for these moneyed men to expropriate landed property in the settled South. That would not only set too dangerous an example of confiscation but might endow the small cultivators of the soil with too much potential political weight.

After using the freed slaves and the poorer whites to hold the ex-Confederates down, the northern capitalists left them in the lurch. They turned away while the Ku Klux Klan instituted a reign of terror, deprived the Negroes of their gains, and drove them back into oppression. Finally, in the disputed presidential election of 1876, the Republican and Democratic chiefs sealed a bargain by which white supremacy was relegalized in the South in return for a continuance of Republican rulership in Washington. The robber barons of industry and finance, assured of a divided and destitute working population and a plentiful supply of cheap agricultural labor in the South, then proceeded to harvest and enjoy the golden fruits of their victory.

The Reconstruction period was the final chapter in the Second American Revolution. Its tragic outcome is pertinent to the Negro struggle today. It demonstrated that the capitalist rulers at the peak of their revolutionary vigor would not accord full and enduring equality to the Negroes, or even permit the freedmen to keep the rights they had won in bloody combat. Will their present-day descendants be more inclined to grant genuine integration a century later when they have become the mainstay of the antidemocratic, procolonialist, and antisocialist forces in the world?

The experience of the Civil War is instructive on both the positive and negative sides of the problem of alliances in the fight for freedom. The coalition of the Republican bourgeoisie and the small farmers with the Negroes took time to cement and become effective. But it pulverized the slave system, struck off the shackles of chattel slavery, and protected the most democratic and progressive regimes the southern Negroes have known to this day. With the relationship of forces in the country at that time, these accomplishments could not have been made in any other way.

After advancing the cause of Negro liberation, the upper-class

Republicans broke the alliance and conspired to thrust the ex-slaves back into bondage. They became anti-Negro, antidemocratic, antilabor, not because they were white, but because they were capitalist profiteers bent on their own aggrandizement.

It would be wrong to conclude from this betrayal—and those which have occurred since—that the Negroes are predestined to travel the rest of freedom's road alone. They remain a minority in this country they have helped create and make great. To attain the objectives they seek and overcome the enemies of equality, they can again use reliable and strong allies. Where today are these to be found within our borders?

It is becoming widely recognized that the "liberals" in both the white and Negro communities, who deprecate direct action and pin their hopes on the powers-that-be, are untrustworthy allies and even worse leaders. This is all to the good, since those who look to the beneficiaries of discrimination to end it serve to weaken and derail the struggle against the Jim Crow system.

At the same time many of the best fighters for Negro emancipation have lost all faith in the capacity of the white workers to aid their struggle and have totally canceled them out as possible allies. It cannot be denied that organized labor, and especially its leaders, have given ample grounds for this mistrust. The Negro militants are completely justified in going ahead, as they are doing, to direct their independent actions against discrimination. This same spirit of self-reliance was evidenced by the slave insurrectionists, the runaway slaves, the Negro abolitionists, the delegates to the Colored People's Conventions, the freed slaves who seized their masters' plantations and armed themselves against the resurgent white supremacists.

Will the mutual estrangement between the privileged white workers and the Negro movement, fostered by the divisive strategy of the rich, be everlasting? The Civil War showed what radical reversals and realignments can come about in the course of a life-and-death struggle. We are far from such a situation in the United States now. But the increasingly militant temper of the movement for racial equality does mark the beginning of a deep-going change in American life and politics which has revolutionary implications.

Even at this stage the government has trouble coping with the Negro problem. It will become still more disturbed as the antidiscrimination struggle batters at other parts of the Jim Crow system, North and South.

At some point along the way the reactionary antilabor policies of big business will also shake up the mass of workers and bring them into opposition to the administration. Both segments of the American people will then find themselves arrayed against a common foe. It is an old and often true adage that "the enemy of my enemy is my friend."

However hesitatingly and slowly, these converging antimonopolist forces will have to seek points of contact and mutual support. In the course of practical collaboration, both will have to readjust their relations and revise their opinions of the qualities of the other. As has happened in many union battles—and in the battle for the Union—prejudices will be burned away and new alliances forged in the fires of joint combat.

Just as the Republicans of 1860 underwent a profound transformation and decreed the liberation of the slaves in 1863, despite their earlier indifference, so the participants in a new revolutionary movement would have to recognize even sooner the necessity of achieving solidarity through complete equality. This time, forewarned and forearmed, the Negroes will not be satisfied until that is won.

It would be unrealistic to underestimate the vigilant, unremitting efforts it will take to purge the poison of racial prejudice which capitalism has injected into the bloodstream of American life. Yet the day will dawn when the white workers must come to understand that discrimination is not only a crime against their Negro brothers and unworthy of a democratic society, but injurious and costly to their own welfare. The emancipation proclaimed in the Second American Revolution will be realized for black and white alike in the "new birth of freedom" which a socialist America will bring.

Two Lessons of Reconstruction

George Novack (1950)

As the Negro millions have risen up and their struggles have stirred America from top to bottom, students of past history and participants in current history have turned their thoughts to that epoch when the Negro question also held the center of the stage and the Negro masses first came forward as an independent political power. The forces preparing for new revolutionary collisions are, each in its own way, drawn toward a reexamination and reappraisal of the course of the Civil War, i.e., the Second American Revolution.

From the foundation of the United States the northern capitalists and southern planters had contended for total sovereignty over the nation. By crushing the proslavery rebellion, the capitalists at last gained their prime objective, confirming by armed force the supremacy won through Lincoln's election. Naturally bourgeois historians incline to center their attention upon that part of the revolutionary process by which their own class conquered supreme power and to regard the revolution as virtually completed at that point.

They recoil from the aftermath of the Civil War for still other reasons. Reconstruction not only disclosed the capacities of the Negro people for bold and creative deeds but exposed above all the real nature of the capitalist class. The bourgeois writers fear to dwell upon Reconstruction as a criminal dreads to return to the scene of his crime. For it was then and there that the capitalist rulers killed the hopes of the freedmen for full emancipation and conspired to deliver them back into bondage.

On the other side, by a sure instinct Negro and radical writers have become increasingly absorbed in the study of Reconstruction. Their reappraisal of the period was initiated in 1935 by

W.E.B. Du Bois in *Black Reconstruction,* which remains one of the foremost contributions to American history in our generation.

As Du Bois emphasizes, after the military defeat of the Confederacy had disposed of the contest between the revolutionary and counterrevolutionary forces on a national scale, the battle for supremacy between the people and the planters, the forces of revolution and counterrevolution, still had to be fought out and decided within the southern states.

Following Lee's surrender to Grant early in 1865, it was easily possible to proceed to a thoroughgoing renovation of the South along democratic lines. The former slaveholding potentates had been militarily beaten, economically and politically dispossessed, and were so disgraced and demoralized they could offer no serious political or physical resistance.

At that juncture there were only two real powers in the South. First and foremost was the federal government headed by the Republican Party and controlled by the industrial capitalists. They were the conquerors and the directors of the occupying forces. They had not only the military power but, what was more important, the confidence and allegiance of the progressive forces throughout the country.

The other power was the might of the aroused masses headed by the four million ex-slaves with their allies among the small farmers and poor whites. If these two powers had marched along together down freedom's road, they would have constituted an invincible combination.

But something quite different resulted. What started out, at the close of the Civil War, as an alliance between the northern men of means and the black and white plebeians of the South against the landed aristocracy terminated in 1876 with a union between the capitalist magnates and the planters against the southern masses and their Negro vanguard.

The eleven years of Reconstruction fall into three main stages: (1) the years 1865-66, when the revolution in the South was arrested by the conservative northern bourgeoisie, marked time, and missed its most favorable opportunities; (2) the years of revolutionary resurgence from 1867 to the early 1870s, when the Radical Republicans gained full command of the situation at Washington and joined with the Negro masses and their white allies to institute through armed force the first and only democratic regime in the South; (3) the years of revolutionary recession ending with 1876, when northern capitalism definitively broke with the southern masses, threw its decisive weight against their struggles, and finally concluded a pact with the planters which sealed the fate of the revolution and reestablished the white supremacists in the South.

The various elements in the antislavery coalition were animated by different and at times conflicting interests and purposes. The main driving force of the revolutionary movement emanated from the four million former slaves in the South. They wanted relief from age-old oppression and insufferable exploitation. They desired land, jobs, a decent living, civil rights and political power as represented by the vote, legal and racial equality, educational and cultural opportunities. These demands were eloquently voiced during the canvass for the Constitutional Convention of 1867 by a Negro voter at Selma, Alabama, who held up a red (Radical) ticket and shouted: "Forty acres of land! A mule! Freedom! Votes! Equal of white man!"

These measures necessitated turning the entire structure of the old South upside down. The confiscation of the land owned by the big proprietors, its partition and distribution among the landless laborers, meant an agrarian revolution. The ballot and freedom of organization meant the transference of political power into Negro hands, especially in states where they were the majority. Ex-slaves on an equal footing with their former owners and taskmasters meant undermining the pyramid of class rule and privilege.

The northern rulers had different aims, now that they had been lifted to the top by the antislavery movement. The triumphant capitalists wanted to perpetuate their grip upon the national government, increase their control over industry and agriculture, and grab the natural resources. In order to promote this program their political representatives had to maneuver with the other forces in the country. On the right, they had to prevent the revival of the political influence of the southern planters and their northern accomplice, the Democratic Party. On the left, they had to curb the demands of the lower classes, North or South. The Republican bourgeoisie was willing to use any of these other classes as tools in the furtherance of its own aims, but was determined to keep them all in a subordinate position.

Most of the Republican leaders had been reluctant to emancipate the slaves; during the Civil War they had tried to keep Negroes in the background and even out of the Union army. Now that the menace of the Confederacy had been eliminated, the

Republican bourgeoisie sought to hold the Negroes on a leash, lest they overstep the bounds of bourgeois proprieties.

Thus in the early part of Reconstruction the most moderate elements, through President Johnson and Secretary of State Seward, moved to effect a speedy reconciliation with the defeated planters and bring them back into the state and national administrations. They sponsored constitutional conventions in the southern states in 1864-65 toward this end.

The conservative Republicans sought to hold reconstruction of the seceded states to the minimum, without even granting voting rights to the freedmen. Johnson condoned the new Black Codes passed to police and suppress the Negroes, did little to help improve their conditions, and went so far as to veto the Freedmen's Bureau and Civil Rights bills.

The subservience of the president to the counterrevolution endangered all the fruits of victory. He was abusing the executive powers swollen by the war to reverse the course of the democratic revolution. Charles Sumner aptly wrote that the Negroes "should have had a Moses as a President; but they found a Pharaoh."

President Johnson's reactionary course encountered massive resistance from the people, both North and South, as well as in his own party. The opponents of Johnson's conciliatory course, however, did not all have the same attitude toward the Negro struggle and the democratization of the South. The majority of Radical Republican leaders were primarily concerned with preventing the Democratic Party from regaining power in Washington. Howard Beale explains their social motives:

> Stevens at least was genuinely a radical. He wanted to confiscate planter property and divide it among Negroes. The Republican Party never seriously considered this, because, while it would have served certain party purposes, the majority of Republican leaders and party members had not the least interest in social revolution, even in a distant section. They were men of property who would not endanger the sanctity of property rights for Negroes or poor Southern white men any more than they would divide ownership of their own factories or farms with Northern workingmen. There were sighs of *Northern* relief when death removed Stevens' troublesome radicalism. The Negro wanted forty acres and a mule, but his Republican backers had no serious thought of turning political into social and economic revolution. ("On Rewriting Reconstruction History," *American Historical Review,* July 1940.)

The more militant Radical leaders like Stevens and Sumner were the last of the great line of resolute representatives of the revolutionary bourgeoisie, like Cromwell, Robespierre, and Sam Adams. Stevens was a true friend of the Negro all his life, but he also recognized that the interest of capitalist industry could best be promoted by exterminating the slave power root and branch.

Fortunately, the Radicals had control of Congress. Directed by Stevens, Sumner, and their colleagues, prodded by the abolitionists led by Wendell Phillips and Frederick Douglass, and urged onward by the Negro masses, the Radicals set up a Congressional Committee of Fifteen. This Republican "Directorate" pushed through a series of measures to prolong military rule in the South; exclude the secessionist states until they had been remodeled to their satisfaction; establish regimes which gave the Negroes freedom, the vote, legal and civil rights, and aid through the Freedmen's Bureau and similar agencies.

At the same time, the efforts of Sumner to get schools and homes, and of Stevens to get land for the Negroes were turned down.

The conflict between President Johnson and the Radicals continued through 1867, during which the Radicals impeached Johnson but failed to remove him by a single vote in the Senate.

Direct Action by the Masses

While this struggle was going on in the government circles at Washington, the masses in the South were on the move. Direct action by the insurgent people is the most salient feature of a revolution. The Negroes, whose vanguard had fled the plantations to find freedom, who had fought in the Union armies and were uplifted by the vision of a new world, started to reconstruct the South they longed for.

As early as 1864, free Negroes in the North had held Equal Rights Conventions which were sharply critical of Republican policy and energetically set forth their own demands. Southern Negroes began to organize politically as soon as they could. Beginning with the summer and fall of 1865, Colored People's Conventions in most southern states outlined a new Bill of Rights which included repeal of the Black Codes, the right to serve on juries, to vote, to own land, to bear arms, free public education, etc.

The Negroes did not always wait for sanction or approval of any constituted authorities or laws to secure these rights, especially with regard to the land and the right to bear arms. In a number of areas they seized possession of the plantations, divided the land among themselves, and set up their own local forms of administration. On the Sea Islands off Georgia and South Carolina, for example, forty thousand freedmen each took 40 acres of land and worked it on their own account. When the former owners came later to claim their plantations, these new proprietors armed themselves and resisted. Similar expropriations and clashes took place elsewhere, not only with planters but with federal troops. Land seizures would have taken place on a far larger scale if the freedmen had not had faith in the Republican promises and expected that land would be handed to them as it was to the homesteaders in the West.

At the same time, Negro troops held on to their rifles and Negro civilians began to arm themselves. Citizens' committees were formed or sprang up spontaneously to guard Negroes from actual or threatened assaults, which were not always energetically repulsed by federal commanders.

The initiative shown by the emancipated Negroes, their rapid overcoming of handicaps and achievements under the Reconstruction governments have been cited by sympathetic observers as evidence that, given equal opportunities, black citizens can prove themselves equal to whites. It is good of them to recognize this—but there is more to the matter than that. Even Du Bois insists that the ex-slaves were just ordinary folk no better and no worse than their white counterparts. This may serve to refute the doctrine of racial inferiority, but it is inadequate for a correct appraisal of the Negro's role during Reconstruction. Conditions make people as much as people make conditions—and revolutionary upheavals place ordinary human beings in exceptional situations, which make unusual demands upon their capacities, call forth greater efforts, and result in remarkable deeds. That was the case with the southern Negroes. They became the vanguard of the revolutionary forces, not because they had been prepared by experience and education to assume that role, not because they had intended to, but because their social situation and the tasks of the times thrust them to the forefront of the mass movement.

The most significant aspect of Negro participation in these events is the fact that, because of their social status as the most exploited and oppressed section of the laboring population, the Negroes and their leaders were compelled to go farthest in seeking satisfaction of their needs. They thereby occupied the most advanced political positions and advocated the most progressive measures.

This highly radical quality was unmistakably clear on the crucial land question, the touchstone of the agrarian revolution. While the Republican bourgeoisie dickered and evaded decision, rejecting Stevens's proposals, the most audacious Negroes proceeded to settle the issue by taking land and cultivating it. While the Republicans debated how much—or how little—liberty they could safely extend to them, the Negroes voiced demands, not only for themselves but for the whole people, for free public education, correction of criminal codes, and many other reforms which far outstripped the ideas and intentions of the northern overlords. Throughout the South, Negroes took the lead in establishing and extending the power of the masses and instituting democratic forms of administration.

As they became more independent and formidable, determined to carry democratization to its limits, they not only terrified the planters but alienated their northern patrons. Just as the northern capitalists held down the industrial workers and small producers in the North and West, so they strove to keep in their place the black agricultural toilers of the South. However, so long as they had not settled accounts with the "lords of the lash," they could not completely ignore the demands raised by the black millions. These masses were a vital force which kept exerting tremendous pressure upon Washington.

The conventions of 1867-68, composed of Negro and white delegates, and the state governments issuing from them, instituted a new type of government in the South. Describing their remarkable activities in *Black Reconstruction,* Du Bois incorrectly defines these radically reconstructed governments as "dictatorships of labor," analogous to the Soviet dictatorship of the proletariat.

The Radical governments were dictatorial in the sense that they rested on the bayonets of the northern troops and held down the disfranchised ex-slaveholders by direct force. However, the central and dominating role in these governments belonged to the bourgeois elements. And the plebeian participants were not industrial proletarians but landless farmers who aspired to become small owners and producers. Thus these governments can be more properly characterized as dictatorships of the bourgeoisie, democratically supported by the Negro and white masses of actual and potential small farmers.

The southern revolution was not proletarian in its character or socialist in its aims, as Du Bois believed, but plebeian and petty-bourgeois in its social basis and bourgeois in its tasks. It did not pass beyond the foundations of private ownership, production for the market, and capitalist relations. But within the broad framework of these bourgeois relations, the revolution could take on different forms and proceed in different directions according to the forces and policies that predominated.

While the bourgeoisie debated whether to effect immediate reunion with the landed aristocrats, or to hold back the ex-slaveholders and support the freedmen until their own supremacy was nailed down, the bourgeois-democratic coalition contended over two methods of reconstructing the South. The first was the bourgeois-bureaucratic policy of those Radicals who used the masses as a counterbalance and weapon against the old rulers; the other was the plebeian-democratic policy of the abolitionists and Negroes, who wanted to push democratization to the very end through united struggle against all the possessors of privilege. This struggle to determine whether the southern revolution would be consummated according to the needs of the masses, or be manipulated and restrained by the big bourgeoisie, came to the fore during this period of Reconstruction.

What Was Accomplished

The Radical Reconstruction governments had tremendous achievements to their credit, which proved what could be done even with the beginnings of unity between Negro and white. They registered progress in the field of education and in the tax system, cut down illiteracy, abolished imprisonment for debt, did away with property qualifications for voting or holding office, and instituted other progressive reforms in city, county, and state governments. As Du Bois notes: "There was not a single reform movement, a single step toward protest, a single experiment for betterment in which Negroes were not found in varying numbers."

"The story of the last six years of the period of Reconstruction is one of counter-revolution—a counter-revolution effected under the forms of law where that was possible; effected by secrecy and by guile, where that would serve; effected openly regardless of the forms of law, with violence or the threat of violence, where that had to be." So a recent writer, Ralph Selph Henry, candidly summarizes the last chapter of Reconstruction. And he defends this historical crime as a lesser evil. "But the counter-revolution was effected, at a cost to the South and its future incalculably

great, justified only by the still greater cost of not effecting it."
(*The Story of Reconstruction,* p. 401.)

The growing conservatism of the Republican leaders changed
the relation of forces in the South. The white supremacists
became considerably more bold, outspoken, unrestrained, and
powerful. They revived the Ku Klux Klan in the form of "White
Leagues" and applied naked terror to rob the Negroes of their
rights and gains and to cow them into submission. For example,
in the Mississippi elections of 1875, "nearly all the Democratic
Clubs in the state were converted into armed military companies," wrote John R. Lynch, Negro representative in Congress.

The Negroes put up a stubborn and heroic resistance. But the
revolutionary coalition grew weaker; within its ranks disintegration, demoralization, and disillusionment set in. There was a
series of splits in the Republican Party.

This process was crowned in 1876 by the deal between the
managers of the Republican Party and the Democrats. Hayes
was permitted to assume the presidency in return for acquiescence in the restoration of white supremacy in the South.

Two important lessons flow from this sketch of Reconstruction.
One pertains to the relations between democracy and dicta-
torship; the other concerns the role of the capitalist rulers of the
United States:

1. It is customary to counterpose the bare abstraction of
democracy to dictatorship as though these two forms of rule were
everywhere and under all conditions irreconcilable opposites.
Reconstruction demonstrates that reality is more complex. The
slaveholders' despotism smashed by the Civil War was utterly
reactionary; so was the Bourbon-bourgeois autocracy which has
dominated the South since the restoration of white supremacy,
although both these dictatorships tried to disguise themselves
behind democratic forms.

On the other hand, the bourgeois-military dictatorship backed
by the masses which dominated the South at the flood tide of the
revolution was the shield and support of democracy, the
indispensable form of the people's rule. It is an indisputable
historical fact that the only time Negroes have ever enjoyed
democracy in the South and effectively participated in its
political and social life was under the bayonets of the federal
armies and under the protection of their own organized defense
forces.

2. Nowadays the Trumanites advise the Negroes to look toward

the liberal capitalists and their political agents in Washington for equality. Much disillusionment in regard to the current civil rights struggle might have been avoided if the following lesson of Reconstruction had been known and assimilated. The Northern capitalists feared and failed to give real equality and enduring freedom to the Negroes during their progressive days in the mid-nineteenth century. How, then, can the present imperialist autocrats at Washington be expected to grant equality and freedom in the middle of the twentieth century when big business not only tyrannizes both North and South, but has become the foremost foe of liberty on a world scale?

THE TRIUMPH
OF THE MONOPOLISTS

Historians and the Belated Rise of American Imperialism

George Novack (1935)

In the course of its development every class creates a view of the historical process corresponding to its own fundamental interests, a world outlook that does not remain constant but changes in accordance with the development of the class itself. This can be clearly seen in the careers of the two great classes of modern society, the capitalists and the working class.

As soon as the bourgeoisie has attained a consciousness of its aims and begins to struggle for political power, historians spring up within the nation and take the field in its behalf. These historians are important agents in awakening bourgeois class consciousness and stimulating national pride in the lower classes who follow the lead of the bourgeoisie and share its prejudices. Wherever the bourgeoisie has consolidated its power, the nationalist historians of this school become the celebrators of its achievements and official spokesmen for its regime. Thus the most popular of contemporary American historians, James Truslow Adams, author of *The Epic of America,* voices in every essential respect the viewpoint of the capitalist masters of the United States.

Consciously or not, the bourgeois historians limit their horizon to the classic framework of bourgeois rule, the national state. They adopt an internationalist point of view only incidentally and occasionally—in the same abstract fashion, and with the same obscuring of the real state of affairs, as a bourgeois politician might advocate entry into the League of Nations. This school of historians seeks an understanding of their national history, not in its development as an integral and subordinate part of a worldwide social system governed by its own general laws of development, but somewhere within the sacred body of the nation itself—in its political institutions, laws, racial composition, material resources, or an ensemble of these elements called "the national spirit." They regard the national state not as a transient form of social organization, the product of a particular social order, but as the inevitable and final form of human society. In their investigations these scholars treat the nation as an independent organism, bearing within itself the forces of its own development, and having only casual relations with the outside world.

In the eyes of these historians their own nation has not only an exceptional character, but a special destiny or mission that fundamentally distinguishes it from all other nations. Whatever the particular character of this mission, which has ranged from the conversion of the infidels to Christianity in the early days of capitalism to the bringing of "civilization" to backward colonial peoples in the imperialist fashion of Mussolini, it will be found to coincide in content with the material interests of some section of the ruling class.

Frederick Jackson Turner, the author of *The Significance of the Frontier in American History,* was the father of the present school of nationalist historians in the United States, a school which includes among its ideological precursors Hegel and Lamprecht in Germany, Taine in France, and Macaulay in England. Although Turner himself had the mind of a petty bourgeois of the period of capitalist expansion, his ideas have been taken over and are used today as protective coloration by the big bourgeoisie. Today the Turner school reigns in the universities, the schools, and the popular press. Its ideas have seeped into the minds of the American people through a thousand different channels. Our two historian-presidents shared Turner's ideas. Woodrow Wilson was Turner's close friend and avowed disciple; Theodore Roosevelt's *Winning of the West* was a contribution to the Turneresque history of the frontier. So pervasive has Turner's influence been upon the present generation of historians that Benjamin Stolberg has denominated the American Historical Society a "Turnerverein."*

To Turner, the United States is originally and essentially a nation of pioneers and a pioneer among nations, the standard-bearer of progress in Western civilization. His philosophy of American history rests upon two main conceptions, the frontier

---

* In German, a *Turnverein* is a gymnastics club.—*Ed.*

and the section. These two categories account for all the peculiarities of American life from the character of its people to the character of its conflicts. The frontier is a cause of the distinctive character of American development only until its disappearance at the end of the nineteenth century, while contests between geographical sections continue to shape our national life thereafter. The frontier, however, remains the key concept of the Turnerites.

The frontier is an extremely vague and confused category, which Turner himself never clearly defined. Theoretically, it covers a diversity of economic relations; historically, it includes numerous different forms of civilization. In the main, when the Turnerites speak of the frontier, they have in mind a society of independent and democratic freehold farmers, such as existed in many midwestern states during the last century.

The Turnerites, however, fail to analyze or to understand the economic character of this pioneer agricultural society or the economic causes of the westward movement of the frontier. In the first place, the frontier was not simply the expanding edge of American capitalism; *it was one of the primary factors in the expansion of world capitalism.* In the second place, *more than any other agriculture the world has ever seen, American agriculture has been a commercial capitalist agriculture.*

When the frontier "moved forward," that meant that agriculture was expanding in response to the pressure of the world market. From the days of the first tobacco plantations in Virginia and Maryland until the present century, commercial agriculture has played the leading role in the development of the American economy and has been the principal source of its peculiar social, political, and economic traits. It is impossible to explain the development of American society without a correct appraisal of the economic character and function of American agriculture on both a national and an international scale.

The Turner school is materialist insofar as it recognizes that the unique qualities of American civilization have a material origin and basis in the conditions along the frontier. But the Turnerites do not understand the economic character of these conditions, since their materialism is not historical-economic but territorial. Even this halfhearted materialism is discarded for an idealistic standpoint when they come to consider latter-day America. Turner quite correctly holds that (bourgeois) democracy in the United States had its economic basis in cheap land and its social support in the small farming class. But what becomes of such democracy when the free land is gone and the farmers fall under the domination of industrial and financial capital? Turner's only answer was to exhort his countrymen to remain true to the democratic ideals of their pioneer forbears in the same futile manner as the earlier school of New England historians begged their contemporaries to adhere to the faith of the Puritan fathers.

At the opposite pole from the bourgeois historians are the Marxists, who place themselves at the standpoint of the international working class. They realize that American history and world history are inseparable. American society is the offspring of European society economically, politically, and culturally; it has never been isolated or independent from Europe.

This does not mean that the Marxists deny or ignore the peculiarities of American development. These indubitably exist and it is the task of the historian to explain them. But how? Bourgeois historians seek their explanations in the nation alone, in its unique character. Marxists, on the other hand, locate them in the world-historical process of which American history is a component part.

Between the bourgeois-nationalist and the Marxist historians stands a third group, which we may call the liberals. This school, which reflects the ideas of the middle class, attempts to combine eclectically the viewpoints of the two chief historical tendencies. As might be expected from the variegated nature of the middle classes, the representative productions of this school exhibit the most diverse qualities. On many questions it is difficult to distinguish any differences between them and their bourgeois-nationalist brethren. On the other hand, the best of the liberal historians frequently approximate the Marxist position in their historical analyses.

Charles Beard is the acknowledged leader of the liberal school. The book he coauthored with Mary Beard, *The Rise of American Civilization,* is the greatest American historical work of our time. The liberal historians of the Beard school often adopt a materialist point of view. The chapters on the Civil War in *The Rise of American Civilization,* which are the high-water mark of American historiography, constitute almost a complete Marxian analysis. But these liberal historians recognize the reality of class antagonisms only in the past, over their shoulders. Even James Truslow Adams had a keen eye for the workings of the class struggle in his excellent earlier books on revolutionary New England. But this vision dims as they approach the present, and, like the other bourgeois historians, they ultimately take refuge in an idealist point of view. Thus Beard puts individual ideas on the same plane as class interests. Quite logically, he has written two big books embodying his ideas of what "the national interest" should be and recommending his program to the political representatives of the ruling class. Since his ideas flagrantly contradict the interests of that class, we may rest assured that, although President Roosevelt has read his books attentively, Beard's program will not be put into practice.

Out of the left wing of the liberal school there has recently emerged a group of young historians who are endeavoring to pass beyond the limitations of bourgeois history and assimilate the Marxist method. They inaugurated their theoretical work by attacking and criticizing the prevailing ideas of the Turner and Beard schools, but they have not yet had time to rid themselves completely of the preconceptions inherited from their old teachers. When this necessary stage of mental moulting is over, there should be many full-fledged Marxists among them. The ablest of these younger historians is Louis Hacker; his remarkable pamphlet *The Farmer Is Doomed* is the finest production of this group to date.

Unfortunately, the United States has not yet given birth to a school of Marxist scholars and historians whose work is at all comparable to that of the bourgeois historians. We have only the scanty, isolated productions of an A.M. Simons, a De Leon, a Schlüter. The backwardness of the American labor movement (one of its most important peculiarities from the standpoint of revolutionary strategy!) is reflected in the ideological, as well as the political, sphere,

Recently, however, under the influence of the same general social causes that are removing the backwardness of the American working class and educating it politically, Marxist works are beginning to appear which herald a renaissance of Marxist scholarship in the New World. Such a work is Lewis Corey's *The Decline of American Capitalism*. It is an interesting commentary on the theoretical backwardness of the American labor movement that, whereas Lenin's *The Development of Capitalism in Russia* appeared in the youth of Russian capitalism, the first extended survey of the evolution of American capitalism was not written until the colossus had already passed its prime. The very title suggests its belated appearance.

Corey's book is an important addition to the treasury of Marxist literature and merits the closest critical study by every thinking revolutionist. It is the first comprehensive treatment of the development of American capitalism, particularly in its later stages. In scope, it towers above the other productions of American Marxists like a giant sequoia. It is especially valuable for its graphic and statistical demonstrations of the general laws of Marxist political economy as they have actually unfolded in the course of American capitalism.

We do not propose to discuss the many merits of Corey's book in this article. We wish rather to consider some serious errors in Corey's theory of the development of capitalism, and of American capitalism in particular. Corey's mistaken conceptions lead him into error and confusion when he comes to deal with the most important problem in the development of American capitalism, the question of imperialism.

These errors spring from two different but closely related sources. In the first place, Corey takes a wrong methodological approach to the subject, abandoning the international standpoint of Marxism for a national point of view. In the second place, his mind retains residues of some incomplete and erroneous notions popularized by Turner. While Corey recognizes the inadequacy of these ideas, he inclines to return to them whenever he is confronted by a particular difficulty in the development of American capitalism. This can be seen in his reliance upon "the frontier," that philosopher's stone of the Turner school, in order to explain the specific peculiarities of nineteenth-century American capitalism.

The International Roots of American Capitalism

Corey's theory of capitalist development is fundamentally weakened by a false dichotomy between the "inner" and "outer" forces of capitalist expansion. This distinction is untenable. It is theoretically impermissible to take the boundaries of the national state as the limits of the productive forces of capitalist economy. The national state is the political instrument of bourgeois rule, not its exclusive economic basis. According to Marx (*Capital,* Vol. III), "the expansion of foreign trade, *which is the basis of the capitalist mode of production in its stages of infancy,* has become its own product in the further progress of capitalist development through its innate necessities, through its need of an ever-expanding market." In other words, capitalism had an international foundation from its very beginning. From their first appearance and in all the subsequent stages of their development, the economic forces of capitalism transcend national boundaries.

This is apparent the moment we consider the history of English capitalism, not to speak of the continental countries, whose economy assumed an international cast in proportion to the inroads capitalism made upon feudal society. English commercial capitalism rested upon the colonial system, which was not only worldwide but was established as the result of a long series of commercial wars with other European powers, fought all over the globe. The dependence of English industrial capitalism upon the world market is too obvious to dwell on.

It is often forgotten that commercial and industrial capitalism were, no less than the present monopoly capitalism, international in scope. Monopoly capitalism, of course, binds the world together more tightly in imperialist chains. One of the great differences between the earlier forms of capitalism and monopoly capitalism lies in the superior mechanisms of exploitation developed by the latter. Although the difference is of extreme importance, it should not obscure the fact that capitalism, from its very beginnings, is an international form of economy. The transition from feudal to capitalist society was made possible only through the creation of the world market, which grew up with commercial capitalism.

The distinction between the "inner" and the "outer" forces of expansion has an important function in Corey's account of American capitalist development. It opens the door to a theory of American exceptionalism. While the European nations were compelled to turn early in their history to "the outer long-time factors of expansion," American capitalism, according to Corey, pursued a different course and developed on a different basis. Thanks to its rich natural resources and vast continental areas, American capitalism had a relatively autonomous and self-contained character in the early stages of its development. It did not have to acquire an international foundation and join the mainstream of capitalist development until it had reached the stage of monopoly capitalism.

As a matter of historical fact, the truth lies in the opposite direction. From its origins the American economy has been either capitalist in character or a subsidiary part of the world capitalist economy. American capitalism, no less than European capitalism, had an international foundation throughout all the stages of its evolution. It is fundamentally wrong to regard it as economically independent or self-sustaining. Let us take a look at the colonial economy.

From the huge agricultural area already occupied in 1765 flowed annually an immense stream of produce. All the sections save New England raised more provisions than they could consume. The middle colonies sent to port towns for shipment mountains of corn, flour, salt pork, flax, hemp, furs, and peas, as well as live stock, lumber, shingles, barrel staves, and houses all shaped for immediate erection. Maryland and Virginia furnished the great staple, tobacco, the mainstay of their economic life—an article for which the planters had a steady demand unhampered by competition. . . . North Carolina offered farm produce and some tobacco in the market, but paid its London bills mainly in tar, pitch, and turpentine. South Carolina and Georgia furnished rice, shingles, bacon, and salt beef to the Atlantic and Mediterranean trade, and later added indigo to their profitable staples. (Charles and Mary Beard, *The Rise of American Civilization*, pp. 89-90.)

New England ships carried fish and lumber to England, Spain, and Italy; went whaling through the seven seas to get oil and candles for Europe; sailed to Africa and the West Indies in the slave, rum, and molasses trade; and competed with French and English bottoms for the lion's share of the carrying trade in all the principle ports of the Western world. One single fact will illuminate the colonial scene. As early as 1740, taxes in the colonies were no longer paid in kind (produce) but in money, i.e., there existed a money economy based on production for the international market.

Let us view the matter from another angle. While it is true that America possessed richer natural resources than Europe, it lacked the most important of all productive forces—and the indispensable element in capitalist production—a supply of living labor power. Labor had to be imported from Europe by immigration or indenture, or from Africa through the slave trade, before this natural wealth could be exploited. This fact alone disproves any theory, like Corey's, which makes the early development of the American economy depend primarily on its internal natural resources.

The dependence of the American economy upon the world market increased, rather than diminished, after the colonies had achieved political independence from England (incidentally, only by means of the decisive intervention of French money and French arms). The whole development of the American economy from the War of 1812 to the Civil War was largely a product of European large-scale industry and of English industry in particular. The form of agriculture that was the predominant part of the American economy during this period was not the subsistence farming of isolated pioneers, but was primarily capitalist cash-crop production. The principal crops, cotton from the South and foodstuffs from the West, were shipped not only to the North but to Europe to provide raw materials for its textile mills and food for its laboring population.

The main features of the American economy during this period were shaped not simply by the richness and diversity of the resources to be found upon the continent, but by the demands imposed upon these internal economic factors by the world market, above all by the more highly developed countries across the Atlantic. Europe was the sun, America the earth, of the capitalist system. The orbit of the American economy was fundamentally determined by the attraction exerted upon it by the economic mass of Europe. American agriculture and industry grew not only because of the richness of the earth, but according to the amount of energy radiated from the solar center of the capitalist system. The direction and the degree of development of the productive forces within America were determined by the economic needs of the parent body.

The fountainhead of Corey's errors is his habit of treating the development of American capitalism not as an integral part of the evolution of world capitalism, but apart from it. He first abstracts the American economy and its main attributes from the world economy and then views it as an isolated, self-contained entity, evolving according to a preconceived pattern, for the most part out of its inner forces alone, until these inner forces were exhausted. For Corey, world economic forces play a decisive role in the American economy only in its imperialist stage.

This national point of view is maintained throughout the work and is the underlying tendency of its thought. The organic connections between the American and world economies are touched upon as an afterthought and in the most eclectic and abstract fashion. For example, in Corey's survey of the major aspects of capitalist development in the United States from the Civil War to the World War of 1914-18, he hardly casts a glance at world economic conditions. The national and international processes of capitalist development are considered apart from each other, as though they were parallel and not interpenetrating processes.

One of his few extended references to the part played by foreign trade in the expansion of the American economy (contained, significantly enough, merely in a footnote on p. 278) confirms this judgment:

> It must not be assumed that foreign trade was not an important factor in American economic development. It was. The United States, *in spite of its peculiarities* [italics ours], was inseparably bound up with the world market. Agriculture exported its surplus to Europe, without which its expansion would have been limited. Capital, raw materials, and manufactures were imported, accelerating industrial development. After the 1870's the American scale of production was enlarged by an increasing cultivation of export markets, particularly for textiles, meats, boots and shoes, petroleum, and metal products, including agriculture machinery.

In the first place, it must be observed that foreign trade was far more than "an important factor" in American economic development. It was the *decisive* factor. In the second place, although Corey *abstractly* recognizes the inseparable connection between American economy and the world market, he does not grasp the effects of this in America's *concrete* peculiarities. For him these evidently originated and existed apart from the world market.

In reality, the special peculiarities of American capitalism were a product of the given constellation of economic forces constituting the world market, in which the economic forces of the United States were throughout this period a subordinate factor. American capitalism has always been an organic part of world capitalism. The peculiarities of its economic development were not spontaneously generated from within itself alone, but were the outcome of the interactions between the national and the international productive forces and relations. This we hope to make clear when we consider the peculiarities of American imperialism.

The Theory of "Inner Imperialism"

We shall not linger over Corey's general theory of imperialism, except to observe, in passing, that it shares the same defects, since it is based upon the same false antitheses, as his general theory of capitalist development. Instead, we shall pass on directly to the concrete application of his theory in the case of American imperialism, where he is led astray by his false methodological approach.

According to Corey, there have been two distinct phases in the evolution of American imperialism, an earlier and a later, an inner and an outer. The first or "inner imperialist" stage was concentrated within the borders of the United States. The economic relations between the more highly developed northeastern section and the inner continental areas reproduced *within* the United States the relations of exploitation that existed *between* the European nations and the colonial countries. The industrial and financial region exported goods and capital to the frontier in the same way and with the same results as the highly industrial nations exported goods and capital to the colonial regions. "The inner continental areas were the American equivalent of Europe's overseas markets." (p. 278.) Corey develops the parallel to the point of identifying the relative economic decline of New England's agriculture and textile industry with similar phenomena in imperialist England.

Upon examination, Corey's evidence for the existence of an "inner imperialism" in the United States turns out either to be unfounded or to be nothing else than the normal conditions and consequences of capitalist development under assumed names. In both cases, the peculiar characteristics of imperialism are conspicuously absent.

Just as there have been two stages of "imperialism," so, Corey informs us, there have been two stages of "colonialism" within the United States—an earlier phase from 1820 to 1850 and a later phase from 1860 to 1890. In the first colonial period the "East" exploited the "West" commercially by exporting settlers and manufactures in exchange for foodstuffs and raw materials. But where are the specific characteristics of imperialism in such normal capitalist relations? If Corey is looking for "imperialists" before the Civil War, he will find them, not in the Northeast, but among the slaveowners of the South, who instigated the War of 1812 with England and the War of 1845 with Mexico—against the violent protests of the northern capitalists.

Corey is hopelessly at sea by the time he reaches the second stage of "colonialism." Here he also finds that the major colonial relation was the exploitation of the agricultural West by the capitalist East. Betrayed again by his fatal theory, he speaks of the struggle between the western farmers and the eastern capitalists as a sectional struggle, or as a struggle between agriculture and industry, instead of as a class struggle. Yet, elsewhere in his book, he specifically states that the so-called struggles between the East and West, and the North and South, were fundamentally class struggles.

As additional proof of the "inner" imperialist character of American capitalism after the Civil War, Corey cites the exploitation of immigrant and Negro by monopoly capital. But surely, the exploitation of the proletariat by industrial capital, no less than the exploitation of the lower orders of the bourgeoisie by their capitalist superiors, is a general characteristic of capitalism and cannot be considered the distinctive mark of its imperialist stage.

The whole fabric of Corey's theories of "inner colonialism" and "inner imperialism" is woven from such superficial and misleading analogies, which serve only to conceal the genuine differences between disparate phenomena and different stages of capitalist development. The common traits which Corey discerns, for example, in the economic decline of New England and old England are the results of the same general processes of capitalist development. But at this point their resemblances end and their all-important differences begin. They cannot be considered identical in kind, as the results of two forms of "imperialism," without causing the greatest confusion. The lion and the mouse are both products of biological evolution and members of the animal kingdom. But what would we say of a biologist who contended that the mouse belonged to the same species as the lion?

Nothing is gained by quarreling over words. No one can deny Corey his right to use the word "imperialism" to denote two different kinds of phenomena. But Marxism also has its rights, in this particular case the right of priority. When a specific term is stretched to include its opposite within its own meaning, it is useless for scientific purposes. The terms "colonialism" and "imperialism" have precise meanings in the vocabulary of scientific socialism. Instead of limiting himself to those clear, concrete meanings, Corey uses these terms in a double sense. This abuse of the established terminology introduces the utmost confusion into the subject under investigation.

It is not difficult to understand why Corey violates the

customary terminolgy of Marxism and invents a new species of "inner imperialism." He is genuinely puzzled by an important peculiarity of American imperialism. Monopolies took possession of the American economy more rapidly and to a greater extent than in any other capitalist country. Nevertheless, the United States did not pursue an aggressively imperialist policy until the end of the nineteenth century, and did not join the front rank of imperialist nations until the World War of 1914-18. How shall we explain this apparent contradiction between the domestic development of American capitalism and its foreign policy? Why did the United States enter the imperialist arena so much later than the European powers?

Corey answers the problem in the following manner. "American imperialism lagged behind the European . . . [due to] an inner imperialism, or in other words to conditions whose economics resembled that of the export of capital." (p. 421.) The great opportunities for exploitation and the high rate of profit obtainable within the United States absorbed surplus American capital and made its export unnecessary. As soon as the "short-time internal factors" began to be exhausted, American capitalists were compelled to turn, like their European rivals, to the "long-time outer factors" beyond their borders. At this point, the sham phase of American imperialism dissolved and the real era of American imperialism began. "The real outer imperialism was only emergent at a time when, from the 1880's to 1910, it was being consolidated in the economy of the highly industrial nations of Europe." (p. 422.)

What has Corey done here? Troubled by the fact that the United States, despite the predominance of monopoly capitalism, trailed far behind the European nations in its imperialist policy, he attempts to cover up the contradiction by giving the United States an imperialist uniform too. Unable, however, to outfit it in full imperialist regalia, he clothes it in a juvenile imitation, made of homespun, which it soon outgrew and discarded. Corey himself should discard it along with his other analogies. It is both false and unnecessary, and serves only to obscure the real processes of the economic and political development of American imperialism.

Although Corey's answer is unsatisfactory, the problem is real and demands an answer. The answer can be obtained in only one way—not by relying upon analogies derived from some general scheme of imperialist development, but by a concrete analyses of the peculiar conditions of American capitalist development.

Why American Imperialism Arrived Late

The United States entered upon its imperialist career later than the European powers because industrial capitalism held the center of the stage much longer here than in England, France, or Germany. Although the concentration of industry began relatively earlier and proceeded at a more rapid rate in the United States than in Europe, and trustification was more highly developed, finance capital did not begin to shoulder aside industrial capital in the sphere of monopolized industry until the close of the century, and did not completely control the strategic centers of national economy and the state until the World War. Since imperialist policies are an outgrowth of the domination of finance capital, the key to the relatively slow development of American imperialism is to be found in the late blooming of finance capital.

We need hardly go outside the pages of Corey's book to collect the evidence for this thesis. Corey himself informs us that: "In the United States, before 1898, trustification was primarily industrial concentration, under control of industrial capitalists; after 1898 trustification was primarily financial combination under control of financial capitalists, promoters, and bankers." (p. 374.) "The 1860's-1890's was the epoch of the industrial capitalist, who participated directly in production. . . . By 1900, the industrial capitalist was swiftly receding into the limbo of small-scale industry, or was becoming a financial capitalist, with interests in a multitude of enterprises, promoting, speculating, financing, *not* engaged directly in production." (pp. 360-61.)

Industry, then, was trustified after the Civil War under the supervision of industrial, rather than financial, capital. The giant monopolies of the period, Standard Oil, Carnegie Steel, Armour & Company, the American Sugar Refining Company, were organized and controlled by industrial capitalists like Rockefeller, Carnegie, Armour, and Havemeyer, and the new capital poured into them came from reinvested profits or from foreign capital directly invested in the industry, rather than from the flotation of bond and stock issues by banks and investment houses. The outstanding exception to this rule was the railroads, because of their greater capital requirements.

Finance capital began to supersede industrial capital and take the initiative in forming monopolies about the beginning of the century. The organization of the Steel Trust in 1900 by the House of Morgan was the first large-scale operation in this field by finance capital. When Carnegie sold his steel companies to the banking syndicate headed by Morgan and retired to his philanthropies, he symbolized the retreat of the industrial capitalist before the invasion of the financier. It is equally significant that Carnegie was, politically, an outspoken anti-imperialist and one of the chief financial backers of the Anti-Imperialist League, which organized the opposition to the Republican Party's imperialist policies—until the Morgan partners forced him to withdraw by pointing out that such propaganda was jeopardizing McKinley's reelection and the tariff essential to the Steel Trust.

While Morgan and Company were preparing to launch the Steel Trust in 1899, they floated the first important foreign loan issued in this country, the bonds of the Mexican Republic. This was followed two years later by a fifty-million-dollar loan to Great Britain to help pay the costs of the Boer War, the father of the Morgan war loans to England that helped suck the United States into the World War.

But although financial capital began to get a foothold before the 1914-18 war, it did not become the absolute governor of American economic and political life until the war. The transformation of American capitalism from the commercial-industrial (colonial) stage to the industrial-financial (imperialist) stage was accomplished in two separate steps. The period from the Civil War to the turn of the century completed the transfer of the American economy from a predominantly agricultural to an industrial basis. The period preceding the World War marked the beginning of its transformation from an industrial capitalist into a financial capitalist, imperialist nation.

Economically speaking, the United States did not shed all its colonial characteristics until the World War. It was a debtor nation and imported tremendous quantities of capital from Europe. Throughout the nineteenth century, foreign capital poured in an unending stream into the United States and was one of the most potent factors in its rapid economic development. Canals and railroads, extractive and manufacturing industries, southern plantations and western ranches as big as baronial domains sprang into being at the touch of the magic wand of foreign capital, and English capital in particular. The New York money market was but a satellite of the London and continental money markets.

Before the World War the United States was an industrial

rather than a financial competitor of the European powers. This can be seen in the comparatively small part played by American capital in the transformation of Japan from a tiny feudal island empire into a world power, although the guns of the United States Navy first battered down the gates of Japan and opened them to foreign trade. The United States remained in the ranks of the second-rate powers until it appeared on the scene of military operations in Europe to save the Allies—and its own investments.

The diplomatic policies of the United States before the World War had a provincial stamp and limited objectives, corresponding to the degree of its internal economic development. The ambitions of American imperialists did not extend beyond the domination of the Western Hemisphere and the freedom to exploit the markets of the Far East. The Monroe Doctrine and the Open Door in China were its guiding lights, "America for the Americans" was its slogan. Hawaii furnished the typical example of imperialist penetration by American capital during this period; "the bully little war" against the decrepit Spanish empire was the extreme limit of its military operations; the islands of Cuba, Puerto Rico, Hawaii, the Philippines, and Guam constituted the petty extent of its colonial acquisitions. Although Theodore Roosevelt was the most conscious and aggressive imperialist among the American presidents, his private schemes were limited by the objective development of American capitalism. He could seize the Panama Canal and wave "the big stick" at England and Germany over Venezuela, but he remained nothing more than the watchdog of the Western Hemisphere for American interests.

The decisive qualitative change in the character of American capitalism occurred during the war, which reversed the political and financial relationships between America and Europe and transformed the United States from a provincial parvenu in the society of the Great Powers into the colossus of the capitalist world. Today, when American capital has taken the whole world for its province, the tasks of Roosevelt II are correspondingly greater.

The relatively meager development of finance capitalism in the United States compared with European finance capitalism before the war, and its gigantic strides forward after the war, are shown by the following statistics of the export of capital, taken from Corey's book. By 1900 only $500 million of American capital was invested abroad, including government loans, compared with

England's $20,000 million, France's $10,000 million, and Germany's $5,000 million. The export of capital from 1900 to 1910 was "almost negligible," although "by 1913 American foreign investments amounted to $2,500 million, mainly the direct investments of dominant combinations." (p. 247.) By 1932, however, American foreign investments had mounted to $17,967 million (excluding the extremely important intergovernmental loans), of which more than one-half represented direct investments of monopolist combinations. What a tremendous leap forward!

The Real Significance of the Frontier

American imperialism lagged behind European imperialism, therefore, owing to the delayed development of finance capitalism. But what retarded the growth of finance capital and the export of large quantities of surplus capital, which paves the way for imperialist politics? Obviously, the high rate of profit obtainable within the United States. But why did capital, and especially monopoly capital, continue to command a high rate of profit during this period?

In his discussion of "the law of the falling tendency of the rate of profit" in *Capital*, Marx singles out six causes which counteract the effects of this general law of capitalist development. These are: (1) raising the intensity of exploitation; (2) depression of wages below their values; (3) cheapening the elements of constant capital; (4) relative overproduction; (5) foreign trade; (6) the increase of stock capital. All of these agencies were at work to a greater or lesser degree in the United States after the Civil War, checking the tendency for the rate of profit to fall. Corey systematically ignores one of the most important factors—foreign trade—precisely because it is not "internal."

According to Corey, the cause of the progress of American capitalism and the source of its peculiarities lie not in the organic connections between the American economy and the world market, but in Turner's universal solvent, "the frontier."

While it existed, the frontier was one of the major peculiarities of American capitalism. Its conditions of life renewed economic opportunity and progress. It provided almost unlimited possibilities for industrialization and the accumulation of capital and created constantly larger mass markets. The industrial Eastern states exported manufactures to the newly settled regions and imported raw materials and foodstuffs. This permitted an enlargement of the scale of production and an increasing realization of profit and accumulation of capital. . . . The expansion of the frontier was a perpetual rebirth of capitalism, energizing its upward movement, strengthening capitalism economically and ideologically; and its continental area and resources performed, up to the World War, the same economic function that colonialism and imperialism did for the industrial nations of Europe. (p. 51.)

But what is the economic character of this bountiful frontier, from which all blessings flow? "The expansion of the frontier depended upon the development of agriculture (mining), which in turn depended upon the markets of the industrial Eastern states and Europe." (p. 50.) We have already pointed out that Corey does not understand the important function of foreign trade in the development of American capitalism. Here he fails in a test case. By putting the markets of the industrial East on a par with the European (that is, the world) market, he completely misses the significance of "the frontier," that is, of agriculture, in the expansion of American capitalism.

Again, there is not simply one, "there are really two frontiers. The older frontier, before the 1850's, built up an essentially self-sufficing agricultural economy . . . the newer frontier, after the 1850's, was increasingly dependent upon the market and price." (p. 518.)

The existence of two different kinds of frontier is as imaginary as Corey's two different stages of imperialism. There has always been a peripheral class of self-sufficient farmers in the United States. But by its very nature this class could have little or no effect upon the *expansion* of American economy, since they bought and sold almost nothing on the market. However, unlike the isolated farmers in the Kentucky and Tennessee hills, even the self-sufficing farmers on the very fringe of the frontier performed important economic functions in the expansion of commercial agriculture. They were the advance scouts of the agricultural army, clearing the forest lands and preparing the soil for the oncoming wave of permanent settlers, the producers for the market. As the main army advanced, the frontier farmers often sold their improvements to them and moved to new lands, where they repeated the operation. It must be remembered, however, that the center of American agriculture before the Civil War was in the Cotton Kingdom of the South. The Wheat Kingdom of the West was just beginning to arise.

Even so, was it true, as Corey claims, that western frontier agriculture was essentially self-sufficient before 1850? Let us consult Turner himself for information on this period:

> The surplus of the West was feeding the industrial Northeast and finding an urgent demand in Europe. In 1830, breadstuffs to the value of only $7,000,000 were exported; but, in 1847, they had risen to over $50,000,000. This was exceptional due to the European crop failures and the opening of English ports, and the figures dropped in 1848 and 1849 to $22,000,000. But the capacity to supply such a relatively large surplus of breadstuffs indicated the new resources of the West, *and its need of a market.* Even the lower figures represent threefold the export of 1830. . . .
>
> Cotton had risen from a production of less than 800,000 bales, around 1830, to over 2,000,000 bales, in 1850. As over two-thirds of the crops was exported, this furnished the most important single factor in our foreign exchange and an essential basis for the use of bank credit in domestic business. The value of the cotton export was, by the close of the period, over three times the value of the exports of foodstuffs. In short, *during these two decades* an enormous and transforming increase took place in the agricultural production of the interior of the United States, due to the opening of virgin soils in regions equal in size to European countries, and furnished new *exports,* new *markets,* new *supplies to the manufacturing cities,* and new fields for *investment to the capitalists* of the coast. (*The United States, 1830-1850,* pp. 586-87; our emphasis.)

So much for the period before 1850 on the western frontier. If we analyze the movement of the American economy from 1850 to the World War, we see that commercial agriculture remained the mainspring of the movement. American capitalism expanded and contracted in response to the impulses of American agriculture, which expanded and contracted according to the demands made upon it by industrialized Europe. American industry was able to keep operating and expanding behind high tariff walls, and American capital to enjoy a high rate of profit, thanks, above all, to the position occupied by American agriculture in the world market. Cotton from the South and foodstuffs from the Middle West were the principal American exports during this period. American manufacture and American capital did not displace agricultural commodities from this position until the World War.

The leading role of American agriculture is demonstrated by the fact that American capitalism was enabled to emerge from its periodic crises mainly by virtue of the restoration of the European agricultural market. In one such specific case, Corey himself informs us that "in 1879 the large exports of wheat, the result of a serious grain shortage in Europe which created an increased demand for American wheat, played an important part in the renewal of the upward movement of prosperity." The extraordinary burst of prosperity that followed the Spanish-American War was caused by the failure of the wheat crop in Russia and Australia, resulting in heavy exports of wheat and a rise in price. With wheat at a dollar a bushel, the farmer could pay his debts and spend money to start the wheels of industry and finance whirling again.

This is only one side of the picture. Until the World War a three-cornered relationship existed: the advanced industrial countries of Europe exported capital to finance American railroads and industries (and labor to operate and build them); American financiers loaned money and American industrialists sold manufactures and services to the farmers; who shipped their products abroad to pay off the debt charges on the capital borrowed from Europe. As usual, the middlemen in this chain of transactions, the strategically located financial and industrial capitalists, harvested the major share of profits. Thus the two decisive factors in the period which really saw the development of American capitalism to its present estate—import of capital from Europe and export of agricultural commodities to Europe—depended upon European capitalism and its needs.

This triangular exchange relationship produced an economic balance between agriculture and industry within the United States, and between the United States and Europe. The relatively proportionate development of American capitalism was but the reverse side of the uneven development of European, and in particular English, capitalism. English capitalism had been forced to sacrifice its agriculture to the Moloch of the falling rate of profit with the repeal of the Corn Laws in 1846. Free trade with England, on the other hand, opened up an extensive foreign market to American agriculture, enabling it to march forward at the head of the American economy until it was overtaken by American industry and, later, by American capital. The equilibrium between industry and agriculture in the United States was maintained until the international postwar agricultural crisis ruptured it beyond repair.

The basis of American prosperity, that is, the high rate of profit obtainable by American capital, therefore, lay in the continual expansion of American agriculture, which was a product of the world market. And the internal relations of American capitalism, out of which its peculiarities arose, were rundamentally shaped by international economic conditions.

Theoretical errors take their revenge all along the line. It is a cardinal principle of Marxism that national peculiarities are, in Trotsky's words, "a unique combination of the basic features of the world process." Corey, however, forsakes the Marxist position for a nationalist standpoint. Instead of regarding the American economy as a component of the world economy, he views it as a microcosm, mirroring within itself all the economic relations of the world outside. Except in the imperialist stage of its development, this self-enclosed organism has for him only incidental connections with the rest of the world, and its internal relations are self-determined. Consequently, Corey is prevented from seeing the primary cause of the expansion of American capitalism; it lies outside his field of vision in the world market. He can explain the peculiarities of American capitalism only by resorting to a theory of American exceptionalism, which discovers in Turner's unique frontier the solution of all its problems. If Corey had purged his mind of such limited conceptions, which conceal more problems than they explain, and consistently adhered to an international standpoint, his work, valuable as it is, would have been considerably more valuable and penetrating.

Big Business and the
Two-Party System

George Novack (1938)

The radical ferment in the United States during the past decade has given rise to a new school of historical writing for the literary public of the left. In their general approach the biographers of this tendency have advanced a step beyond the "debunkers" whom they have superseded in popular favor, being far less preoccupied with the purely private sides of their subjects, their psychological quirks, sexual peccadilloes, and quaint characteristics than with the socially significant aspects of their careers. Their works are written, that is to say, not during the reactionary 1920s but in the crisis-torn 1930s, and under the intellectual influence not of Freudianism but of Marxism.

The influence of Marxist thought upon most of these authors has been extremely slight and casual, and indeed the majority have never professed to be Marxists. On the contrary, they condemn Marxism for its "one-sidedness," for its obsolete Hegelian philosophy or its equally outmoded nineteenth-century economics, for its revolutionary proletarian politics, and in general for its unyielding scientific materialism. The hundred and one doctrines they present as improvements over orthodox Marxism are potpourris of notions thrown together from diverse sources—Marx, Weber, Sombart, Veblen, Beard—in proportions varied to please the individual taste. These anti-Marxists, no less than the minority of self-avowed Marxists in this group, borrow from the treasury of Marxist thought, as from everywhere else, only those elements suited to their momentary needs and petty-bourgeois outlook, which they quote learnedly and plaster upon their works for radical decoration.

In revising past events and personalities, the writers of this school refrain from overstepping certain inviolable limits. They are bold—but not overbold; "radical" without being revolutionary. These limits are prescribed for them by their social outlook as petty-bourgeois intellectuals, by their intellectual indolence, and by their reformist politics. If they often plumb deeper than their predecessors, they still do not touch the bottom of most historical problems but dangle between the surface and the depths at the mercy of conflicting currents.

Caution and intellectual confusion characterize their political thinking no less than their historical investigations. The purely retrospective character of their wisdom is most clearly shown in their present politics, which consists of New Dealism, Stalinism, and often an amalgam of both. Thus John Chamberlain, who in 1932 performed an autopsy upon the Progressive movement in *Farewell to Reform,* pronouncing it dead beyond recall, comes forward in 1938 to cheer for Roosevelt and the New Deal.

Matthew Josephson, who stands with one foot in the Stalinist camp and the other in the liberal morass of the *New Republic,* is a virtuoso of this tendency. This biographer of Zola perceives no parallel to the Dreyfus case in the Moscow Trials, and no identity between his hero and John Dewey. On the contrary, he emulates the reactionary French scribblers he once excoriated by lending his pen to cover up these frame-ups in the *New Republic.* Nor do his two fat volumes on the patriarchal relations between big business and the twin capitalist parties, and on the futility of late nineteenth-century reformism, at all deter him from being well disposed toward the Roosevelt regime and its left wing.

These pseudoradical intellectuals are no better than the Bourbons: they have forgotten nothing and learned nothing. However perspicacious they may be in respect to the past, however bold in their criticism of their precursors, they are blind and timid as newborn kittens before the great problems of the present. Overwhelmed, disoriented, and unnerved by the prospective war and the onrushing social crisis, they are unwittingly taken in tow by conservative forces far stronger than themselves and involuntarily converted into accomplices of reaction. Likely at any moment to go astray in the tangled thickets of history, they are even less reliable guides amidst the mighty contending forces of today.

Matthew Josephson's latest production, *The Politicos,* is an excellent specimen of the historical work of this school. In *The Robber Barons,* he presented the economic development of the United States from 1865 to 1896 in terms of its principal figures.

Now he has aimed to interpret the political history of the same period. It is extremely hazardous to approach either history or politics in this manner. Its fruitfulness depends upon the measure of the author's insight into the social struggles and class dynamics of the time and upon his ability to correlate the ideas, character, and conduct of his subjects to them.

Josephson best fulfills these requirements in his portrayals of the Republican and Democratic chieftains, Grant, Harrison, Cleveland, and McKinley, who held the center of the national stage, and Blaine, Conkling, Olney, W.C. Whitney, and Mark Hanna, the stage managers who directed them. He delineates their personal and political traits with commendable care and skill. He thoroughly demonstrates the double dealing of these presidential figureheads who publicly posed as servants of the people while privately promoting the interests of the plutocracy together with their own personal or factional ends.

They presided over a carnival of corruption unprecedented in American history, aptly characterized by V.L. Parrington as "The Great Barbecue." Under the protecting wing of the government, the conquering army of spoilsmen overran the South like locusts; flung themselves with unleashed appetites upon the national resources; plundered the people; auctioned off or gave away lands, choice appointments, railroad charters, tariffs, and privileges of all kinds. The Credit Mobilier scandal in connection with the building of the Union Pacific Railroad, along with the operations of the Whiskey Ring, disclosed the intimate connections between the highest officeholders and the capitalist interests.

By tracing the activities of the go-betweens of high and low degree in the administrations from Grant to McKinley, Josephson exposes the complicated, costly, concealed machinery of transmission whereby the demands of the real rulers of the state, the captains of industry and finance, were impressed upon their political agents and translated into the law of the land. He shows the wheels within wheels of the administrative apparatus: the party dominating the government, the faction ruling the party, the boss or clique of bosses running the faction, who, by means of their control over the national conventions, nominated their candidates for president and named cabinets.

How instructive a handbook for an aspiring capitalist politician! From these pages he could learn how patronage should be allotted, how privileges must be marketed, and what kind of deals must be made to oil the party machinery and keep it running smoothly. He can see how the big party bosses establish regular business relations with the big capitalist bosses, who act as executive heads for their class. He can find out how a cabal of senators can exercise a dictatorship over Congress, opening or closing the sluices of legislation as they ordain.

The wealth of material Josephson has assembled on the personnel and methods of operation of the capitalist parties constitutes the valuable part of his work. Here we see bourgeois democracy not in an unrealizable version begotten in some idealist's imagination, but as it actually existed in the heyday of its development in the United States, when it had freshly issued from a revolutionary purging. What a repulsive spectacle of duplicity, demagogy, and venality is unrolled before our eyes! The final judgment upon the politics of this period, and upon this form of capitalist domination in general, was uttered by "Dollar Mark" Hanna, the kingfish of the big bosses: "All questions of government in a democracy are questions of money."

The serious shortcomings of *The Politicos* arise from Josephson's theoretical limitations, which prevent him from perceiving the basic historical tendencies at work from 1865 to 1896. This epoch breaks into separate parts. The first, which extended from the close of the Civil War to Hayes's assumption of power in 1877, belonged to the final chapters in the development of the Second American Revolution inaugurated by the Civil War. The political essence of this period, which marked the culmination of the bourgeois-democratic revolution, consisted in the direct dictatorship of the triumphant northern bourgeoisie over the conquered South and thereby over the rest of the country. The instrument for the exercise of this dictatorship was the Republican Party; its wielders, the Radical faction. Josephson, who tends to identify the revolution with the Civil War alone, does not comprehend the real disposition of the social forces in conflict during this period or the significance of their political battles. He is consequently unable to answer the key questions posed by the political developments of the time.

His theoretical helplessness is most clearly manifested in his treatment of the conflict between President Johnson and the Republican Radicals. He views this crucial contest as a purely administrative matter in the same bureaucratic way that contemporary liberals interpret the struggle between Roosevelt and Congress. According to him, it was but another episode in the recurrent struggle between a popular, independent, and democratic executive and a partisan, scheming, and autocratic senatorial clique.

Josephson unmistakably, if indecisively, places himself on the side of Johnson, the "man of the people" and "radical agrarian." The main reason for his stand is not difficult to discern. Believing, in his liberal simplicity, that formal democracy must always be on the progressive side, he must be for Johnson rather than the Radical advocates of military rule, congressional control, and dictatorship.

Yet Johnson, who proposed to revert to the political status quo before the Civil War, was counterrevolutionary compared with the Radical leaders, who aimed to monopolize their hard-won state power instead of sharing it with their vanquished foes. Josephson's perplexity in the face of this situation demonstrates that he has not yet attained the degree of historical insight possessed by the most resolute and farsighted leaders of the radical bourgeoisie at that date. They were sagacious enough to recognize that their revolutionary conquests could be safeguarded and extended only by maintaining a dictatorship over the South, and audacious enough to enforce that program over all opposition. While the Radicals pushed forward along the revolutionary road until they had utterly annihilated their class enemy, and cushioned their political positions against the inevitable recoil, Johnson and the faltering conciliators around him, leaning upon the reactionary sections of the petty bourgeoisie and upon the fallen slave oligarchy, wanted to stop the revolution short and welcome back the southern rebels. By placing himself at the head of the restorationist forces, Johnson, the formal democrat, was patently reactionary.

Josephson's incapacity to distinguish between the basically counterrevolutionary role of Johnson and the relatively progressive position of the Reconstructionists shows how shallow his understanding of the Second American Revolution is, and how alien to Marxism is his entire outlook. He cannot reconcile, either in theory or in reality, the contradictory concepts of dictatorship and democracy, although the history of this very period demonstrates that under revolutionary conditions a dictatorship of the advanced class is the only serious way to guarantee the social gains acquired by bloody struggle.

The dictatorship of the Radical bourgeoisie had its reactionary as well as its predominant progressive side. While the Radicals worked to complete the subjugation of their rivals on the right and directed their deadliest blows against them, they also strove to protect themselves and the material interests of the big bourgeoisie against their allies on the left flank, the discontented workers and farmers who instinctively struggled to carry the revolution forward along the lines of their own class interests. The capitalists needed the dictatorship to fight the counterrevolutionists on the one hand and the rebellious plebeians on the other. This dual function of the Radical regime, which flowed from the political and social necessities of the upper bourgeoisie, accounted for its contradictory character.

Josephson describes this dual character in the following paragraph:

The politicians in those stormy years of reconstruction were as men afflicted with dual identity: they were literally Jekylls and Hydes. As Dr. Jekyll, with a generous impulse they emancipated Negro slaves, swept away the feudal, landed order of the South; as Mr. Hyde, they deliberately delayed the recovery and restoration of the conquered states, whose economy languished during many years of disorder; imposed military rule; and established a network of Freedman's bureaus and Carpetbag local governments which were subject to the central Republican Party Organization at Washington and paid tribute to the same. As Dr. Jekyll, they stirred the masses of voters to their support by use of a humane and libertarian ideology of a revolutionary American pattern; as Mr. Hyde, they planned and built coolly, at the height of deliberately invoked, turbulent electoral struggles and parliamentary storms, measures of high capitalist policy, to stand "not for a day, but for all time"; they worked to implant in the covenant of our society safeguards to property and capital which might hold against all future assaults.

Just as he cannot grasp the fact that the Radical dictatorship was the dual shield of democracy, so Josephson is completely bewildered by the dual personality of the Radical politicians. In short, he does not understand the dialectics of the situation.

Since it lacks the dramatic values and picturesque color of the Republican regency, Josephson slights the history of the Democratic organization from 1864 to 1876. Yet the resurrection of the Democratic Party was not the least remarkable political phenomenon of the period. This party, which had been split in two by the revolutionary crisis and discredited by its policies during the war, rose from its ruins and returned to challenge the victor. Josephson offers no better explanation for the resurgence of the Democratic Party than the immortality of the two-party system. The profound regroupings of social forces that expressed themselves in the political realignments after the Civil War are left obscure and unregarded.

Finally, Josephson only partially appreciates the historical significance of the disputed Hayes-Tilden election of 1876. He correctly points out that the secret bargain between the Republican and Democratic chiefs sealed the reconciliation between the sundered ruling classes of the North and South over the prostrate bodies of the Negroes, the wageworkers, and the poor farmers. But he fails to note that, by withdrawing the federal troops from the South and permitting the Carpetbag governments to collapse, the Republicans relaxed their outright dictatorship and thereby terminated the last chapter of the revolution. Having consolidated their conquests and securely entrenched themselves in power, menaced far more by the plebeian left than by the planters on the right, the capitalist oligarchy was moved to restore "formal democracy" to the South. From then on, their reactionary dictatorship masked itself behind democratic processes—except in those instances of acute class conflict when the president called out federal troops against striking workers. The edge of the dictatorship was turned almost entirely against the rebellious proletariat.

The political axis of the next twenty years, from 1876 to 1896, evolved around the struggle of the plebeian masses against the rule of the plutocracy. The rural petty bourgeoisie took full command of the parliamentary fight against the big bourgeoisie, leading the proletariat behind it. Their revolt expressed itself in the Greenback, Granger, Populist, Single Tax, and Free Silver movements.

For the first sixteen years of this period the political security of the big bourgeoisie at Washington remained unshaken. During this age of economic progress, they ruled indifferently through the Republican and Democratic parties without serious threat from the workers and farmers. Then the crisis of 1893 cut across this comparative calm, resulting in a speedy and sharp consolidation of the opposing forces.

In 1896 the plebeian hosts rallied under the banner of the Democratic Party and the leadership of Bryan to storm the citadel of monopoly capital. Their campaign was subsidized and supported by big mining interests. Bryan's crusade against the Goldbugs was the high-water mark of the postrevolutionary struggle of the lesser bourgeoisie. Their failure to dispossess the direct representatives of big business from power underscored their impotence and initiated their political decline.

This period properly ends, however, not with McKinley's election, bought with Mark Hanna's funds, but with the Spanish-American War. This inglorious adventure was the imperialist solution to the social crisis precipitated by the economic panic of 1893 and aggravated by the bitter contest of 1896. By arbitrarily cutting short his exposition at McKinley's victory, Josephson indicates his incapacity to understand the stages of development and grasp the great turning points in the political history of the time.

Classes and Parties

The political spokesmen for the plutocracy foster two ideas that help perpetuate their authority over the minds and lives of the American people. The first, which is the essence of democratic mythology, is that one or both of the two capitalist parties have a classless character. The second is that the two-party system is the natural, inevitable, and only truly American mode of political struggle. The Democratic and Republican parties are granted the same monopoly over political activity that CBS and NBC have acquired over radio broadcasting.

The theoretical underpinning of *The Politicos* is constructed out of these two propositions, which Josephson affirms in a special version of his own. The central thesis of his book is that "neither of the two great parties in the United States" was "a class party," such as were common in Europe. They were competitive cartels of professional spoilsmen independent of all classes and primarily concerned with looking out for themselves and their political outfits. Only incidentally, as it were, did they also cater to the plutocracy or the people.

By 1840, Josephson remarks, "the professional or 'patronage' party had been forged in America, had become part of the fabric of government itself, wholly unlike parties elsewhere which labored primarily for 'class' or 'ideas.'" Further, "the historic American parties were not 'credo' parties, as Max Weber has defined them, parties representing definite doctrines and interests or faiths in a church, or a monarchical or traditional aristocratic caste principle, or a rational liberal capitalist progress; they now paralleled and competed with each other as purely *patronage parties*."

This is an utterly superficial and one-sided appraisal of the bourgeois parties. While it is true that in the classic land of big business, politics itself became the biggest of businesses, the two great political firms that contended for possession of the enormous privileges and prizes of office were no more independent of capitalist interest and control than are the two mammoth broadcasting corporations. On the contrary, they vied with each other to render superior service to their employers.

The all-important point is that the big business of politics was at one and the same time the politics of big business. This applied in petty matters as well as in the most vital affairs, whether it was a question of assigning a local postmastership, fixing tariffs, or declaring war. The real relations between the party bosses and the capitalist moguls were similar to those between an agent and his principal. While executing the orders of their employers and attending to their affairs, the agents, who were powers in their own right, did not hesitate to pocket whatever they could for themselves and their associates. The ruling caste was willing to wink at these practices, even encourage them, so long as they were not too costly or did not create a public scandal.

Josephson's theory, however, not only denies this intimate relationship but even inverts it. According to his conception, it was not the capitalists but the party bosses, not the big bourgeoisie but the parties, that were politically paramount. Josephson invests this thesis with a semblance of plausibility by drawing a whole series of incorrect conclusions from a number of indisputable but isolated facts of a secondary order. From the relative autonomy of the party organizations, he deduces their absolute independence of the ruling caste; from the episodic antagonisms of particular bourgeois politicians to certain demands, members, or segments of the capitalist oligarchy, he deduces a fundamental opposition between them.

Throughout his work Josephson displays a very meager understanding of the interrelations between political parties and the class forces they represent. These relations are not at all simple, uniform, or unvarying but extremely complicated, many-sided, and shifting. In the first place, it is impossible for any bourgeois party to present itself to the electorate as such. The capitalist exploiters constitute only a tiny fragment of the nation; their interests constantly conflict with those of the producing masses, generating class antagonisms at every step. They can conquer power and maintain it only through the exercise of fraud, trickery, and when necessary brute force. Their political representatives in a democratic state are therefore constrained to pass themselves off as servants of the people and to mask their real designs behind empty promises and deceitful phrases. The official actions of these agents negate their democratic pretensions time and time again. Opportunism, demagogy, dupery, and betrayal are the hallmarks of every bourgeois party.

Since the masses sooner or later discover their betrayal and turn against the party they have placed in power, the ruling class must keep another political organization in reserve to throw into the breach. Hence the necessity for the two-party system. The Democratic and Republican parties share the task of enforcing the domination of big capital over the people. From the social standpoint, the differences between them are negligible.

The apparent impartiality and independence of the twin parties and their leaders is an indispensable element in the mechanics of deception whereby the rich tyrannize over the lesser orders of the people. In affirming the classless character of the capitalist parties, Josephson shows himself to be no less enthralled by this fiction than the most uneducated worker. The worker, however, has had no opportunities to know better.

In the second place, no party can directly and immediately represent an entire class, however great a majority of suffrage it enjoys at any given moment. Intraparty controversies and splits, no less than interparty conflicts, reflect the divergences between the component parts of a class as well as the opposing interests of the different classes that constitute the coalition parties of the bourgeoisie.

A new party, made up of the most conscious and advanced members of a class, frequently comes into violent collision with the more backward sections of the same class. This was true of the Republican Party throughout the Second American Revolution. Thus Josephson's contention that "the ruling party often vexed and disappointed the capitalists as in the impeachment action itself, in its 'excesses,' or pursuit of its special ends" does not at all demonstrate the supraclass position of the Radical Republicans. It goes to prove that they were more intransigent and clear-sighted defenders of northern capitalism than many hesitant and conservative capitalists.

Finally, the independence of any party from the social forces it represents is always relative and often restricted within narrow limits. However long or short the tether, however loose it may be at any given moment, the leaderships of both parties are tied to the stake of the plutocracy. Whenever important individuals or tendencies begin to assert themselves at the expense of the capitalist rulers or in opposition to their interests, countermovements inevitably arise to bring them to heel, cast them out, or crush them. Josephson reports a hundred instances of this process in his book. Wherever the spoilsmen grabbed too much or too openly, they evoked Civil Service or reform movements, initiated or supported by those bourgeois groups demanding honest, cheap, or more efficient administration of their affairs.

The sovereignty of the capitalists stands out in bold relief in many individual cases described by Josephson. When Johnson dared oppose the Radicals he was fought, impeached, and then discarded. When his successor, Grant, endeavored to assert his independence of the senatorial cabal, he was quickly humbled and converted into a docile tool of the plutocracy. J.P. Morgan broke Cleveland's resistance to his financial policies after months of struggle and bent the president to his will.

Even more instructive is the example of Altgeld, recently resurrected as a liberal hero. Those who recall his pardon of the Chicago anarchists conveniently ignore the cause and outcome of his controversy with President Cleveland during the railroad strike of 1894, led by Debs. The governor of Illinois wanted to use the state guard alone to break the strike; the president insisted on sending in federal troops as well. Their quarrel amounted to a jurisdictional dispute as to which was to have the honor of suppressing the strike. Both state and federal troops were finally used. Thus the radical petty-bourgeois leader vies with the conservative commander of the big bourgeoisie in protecting the interests of the possessing classes against the demands of labor.

After annihilating the slavocracy, the reigning representatives of the big bourgeoisie set about to reinforce their supremacy. While the masters of capital were concentrating the principal means of production in their hands and extending their domination over ever-larger sectors of the national economy, their political agents were seizing the controlling levers of the state apparatus in the towns, cities, states, and federal government. The simultaneous growth of monopolies in the fields of economics and politics was part and parcel of the same process of the consolidation of capitalist rule.

The two major parties became the political counterparts of the capitalist trusts. Functioning as the right and left arms of the big bourgeoisie, the Republican and Democratic parties exercised a de facto monopoly over political life. The masses of the people were more and more excluded from direct participation and control over the administration of public affairs. The capitalist politicians did not attain this happy result at one stroke or without violent struggle within the two parties and within the nation. Overriding all opposition, outwitting some, crushing others, bribing still others, they succeeded in thoroughly domesticating both organizations until the crisis of 1896. The two-party system of capitalist rule was the most characteristic product of the political reaction following the great upheaval of the Civil War. This mechanism enabled the plutocracy to maintain its power undisturbed during an epoch of relatively peaceful parliamentary struggle.

The managers of the two parties had two main functions to perform in defense of the bourgeois regime. First of all, they had to safeguard the bourgeois parties against the infiltration of dangerous influences emanating from the demands of the masses. In addition, they had to head off any independent mass movement which jeopardized the two-party system and therewith the domination of the plutocracy.

The monopoly of the two great political corporations was accompanied by the ruthless expropriation of political power from the lower classes, the strangling of their independent political enterprises, and their more intensive exploitation in the interests of the commanding clique. This state of political affairs, combined with the periodic economic crises, generated the series of popular revolts culminating in the campaign of 1896.

We can discern two dominant tendencies in the political turmoil of the times. On one side, the two major parties, despite their secondary differences, cooperated in promoting the ascendancy and interests of the big bourgeoisie. On the opposite side, various popular movements welled forth from the lower classes in attempts to reverse the process of capitalist consolidation and to assert their own demands in opposition. Although these two tendencies were of unequal strength, corresponding to the disparities in the social weight and influence of the farmers and workers as against their oppressors, it is the struggles between these two camps, and not the secondary and largely sham battles between the two capitalist parties, that constitute the socially significant struggles of the epoch.

Bourgeois historians, however, focus their spotlight upon the contests of the monopoly parties which crowd the foreground of

the political arena, leaving obscure the popular protest movements which agitated in the background and emerged into
national prominence only on critical occasions. Josephson has
not freed himself from this preoccupation. While *The Politicos*
presents an illuminating picture of the top side of American
politics, revolving around the inner life of the plutocratic parties
and their struggles for hegemony, it systematically slights the
underside of the political life of the same period.

Josephson devotes attention to third-party movements that
expressed the aspirations of the plebeian orders and embodied
their efforts to emancipate themselves from bourgeois tutelage
only insofar as they affected, approached, or merged into the
channels of the two-party system. He shows himself to be
considerably more enslaved by bourgeois standards of political
importance and a far less independent, critical, and astute
historian of post–Civil War political life than the evangelical
liberal V. L. Parrington, who, for all his deficiencies, is keenly
conscious of major issues and alignments.

This is not an accidental error on Josephson's part but an
offshoot of his theoretical outlook. He draws the same fundamental conclusions from the political experiences of the postwar
epoch as other bourgeois historians. American politics moves in a
bipartisan orbit; third-party movements are short-lived aberra-
tions from the norm, predestined to disappear or to be absorbed
into the new two-party alignments; power oscillates between the
"ins" and "outs" in a process as recurrent and inevitable as the
tides.

Josephson even regards the two-party regime as "a distinct and
enduring" contribution of American statecraft to "realistic social
thought," although the American bourgeoisie borrowed this
system from the British ruling class, who fixed the pattern of
parliamentary government for the rest of the Western world.

Superficially considered, American politics since the Civil War
tends to confirm these conclusions. Despite their promising
beginnings, none of the third-party movements developed into an
independent and durable national organization, let alone succeeded in uncrowning the plutocracy. Even the mighty Populist
flood, with its millions of voters and followers, was sucked into
the channels of the two-party system in 1896, where it ebbed
away into nothingness after Bryan's defeat. The two-party
system has remained intact and triumphant until today.

These third-party movements were, to be sure, chiefly responsible for whatever political progress was achieved during this period. Their militancy kept alive the spark of revolt against the existing order. They provided the experimental laboratories in which the creative social forces worked out their formulas of reform. Some of these minor reforms even found partial fruition through the two major parties. Exerting pressure upon their left flanks, the third-party movements pushed the monopolist parties forward step by step, exacting concessions from them. Nevertheless, the fact remains that none of the third-party movements blossomed into a full-blown national party on a par with the two big bourgeois organizations.

The situation appears in a different light, however, upon a critical examination of the causes and conditions of their failure. First, the aims, programs, composition, and leadership of these movements were almost wholly middle class in character. The heterogeneous nature of the middle classes hindered them from welding together their own forces in a permanent organization. Their interests as small property owners and commodity producers set them at odds with the industrial workers. A fundamental community of interest deterred them from conducting an intransigent or revolutionary struggle against their blood brothers, the big property owners.

Second, these petty-bourgeois protest movements lacked the stamina, solidity, and stability to weather boom periods. Blazing up during an economic crisis, they died down during the subsequent upswing. The upper strata of the middle classes were satisfied with higher prices or petty reforms; the masses sank back into political passivity.

Third, the history of third-party movements is a sorry record of the betrayal of the plebeian masses by their leadership. This leadership was largely made up of careerist politicians or representatives of the upper middle classes, who were usually ready to make unprincipled deals with the managers of the two big parties; to forsake their principles and the interests of their followers for a few formal concessions or promises; to quit the building of an independent movement for the sake of a cheap and easy accession to office. An almost comic example of this was the fiasco of the Liberal Reform movement of 1872, which, originating in revulsion against the degeneracy of the Republican Stalwarts, ended by nominating Horace Greeley as a joint candidate with the Democrats in a presidential convention manipulated by wire-pulling, ruled by secret diplomacy, and consummated in an unprincipled deal that totally demoralized the movement and disheartened its sympathizers. Even more striking was the decision of the Populist Party in 1896 to abandon its identity and support Bryan, the Democratic nominee.

Finally, the mesmerizing effect of the two-party system and the activities of the capitalist politicians must be taken into account. They threw their full weight against every sign of independent political action reflecting mass discontent, crushing (wherever they could not capture or head off) the nascent movement of rebellion.

The social force capable of forging and leading a strong, stable, and independent movement against the plutocracy, the proletariat, was too immature to undertake that task. As a rule, the industrial workers remained politically subservient to bourgeois interests and influence. They limited their field of struggle to the economic arena, with their trade union leaders adhering to the policy of begging favors from the two parties as the price of their allegiance. The left-wing labor and socialist parties remained insignificant sects.

The two-party system was therefore perfected under certain specific social, economic, and political conditions, and its perpetuation depends upon the continuation of these conditions. The two-party regime is no more eternal than the bourgeois democracy it upholds. Its stability is guaranteed only by the relative stability of the social relations within the nation. The two-party system consolidated itself when American capitalism was ascendant; when the masters of capital sat securely in the saddle; when the proletariat was weak, disorganized, divided, and unconscious; when the direction of political mass movements fell to the middle classes. There was plenty of room for class accommodation; ample means for concessions; opportunities and necessities for class reconciliation. Consequently, the political equilibrium was always restored after it had been upset by severe class conflicts.

These circumstances either no longer prevail or are tending to disappear. American capitalism is on the downgrade; the proletariat is powerful, well organized, militant; the capitalists are in a quandary; the middle classes are nervous and restless. All the antagonisms that slumber in the depths of American society are being awakened and fanned to a flame by the chronic social crisis. The forces formerly confined within the framework of the two-party system are pounding against its walls, cracking it in a hundred places. The sharpening class conflicts can no longer be regulated inside the old political setup. The leading elements of the contending forces are straining to break the bonds which tie them to the old parties and to forge new instruments of struggle better adapted to the new situation.

While the trend toward new forms of political action and organization is common to all classes, the movement most fraught with significance for the future is the manifest urge of organized labor to seek the road of independent political action. Skeptics, conservative-minded pedants, Stalinists, interested trade union bureaucrats, and all those under the spell of traditional bourgeois prejudices point to the futility of third-party movements in the past in an attempt to discourage the workers from taking this new road and keep them in the old ruts. Their historical arguments are based entirely upon conditions of a bygone day.

Viewed on a historical scale, American society and therewith American politics are today in a transitional period, emerging out of the old order into a prerevolutionary crisis. This new period has its historical parallel not in the postrevolutionary epoch following the Civil War, but in the period preceding it. The "irrepressible conflict" between the reactionary slaveholders and the progressive bourgeoisie has its contemporary analogy in the irrepressible conflict between the capitalist and working classes.

The class showdown which then shook the social foundations of the Republic shattered all existing political formations. The Whigs and Democrats had, like the Republican and Democratic parties, monopolized the political stage for decades in the service of the slave power; they were pulverized by the blows delivered from within and from without by the contending forces. The turbulent times gave birth to various kinds of intermediate parties and movements: Free Soil; Know Nothing; Liberty. The creators of the Republican Party collected the viable, progressive, and radical forces out of these new mass movements and out of the old parties to form a new national organization.

As the abolitionists knew and declared, the Republican Party was not revolutionary in its principles, program, or leadership. It was a bourgeois reformist party aiming to alter the existing political system for the benefit of the bourgeoisie, big and little, not to overthrow it. This did not prevent the slaveholders from regarding this party as a revolutionary menace to their rule. From 1854 to 1860 the political atmosphere within the United

States became totally transformed by the deepening social crisis. Six years after the launching of the Republican Party came its formal assumption of power, the rebellion of the slaveholders, civil war, and revolution. All this occurred as a result of objective social conditions, regardless of the will of the majority of the participants and contrary to their plans and intentions.

The national and international conditions of the class struggle are too radically different today for the forthcoming period to reproduce the pattern of pre-Civil War days. It is certain, however, that its revolutionary character and tendencies are considerably closer to the present situation and problems confronting the American people than are the conditions and concepts stemming from the post-Civil War era of capitalist consolidation and reaction.

Matthew Josephson and his school operate almost exclusively with ideas derived from the conditions of the postrevolutionary period and tacitly based upon a continuation of them. Their writings are permeated with the same spirit of adaptation to the reigning order as their politics. A resurgent labor movement struggling to free itself from capitalist control must first cast off the obsolete prejudices inherited from its past enslavement. For a thoroughgoing, critical revision of such antiquated ideas, the advanced intellectual representatives of labor among the rising generation will have to look elsewhere than in the pages of *The Politicos.*

The Spanish-American War

John G. Wright (1936)

As late as the year 1895 the English historian Bryce was able to announce in his well-known work, *The American Commonwealth,* that the same thing could be said about American foreign policy as about the snakes in Ireland: there was no such creature.

In 1898 the United States was a world power conducting a colonial policy with perfect consciousness of its major imperialist interests.

The factual history of this seemingly astounding transformation is very simple and quite transparent. But the American—i.e., capitalist—school of historians persists in pretending that it was sheer coincidence that America entered the Spanish War to emancipate "little" Cuba and concluded it by a bloody subjugation of the Philippines. The liberal historian Beard (a very "critical" man) does not go beyond a mild surmise that a "number of active politicians had early perceived the wider implications of a war with Spain"; and he denies that there is any reason for even "believing that all who sat at the President's inner council table had at the time any such definite imperial design."

The Spanish-American War is vaguely explained, as a rule, by the hysteria drummed up by the "yellow press" (Hearst, Pulitzer, and Company). Says a professor at Clark University: "The newspaper press of the time inflamed popular passion till almost any lie received currency." (A.L.P. Dennis, *Adventures in American Diplomacy,* p. 63.) "Certain newspapers, notably those owned by William Randolph Hearst, fanned the flames." (L.B. Shippee, *Recent American History,* p. 238.)

But of course they all insist that there was no connection at all between a campaign in the press and the policy pursued by the government. "No considerable group of people or politicians talked of annexation or conquest." (F.L. Paxson, *Recent History of the U.S.*, p. 275.) A Harvard historian, Archibald C. Coolidge, remarks blandly: "It was not merely that the Americans had a natural sympathy for the insurgents as a people striving to free themselves from tyranny, but they were tired of a commotion at their very door." (Archibald C. Coolidge, *U.S. As a World Power*, p. 128.) And Chester Lloyd Jones ably sums up as follows: "At the end of the century the U.S. came into conflict with Spain the results of which made her a holder of both Caribbean and Asiatic colonies. This war, however, was a development of no conscious imperialism, and one but slightly, if at all, connected with the movement for increased colonial holdings in which the European powers had been engaged." (Jones, *Caribbean Interests of the U.S.*, p. 19.)

And to prove that the American people were acting from no selfish motives, Congress proclaimed that it had no annexations in mind, passing the Teller Resolution on April 18, 1898, after a week's debate on McKinley's war message.

The Teller Resolution stated: "That the U.S. hereby disclaims any disposition or intention to exercize sovereignty, jurisdiction or control over said Island except for the pacification thereof and asserts its determination, when that is accomplished, to leave the government and control of the Island to its people." The authority from Harvard tells us that "this self-denying ordinance was voted in a moment of excitement, and in all sincerity." (Coolidge, p. 129.)

And another authority swears, "This . . . resolution gave the war the appearance of altruism and was undoubtedly sincerely approved by the great majority of Americans." (A.L.P. Dennis, p. 75.)

To introduce a slightly sour note into this symphony of excitement, altruism, and sincerity, we quote from still another authority. Months before the battleship *Maine* was sunk (on September 21, 1897), one Theodore Roosevelt, the then assistant secretary of the navy, wrote to another gentleman not unknown to Harvard, Henry Cabot Lodge, that in the event of war: "Our Asiatic squadron should blockade and if possible take Manila." Lodge, replying a little later, remarks with satisfaction: "Unless I am utterly and profoundly mistaken, the Administration is now fully committed to the *large policy* that we both desire." (Our emphasis.) They at least seemed to know what was at stake, and how to get it.

As we already know, an uprising occurred in Cuba. Spain was

very sorry, and very ready to conciliate. Suddenly the *Maine* blew up in Havana harbor.

Remember the Maine! To Hell with Spain! To hell with peace talk. The war was on. No sooner were hostilities declared than, strange to tell, a national uprising immediately flared in the Philippines—far, far away in the Pacific Ocean, and belonging to Spain. Through a mysterious coincidence, the American "Asiatic" fleet happened to be nearby. Battleships and revolutions have an affinity. Since the Americans did not want to have their ships blown up, there was nothing to do except to attack Manila and blow up the Spanish fleet . . . although, as a newspaper wit remarked at the time, the American people "didn't know whether they [the Philippines] were islands or canned goods."

The American people were dumbfounded. "Astonishment bordering upon bewilderment seized the American public. . . . that it [the war] should have reverberations in the Orient was beyond comprehension. Slowly it was understood that freeing Cuba was not a simple proposition." (Shippee, p. 244.)

Such a slow and complex proposition deserves a little attention. We shall try to establish a few facts about this happy coincidence. Everybody knows what Dewey did once he got to Manila and fired another "shot heard around the world." But who got Dewey to Manila? Who timed the long, long journey so nicely? None other than our frank correspondent, the mere assistant secretary.

"The vessels on the Asiatic station had recently received a *new commander,* after a fortunate selection which was *less due to merit than to politics.* Assistant Secretary Roosevelt was reponsible for the detail of George Dewey to post. . . ." (F.L. Paxson, p. 279.)

Obviously, we are dealing with people who are fortunate in everything they do!

But let us hear more about Roosevelt's "own" actions: "*In advance* of the message of April 11 [McKinley's war message to Congress] he [T.R. himself] had taken the responsibility of ordering Dewey to proceed to Hong Kong there to clean ship and outfit, and thence in the event of war to proceed to Manila. . . ." (Ibid.)

When Dewey, who was appointed not so much on merit as because of "political considerations," arrived in Hong Kong, he was shocked by the news that the eventuality had become a fact. "Three days after the beginning of the war, on April 25, a British proclamation of neutrality made it impossible for Dewey to continue at Hong Kong. The war itself had brought into operation the orders he had received from Secretary Roosevelt." (Ibid., p. 276.)

This is corroborated by L. B. Shippee who says: "In accordance with plans worked out largely [!!!] by Theodore Roosevelt, Assistant Secretary of the Navy, Commodore Dewey, commanding the Asiatic squadron, proceeded from his station at Hong Kong to the Philippines. There was little else to do: Dewey could not remain at Hong Kong without being interned for the duration of the war; the only alternatives were making for a home post, thousands of miles away, or striking at and securing some position upon enemy territory. . . . " (*Recent American History*, p. 244.)

But Dewey apparently did more than he was instructed. For in addition to "cleaning ships, etc.," he somehow got in touch with Aguinaldo, who was the leader of the previous native revolt against Spanish rule. Dewey made a deal with Aguinaldo. There has been considerable controversy over this deal. "Even today just what sort of arrangement was made between Dewey and the Filipinos is in doubt." (Shippee, p. 257.) It is generally agreed that it was an unfortunate misunderstanding. Aguinaldo insists that Dewey had promised him independence for the Philippines. Dewey on his part violently denies this. True, a misguided historian like N. W. Stephenson asserts rashly that Aguinaldo set up a nominal republic which "Dewey recognized as if it were an actual state." (*A History of the American People*, p. 989.) But as Archibald C. Coolidge correctly points out: "The American government . . . gave Aguinaldo no promise whatever. Indeed, Admiral Dewey and the consul at Hong Kong could in no wise commit the administration in a matter of such importance." (*U.S. As a World Power*, p. 153.)

The entire trouble arose as a result of the fact that the negotiations were carried on by word of mouth through an interpreter. We cannot do better than quote Coolidge again:

> There has been much heated discussion about the extent to which the Americans committed themselves to the support of Aguinaldo in their original compact with him. . . . In trying to reconcile the different versions of what was agreed upon, it must be remembered that the negotiating was done through an interpreter. Translations of this kind, with the best of intentions and every precaution are notoriously unsafe. . . . We have no proof that the words exchanged between Aguinaldo and Mr. Wildman in Hong Kong, in May 1898, were correctly rendered from one to the other. Who knows whether the interpreter even

tried to be exact? And admitting he did, a misunderstanding is easy to conceive. (p. 153.)

One thing is clear: Aguinaldo was left with the consoling thought that "misunderstandings" of this sort must have played a considerable role in the history of capitalist expansion. Thanks to this misunderstanding the Filipinos fought and died for the rule of the Yankee imperialists while thinking that they were fighting for their own independence.

Aguinaldo and his Filipinos were very badly needed. The American imperialists had a few difficulties to overcome before their plans could be smoothly realized. First, there were the dumb and pathetic Populists and Democrats, who unfortunately had too many votes in Congress, and who had to be led by their noses carefully lest they upset the applecart. They made enough trouble as it was with their "altruistic" revolution, which made Whitelaw Reid foam at his mouth. But worse yet, McKinley, the figurehead as president, was in a constant panic lest somehow the entire sincerity and altruism should plop into the open. He was constantly getting down on his knees and praying, while others, like Roosevelt, were working away like beavers to provide against every possible contingency. Small wonder that our frank assistant secretary lost his temper and barked: "McKinley had no more backbone than a chocolate eclair."

True, Lodge kept hammering away, prodding and planning. Puerto Rico was already secure, but the Philippines were not quite so safe. In May 1898 (and a merry month it must have been!) he writes to Theodore, who was then aching to become a real Rough Rider, that there was no hurry about Cuba but that substantial land and naval forces should be rushed to the Philippines. (See Beard, *Rise of American Civilization*, p. 375.)

But one cannot do everything at once . . . not even if one happens to be an imperialist par excellence, as all these gentlemen were. One has to wait for "consequences," and the "needs" that they engender.

"The immediate consequence of Dewey's victory at Manila was a need for an occupying army. . . . the fleet was destroyed but Dewey had no troops to grasp the fruits of victory. . . ." Emilio Aguinaldo was brought to the islands (what foresight!) "for the purpose of keeping the revolt alive." (Paxson, p. 277.)

In short, no Filipinos "revolting"—no fruits to be plucked! But fortunately they were there to fight. Dewey made sure of that by bringing Aguinaldo on a warship. He also supplied him with money and ammunition. Meanwhile, McKinley made speeches. Said he: "There is a very general feeling that the United States, whatever it might prefer as to the Philippines, is in a situation where it cannot let go." Meanwhile, Secretary of State Hay first proceeded to write remarkable diplomatic documents in which he said that the Philippine Islands must be allowed to remain with Spain, only to understand suddenly (on June 3, 1898) that this would have to be "modified" because "the insurgents there have become an important factor in the situation and must have just consideration in any terms of settlement." And finally (thank God), Lodge's instructions were carried out. General Merrill set sail with "an advance guard of two regiments" and arrived at Manila with "instructions to ignore Aguinaldo and establish a provisional government under American auspices." (Stephenson, p. 982.)

When we consider the difficulties under which this phase of American history was made, we stand aghast. One unforeseen difficulty after another! No sooner was Dewey really equipped to "grasp the fruits of victory," than the war unfortunately came to an end, that is to say, an armistice had been signed. (Lodge had warned that there was no hurry about Cuba, but even Roosevelt, it seems, was fallible.)

However, this was a mere technicality. Due to faulty communications the news did not arrive in time, and three days after the signing of the armistice, Merrill stormed Manila. Of course, the Filipino army was already there. But "Aguinaldo was induced to withdraw from Manila, pending the completion of the treaty." (Ibid., p. 982.)

The inefficient Spaniards raised a howl, insisting that an armistice was an armistice, no matter what sorts of faulty communications obtained, let alone "misunderstandings." But the American government flatly refused to accede to the demand that the status quo of August 12 be restored. However, it was ready to be broadminded. The American government accepted the "principle" that the islands had not been conquered. The Spaniards collected $20 million. But no doubt, the enlightened American commissioners all felt that it was not the money but the principle that counted. This commission was composed of Day (first secretary of state under McKinley), Davis (senator from Minnesota), Frye (senator from Maine), and Whitelaw Reid (editor of the *New York Tribune*)—all these men are admitted even by capitalist historians to have been "avowed imperialists."

No one was more qualified to settle the war than those who had started it. Besides, no one else could be trusted.

It transpired during the negotiations that Aguinaldo and his friends had entirely false notions on many subjects, their own importance included. "The insurgents, moreover, represented a relatively small group." (Shippee, p. 252.) And Paxson is able to say with a sigh of relief and sorrow in retrospect that: "The date of victory at Manila marks the entry of the United States *against its will* upon an imperial course." (*Recent History of the U.S.,* p. 277.)

When the unenlightened Filipinos finally realized what had happened to them "against their will," they tried to turn their guns against the Americans. And the unwilling Americans proceeded to teach them a few things about American concentration camps and American methods of civilizing backward peoples. Aguinaldo himself was finally captured in February 1901. Perhaps by then he was no longer capable of becoming astonished. After all, accidents can happen. But these are merely the flowers; the berries are still ahead.

If it was not another misunderstanding, it was certainly at least an accident that during this self-same Spanish-American War a revolution broke out . . . this time in the Hawaiian Islands, also in the Pacific Ocean; not, it is true, the property of Spain; yet, on the other hand, of tremendous naval importance.

Coolidge, the historian, informs us that according to the opponents of imperialism in the United States, "the revolution by which the Queen had been overthrown was a usurpation of power by a handful of foreigners who would never have succeeded but for the landing of American troops." (p. 134.)

The anti-imperialists were not merely muckraking. In 1893, a Committee of Public Safety "largely [!!!] composed of Americans and having the support of the American Minister Mr. Stevens, seized control of the government in Honolulu" and overthrew Queen Liliuokalani. (Dennis, *Adventures in American Diplomacy,* p. 103.)

Said Minister Stevens at the time (1893): "The Hawaiian pear is now fully ripe, and this is the golden hour for the U.S. to pluck it." The eloquent minister was a connoisseur of fruit, but he was mistaken in his "golden hour." Cleveland was then president, a man of inadequate girth and vision; a "larger" man was needed to herd the recalcitrant petty bourgeois in Congress.

Said McKinley in 1898: "We need Hawaii just as much and a

good deal more than we did California. It is manifest destiny."
The accommodating press screamed about the designs of the
Japanese (to say nothing of the Germans) on Hawaii. "Extravagant tales," comments one historian. Even more extravagant
congressmen yelled that American speculators had purchased $5
million of Hawaiian bonds at thirty cents on the dollar, and it
was they who wanted to annex Hawaii so that the United States
treasury would have to assume the responsibility for the
worthless Hawaiian paper. Of all creatures, the petty bourgeois is
the most extravagant! Sober men (Republicans) pointed out that
the "Hawaiian Islands were necessary to the defense of the
Philippines, which in turn were necessary to defend American
interests in the Far East." (Beard, *Rise of American Civilization,*
p. 375.) And sobriety carried the day.

"The annexation was carried out during the excitement of the
Spanish War, not by treaty—for fear that the necessary two-
thirds majority could not be secured in the Senate—but by joint
resolution of the two Houses of Congress." (Coolidge, p. 135.) As a
matter of fact it was *impossible* to secure the two-thirds vote of
the Senate, and that is why recourse was had to the device of
1845. McKinley signed the "joint resolution of annexation" on
July 7 (a few days after General Merrill had reached Manila).

All of which entitles American historians to say in chorus:
"Another unforeseen [?] result of the war affected the Hawaiian
Islands." (Shippee, p. 245.)

The Peace of Paris, December 10, 1898, liquidated completely
the colonial empire of Spain, the empire that had been crumbling
to pieces while so many hungry mouths were slavering. American
imperialists took practically everything: Cuba, Puerto Rico, the
Philippines (three thousand-odd islands), Guam, etc. What an
extraordinary and choice selection! An astounding harvest,
plucked in one "Golden War"! "Internationally there was
astonishment at the outcome." (Shippee, p. 245.) "To the greater
part of Europe the war itself, and the course which it took came
as an unpleasant surprise." (Coolidge, p. 130.)

There was good reason to gloat. A single glance at a map is
sufficient to make clear that here was no accidental colonial
grab—like that perpetrated by the German imperialists in their
day, or by Mussolini and his crew today—but a painstaking, fully
considered, consciously planned and executed preparation of U.S.
imperialism for its struggle to obtain the richest colonial prize in
the world—the outlets of the Orient fronting the Pacific Ocean.

"They gave the Americans a stronger strategic position in the Gulf of Mexico, and in the Caribbean sea, coaling stations in the Pacific, and a base of operations in the Far East." (Coolidge, p. 130.)

The Philippines are strategically located in respect to the most developed section of China, its southern section (Canton), just as Japan is located strategically in respect to northern China and Manchuria. At the same time the Philippines provide a "base of operations" in the struggle for the Dutch Indies, and (whisper it!) India itself.

The Hawaiian Islands are a midway base en route to the Far East of vital naval and military importance. Between the Hawaiian Islands, Asia, and Australia there is nothing except the Islands of Fiji. Therefore, as Mahan, the American naval expert, states, "the Hawaii are of utmost importance." As far back as 1892, when England and France toyed with the idea of plucking the Hawaiian "pear," the U.S. government flatly declared that it would not tolerate the colonization of these islands by any European power, and would intervene with force of arms if need be.

Puerto Rico flanks the British and French possessions in the Antilles. And as for Cuba, "Pearl of the Antilles," let us have an expert's appraisal of a jewel like that! "A glance at the map is enough to convince anyone of the unique importance of this island to the United States. Strategically it commands at one end the entrance to the Gulf of Mexico—the outlet to the huge Mississippi Valley—and at the other it fronts on the Caribbean Sea, and any *future isthmian canal*." (Coolidge, p. 124.)

The American imperialists could not take the bull by the horns and set to the task of solving the question of the Panama Canal, that is, of a direct route to Asia, unless they had first seized Cuba and Puerto Rico, unless they had beforehand guaranteed their key harbors to the Orient, and had established their "interests in the Far East" that must henceforth be so preciously protected.

After the Spanish-American War, "it [the United States] was now in a situation, as well as in a mood, to take up the *canal question* with an energy it had never before shown." (Coolidge, p. 275.) "The lessons of the Spanish-American War were clearly before the American people: *a canal* was an urgent necessity both from a naval and commercial point of view." (Dennis, p. 157.)

Thus the spoils of the Spanish-American War set the stage for the expansion of U.S. imperialism on the world scene.

A Forgotten Fighter
Against the Plutocracy

George Novack (1949)

Recent converts to capitalist "free enterprise" glorify this system of robber rule as the foundation of American democracy. However, the real traditions of plebeian democracy in the United States, especially since the Civil War, have been bound up with mass struggles against big business. Many antimonopolist battles have been waged under the banner of democracy by movements and individuals apart from the tendencies inspired and guided by Marxism.

However great their deficiencies in other respects, these forces at least correctly viewed the plutocracy as the deadliest enemy of the rights of the people. Until recently they occupied the foreground in American thought and politics. Their eclipse has been an integral part of the process by which the representatives of big business have sought to shove aside all critics and opponents of its regime.

The best of these standard-bearers of the antimonopolist crusade were known beyond the borders of this country. One of them was Richard Franklin Pettigrew, the first United States senator from South Dakota. Even in the midst of the reconstruction of the Soviet Union, Lenin, for example, found time to read Pettigrew's *Triumphant Plutocracy.*

In October 1922, Oscar Cesare, the American artist, went to sketch Lenin in his Kremlin office. Cesare told Walter Duranty the next day that he had murmured something about political opinion in America. Duranty quotes Cesare as saying that Lenin replied, " 'Yes, I've just been reading this,' and he held up a red-bound copy of Pettigrew's *Plutocrat Democracy* [sic]. 'It's a very fine book,' he said—and his eyes sparkled as he looked down at it." "I got the impression," Cesare commented, "that Lenin didn't admire the American political system as much as he admired the book."

Who was Pettigrew? What sort of man was this Republican senator that he could call forth Lenin's admiration? Lenin was not in the habit of praising bourgeois politicians or their works.

You will not find the answer to these questions in the best-known liberal histories of Pettigrew's period—in the Beards' *Rise of American Civilization,* in Kendrick and Hacker's *History of the United States Since 1865,* or in John Chamberlain's *Farewell to Reform.* As though to emphasize his obscurity, Pettigrew's name remains misspelled and the title of his book misquoted in Duranty's Moscow dispatches published in book form twelve years after Cesare's interview with Lenin.

It is only when we turn to Pettigrew's book that we begin to see why he has been obliterated from official historical memory. His book is a scathing indictment of monopoly rule besides which the writings of the muckrakers and speeches of the reformers seem pale and harmless.

As we delve deeper into the events of Pettigrew's career, we understand still more clearly why he has been cast into obscurity. Richard Franklin Pettigrew was not only a picturesque personality but an influential figure in national politics at the turn of the century.

Pettigrew's elimination from the political arena coincided with the defeat of the middle-class radicalism he represented. He was crushed by the political steamroller of the plutocracy as an obstacle to its concentration of power. In the process his reputation was so dishonored and his deeds so distorted that he has never been accorded his rightful place as one of the staunchest opponents of monopoly domination in American public life.

Pettigrew's resistance to tyranny carried forward his family traditions. Several ancestors fought in the Revolution and his father was an abolitionist who helped many slaves to escape through the Underground Railroad. Pettigrew was born in Vermont in 1848 and spent his boyhood in Wisconsin. After studying law at the University of Wisconsin and teaching school for a year in Iowa, he went to Dakota in 1869 to help in the government survey of the territory. At that time Dakota was on the fringe of the frontier, a region of wind-swept plains and badlands, dotted with military posts and sparsely settled with unfriendly Indians and homestead farmers.

Pettigrew started a law office and real estate business in Sioux Falls, the urban center of the territory, and lived there most of his life, practicing law, promoting business enterprises such as the Midland Pacific Railroad, and participating in the territorial government. When South Dakota attained statehood in 1889, he was elected to the U.S. Senate.

He served in that millionaires' club for twelve years from 1889 to 1900, when he was defeated for a third term. Although removed from the national scene at that time under circumstances we shall soon set forth, he kept in close touch with the major political events and personages until his death twenty-six years later. Thus for over fifty years Pettigrew had his finger on the pulse of American politics, during a period of tremendous transformations in American society.

Pettigrew entered public life as a member of the Republican Party, which had been launched as the upholder of freedom against slavery on the basis of an alliance between the northern bourgeoisie and the Free Soil farmers of the West. However, he was an independent Republican, never hesitating to oppose party policy on any issue that ran counter to his convictions or to the interests of the farmers and merchants of South Dakota.

His first major conflict with the Republican Party leadership and its boss, Mark Hanna, came in the presidential campaign of 1896 when Pettigrew led a large group of Free Silver Republicans in a dramatic walkout from the party convention, which nominated McKinley, into the camp of the Bryan Democrats. He quit the Republican Party forever once he saw that it had been totally converted into a tool of the capitalist oligarchy.

The campaign of 1896 was fiercely fought. The Populists, who had polled over a million and a half votes in the preceding presidential election, endorsed Bryan along with the Free Silver Republicans, while the Gold Democrats went over to McKinley's side. In this realignment of political forces only the Socialist Labor Party of De Leon retained its independence.

For the first time since the Civil War the masters of industry and finance felt that the machinery of the federal executive threatened to fall into unreliable hands. Two weeks before election day John Hay wrote to Henry Adams that Cleveland capitalists had visions of themselves hanging from lampposts on Euclid Avenue. The rulers of America had become frightened by their own propaganda; McKinley was reelected.

Although Bryan and his cohorts were repulsed, the insurgent

agrarians won victories in several western states. The most notable was South Dakota, Pettigrew's bailiwick, where the legislature had been captured by a Democratic-Populist coalition headed by former leaders of the Knights of Labor and the Farmers' Alliance, which proceeded to enact the first initiative and referendum measure in the United States. Populism in the West, as well as Pettigrew in the Senate, remained to plague the Republicans.

While the monopolists were consolidating their economic and political supremacy at home, they had been reaching out beyond the national boundaries for fresh markets and sources of raw materials, planting the first seeds of imperialism which were soon to flower in the "splendid little war" against Spain. For five years before the battleship *Maine* exploded in Havana harbor, the Senate had been the arena of combat between the imperialists and anti-imperialists over the question of Hawaiian annexation.

Pettigrew was the leader in the rancorous debates that punctuated the struggle in the Senate and cast the lone Republican vote in the last desperate filibuster of the anti-imperialists against the adoption of the annexation resolution in July 1898. His anti-imperialist speeches, gathered by Scott Nearing in a book entitled *The Course of Empire,* constitute a valuable record of the first steps of American imperialism in Hawaii, Cuba, and the Philippines.

A study of Roman and European history, a first-hand acquaintance with British imperialism gained from a trip to the Far East in 1897, and his daily contacts with the agents of the corporations had made him familiar with the forces behind imperialist enterprise. With the Pullman and Homestead strikes fresh in his mind, Pettigrew asserted that "the sum and substance of the conquest of the Philippines is to find a field where cheap labor can be secured, labor that does not strike, that does not belong to a union, that does not need an army to keep it in leading strings, that will make goods for the trusts of this country; and as the trusts dominated the St. Louis Convention and own the Republican Party, it is a very proper enterprise for them to engage in." Pettigrew warned the Republican Party that even as it "had come into being as a protest against slavery and as the special champion of the Declaration of Independence, it would go out of being and out of power as the champion of slavery and the repudiator of the Declaration of Independence."

He helped found the Anti-Imperialist League, which attracted a membership of over half a million people and became a center of popular agitation against McKinley's administration. Pettigrew received another lesson in the interrelations between imperialist politics and monopoly when Andrew Carnegie, one of the League's original backers, withdrew financial support after the House of Morgan, organizers of the Steel Trust, warned him that the tariff dependent on McKinley's reelection was essential to the consummation of their plans.

In following the trail of corruption left by the captains of industry and finance, Pettigrew was led to the inner sanctum of the Republican high command and the Senate seat of Mark Hanna himself. Hanna was the Bismarck of big business. Ever since "Dollar Mark" had come forward, Pettigrew hated him and all he represented. When Hanna entered the Senate, a clash between the two was unavoidable, and they soon engaged in a duel epitomizing the struggle between the declining agrarian democracy of the West and the industrial magnates of the East.

Pettigrew first grappled with Hanna during the spring session of the Senate in 1900 in a dispute over antitrust legislation. The Steel Trust had been caught submitting bids to the Navy Department asking four times the average cost of production for armor plate. The antimonopolists countered with a proposal to build a government armor-plate factory unless the steel manufacturers reduced their prices.

As Hanna was marshalling his men to combat this move, Pettigrew hurled a thunderbolt into the Senate. He told how a wealthy shipbuilder named Cramp had given $400,000 to the Republican campaign fund of 1892 in return for promised contracts from the incoming administration. Cramp had complained to Pettigrew that his contribution had been "misused" to line the pockets of members of the Republican National Committee.

The Republican leaders tried to ignore this accusation until they began to be baited by the Democrats for their failure to reply. In view of the approaching fall election, this challenge from the Democratic side of the Senate could no longer be left unanswered. Thereupon Senator Carter, who had received the $400,000 from Cramp, rose to defend the honor of his party by an attack upon Pettigrew's character and a shout that "those who lie down with dogs must expect to get up with fleas." Hanna followed with the curt statement that "he considered the accusation unworthy of notice and declined to dignify it with a reply." He neglected to mention that an investigation might have proved extremely embarrassing since Cramp, who had been visited in the interim by a Republican delegation, stubbornly declined to deny Pettigrew's story until he got back his $400,000.

After Carter and Hanna had spoken, Pettigrew delivered his second blow. He charged that Hanna had bought his way into the Senate. His assertion was based upon a pending petition, signed by four out of the five members of the Ohio Senate Committee on Elections, asking the U.S. Senate to inquire into Hanna's bribery of two members of the Ohio legislature. Hanna dared not keep silent in the face of this personal accusation. Flushed with anger, he jumped up from his chair, which happened to be directly in back of Pettigrew's, and began an indignant but inadequate defense of his probity in business, politics, and personal life. He wound up with a warning to Pettigrew that judgment day was at hand and accounts between them would be settled at the coming election.

This was Hanna's maiden speech in the Senate. Chauncey Depew later characterized it as "not so much of a speech as an explosion." Luckily Hanna did not have to rely on his speeches to retain his seat. The Senate Committee on Elections, packed with regular Republicans, refused to pursue the investigation further, despite protests from the Democratic minority.

The presidential campaign of 1900 caricatured the contest of 1896. The same candidates, the same issues; but four years of prosperity and a successful war against Spain had seated the Republicans firmly in the saddle.

McKinley's reelection was a foregone conclusion. The chief task of the Republicans was to sweep away the strongholds of populism in the Middle West. Political strategy and personal hatred combined to make Pettigrew and his fellow agrarians the focus of attack; Mark Hanna, as campaign manager, was eager to drive the nails into their political coffins with his own hands.

When the rumor spread through Washington during the summer of 1900 that Hanna was preparing to make a speaking tour of the farm belt, the Republican leaders were alarmed. Hanna might be shot by one of those crazy Populists, and even if he was unharmed his presence might offend the farmers and turn them against the Republican ticket. His already celebrated feud with Pettigrew was more than likely to redound to Pettigrew's favor if he showed himself in South Dakota. Armed with these arguments, Hanna's friends protested in person and by letter against the expedition—and Hanna growled: "Isn't it nice to be told that you're not fit for publication?" McKinley himself sent the postmaster general to dissuade Hanna. "Return to Washington and tell the President that God hates a coward," was Hanna's command to the envoy.

Amid the fears and prayers of the Republican leaders Hanna set out after his prey. Lest the goal of his trip seem too manifest, Hanna looped his itinerary through Iowa and Nebraska, Bryan's home state. But his route converged on the den of the "rattlesnake Pettigrew" in South Dakota. Teddy Roosevelt, the vice-presidential candidate, exposed the animus behind Hanna's mission when he joined the chorus howling for Pettigrew's scalp. "Good Lord," he telegraphed Boss Platt of New York, "I hope we can beat Pettigrew for the Senate. That particular swine seems to me, on the whole, the most obnoxious of the whole drove."

Hanna mobilized his full resources to effect Pettigrew's defeat. He handed out free railroad passes, reckless promises, adroit flattery to key citizens. A battery of celebrities was brought into South Dakota to blast away at Pettigrew. Vast sums of money were put in the hands of local leaders to buy votes.*

Shortly before the election, Hanna had the state polled and discovered that Pettigrew might win by a few thousand votes. The alarm was sounded. Hanna raised a special fund of $500,000 among the railroad interests, trusts, and financial institutions. According to Pettigrew, the Republicans visited every banker in every country town of the state and deposited a sum of money together with instructions on the part they were to play in the campaign. Farmers were promised ten dollars before and ten dollars after the election if they voted right. After these preparations, Hanna returned home and awaited the results.

About ten o'clock on election night, Hanna telephoned from Cleveland to his private secretary in Chicago for news of the balloting. He was told that McKinley was undoubtedly elected. "Oh, I know that," Hanna replied, "but how about Pettigrew?" "Pettigrew is undoubtedly beaten," his secretary assured him. "If

---

*Although the Seventeenth Amendment to the Constitution was not ratified until 1913, many states, especially in the West, had already adopted the direct election of U.S. senators by the year 1900. In these states the legislators, who were empowered by the Constitution to elect U.S. senators, were required to cast nondiscretionary ballots in accordance with mandatory instructions from the voters.

you are sure of that," said Hanna, "I can go home and to sleep. I wanted to accomplish two things in this election—to elect McKinley and to beat Pettigrew—and I did not know which I wanted most!"

Dollar Mark's hatred of Pettigrew lasted to his dying day. In an oration at Hanna's funeral in 1904 Chauncey Depew alluded to their feud, stating that Pettigrew had written his political epitaph by opposing Hanna. "The titanic power the Dakota Senator had evoked was his political ruin."

Pettigrew's defeat at the polls climaxed the long campaign directed against him by the political hacks of big business. They could not enjoy the sweets of office in comfort so long as he remained in the Senate. They winced whenever he arose, not knowing what he might reveal nor whom he might attack. As he unfolded his exposures, according to Washington correspondent Charles Willis Thompson, "they shivered silently and were thankful when he was through with them." Thomas Beer relates how Senator Cushman Davis, the wit of the Senate, greeted Pettigrew's approach one day with the remark: "Here comes pale malice." John Hay described him as "a howling lunatic."

During the Spanish-American War the yellow press damned Pettigrew as pro-Spanish and pro-Filipino. Soon the respectable journals set to work discrediting him. They manufactured a picture of Pettigrew as a venomous fanatic. The following portrait of Pettigrew by Thompson, a conservative, shows how his chromo was tinted and twisted.

Pettigrew was a malicious minded man whose guiding star was hatred. His sole pleasure lay in hurting somebody. He was suspicious to an almost insane degree, and saw evil in every action of other men. He had an uncanny genius for tormenting people. He was so skillful in hurling his poisoned darts that men were afraid of him, and let him go unrebuked; though one day a Senator who was his direct antithesis in character, sturdy, jolly, open-hearted Ed Wolcott of Colorado, who feared no man, woke the Senate echoes with a speech painting Pettigrew as one "who views the world with jaundiced vision" and who, "when the sun shines sees only the shadow it casts." Pettigrew listened with a white face that grew whiter, and when Wolcott ended, he made a low-voiced bitter reply that sounded to me like the hiss of a rattlesnake.

The facts we have presented enable us to see the reality behind this malicious caricature. Pettigrew's "insane suspiciousness" meant that he was alert to the maneuvers of the money power and ready to expose them fearlessly. He was called a "rattle-snake" not because he menaced the people, but because his thrusts were dreaded by the sycophants of the rich and the purveyors of corruption in high office.

Estimates of Pettigrew differed according to the reporter's sympathies. Charles Edward Russell, a socialist journalist, declared that Pettigrew had one of the coolest, clearest, and steadiest minds he had ever encountered in a long acquaintance with public men of affairs. His speeches confirm that impression. They are eloquent, firmly knit, well informed, and keenly perceptive of the immediate and long-range bearing of the issues involved. No, Pettigrew was regarded as a Wild Man from the West, defamed, and driven from public office not because he was a half-demented crank, but because he would not bend his knee in homage to the plutocracy.

During his active political life, Pettigrew moved in the social orbit and shared the political point of view and provincial prejudices of the middle western farmers and merchants among whom he lived. He was an ardent patriot given to spread-eagle spouting ("I yield to no man in my devotion to my country and my flag"), an antimonopolist, Free Silverite, Single Taxer, and semiprotectionist. His prejudices stand out in his mixed motives for opposing Hawaiian annexation. He not only declared that imperialism endangered democracy, violated the Constitution, threatened the dignity and character of American labor, but that the tropical natives were debauched, unchaste, unfit, and incapable of self-government.

Like other reformers he sought to curb the power of the trusts by placing the bridle of government regulation upon them. He had yet to realize that the monopolies could not operate without controlling the federal government which was supposed to control them. In 1897 Daniel De Leon saw in the trusts not only the growing centralization of capitalist ownership and wealth, but also the material prerequisite for socialized industry. The task was not to break up the capitalist combines or regulate them, but to deprive the monopolists of their economic and political strangleholds through the rule of the working class. While not unsympathetic to De Leon's socialist viewpoint, Pettigrew still hoped to reverse the wheels of economic development and return to the bygone era of free competition.

Although Pettigrew lacked the insight into the laws of capitalist development and the nature of the state which

Marxism had given De Leon, he nevertheless learned many things in the harsh school of struggle with his own bourgeoisie. He grasped the character of capital ("capital is stolen labor and its only function is to steal more labor") and the connection between free land and capitalist democracy ("free land makes a free people").

In 1900 the American Red Cross invited Pettigrew to contribute to a symposium on the topic of progress in the nineteenth and twentieth centuries. Here is the essence of his views on the character of our epoch:

> The early years of the century marked the progress of the race toward individual freedom and permanent victory over the tyranny of hereditary aristocracy, but the closing decades of the century have witnessed the surrender of all that was gained to the more heartless tyranny of accumulated wealth. . . . I believe the new century will open with many bloody revolutions as a result of the protest of the masses against the tyranny and oppression of the wealth of the world in the hands of the few, resulting in great progress toward socialism and the more equal distribution of the products of human toil and as a result the moral and spiritual uplifting of the race.

After leaving Washington, Pettigrew went to practice law in New York City, where he could observe the capitalist overlords at work in their private demesnes. Although he never again held public office, he participated in all the movements of middle-class insurgence against the unrestrained domination of Wall Street. He was a delegate to the Democratic national conventions of 1904 and 1908, serving as a member of the platform committee and chairman of the subcommittee on the tariff planks and the Philippines.

When Woodrow Wilson became the Democratic nominee in 1912, he concluded that the Democratic Party was no less irremediably tied up with big business. He termed Wilson "the worst Tory in the United States." He transferred his allegiance to Theodore Roosevelt's Progressive Party, wrote the original draft of its platform, and helped carry South Dakota for Roosevelt in 1912 as he had carried it for Bryan in 1896. With the collapse of the Progressive Party venture, he severed all political affiliations and became a man without a party.

The outbreak of the First World War and the entrance of the United States into the conflict came as no surprise to this old student of imperialism. Early in the nineties he had predicted that the first step of the United States in acquiring "the tainted territory of Hawaii by a robber revolution" would be fast followed by the taking of the Philippines, Puerto Rico, and Cuba and the conquest of South America. The first parts of his prophecy were fulfilled in short order; the second was being realized during the early decades of this century.

When the United States went into the war, Pettigrew openly declared that if he had been in the Senate he would have voted against entry. He was indicted for sedition in Sioux City for making statements like this to a reporter: "We should never have gone into a war to help the Schwabs make $40,000,000 a year." He was never tried and the indictment was dropped. But he remained proud of his antiwar stand and kept the indictment framed in his home as one of his treasured possessions.

Later he wrote: "Capitalism produced the war. Capitalism profited by the war." He saw that the imperialist powers were preparing bigger and bloodier wars through the Versailles treaty and the League of Nations, which he characterized as another Holy Alliance against Soviet Russia, the backward countries, and the defeated nations for the purpose of crushing socialism, safeguarding the British Empire, and uniting the exploiters against the exploited.

Upon Harding's election in 1920, Pettigrew had to admit that his fight for the preservation of democracy within the framework of bourgeois politics had been irrevocably lost. Like Grant and McKinley before him, Harding was nothing but the puppet of the political gang who ran the Grand Old Party and acted as orderlies for the financial aristocracy. This aristocracy itself was no longer the invisible government but the open and undisputed possessor of state power. As Lincoln Steffens observed, "Washington was no longer the kept woman but the legally wedded wife of Wall Street."

Guided by these experiences and reflections, in the evening of his life Pettigrew sat down to review the political development of the United States since his youth. He was well equipped for the task. For a half century he had observed the real rulers of America. He had been on the inside of the big business of politics and the politics of big business. He had been personally acquainted with all the important men in the major parties, the members of the diplomatic corps, ten presidents, and the industrialists and financiers who oiled the political machines and made and unmade presidents. The fruit of this knowledge was his book *Triumphant Plutocracy,* privately published in 1922, and reprinted by Charles H. Kerr under the title of *Imperial Washington.*

Triumphant Plutocracy is Pettigrew's minority report on the degradation of American bourgeois democracy, a documented exposure of the methods used by the rich to capture the ship of state and steer it in line with their greedy desires. The book is like a magnifying glass which concentrates hitherto scattered rays of light on the dark deeds and hidden recesses of national politics since the Civil War.

Pettigrew was a homespun democrat of the frontier, truckling to no man and to no party, and standing unawed before official authority and manufactured reputation. He had known all the presidents from Andrew Johnson to Woodrow Wilson. This is his judgment of them: "These ten presidents were not brainy. They were not men of robust character. They were pliable men, safe men, conservative men. Many of them were usable men, who served faithfully the business interests that stood behind them."

Grover Cleveland he recalls as the chief actor in the scandalous bond transactions of 1894 and 1895, whereby Morgan and his fellow financiers dipped their endless chain of buckets into the treasury for a cool thirty million.

Teddy Roosevelt seemed to him an egotistic poseur who permitted lies to be spread about his heroic feats in the taking of San Juan Hill, using them as a political stepladder in his career, and who talked of "trust-busting" while sanctioning the purchase of the Tennessee Coal and Iron Company by the Steel Trust.

Wilson was a southern aristocrat who feared and despised the masses and who ran for reelection on the slogan "he kept us out of the war" while making preparations to enter it.

Even Bryan, whom he twice supported for president, was only "an American politician, vacillating, uncertain, overlooking the fundamental things, ignorant of the forces that were shaping American public life, incapable of thinking in terms of reality, but making phrases a substitute for thought."

There is scarcely a method of swindling the masses and appropriating the public wealth that Pettigrew did not encounter in his career and describe in graphic detail: land-grabbing by the railroads; the preemption of mineral lands and natural resources by predatory individuals and corporations; tariffs, trusts, and monopolies; railroad reorganization proceedings; the centralization and control of credit in Wall Street through the national bank system; the creation of a huge national debt; control of political parties by campaign contributions and of the judiciary by rewards of fat fees and sinecures. His book is a guide to the grand larceny practiced by the chief citizens of capitalist America between the close of the Civil War and the beginning of the First World War.

Pettigrew analyzes the roles played by the various branches of the government in defending and extending the power of the plutocracy. He spares no category of officeholders in his investigation: county and state officials, governors, representatives, senators, presidents, justices. He censures the lawyers for prostituting themselves and shedding all vestiges of integrity. "Under the ethics of his profession," he says scornfully, "the lawyer is the only man who can take a bribe and call it a fee." He lets loose ferocious blasts upon that holy of holies of the propertied classes, the Supreme Court, asserting that it usurped the lawmaking powers from the elected representatives of the people and ran roughshod over the Bill of Rights in one case after another.

Pettigrew did not confine his criticism to the bourgeoisie and its political servants. He pointed out the part assigned to the officials of the American Federation of Labor in fixing the yoke of capitalist control upon the shoulders of the working class. Gompers and the labor aristocracy, he says, entered into combination with the industrialists and aided their exploitation of the unorganized masses. The capitalists were thus enabled to buy off the upper crust of the working class by giving them a small share of their profits. The policy of pure and simple unionism, restricting trade union struggles to higher wages and shorter hours, played into the hands of the capitalist parties and helped perpetuate the system of wage slavery. When Gompers solicited his opinion on the trade union movement in 1911, Pettigrew insisted that trade unions should be universal, embracing everyone who toils in either farm or factory. Labor could not be emancipated, he said, until the lands and implements of production were cooperatively used and publicly owned. When Gompers denounced this as socialism, Pettigrew wrote him in 1916:

The position of the American Federation of Labor as represented by you is that of standing in with the corporations who employ labor to secure a part of what labor is entitled to and make the corporations divide with organized labor what they take from the public. . . . The only way to make a federation of labor effective is to combine all those who are producers of wealth in a political organization and take charge of the government and administer the government in the interests of the rights of man. It is now being administered in the interests of the rights of property and administered by the men who did not produce any of the property, but have stolen it from those who did produce it.

When the Bolsheviks took power in Russia, Pettigrew hailed the event as a beacon of hope for the international working class. "The war," he wrote, "was an affirmation of capitalism. The Russian Revolution was the answer of the workers. . . . It is the greatest event of our time. It marks the beginning of the epoch when the working people will assume the task of directing and controlling industry. It blazes a path into the unknown country, where the workers of the world are destined to take from their exploiters the right to control and direct the economic affairs of the community."

With these resounding revolutionary words Pettigrew draws to a close his story of public life in America from 1870 to 1920. His conclusions are clear and decisive. Democracy had been strangled by plutocracy. The society of free land and free competition that had inspired the democratic dream of the pioneers had been transformed into a society owned and ruled by a small oligarchy, which, in its insatiable greed for profits and world domination, was driving the United States toward the shambles of imperialism.

The issue before the American people was no longer democracy versus class rule, but socialism—the rule of the working class—or barbarism. With Jefferson and Lincoln, Pettigrew appealed to the historic and democratic right of revolt by the people against a governing class which represented neither the interests of the people nor the necessities of social progress. He urged the masses to rise from their enslavement and seize the power and property that were rightfully theirs. A half century of struggle had convinced him that the entrenched plutocracy could not be otherwise overthrown.

Triumphant Plutocracy was Pettigrew's last testament to the American people. He died four years later in 1926 at the age of 78. He had traveled a long and winding road in the course of his political career and his final position was far from his starting point. He had entered the Republican Party soon after the Civil War, a devout believer in the virtues of capitalist democracy, the

Constitution, and the flag. As the bankers and industrialists tightened their grasp upon the economic and political life of the nation, throttling resistance to their ever-expanding power and plunder, extending their sphere of exploitation around the globe, Pettigrew, fighting them all along the way, gradually shed his illusions.

The clarity of his insight into the development and destiny of American monopoly capitalism deepened until at the end of his life this plebeian fighter for democracy began to see the dawning of a new light and a new era.

The Rise and Fall of Progressivism

George Novack (1957)

The present political course of the Communist Party of the United States is characterized not only by the crassest opportunism but by willful disregard for the lessons of our national past. The main political task of progressive Americans, declare the CP leaders, is the building of an antimonopoly coalition to curb the corporate interests and dislodge them from power. This is a praiseworthy objective, though it is hardly a new discovery. This same problem has faced the American people and the socialist movement ever since industrial capitalism acquired national supremacy and the trusts took over the economy following the Civil War.

From the 1870s on, there have been more than a few attempts to assemble an alliance of forces enduring and strong enough to defeat the monopolists. The highway of protest from the Greenback Party through the Populists up to Henry Wallace's Progressive Party is littered with the wreckage of the political vehicles patched together to do that job. None of them succeeded.

The Communist Party now proposes to succeed where all these failed by entering the Democratic Party and working in its left wing with other "progressive" elements. According to its representatives, the desired "people's antimonopoly coalition" may come about either by driving the reactionaries out of the Democratic Party or through the formation of a new third-party movement opposed to the old parties.

Neither of these programs is very new, although they may seem so to inexperienced people unacquainted with the American politics of the past seventy-five years. The history of the traditional left since the 1870s has been marked by oscillations between the alternatives of reforming the Democratic Party (and

349

even, on occasion, the Republican Party) or challenging the "Gold Dust Twins" with a "progressive" third-party coalition on an antimonopolist but not anticapitalist program. Both confined themselves to the aim of reforming capitalism, not replacing it with a workers' government and a publicly owned economy.

The Communist Party itself has gyrated from one of these positions to the other since the mid-1930s. From 1936 through 1944 it backed the Democratic candidates as the lesser evil and the more progressive hope in the national elections. Then in 1948 and 1952 it shifted a few degrees leftward by supporting the Progressive Party. Repentant, the CP has now swung back to more unabashed allegiance to the Democratic Party.

The CP leaders promise that the conditions are ripe this time for the realization of big gains for the working people and the Negroes through pressure-politicking within the Democratic machine. Before leaping back into the party of the plutocrats and the Dixiecrats, it might be helpful to appraise the results of previous efforts along this line by reviewing the state of the nation today.

The reformers opposed the growth of monopoly in our economic system and defended small business. Today big business and high finance are stronger than ever. In an editorial on May 13, 1957, *Life* magazine reported: "Big companies are getting bigger (the 50 biggest got 27% of all sales) and the smaller ones are having a tougher time, reflected at the moment in a rising rate of business failures."

Were the Progressives more effective in politics than in economics? Their principal aim was to oust the plutocrats from Washington and place the power of deciding national policies in the hands of the people. Today the monopolists and militarists dominate the government completely, ruling through a coalition of the two capitalist parties, which differ on incidental domestic issues but have basic unity on foreign policy. The liberals dedicated their movements to the defense and extension of democracy at home. Yet it was the most "liberal" Democratic presidents—Wilson through the Palmer Raids, Roosevelt through the Smith Act, and Truman through the loyalty purge—who delivered the greatest blows to civil liberties. Finally, the Progressives aimed to maintain peace within the framework of reforming capitalist imperialism. The United States has had three wars in this century. All of them were headed by Democratic presidents, favorites of the liberals.

Such are the facts. How are they to be explained?

The CP leaders talk glibly nowadays of the need to "apply Marxism-Leninism creatively" to the problems of American politics. They ought to start by using the methods of Marxism to analyze why all previous efforts to capture the Democratic Party for progressive purposes and to reform monopoly capitalism ended in bankruptcy. But they have reasons for refraining from such an investigation. For a Marxist examination of the rise and fall of the Progressive movement would not only illuminate the causes of the failure of reformism but likewise expose the fallacies of the current CP line, which follows in their well-worn track. Since they cannot be expected to perform this essential inquiry, we shall try to do it—not for the enlightenment of incorrigible opportunists, but for the education of the younger generation.

The last three decades of the nineteenth century were basically a period of tightening political reaction following the colossal revolutionary leap of the Civil War and Reconstruction. This "Gilded Age" saw the impetuous, almost uninterrupted rise of capitalist forces in the United States and on a world scale. Despite minor and puffed-up reforms, the triumphant plutocracy was energetically consolidating its grip over the major spheres of our national life.

The ever-harsher domination of the capitalist oligarchy encountered resistance all along the way from the masses. These were divided into three important sections: the agrarian producers, the urban middle classes, and the industrial workers. The currents of protest welling forth from the depths of the people were mostly movements of reform which aimed to curb, control, or reverse the processes of capitalist concentration in economic, political, and cultural life. Outright revolutionary voices were rare, and working-class tendencies bent upon the abolition of capitalism were in their infancy.

The principle large-scale political struggles were waged between the agents of the plutocracy and the representatives of the liberal petty bourgeoisie who headed the plebeian masses. Except in industry itself, the proletariat was as yet a subordinate factor in national affairs. The mainstream of political opposition came from the Populist-Progressive movement, which had its direct social base in the middle-class elements of the country and city. The proletarian currents at various times ran parallel to this mainstream, fed from it, or even emptied themselves into it.

The life cycle of the Progressive movement, its rise, its periodic fluctuations from effervescence to stagnation and back again, its decline and disintegration, can be charted in close connection with the economic development of American capitalism. The Progressive movement was a political product of the post–Civil War era. It was born during the hard times following the panic of 1873 and gained new impetus from each succeeding economic crisis.

The 1892 platform of the Populist Party, as summarized by Charles and Mary Beard in *The Rise of American Civilization*, made the following indictment of the "Gilded Age" of capitalism.

. . . that America was ruled by a plutocracy, that impoverished labor was laid low under the tyranny of a hireling army, that houses were covered with mortgages, that the press was the tool of wealth, that corruption dominated the ballot box, "that the fruits of the toil of millions are boldly stolen to build up colossal fortunes for a few unprecedented in the history of mankind; and the possessors of these in turn despise the republic and endanger liberty." (p. 210.)

The movement reached the peak of its social energy and political influence in 1896, when its aims ostensibly were adopted by the Democratic Party, and Bryan led the Progressive hosts in an attempt to dislodge the finance capitalists from power in Washington. After Bryan's defeat, the Spanish-American War, and the ensuing prosperity, the Progressive movement died down except in the rural districts. It was revived by the crisis of 1907 and took on several new shapes, culminating in 1912 in Theodore Roosevelt's Bull Moose crusade and Wilson's New Freedom.

The entry of the United States into the First World War dealt a mortal blow to the Progressive cause but did not completely dispose of it. After a regional revival in the agrarian Northwest, the movement had a spasmodic national resurgence in the La Follette campaign of 1924, which was a belated response to the consequences of the postwar crisis of 1921. Even then the force of the movement, which had so many decades of struggle behind it and so many hopes deposited with it, was not wholly spent. In his speeches against "the economic royalists," Franklin D. Roosevelt skillfully exploited Progressive sentiments and traditions to win support for his New Deal. His ex-vice-president, Henry Wallace, aided by the Stalinists, sought in vain to resurrect the corpse of Progressivism as late as 1948.

In all these incarnations, the Progressive movement has been middle class in body and spirit. In the earlier stages of its career, in the Greenback, Granger, and Populist trends of the seventies and eighties, it was based upon the farmers of the Middle West and South, pulling behind it the radicalized workers and urban middle classes and effecting alliances with them. The programs of the Greenback, Granger, and Populist movements largely expressed the interests and formulated the demands of these aroused and oppressed small farmers, and they had rural leaders.

Later the Progressive movement came to lean more and more upon the city masses and the rising industrial workers. This shift in the base of the Progressive movement resulted from the diminishing importance of the rural population and the increasing power of labor in American society. This change in the social composition of the Progressive ranks was reflected in the character of its principal leaders. "Sockless" Jerry Simpson, General Weaver, Ignatius Donnelly, Mary Ellen Lease ("Let's raise less corn and more hell"), and Tom Watson were representative figures of its Populist period. Robert La Follette, Sr., may be regarded as a leader who bridged the country and the city—a link between organized labor and the rural sections of the movement.

In their heyday the Populist-Progressives constituted the left wing of the capitalist regime. As a loyal opposition, they did not desire to abolish but rather to moderate the despotism of the plutocracy, to curtail its powers and reduce the privileges of the magnates of industry and finance. The principal planks in their economic platforms expressed the interests and put forward the demands of various sections of the middle classes—from the farmers to the small businessmen. This was true of such Populist money panaceas as greenbackism and bimetallism and of such reforms as the graduated income tax and the regulation of the monopolies.

The Progressives did not dream of going beyond restricting the power of King Capital, his moneyed aristocracy, and his favorites. To dethrone this despot by expropriation and thereby end the rule of his nobles forever—that was regarded as socialism, anarchism, the end of civilization!

Even at their most radical, the political ideas of Progressivism did not transgress the boundaries of that bourgeois democracy which had been built upon competitive capitalism. The Progressives restricted their proposed reforms within the constitutional framework of the regime which had been laid down by the architects of the Republic following the First American Revolution, as defended and amended by the Civil War.

The Progressives sincerely believed—and still do—that the capitalist republic of the United States is the highest and final form of political organization. They could not conceive that progressive humanity might desire or create any other or better kind of government. As a gauge of their provincial backwardness in this respect, when Robert La Follette went to the Soviet Union in 1922, he invited the Soviet leaders to come and repay his visit in Wisconsin where, he assured them, they could see "a really progressive state"!

The Progressives wanted the machinery of the United States government cleansed of its more glaring aristocratic vestiges and its democracy perfected by the introduction of such reforms as the direct election of senators and judges. They sometimes stopped halfway even in the direction of democratizing the state apparatus. They campaigned, for example, to abolish the Supreme Court's veto power over congressional enactments but upheld the president's veto power, which is a relic of monarchical rule; they asked for direct election of senators on a state basis, but not the president on a national scale; they did not call for a single instead of a double system of national legislative bodies. Their demands for civil service reform and for cheap, honest, efficient administration even pleased a part of the ruling class which could get along without direct corruption or coercion of their political servitors.

Armed with these reform programs, the Progressives vainly stormed the fortresses of plutocratic power at periodic intervals from 1872 to 1924. They did manage by tremendous exertions to exact a number of concessions and reforms from successive administrations which felt their pressure. Occasionally, they even controlled some of the state governments.

Nevertheless, these reforms did not result in any basic changes in American life or reverse the processes of capitalist centralization and control. In some cases they even produced consequences contrary to those expected or promised. The laws curbing or breaking up the trusts did not halt but rather facilitated the growth of the monopolies. The income tax, which was to make the rich pay more for the costs of running the government, became converted into an engine for extorting the pay of the workers. The various electoral revisions failed to make the system more responsive to the voters' will; instead of breaking up the party machines, the primaries gave the bosses an additional instrument for handpicking their candidates.

Why did the Progressive movement display so little stability and stamina and end up in futility and despair? First, because of its class basis and social composition. The small property owners and those imbued with their psychology could not conduct a fight to the end against the big bosses. That would have involved abolishing the economic and social ground upon which they themselves stood.

Their interests, their hopes, and their outlooks were bound up with the maintenance of the capitalist system, whose prosperity they wanted to share. They showed this by dropping the struggle time and again, whenever the system temporarily showed its smiling side to them. Just as every economic depression reanimated the fighting spirit of the Progressive forces, so every period of capitalist revival cooled them off.

Moreover, when the fate of the capitalist regime was at stake, the Progressives did not intervene as a decisive and independent power, following their own line, but rallied to the side of the plutocratic rulers. This happened at every great historical turning point, from the first imperialist venture—the Spanish-American War—to preparation for a Third World War. John Dewey's support of the Democratic administrations in all the wars of the twentieth century was typical of the entire movement.

Progressivism, as a social movement and a political product, belonged to the epoch of ascending competitive capitalism and was laid low by the subsequent epoch of monopoly capitalism in the United States. Its fortunes were bound up with the status of the middle classes which were first being uplifted by capitalist expansion (this gave them hope), and then being oppressed and ruined by the plutocracy (this gave them wrath and militancy).

As monopoly capitalism grew, the plutocracy heightened its power while the numbers and influence of the industrial proletariat expanded as well. But the economic, social, and political power of the middle classes, which were the backbone of the Progressive forces, declined, dragging their movement down with them.

After every losing battle with the entrenched plutocracy or ignoble surrender to its war program, the Progressives lost more of their strength, self-confidence, and mass support. Without broad historical perspectives or bold revolutionary aims, unable to grasp the dynamics of the principal forces at work in the world and in American society, the movement progressively lost whatever progressive aspects it once possessed.

On the one hand, its traditions shriveled into empty phrases which served to cover the procapitalist policies of such Democratic demagogues as Roosevelt and Wallace. On the other hand, whatever was vital in those traditions was absorbed by the Socialist, Communist, and labor movements.

The fundamental reason for the failure of Progressivism lay in the fact that it was progressive only in its incidental features. At bottom it was a retrograde movement which aspired to turn back the wheel of history and reverse the development of modern society. The Progressives longed for a return to the childhood of American capitalism while it was maturing into imperialism. This impotent yearning for an irrecoverable past gave the movement its basically reactionary direction and enveloped it in a utopian atmosphere.

The Progressives demanded greater equality, wider opportunities, peace, the extension of democracy, the sharing and spreading of wealth—all within the boundaries of capitalism. They received in increasing measure more inequality, fewer opportunities for fewer people, wars, the growing concentration of wealth, and political autocracy along with it. These were the natural fruits of monopolist rule launched upon its imperialist phase.

The Populist-Progressive movement had a colossal significance for the American people in the late nineteenth and early twentieth centuries. This many-sided mass movement of protest against the reactionary rule of big business and high finance made a deep impression upon cultural and intellectual activity, providing the impulse for many creative forces and ideas and giving support to advanced tendencies and causes in American thought. The rebellion of the oppressed against the ideas, attitudes, and practices of the tyrannical money-masters was conducted on many fronts. This class struggle penetrated and modified not only economics and politics, but also the higher realms of education, morals, religion, literature, art, and philosophy.

This tremendous and sustained movement enlisted and engrossed the services of several generations of the best minds in many fields: politicians, economists, journalists, historians, writers, poets, philosophers. Indeed, in the balance sheet of the Progressive movement as a whole, its most fruitful and enduring work was accomplished in the field of general culture.

The Progressives didn't and couldn't create any lasting

political party of their own. Nor did they make any substantial changes in the American economy. They lacked the power and the will to revolutionize the political system and the economic structure of capitalism, or even to break with the basic ideas of bourgeois life. But they could and did strive to push the ideas and cultural institutions belonging to petty-bourgeois democracy to the limits of their development under the given conditions.

The expansion of free public education from the kindergarten to the state universities, the development of progressive education, the building of free public libraries, settlement houses, extension of the franchise, prison reform, the renewal of realistic literature, the revision of American history, the creation of pragmatism— these were typical accomplishments of the leading figures of Progressivism.

The instrumentalist philosopher John Dewey, for example, belongs wholly to this movement. He was a foremost participant in many of its most important enterprises. In time he became the supreme and unchallenged theoretical head of the movement. Dewey was not a leader of its plebeian masses, like Weaver or La Follette. He was rather the ideologist of the advanced intellectuals who worked out the theoretical premises and formulated the views corresponding to the mass movement in their respective spheres of Progressive activity. Dewey performed for the philosophy of Progressivism the same great work as Henry George and Veblen for its economics, Beard for its history, Parrington for its literary criticism, Holmes and Brandeis for its jurisprudence, Sandburg for its poetry.

This summary of the Progressive movement contains nothing essentially new; it reproduces ideas and observations made by scores of socialist writers in earlier decades which became commonplaces of radical thought. But all this is being obliterated by the new advocates of opportunism.

They argue that the Democratic Party provides the best arena for political activity because the masses of workers and Negroes support it. But this was no less true in earlier decades. Only a small minority of workers in this country have ever yet supported socialism.

The Communist Party's policy not only flies in the face of the urgent needs of organized labor and its socialist vanguard; it nullifies the advances achieved by previous socialist movements. It even denies the significance of its own origins. For it was precisely the recognition of the inadequacies of the middle-class reform crusades in theory and in practice that provided the impetus and the pioneer forces for the formation of separate labor parties and socialist parties from the 1880s on.

If it was realistic to transform the Democratic Party into an agency for working-class politics or to organize a "people's antimonopoly coalition" in some other way, then what was the point of building a Socialist or Communist Party on a working-class program? Why did Eugene Debs have to reject Populism and Bryanism and help launch the Socialist Party at the beginning of this century? Why did the left-wing forces have to form a Communist Party on an independent Marxist basis twenty years later? (We are not speaking of educational and propaganda groups spreading socialist ideas but of Marxist parties set up to challenge capitalist and reformist parties in elections, etc.)

We raise these questions to indicate that the uneasiness of so many Communist Party members over its present political course is well founded. The policy of penetrating and transforming the Democratic Party is unrealistic even on a pragmatic basis; it has been tried often enough before by other and more influential forces than the CP and found wanting.

If the conclusions of past experience do not suffice, then the fallacies of this project can be demonstrated on theoretical grounds by a Marxist analysis of the relations and requirements of the class forces at work in the United States today.

THE FIRST WAVE OF FEMINISM

The Suffrage Movement, 1848-1920

Debby Woodroofe (1971)

In spite of the important victories of the woman's rights movement, it is one of the most ignored and maligned chapters in American history. We grow up mocking our sisters who went before us, taught to think of them as sexually frustrated, hawk-faced spinsters who carried hatchets. We learn about Lincoln's self-sacrificing mother, but never about Charlotte Perkins Gilman. Our history has become an anecdote, thrown in for amusement between the lengthy descriptions of men's accomplishments. Morison's *Oxford History of the American People,* for example, gives the woman's suffrage movement a few sentences under a section on "Bootlegging and other sports."

The very name history has given our sisters—"suffragettes"— is itself a slander. "Suffragettes" was what the opponents of woman's rights called them. It was an epithet, coined to downgrade their historical significance. The women called themselves "suffragists," except in England where women in the most militant wing of the movement, the Women's Social and Political Union, led by Emmeline Pankhurst, called themselves suffragettes so they would not be confused with more moderate groups.

Our history is a weapon in our liberation. Dependent on the oppression of women, the rulers of this country do not want us to know that we have a history. They do not want us to know that through united struggle we have won important victories for our sex and can do it again.

We must recover our history ourselves. No one else will do it for us. The sources we have been given are full of falsifications which we must correct. And many we could learn from, such as the writings of the early suffragists themselves, have been relegated to obscurity. For example, when several Michigan feminists went to the library in Kalamazoo, where Lucy Stone once lived, to see if it had any of her papers, they found forty-three boxes of her writings in the library basement, long forgotten. It is up to us to bring our history out of mothballs, up from the dusty cellars, and learn from it so we can most effectively continue the struggle our sisters began.

Throughout history, the struggle of women for their liberation has waxed and waned according to the extent of general political radicalization in the society. The women's rights movement of the past century emerged at the height of the abolitionist struggle and ended in the 1920s—a period of deep reaction and conservatism during which most radical movements declined. It was not until another period of radicalism, the late 1960s, when young people were propelled into action by the Vietnam War, the oppression of Third World people, the reactionary role of the universities, that the women's movement regained the momentum it had lost fifty years earlier.

The founding members of the women's rights movement were active in the antislavery struggle. In fact, it was at an abolitionist conference in 1840 that the women's movement was given the initial impetus to move into action. A World's Anti-Slavery Convention was held in London that year. Several American women, among them Lucretia Mott, had been elected as delegates by their chapters. The convention, however, flatly refused to seat female delegates and relegated all the women to a remote gallery, sealed off from public view by a curtain, where they were to sit as silent spectators.

Lucretia Mott and Elizabeth Cady Stanton met in the gallery and spent many afternoons walking through the streets of London discussing their treatment at the conference. It was not the first time that women had run into male chauvinism in the antislavery movement. Many chapters refused to accept female members, forcing women to form their own societies. Mott and Stanton decided that women needed a convention of their own to demand equality and vowed to call one when they returned to the United States.

It was not until eight years later, however, when Lucretia Mott visited the Stantons at their home in Seneca Falls, New York, that the two finally began to put into practice what they had discussed in London. They placed an ad in the *Seneca Falls Courier* calling for a Woman's Rights Convention July 19-20,

1848. Over three hundred men and women from a fifty-mile radius traveled in wagons and on foot to this conference, which Stanton described as "the first organized protest against the injustice which had brooded for ages over the character and destiny of half the race." A Declaration of Sentiments, which has become the most famous document in the history of American feminism, was passed. It stated in part: "The history of mankind is a history of repeated injuries and usurpations on the part of man toward woman, having in direct object the establishment of an absolute tyranny over her."

The Declaration was modeled after the Declaration of Independence, and expressed the same demand for certain basic and inalienable rights. It asserted that the democratic freedoms won by the French and American revolutions should be applied to women also. A list of demands, including equal access to education and the professions, legal rights in marriage, the right to own property, to control one's own wages, to initiate court suits, and to speak in public, was passed unanimously. In fact, the only disagreement was over a demand raised by Stanton— woman's right to vote. Suffrage was considered "excessive," "premature," and an issue that would subject the movement to ridicule. This demand was very narrowly approved.

The Seneca Falls Convention did not come about simply as a result of the chance meeting of Mott and Stanton in that London gallery. To understand why that conference took place we have to look at its historical context. This was a period of extraordinary social ferment. In 1848 Karl Marx and Frederick Engels published the *Communist Manifesto*. In the United States, there emerged a plethora of reform movements, utopian communities, religious experiments, and a general attack on the laws inherited from England. Freedom for the slaves was the key social issue. In this general upsurge women played a major part. There were thousands of women's clubs—church auxiliaries, missionary societies, and cultural discussion groups. The most socially conscious women worked in the abolition movement, where they learned to conduct petition campaigns and organize public meetings—skills they would later use in their own interests. In speaking out against slavery, women won the right to speak in public.

It was also a period of expansion of educational opportunity for women. Oberlin College, the first to admit women, graduated its first female in 1841. Lucy Stone entered Oberlin in 1843. A few years before, she had sat in a sewing circle in Massachusetts, painstakingly making shirts to finance male students through theological seminary. One day she left unfinished the shirt she was working on and decided to go to college herself, even if she had to go to Brazil, at that time the only place women could study. When she left Oberlin, she vowed, "Especially do I mean to labor for the elevation of my sex." Gradually other colleges opened their doors to women, and many of the "Seven Sisters" women's colleges originated in this period.

Women were also entering industry in growing numbers. The textile mills of New England were among the first factories in the United States. With the invention of the power loom, the clothing industry shifted from the home to the factory, bringing many women with it. "Factory girl life" was packaged and sold to New England farm girls as a glamorous existence where one would live with other girls in a factory-run boarding house and participate in self-improvement, educational, and literary pursuits. Some justified the relegation of such menial, tedious factory work to women by assuming they would work for just a few years, experience economic independence, and then marry and return to the home. In this way, they felt, American industry could avoid the permanent class of wretched wageworkers that was developing in England.

Women workers of this period often worked from 4:30 a.m. to 7:30 p.m., averaging thirty-seven and a half cents a day, most of which they paid back to the factory for their room and board. Histories of women in the labor movement, however, record a not always docile response to these conditions. Dozens of strikes and walkouts protesting the frequent speedups and wage cuts occurred during the 1830s and 1840s.

As a result of expanding educational opportunity, the entrance of women into industry, and involvement in the ferment for social reform, many women developed a life outside the domestic circle. Expectations of equality were heightened. Women began to see themselves as having an existence independent of their husbands. The Seneca Falls Convention reflected this new consciousness.

In general, however, the Victorian concept of woman's role—as wife and mother—remained unchallenged. Women were looked upon as females who incidentally happened to be human. It was taught that God *Him*self had ordained that men and women have different roles, with man's realm being the world and woman's the home. As is still true today, all the attributes of a slave—domesticity, submissiveness, incompetence—were assigned to women and then elevated into virtues. As one man of the day said, "It is her province to *adorn* social life, to throw a *charm* over the intercourse of the world by making it lovely and attractive." Man's power over woman was taken for granted in much the same way the divine right of kings once was.

This conception of women as mere ornaments in men's lives was reflected in the law, where women had absolutely no civil status. They were pronounced "civilly dead" when they married, and remained legal minors if they did not marry. When divorced, they were not given child custody.

Their property legally belonged to their husbands and they did not even own the clothes on their backs. Likewise, wages they earned belonged legally to their husbands. Even if a husband was a drunkard who was not providing for the children, he could take his wife's earnings.

This was the context in which the Seneca Falls Convention was held. Considering the ideological and legal barriers against women being autonomous persons, the demands raised there for equality in education, in marriage, in the professions, and under the law were extremely radical. For the first time women saw that the source of their oppression was outside themselves and demanded of men, as Angelina Grimke said, "that they will take their feet from off our necks, and permit us to stand upright on the ground which God has designed us to occupy."

It is indicative of the disdain this society has for the history of women that the church in Seneca Falls that housed this first organizational emergence of the woman's rights movement has been torn down. This society, which makes monuments out of homes in which George Washington slept, let a gas station be built on the site, leaving only a marker on the sidewalk as a memorial!

Seneca Falls was the first of a series of regional and national conferences which took place yearly between 1848 and 1860. In 1850 in Worcester, Massachusetts, the first National Woman's Rights Convention convened. "The time is opportune. Come!" And over one thousand women and men did—Quakers, abolitionists, temperance workers, and housewives. Suffrage was rarely discussed. Elizabeth Cady Stanton remained one of its few advocates. Instead, the conventions focused on questions of poverty, education, employment, and abolition of slavery.

However, no new national organization came out of the gatherings.

One of the differences between the early woman's rights movement and the women's liberation movement of today, which is insisting on the right to all-female meetings where women make their own decisions about their own movement, is that men were always welcome at these conferences of the 1850s. In fact, male abolitionists such as Wendell Phillips and William Lloyd Garrison were regarded as leading spokesmen during this early phase of the woman's rights movement. The one exception to this practice of welcoming the participation of men was an 1850 conference in Salem, Ohio, where men were admitted, but not allowed to speak.

One participant reported: "Never did men so suffer. They implored just to say one word—but no—the President was inflexible—no man should be heard. If one meekly arose to make a suggestion, he was at once ruled out of order. For the first time in the world's history, men learned how it felt to sit in silence when questions in which they were interested were under discussion."

The Second American Revolution—the Civil War—broke out in 1861, interrupting the steady growth of the woman's rights movement. Its activists were drawn into war work, setting up relief camps and hospital services. The few women we do read about in history—Clara Barton, Louisa May Alcott—were part of this service work. Other women were spies, and some, disguised as men, actually fought in the Union army. Elizabeth Cady Stanton and Susan B. Anthony took another course. They distrusted Lincoln, fearing he might settle for a compromise with the southern slave states. Under their leadership, the Woman's Loyalty League was formed to fight for an unconditional end to slavery as the only way to end the war. The League collected over 400,000 signatures on petitions demanding of Lincoln that the slaves be freed immediately.

At the close of the war, women such as Stanton, Anthony, and Lucy Stone decided it was the time to fight for woman's suffrage. Suffrage was no longer considered an inopportune demand. The war raised women's confidence in themselves, and they felt that their war services gave them a claim on the nation. They fully expected the young and "enlightened" Republican Party to reward women with the vote simultaneously with extending it to Black men. But that did not happen.

The Republican Party advised female suffragists that it was now "the Negro's hour"; the vote should be granted to Black men first. They insisted that to add woman's suffrage to the Fifteenth Amendment would lead to its defeat, and accused women such as Elizabeth Stanton of selfishly jeopardizing the Black man's claim to citizenship.

Stanton's incisive reply to the implication that somehow the Blacks' claim to equality was more immediate than that of women was: "May I ask just one question, based on the apparent opposition in which you place the Negro and the woman? Do you believe the African race is composed entirely of males?" She cited the fact that Black women such as Sojourner Truth and Harriet Tubman had been just as involved in the antislavery movement as their brothers.

Even male abolitionists, who were the suffragists' oldest allies and were certainly conscious of their contributions, joined ranks with the Republican Party in asking women to defer their demand for equality to a later time. In many cases, they went so far as to tell women they did not need the vote; they could rule the world "with the glance of an eye."

The controversy over the Fifteenth Amendment created much bitterness and confusion in the woman's suffrage movement. Stanton, who had paternalistically said in 1864, "For the highest virtues of heroism, let us worship the black man at his feet," made the racist comment one year later, "Are we to stand aside and see Sambo walk into the kingdom first?"

Susan B. Anthony proclaimed: "I will cut off this right arm of mine before I will ever work for or demand the ballot for the Negro and not for the woman." The bitterness caused by being told to step aside exacerbated the racist attitudes ingrained in white women by the society of that period.

This tension between male abolitionists and woman's suffrage leaders precipitated a split in the women's movement. At an 1869 convention of the American Equal Rights Association, organized after the Civil War to fight for both Black and female freedom, Stanton proposed that the group focus on getting a woman's suffrage amendment added to the Constitution, no matter what its effect on the Fifteenth Amendment. Her proposal forced the other women present to clarify their position on Black male suffrage and whether or not woman's suffrage should be deferred to it. The result of this debate was the formation of two opposing groups—the National Woman's Suffrage Association and the

American Woman's Suffrage Association—destined to remain separate for twenty years.

The AWSA, hereafter referred to as the American, was centered in Boston. It made Henry Ward Beecher its president and was led by Lucy Stone and Julia Ward Howe, author of the "Battle Hymn of the Republic." The American deferred to the Republican and abolitionist plea to delay demanding a woman's suffrage amendment until Black suffrage was passed. Instead, the organization did propaganda work for woman's suffrage on a state level. Its attitude toward Black suffrage was summed up by Lucy Stone who said, "I shall be thankful in my soul if *anybody* can get out of the terrible pit."

The NWSA, or the National, based in New York, was led by Anthony and Stanton. It excluded men from its membership, convinced that it was the misleadership of men that was responsible for the American group postponing its fight for a woman's suffrage amendment. The National was not willing to wait any longer for woman's rights, and focused its energies on getting a Sixteenth Amendment enfranchising women. As Stanton wrote: "Wendell Phillips says, one idea for a generation, to come up in the order of their importance. First negro suffrage, then temperance, then the eight-hour movement, then woman's suffrage. So in 1958, three generations hence, thirty years to a generation, Phillips and Providence permitting, woman's suffrage will be in order."

A debate has been carried on in historical literature for many years over which group—the American or the National—took the correct position on the dispute over the Fifteenth Amendment. It is impossible to choose sides. Each was partially right; both made some mistakes. The National was absolutely correct to reject the concept of "one idea per generation" and to see no reason why both Blacks and women should not have been given the vote after the Civil War, a war whose ostensible principle had been that all people should be equal under the law. Furthermore, the National rightly understood what we have learned today: women have to depend on themselves and continue to organize against our oppression on a day-to-day basis, even when our allies drop away. This was where the American went wrong. By deferring their demands they gave credence to the notion that woman's suffrage was a secondary issue.

It was wrong, however, for the National to refuse to support suffrage for Black men. The strength of the American's position was its understanding that a victory for any oppressed group—

the fact that at least someone has been lifted "out of the terrible pit," as Lucy Stone put it—should be welcomed and regarded as laying the basis for other oppressed groups to continue the struggle. As historical developments subsequently proved, the victory of Black male suffrage strengthened women's demands for equal citizenship.

But to dwell on which group was right or wrong in this dispute is, in a sense, to make criminals out of victims. The real reason that the two wings of the woman's suffrage movement became set against each other over Black male suffrage lies neither with the National nor the American but with the emissaries of capitalism in the two political parties.

The Republicans were ready to grant the vote to Black men after the Civil War to help clinch their hold on the country. They later acquiesced in taking it away in the post-Reconstruction South. The Republicans falsely claimed that to fight for woman's suffrage would mean the defeat of Black suffrage. When Stanton once confronted a Republican politician with the fact that all the arguments he was using to gain support for Black male suffrage applied equally to woman's suffrage, he replied that he was "not the puppet of logic, but the slave of practical politics."

The Democrats responded no less opportunistically. Some of them spoke in favor of a woman's suffrage amendment, but their motive for doing so was that they thought they could defeat the Fifteenth Amendment by linking it with female suffrage. Thus, both capitalist parties did everything they could to divide the Black struggle and women's struggle, and to play the one off against the other.

Women today must still depend upon themselves to win their liberation. The Democrats and Republicans granted women the elementary right to vote only when suffrage demonstrations became so massive and public opinion so outraged that to continue to deny it became more costly to them than to grant it. They have betrayed us too many times for us not to have learned the necessity of political independence from the capitalist parties.

Most suffragists felt it was best to avoid discussion of the split in the movement and gave the breach little comment in their writings. Most historians explain the split as the result of tactical disagreements over Black suffrage and the Republican Party. Although this was certainly the issue around which the differences were precipitated, there are indications that the split also involved other very major disagreements, which had been brewing for a long time, over the source of female oppression.

That is, those who joined the American wing tended to view woman's subordinate status as based mainly on the fact that she was disenfranchised, while supporters of the National held the institution of marriage responsible for female oppression.

The National saw woman's rights as a broad question involving, as Susan B. Anthony said, "the emancipation from all political, industrial, social and religious subjection." Suffrage was supported not as the magic wand that would erase women's inequality, but as a basic democratic right they should have as citizens. Nevertheless, they were conscious that as long as woman remained tied to the home, she would remain a second-class citizen. As the National's paper stated:

> The ballot is not even half the loaf; it is only a crust, a crumb. The ballot touches only those interests, either of women or men, which take their root in political questions. But woman's chief discontent is not with her political, but with her social and particularly her marital bondage. The solemn and profound question of marriage . . . is of more vital consequence to woman's welfare and reaches down to a deeper depth in woman's heart and more thoroughly constitutes the core of the woman's movement, than any such superficial and fragmentary question as woman's suffrage.

The strengths of the National—that is, its understanding of the necessity for women to struggle day by day for control over their lives—laid the basis for its development into the most consistently radical, vocal suffrage group in history. Under the leadership of Anthony and Stanton, the National was the first (and only) group of that period to challenge the family institution. Feeling strongly that her place was with her sisters, and that her energies belonged to them and should not be exhausted through marriage, Anthony chose to remain single. In a letter to Lydia Mott in 1859, Anthony bemoaned the fact that:

> There is not one woman left who may be relied on; all have "first to please their husband," after which there is but little time left to spend in any other direction. . . . The twain become one flesh, the woman "we"; henceforth she has no separate work. . . . In the depths of my soul, there is a continual denial of the self-annihilating spiritual or legal union of two human beings. Such union, in the very nature of things, must bring an end to the free action of one or the other.

And she realized that this one was always the woman. She wrote later: "Marriage has always been a one-sided matter, resting most unequally on the sexes. By it man gains all; woman loses all; tyrant law and lust reign supreme with him; meek submission and ready obedience alone benefit her. . . . Woman has never been thought of other than as a piece of property, to be disposed of at the will and pleasure of man."

In addition to the women of the National, several individual women challenged the family institution. Charlotte Perkins Gilman carried the challenge further than did the National. Writing during a period of ever-increasing employment of women, she protested that they had to put in another day's work in the home after the day's work at the factories. She favored putting private housekeeping "into the archives of past history," and advocated communal kitchens, public housekeeping services, and child-care centers. She attacked "a family unity which is bound together with a tablecloth" as being of questionable value. And of motherhood, still considered sacred by her society, Gilman said, "Anybody can be a mother. An oyster can be a mother. The difficult thing is to be a person."

Gilman saw that the cult of the home oppressed all its members, stunted women "with the aspirations of an affectionate guinea pig," and was a phenomenon which would be utterly unnecessary in a society where the family was no longer a productive unit. She wrote:

Among the splendid activities of our age [the home] lingers on, inert and blind, like a clam in a horse race. . . . it hinders, by keeping woman a social idiot, by keeping the modern child under the tutelage of the primeval mother, by keeping the social conscience of the man crippled and stultified in the clinging grip of the domesticity of the woman. It hinders by making the physical details of daily life a heavy burden to mankind. Whereas in our stage of civilization, they should have been long since reduced to a minor incident.

Gilman's articles appeared in *The Revolution,* the newspaper of the National, as did similarly iconoclastic ideas. *The Revolution* claimed to speak in the interests of the most wretched of all women, and focused extensively on the double degradation of working women.

It also had the policy of taking the woman's side in controversial issues of the time—something no one else was doing. The Victoria Woodhull case was an example of this. Woodhull was a stockbroker on Wall Street, as well as an advocate of sexual freedom, faith healing, and woman's suffrage, who tended to operate as an individualist. When she announced her intention to run for president in the 1872 elections, she was ridiculed from all sides as a "free-love candidate," and attacked for living in the same house with both her current and former husbands. Only the National defended her right to run for office. Concerning the scandal men tried to make of Woodhull's ideas on sexual freedom, Stanton wrote in *The Revolution:*

> We have had enough women sacrificed to this sentimental, hypocritical prating about purity. . . . This is one of man's most effective engines for our division and subjugation. He creates the public sentiment, builds the gallows, and then makes us hangmen for our sex. We have crucified the Mary Wollstonecrafts, the Fanny Wrights, the George Sands, the Fanny Kembles of all ages. . . . Let us end this ignoble record. . . . If Victoria Woodhull must be crucified, let men drive the spikes and plait the crown of thorns.

The Revolution, based on the motto "Men, their rights and nothing more; Women, their rights and nothing less," was one of the most important contributions of the National. Like many of the feminist journals of today, it provided a forum for debate, gave the movement direction, and was key to reaching out and winning over new allies. Otherwise sympathetic supporters of the National repeatedly urged Stanton to give the paper a more moderate name, but she stood firm, saying: "The establishing of woman on her rightful throne is the greatest of revolutions. . . . A journal called 'The Rose-bud' might answer for those who come with kid gloves and perfumes to lay immortelle wreaths on the monuments which in sweat and tears we have hewn and built; but for us, and that great blacksmith of ours who forges such red-hot thunderbolts for Pharisees, hypocrites and sinners, there is no name but 'The Revolution.'"

After the Civil War, the situation of women workers changed drastically. Production of the equipment required to wage the war had stimulated industrial development in the North. Many women whose husbands had been killed or crippled in the war were forced to go to work, and out of desperation accepted low wages and sweatshop conditions. The range of jobs available to women as a source of cheap labor expanded far beyond employment in the textile industry. The typewriter, originally considered too mechanically complex for women to operate, began to be demonstrated by women in store windows in the 1870s and gradually became our domain. The invention of the telephone opened up jobs as switchboard operators.

Throughout the 1860s and 1870s, countless attempts to form their own unions were made by female sales workers, tailors, textile workers, printers, laundresses, and many others. By 1886, the Knights of Labor had chartered 113 Women's Assemblies.

All these attempts to raise women's wages and upgrade their working conditions, however, proved short-lived and sporadic. Women were not sure of how to organize against their economic oppression, did not have money for strike funds and publicity, and were not supported by male workers.

The National was actively involved in the struggles of working women. Anthony organized many Working Women's Associations and was an invited speaker at some trade-union conventions. The trade-union movement's appreciation of the National's role came to an end, however, when Anthony began encouraging women to break strikes. She claimed scabbing was the only way women would ever learn skilled trades. Anthony was pushed to this decision by the AFL, which had a formal position against sexual discrimination in employment, yet systematically denied women access to skilled jobs or to training programs, viewing them as "temporary" workers in the labor force between pregnancies. Anthony's stand, combined with the disclosure that *The Revolution* was being printed in a "rat" office paying below union-scale wages, brought the wrath of the trade-union movement down on the suffragists.

One cause of this controversy was that neither the feminists nor the trade unionists fully understood the double nature of woman's oppression—that is, both as a female and as an exploited worker. The feminists did not grasp the necessity for the working class to assert its power through weapons such as strikes, and labor ignored the fact that women are a specially oppressed sector of the working class.

Between 1870 and 1910, 480 campaigns in 33 states were undertaken for woman's suffrage. Both the American and the National focused on the frontier states, feeling that equality would be more readily grasped by pioneers who, by necessity, did not consider women helpless creatures with weak nervous systems. Few of us today can imagine the tortuous journeys the suffragists made through the frontier, traveling on sleighs, stage coaches, open wagons and on foot, and speaking from both stages and tree stumps to countless backwoods meetings that were often mobbed by antisuffragists. Often, housewives slammed doors in the faces of the suffrage workers, informing them they had all the rights they needed or that their husbands would provide for them. Other women were more responsive, and it was the pennies and dimes from these women that kept the woman's rights movement alive. Petitions, a way the disenfranchised could be heard, were especially important, but more often than not the petitions were merely laughed out of state assemblies.

It was on the frontier that the first victories for woman's suffrage were won. Both Wyoming and Utah gave women the vote while they were still territories. (There was a severe shortage of women on the frontier, and it has been speculated that Wyoming passed woman's suffrage to encourage a migration of women. There is evidence that the Mormons passed suffrage in Utah to increase the voting weight of their religion.) When antisuffrage forces threatened to block Wyoming's application for statehood because females could vote there, the territorial government vowed, "We will stay out of the Union a hundred years rather than come in without woman's suffrage." Colorado and Idaho in 1893 and 1896 were the next two victories, but between 1896 and 1910 no further states were won over.

Anthony and Stanton were behind these victories. As Stanton wrote in her memoirs, "Night after night by an old-fashioned fireplace we plotted and planned the coming agitation, how, when and where each entering wedge could be driven. Every right achieved . . . was contended for inch by inch." Stanton continues with a description of her working relationship with Anthony:

In thought and in sympathy we were one, and in the division of labor we exactly complemented each other. In writing, we did better work than either could alone. While she is slow and analytical in composition, I am rapid and synthetic. I am the better writer, she the better critic. She supplied the facts and statistics, I the philosophy and rhetoric, and together, we have made arguments that have stood unshaken through the storms of long years; arguments that no one has answered.

The growing strength of the woman's movement and its steady steps toward suffrage forced its opponents (referred to simply as "antis") to make explicit the era's notion of woman's place. At the root of their arguments was the belief that women are by nature infantile and irrational. A minister of the day expressed this: "The excessive development of the emotional in her nervous system ingrafts on the female organization a neurotic or hysterical condition which is the source of much of the female charm when it is kept within due restraint. In moments of excitement, it is liable to explode in violent paroxysms. Every woman therefore carries this power of irregular, illogical and incongruous action and no one can foretell when the explosion will come."

Suffragist Anna Howard Shaw responded to this attack:

Women are supposed to be unfit to vote because they are hysterical and emotional. . . . I had heard so much about our emotionalism that I went to the last Democratic National Convention to observe the calm response of the male politicians. . . . I saw men jump upon the seat and throw their hats in the air and shout "What's the matter with Champ Clark?" Then, when these hats came down, other men would kick them back in the air, shouting at the top of their voices, "He's all right." Then I heard others howling for "Underwood, first, last and all the time." No hysteria about it—just patriotic loyalty, splendid manly devotion to principle. And so they went on until 5 in the morning—the whole night long.

The family was seen as a miniature political unit. The man supposedly cast his vote as a political representative of his family, expressing his wife's opinion for her, and acting as her link to the outside world. It was felt that woman was too delicate for the turbulence of the mire of politics, and that she should be above it, not in it. As a rationalization for her inequality, woman was told that she was the higher form of life, more refined and sensitive than man. For her to invade man's sphere of politics would be retrogressive.

As men came to realize that woman's suffrage would have repercussions beyond a woman's simply dropping the ballot in the box once a year—that it would involve a reassessment of woman's role—they launched a slanderous campaign predicting the dire results of suffrage. They projected women buttonholing strange men on the streets, urging them to vote for "the handsome candidate." They predicted that if women became politically informed in order to cast their vote, political disagreements between husbands and wives would result and the divorce rate would skyrocket. They predicted that suffrage would lead to child neglect as women became politically involved, and this in turn would create juvenile delinquency.

The pioneering days of the woman's rights movement ended around 1890. A new generation of women emerged who were already benefiting from the gains in status that their older sisters had won. By 1890, there were 2,500 women with college degrees. Although they still earned only half of what men earned, women reached 17.5 percent of the labor force, and constituted 36 percent of all professional workers. This figure had only gone up to 40 percent sixty years later.

Rapid industrialization in the United States crowded more and more people, including a huge number of immigrants, into urban centers and created widespread poverty. Many women, alarmed by this trend, became active in combatting such problems as lack of sanitation and disease in the urban slums and child labor, and in supporting labor's right to organize, prison reform, and woman's legal rights.

The Women's Christian Temperance Union, the largest group of the period, has been grossly misrepresented. Rather than being a vehicle for wild-eyed, hatchet-wielding fanatics, as it is depicted, the WCTU tackled a problem especially crucial to working-class women. Alcoholism was one of the many social problems generated by slum life. An alcoholic husband could take a woman's wages away from her, leaving her with no means of feeding the family, since in many states a woman's pay was legally her husband's property. Since with the ballot women could vote the saloons out of business, the WCTU worked closely with suffrage forces.

In 1890 the National and the American healed their twenty-year breach and reunited as the National American Woman's Suffrage Association (NAWSA), marking a new stage in the woman's rights movement. The demand for suffrage became its focus. To both groups it was clear that the contradiction between the Victorian morality which insisted that women were happy slaves, and the increased exploitation of women because of their deepening social and economic independence, had reached a point where masses of women were convinced they deserved the right to vote.

The period following 1890 was one of great contradictions. United States imperialism was on the rise and began to spread throughout Latin America and the Far East. A growing number of strikes made labor a target for government attack. Union organizing attempts during this period were branded as "anarchist plots" and strikers were brutalized.

In order to justify the brutal exploitation of both the working class at home and the colonial peoples, the ruling class whipped up a campaign of racism that permeated all aspects of American life. The right to vote was forcibly taken from many of the recently enfranchised Black men. Jim Crow policies were savagely instituted throughout the South and racist policies intensified in the North.

The depth and all-pervasive character of the racist campaign had a conservatizing effect on all the radical and labor organizations of this period. "Progressivism" was in vogue, offering legislative reform as the means of curing all ills. The Progressives sought to patch up capitalism, to weed out corruption, but not to challenge capitalism in any basic way. The woman's suffrage movement was an integral part of this reformist movement, sharing its strengths and weaknesses.

During this period the Comstock Act was passed. Anthony Comstock was president of the New York Society for the Suppression of Vice, and his act allowed the Post Office to refuse to mail "morally offensive literature." This was construed to mean all literature that attacked marriage and the family. Birth-control pioneer Margaret Sanger was one of the many feminist victims of this strictly enforced law.

The Beecher-Tilton affair indicated the temper of the times. In her paper, Victoria Woodhull exposed the fact that preacher Henry Beecher, first president of the AWSA, was apparently having an affair with one of his parishioners, Elizabeth Tilton, also involved in woman's rights. A close friend of both of them, Woodhull claimed she disclosed the affair because Beecher was not being open, as Woodhull was, about his rejection of monogamy. Before the day was over, copies of Woodhull's paper were selling for forty dollars each. Again, Woodhull became the center of a national scandal. The Beecher-Tilton trial was one of the most sensational in history and everyone involved, including Woodhull, was forced to flee the country to escape the widespread public outrage.

Around this time, Stanton and Anthony's public attacks on marriage and the family came to a halt.

The NAWSA began to propagandize around the moral impact women could have on government. One suffragist went so far as to say, "The state is but the larger family, the nation the old homestead, and . . . in this national home there is a room and a corner and a duty for 'mother.'" Statistics were gathered on the moral superiority of women, proving they were the majority of churchgoers and the minority of prisoners. Suffragists promised that a female electorate would vote for higher penalties for rapists and would end wars forever. They said to the men in power: The government needs woman's virtues. Let us have the vote and we will be housekeepers in politics, and sweep away the corruption of the world.

Thus the NAWSA was no longer demanding the vote as a democratic right in itself, but as a means by which women could help uphold the morality of bourgeois society. No longer stressing the inherent equality between men and women, suffragists dwelt on the ways women were different and accommodated their outlook to the maternal mystique of the Victorian period.

Once having departed from their original arguments, the suffragists' adaptation went one step further. To satisfy its need for a large, docile, easily exploited working class, imperialism made "social Darwinism," construed to indicate that the Anglo-Saxon was the highest form of human being, a popular philosophy. As a result, the suffrage movement began to viciously slander the new immigrants, saying it was an indignity for the daughters of 1776 to be ruled by foreign and Black men. Anna Howard Shaw, onetime president of the NAWSA, said, "Never before in the history of the world have men made former slaves the political superiors of their former mistresses."

Another NAWSA president, Carrie Catt, wrote: "The government is menaced with great danger. That danger lies in the votes possessed by the males in the slums of the cities and the ignorant foreign vote. There is but one way to avert the danger—cut off the vote of the slums and give to women the ballot."

Northern suffragists produced statistics showing there were more native-born women than immigrant men, indicating woman's suffrage could counteract this "menace." In the South, they pointed out that there were more white women than Black men and women combined, which would insure the continuation of white supremacy. Delegates from Black women's clubs were excluded from conventions; Black women were segregated in suffrage parades; and, in certain years, Black woman's suffrage groups were asked not to apply for membership in the NAWSA since it would taint the Association's image.

The fact that suffragists would appeal to the most racist, chauvinistic instincts was especially disgraceful for a group having its origins in the abolition movement. This is one of the most ignoble episodes in the history of the struggle. Fortunately, suffragists retreated from this position around the turn of the century when they realized the need to win support from immigrant voters. In fact, New York State was won for woman's suffrage in 1917 largely through the big immigrant vote in New York City.

One of the many myths perpetuated about woman's suffrage is that the fight for the vote was strictly a middle-class movement, irrelevant to working women. This was far from true. It was clearly in the interests of working women to win suffrage. Mainly, they wanted the vote as women whose equal claims to citizenship were being denied. They also saw the vote as one other way they could improve their working conditions. Lacking the power of the vote, working women's demands were not taken seriously by muckraking reform politicians of the period. This was demonstrated in 1910 when women workers attempted to get the mayor of New York to appropriate funds for factory inspections. He said to them: "Ladies, why do you waste your time year after year in coming before us for this appropriation? You have not a voter in your constituency and you know it, and we know it, and you know we know it."

One of the holidays the women's liberation movement has recently reclaimed had its origins in working women's demand for the vote. On March 8, 1908 (a day German socialist Clara Zetkin was later to declare International Women's Day), women garment workers marched through New York City's Lower East Side protesting sweatshop conditions and demanding the vote. Working women later testified in Albany, New York, at annual hearings on the suffrage bill, sponsored meetings for suffragists, marched in suffrage parades, and organized suffrage rallies outside their plant gates.

During this same period (1890-1910), the number of women workers doubled to eight million and their plight became the focus of much social reform. At a mass meeting in 1890 of female retail shop workers, a Consumers' League was formed to publicize their low pay and hazardous working conditions. Aided by socialists and suffragists, a "White List" was devised, consisting of the names of those few factory employers who met the shop women's demands: complying with protective legislation, not employing child labor, paying a minimum wage, and giving a shorter workweek.

The early 1900s saw the growth of many unions which were largely female, the International Ladies' Garment Workers Union being the best example. At the 1903 American Federation of

Labor convention, a National Women's Trade Union League was formed for women in unions. For many years, the NWTUL functioned as the women's movement within organized labor and labor's voice within the suffrage struggle. Although it worked closely with the AFL, it existed because of the AFL's indifference to women workers. It was thought that women's wages were too low for them to pay full union dues, and that they did not remain in the labor force long enough to be worth organizing. The NWTUL played a crucial role in the many labor strikes of the time, publicizing strike demands and raising strike funds.

The period from 1896 to 1910 is known as the "doldrums period" in woman's rights. Not a single state referendum was won during these years, despite ceaseless campaigns. Susan B. Anthony's death in 1906 seemed to create a void in leadership no one else was able to fill. Her life had spanned almost sixty years of struggle for woman's rights, and the fact that she died without seeing women win one of the most basic of rights—the vote— must have demoralized the second generation of suffragists, many of whom had already fought for twenty-five years. But this slump soon ended and a third stage in the movement began— ushered in by two events in 1910: the victory of suffrage in Washington State and Alice Paul's return from England.

The militant wing of the British suffrage movement, led by the Pankhursts, had abandoned trying to win the vote through gentle persuasion. British women burned down several buildings, including churches and castles, mutilated valued museum art objects, "stormed" the House of Commons, and blew up mailboxes in their attempts to win the vote.

They felt that attacks on property would force the British government to take notice of their demand. Not even high society and diplomatic social occasions were immune from their attack. A common tactic was to infiltrate these tightly guarded receptions, either by using an invitation a wealthy supporter had turned over to them or by posing as a servant. In the middle of the gathering, the secret "suffragette" would jump up on the table, unfurl a "Votes for Women" banner, and launch into a speech. After one such occasion, the headlines read "Suffragette disguised as lady penetrates Foreign Office reception."

So deep was the commitment of the suffragettes to the struggle that one deliberately gave her life to it. On Derby Day in 1913, Emily Davison, wearing the purple, white, and green colors of the suffragettes, threw herself under the King's horse and was trampled to death. For their actions, hundreds of suffragettes were thrown into prison, where they organized hunger strikes.

Alice Paul, an American studying in England, had been among them. Inspired by her experiences in England, she was determined to revitalize the American movement. Until this point, suffrage forces had been working on a state-to-state basis, feeling they had a better chance to win the states one by one than to get a federal amendment passed. Paul criticized this approach, claiming that by confining themselves to a few states at a time, women were not feeling their full force as a national movement, and the powers in Washington, D.C., were escaping attack. She proposed that energies be concentrated on getting a federal amendment passed, followed by state-by-state ratification.

The first step Alice Paul took was to organize a demonstration of ten thousand in Washington, the day before President Wilson's inauguration, to dramatize the large numbers of women expecting the vote from his administration. The demonstrators were attacked by patriotic onlookers, had their clothes torn off, were pelted by burning cigars and knocked to the ground. Troops were sent in to restore order, only to create more of a riot by themselves beating the women.

Finding the NAWSA hesitant to turn toward the national amendment, Paul set up the Congressional Union in 1913 as an auxiliary to the NAWSA. Her strategy was to hold the party in power—with President Wilson as its symbol—responsible for women's being denied the right to vote, and to harass the Democrats until they found it was politically inexpedient to oppose woman's suffrage. Paul's chief contribution to the once again rising suffrage movement was that she persuaded women to stop begging and begin demanding.

In 1914 the Congressional Union was expelled from the NAWSA, charged with refusing to participate in state campaigns and using confrontational tactics that were alienating potential supporters. In 1916 the Congressional Union held its own convention and formed an independent Woman's Party. Not a political party in the usual sense, the Woman's Party had no intention of vying to take power. It had just one plank: winning the vote. Recent victories had given women the vote in twelve states, which composed one-fourth of the electoral college. The tactic of the Woman's Party was to convince the women in these twelve states to vote against, and defeat, Wilson. As the party explained:

One thing we have to teach Mr. Wilson and his party—and all on-looking parties—is that the group which opposes national suffrage for women will lose women's support in twelve great commonwealths controlling nearly a hundred electoral votes; too large a fraction to risk, or to risk twice, even if once risked successfully. If that is made clear, it is a matter of total indifference to the Woman's Party—so far as suffrage is concerned—who is the next president of the United States.

Peace was the major issue of the 1916 Wilson-Hughes presidential election; the slogan was "Vote for Wilson. He kept us out of war"—to which the Woman's Party retorted, "Vote against Wilson. He kept us out of suffrage." The WP, with a membership of over fifty thousand (as compared to two million in the NAWSA), conducted such a vigorous campaign against Wilson in the suffrage states that it was hazardous for him to travel there. One Woman's Party campaigner, Inez Milholland, toured California, speaking night and day and sleeping only on trains. At a rally in San Francisco, she asked "Mr. President, how long must women wait for liberty?" and, with these words, collapsed dead from exhaustion. Mass memorial meetings were held across the country to protest the unnecessary death of this young woman who fell with liberty on her lips.

Wilson was reelected, carrying ten of the twelve suffrage states. In Illinois, however, the only state where votes were tallied by sex, women voted against him two to one. The important thing was that the suffrage movement forced the Democratic leaders onto the defensive. They felt compelled to put out as much literature on suffrage as they did claiming to be for peace.

Then the slaughter of the first imperialist war began; Wilson brought the United States into it in 1917. As in the Civil War, women were asked to defer their own demands to the war effort. Although the NAWSA insisted there was no contradiction between waging the war and giving women the vote, they did enough war work to avoid any questioning of their patriotism.

The Woman's Party, however, continued to fight only on the suffrage front. They picketed the White House with slogans such as "Democracy should begin at home." Noting that women in Russia were given the vote after the tsar was overthrown, they contrasted "free Russia" to "Kaiser Wilson." When envoys representing Kerensky came to the White House and suffragists unfurled banners telling the Russians that the U.S. was a democracy in name only, the Wilson regime began to crack down. Shots were fired into the Woman's Party headquarters. All picketing in front of the White House was made illegal, and mass arrests were made of those who continued.

Nonetheless, on Bastille Day, pickets were there with a banner reading "Liberté, Egalité, Fraternité." When its bearers were arrested, two more women stepped forward to take their place; they were arrested, and so it continued with over five hundred women arrested in all. Those found guilty were sent to prison workhouses where they went on hunger strikes, demanding to be treated as political prisoners, and were force-fed. The arrests never curtailed the movement. There was always another woman who stepped forward and took the place of her arrested sister. The brutal treatment the women received in the prison workhouses became a national scandal. Finally public pressure became so great that all the suffragists were unconditionally released and their sentences nullified.

The NAWSA played no part in the White House demonstrations. Its president, Carrie Catt, visited Wilson quite frequently and felt she was slowly moving him toward active support of women's suffrage. While their sisters were being so brutally treated in jail, the NAWSA never issued a single word in protest or in defense of their right to picket. In fact, they went so far as to carry signs in demonstrations denouncing the left wing of the movement and declaring that they were in no way affiliated with the Woman's Party.

As during the Civil War, the First World War brought large numbers of women out of the home and into either war relief work or industry. Women worked in many fields—from steel mills to explosives factories to the railroads. It would seem that this performance, combined with the large number of states where women were already voting with no disastrous effect on the home, would have put an end to the antisuffrage hysteria. The last ten years of the struggle for suffrage, however, brought forth the most organized opposition.

The opponents represented the interests of a more and more powerful capitalist class which based itself on the permanent existence of an oppressed class of wage earners. Since women were the most underpaid and least organized sector of the working class, American capitalism was not eager to give them the vote. The ruling class feared that the equality of the sexes implied by granting the vote might rouse women from their docility and cause them to start asserting their right to equal wages and job opportunities. They anticipated that women would support protective laws for workers.

This was especially true in the East, where industrial and business interests actively campaigned against woman's suffrage. The oligarchy of wealth began a red-baiting campaign, linking woman's suffrage to struggles to improve working-class conditions, and linking both to creeping socialism. In the South, the racist ruling class was flagrantly defying the Fifteenth Amendment by disenfranchising Black men and was not eager to have to deal with Black women as citizens.

In the West, the liquor industry feared women would vote prohibition in and claimed the woman's suffrage movement was the same organization as the Women's Christian Temperance Union. The mobilization of the Oregon liquor industry to defeat a state referendum on woman's suffrage was typical. They calculated that fifty thousand votes were necessary to defeat the referendum. Each of the two thousand liquor retailers in Oregon was notified and instructed to get twenty-five votes against suffrage—from employees, customers, small businessmen—or else they might be out of business.

This antisuffrage alliance of the South, East, and West was joined by the political machines controlling the government. Women had promised they would clean up politics, going so far as to say that if they had been allowed to vote, Tammany Hall would never have come to power. So woman's suffrage posed a threat to the pillars of the government, based on corruption and bribery.

These forces were careful to disguise the real reasons for their opposition. While behind the scenes they whipped up hysteria in their own ranks and bribed politicians to vote against woman's suffrage, publicly they put out propaganda that was an outrageous insult to the mass woman's suffrage movement. One such leaflet read: "Housewives! You do not need the vote to clean out your sink spout. A handful of potash and some boiling water is quicker and cheaper. Good cooking lessens alcoholic craving quicker than a vote on a local option. Why vote for pure food laws when you can purify your ice box with saleratus water?"

In 1911 the antis set up the National Women's Organization to Oppose Suffrage. Its members claimed to speak for the majority of their sex when they insisted they did not want to be burdened with the vote. They produced "Spiderweb Charts" tracing the suffrage movement straight to Moscow and implying it was a Bolshevik plot aimed at the "nationalization" of women. The NAWSA quickly exposed this group as simply a female front for big money interests, especially the liquor industry.

The urgency with which these interests geared into blocking woman's suffrage indicated that victory was imminent. It was.

The contradiction between the role women were playing in the country and the fact that they were denied the vote became an international scandal which those who claimed the United States was a model democracy were having a hard time explaining. Although the Sixty-fifth Congress had been barred from taking up anything but war measures, it set January 10, 1918, to vote on the woman's suffrage amendment.

The vote itself contained much drama. A New York representative left the deathbed of his wife, an ardent suffragist, to cast his "aye" vote and returned home to attend her funeral. The amendment carried, 274 to 136, exactly the two-thirds majority required.

It took until May 20, 1919, to win the Senate vote. Ahead lay ratification in thirty-six states—the most tedious task of all. The antis made their last desperate attempts to block victory and managed to gain control of all the Deep South states, meaning suffrage had to carry in almost all the rest. Finally, on August 26, 1920, the thirty-sixth state, Tennessee, ratified. Women everywhere voted in elections that year, making the United States the twenty-seventh country to extend the right to vote to women. Despite the fact that women's voting has become so accepted, it was not until 1969 that the last state, Georgia, ratified the Nineteenth Amendment.

An issue which had united women for seventy years was won. The struggle had involved three generations, with none of the founding leaders living to see the 1920 victory. The two wings of the women's movement continued to work separately, and since many women felt the vote was the only change in status women needed, both groups entered the 1920s with their membership severely reduced. The NAWSA changed its name to the League of Women Voters and began encouraging women to register to vote and educating them about the candidates.

The Woman's Party campaigned for further legal rights for women, especially their right to guardianship of their children, and this was won in sixteen states. Soon tiring of working to pass hundreds of individual bills countering sexual discrimination in each individual state, the Woman's Party drafted the Equal Rights Amendment which would make any form of sexual discrimination unconstitutional. The ERA was first introduced to Congress in 1923 (where it was promptly voted down), and for a time it appeared that the women's movement would unite around this issue. But it did not.

Some feminists bitterly opposed the amendment, claiming that equality under the law would be in conflict with and wipe out the special protective laws for women workers that groups such as the Consumers' League had struggled to win. The Woman's Party itself was divided over the issue of protective legislation, with some members favoring the extension of laws to cover male workers as well, and others claiming the laws had only limited women's advancement and should be done away with. That is, the women's movement went through a debate over the ERA similar to that which the feminist movement is carrying on today. The earlier movement, however, was neither on the upswing nor as broadly supported as our movement today, and the debate over equal rights in the 1920s effectively paralyzed the women's movement and demoralized many of its leading activists.

During the past year a debate over the value of the fight for the vote has emerged in the women's liberation movement. Some sisters dismiss the struggle for the vote as reformist, occasionally even implying that women would be better off today if the right to vote had never been won. The decline of feminism after the 1920 victory is blamed on the fight for the ballot. This argument is set forth, for example, in an article by Waltraud Ireland in the May 1970 issue of *Leviathan* titled "You Don't Need the Vote to Raise Hell."

Ireland attacks what she calls "the single-minded preoccupation with suffrage, at the expense of all other and possibly more important struggles to free women." Because of this focus, she asserts, "the feminists failed to produce an integrated, radical analysis either of the nature of women's oppression or its relationship to the basic social and economic structures of capitalist society." This argument leads Waltraud Ireland to conclude that "success killed the women's movement."

The criticisms that Ireland raises are very important. It is true that during the last years of the struggle there were certain issues—most notably the question of the family—that the suffragists did not tackle. It is also true that the movement died out shortly after the vote was won and that it took fifty years for the struggle to be revived. One of the challenges ahead of the women's liberation movement today, in the heat of our struggle to write ourselves into history, is to begin to study the reasons why the movement became conservatized and died out.

One aspect of this work will be to dig out of obscurity the

letters, essays, and novels that former suffragists must have written after 1920, giving their observations on what happened. Lacking such empirical data from the participants, however, we can at this point only begin to discuss some general outlines of an answer.

The first place to look for a partial answer is in the general social and political conditions under which the suffrage movement declined. It has been pointed out that the struggle of women for their liberation has ebbed and flowed according to the extent of general radicalism in the society. It began in the era before the Civil War (a revolutionary period when an entire system—the southern plantation system based on slavery—was challenged and overthrown) and died out in the years of reaction after the First World War. During the 1920s, the liberalism of the Progressive Era was replaced by the hysteria of the Red Scare. Strikes were brutally smashed. Although there were scattered upsurges, such as the Garvey Black nationalist movement (which never spilled beyond the large city ghettos), these were exceptions to the general trend of conservatism. It was clearly not a good period for any movement for social change.

Under these conditions, rebellion and discontent took a personal, rather than organized political form. During the 1920s many feminists who had fought for the vote shifted their rebellion to the realm of individual sexual freedom and dress reforms as embodied by "flapperism." And in a certain sense, the fight against female oppression did continue in this area. For just as the "sexual revolution" of the 1960s contributed to the liberation of women by making us conscious of the need for greater control of our bodies and sexual needs, and by demonstrating to increasing numbers of women that sex need not be linked to reproduction, the flapper era gave women the right to drink and smoke in public, to shed their bodies of restrictive clothing, and to enjoy pursuits beyond the parlor. Of course, like the current "sexual revolution," the increased freedom only highlighted the treatment of women as sex objects. But the fighting spirit of our sisters did not disappear entirely when the flapper came in. It was simply driven underground.

The suffragists had not focused on the vote out of fear of other issues. In fact the woman's rights movement had raised and won other demands: the right to control their own wages, an end to child labor, protective legislation. But our sisters chose suffrage as the focus of struggle because they correctly felt that so long as such a blatant assertion of their inferiority under law existed, their basic dignity and humanity were denied. Their rage over this kept the woman's rights movement going during periods when there were few other struggles for social change.

In her criticism, Ireland is correct in pointing out that one weakness of the woman's rights movement which contributed to its decline was its illusions about the vote and what women would be able to do with it. This reflected deeper illusions about the nature of society itself and the possibility of winning complete liberation under capitalism. Even the most radical suffragists—women such as Stanton and Anthony—did not understand the need for a socialist revolution.

Ireland chides the suffragists for their "lack of response to the development of socialist movements and theory." But this was a two-way street. A look at the Socialist Party, which grouped together most of the progressive forces in society in the period before the war, indicates that early socialists in the United States did not understand feminism, either. An article in the February 1970 *Radical America* by Mary Jo Buhle on "Women and the Socialist Party, 1901-1914" discusses how the SP counterposed feminism to the class struggle.

"Feminism," Buhle claims, "proved as an agitational issue to be unacceptable to the bulk of the socialist movement. . . . Feminism, they held, was middle class, and socialist-feminists were warned that their activity could swamp the party with nonwage earning elements. . . . Thus even a mild variety of Feminism, which clearly disavowed free love and destruction of the family, was feared as a divider of the movement along sex lines." The SP downgraded the Black struggle along similar lines, saying that it took forces away from the larger fight against capitalism. That is, like many groups today that call themselves socialist, the SP saw independent movements of oppressed groups as competitors in the fight for socialism.

Thus both the suffragists and the old SP were one-sided in their understanding. The suffragists did not understand the need for socialist revolution, and many socialists did not see that the feminist struggle and the struggle around the right to vote were part of the struggle for socialism, and therefore did not support the suffragist movement.

It is a serious mistake, however, for feminists of today to claim that the seventy-year struggle of our sisters for the right to vote was not worth the effort. One need only recall the arguments presented against suffrage to see how much winning this fight made inroads into chauvinist concepts men held of women, and women's own feelings of inferiority. We are that much ahead, because if the suffragist movement had not existed, or had failed, the fight for the vote would have to be among our top priorities today.

The great victory of the suffrage movement was that it demonstrated, for the first time, that women can organize *as women* to raise demands that meet our needs, and that through struggle we can *win* these demands.

Unlike those of the 1920s, the conditions today for an all-out attack on women's "traditional" roles are overripe. The tremendous technological expansion and immense social wealth we see in the United States today make demands for birth control, childcare centers, and equal pay for women seem much more reasonable and attainable than ever before. It is only by being conscious of these changes in the objective conditions, which lay the basis for the feminist movement, that we can understand the reasons why the woman's rights movement died out and why the movement of today has so much more potential. It was not the struggle for the vote that killed the woman's rights movement. It was that struggle which kept it alive.

Unlike the movement of the 1920s, the new women's liberation movement has arisen in a period of growing and deepening radicalization. An entire generation of young women is becoming convinced of the fact that capitalism is historically and forever incapable of ending our oppression. The capitalist verbiage of freedom rings hypocritical when this is systematically denied to 51 percent of the population because of sex.

Granting women the vote was something capitalism could do begrudgingly, but the demands that the movement is raising today—for free, twenty-four-hour child care, for free abortion on demand, for an end to job discrimination, for roles beyond that of wife and mother—cannot be fully met under this system. Although important partial victories can be won here and there, the logic of the demands taken together—that women should have full control over their lives, freed from responsibilities within the family—cannot be tolerated by a system dependent on the continued oppression of women. It is participation in struggles to win these things—struggles over such concrete issues as equal pay—that the masses of women will come to an understanding of the need for socialism.

Feminists today already have fewer illusions than our sisters did about what a particular change within the capitalist system can do. No longer seeking simply integration into a rotten system, women today are demanding a total change in the institutions that oppress them. Through the examples of the Black struggle and the antiwar movement, women today have acquired far more faith in themselves and in the power of mass movements to change society. We will no longer tolerate anyone putting our struggle last.

That the struggle for woman's suffrage was unable to end the oppression of women—the oldest, deepest form of oppression in history—does not mean that it failed or should not have been waged. It simply means that those of us in the feminist movement today must pick up our sisters' struggle, inspired by their example, and carry it further. We can be confident that this time around we can carry the revolution they began to completion.

How Women Won the Vote

Stephanie Coontz (1976)

The widespread interest in women's history, stimulated by the feminist movement, has called forth scores of books devoted to the first wave of American feminism—the woman suffrage movement. Many of these add valuable data to the descriptive history of that movement, though the most comprehensive is still Eleanor Flexner's *Century of Struggle* (Harvard University Press, 1959). But there has yet to come out a first-rate, thoroughgoing analysis of the actual process by which woman suffrage was achieved.

The woman suffrage movement offers an instructive case study in how women can fight for their rights and win. The process of winning female suffrage contradicts the view—prevalent among bourgeois politicians, news media, and academics—that the way to win demands for social justice is to curry favor with influential politicians, compromise with reactionary prejudices of sectors of the population, and generally "lie low" so as not to antagonize one's enemies. However, none of the major histories of the suffrage struggle recognize this important lesson.

Most recent historians have correctly rejected the idea that woman suffrage was freely bestowed on the nation by a magnanimous ruling class. They have studied the internal development of the women's movement, assuming, as William O'Neill puts it, "that the choices women made or failed to make were important and deserving of analysis." (*Everyone Was Brave,* Quadrangle, 1971.)

The most widely accepted analysis of the suffrage movement is the one presented by Aileen Kraditor in *The Ideas of the Woman Suffrage Movement 1890-1920* (Anchor, 1971). Kraditor argues that the early women's rights movement was organized around

391

idealistic demands for "justice," but that by the turn of the century the movement had entered a new, opportunistic phase. In this period the suffragists based their case on "expediency," coupling the suffrage campaign with elitist, racist, nativist, and anti-working-class arguments where they believed this would garner support.

She writes: "To win support from needed allies they compromised . . . perhaps more than the requirements of the alliances dictated." But her conclusion remains that "the hard facts of political life" *did* dictate some accommodation to racism and conservatism—"concessions to political expediency."

There are two major problems with Kraditor's thesis. First, her periodization of the movement into early idealism and later opportunism is incorrect. Second, her assumption that concessions to racism and elitism were in fact "expedient" is not supported by the evidence.

The first women's rights convention in America was held at Seneca Falls, New York, in 1848. It was organized by female abolitionists who in the process of working against slavery had also discovered their own oppression as women. There was a close alliance between abolitionism and women's rights up through the Civil War.

At the end of the war, however, the movement was effectively divided by the issue of suffrage for Black males. The women's movement split into two groups over whether to support the Fifteenth Amendment, and did not reunify until 1890, when the two merged into the National American Woman Suffrage Association. During this period a large section of the woman suffrage movement exhibited racism, a reflection of widespread attitudes in American society. This was the period of the final compaigns against the Indians, the consolidation of Jim Crow, the first imperialist ventures, and the anti-Chinese hysteria in the West.

However, contrary to Kraditor's thesis, there was a growing rejection of the most flagrant forms of racism *after* 1900, despite the conservatism of many sections of the movement. For example, although the NAWSA took a hands-off policy toward a 1908 Mississippi scheme to exclude Blacks and to link woman suffrage with opposition to interracial marriage, the plan was opposed energetically by Alice Stone Blackwell, the recording secretary of the NAWSA and editor of *Woman's Journal.*

By 1911 the NAWSA was reorganized, drastically reducing

southern influence. The most virulent racists, led by Kate Gordon, broke off to form the Southern States Woman Suffrage Conference.

Elizabeth Freeman reported in the May 1913 *Socialist Woman,* a Socialist Party publication, that suffragists at conventions held in St. Louis and Chicago had refused to accept the racial barriers erected by the hotel managements.

Kraditor is right to point out that many suffragists argued their case in the most reactionary terms, often claiming that woman suffrage would increase the white and native-born vote. In the South and Midwest many women proposed poll qualifications that would exclude Black and Chicano women from the vote. Some state suffrage organizations gave support to bills that limited voting rights to whites or to the wealthy. Such actions and attitudes marred the woman suffrage movement from its inception right up to the adoption of the Nineteenth Amendment, and it is true that they increased in the latter part of the nineteenth century.

But this is not the whole story, or even most of it. The NAWSA as a national organization never endorsed the limited suffrage bills proposed in some states, and in some cases actually led battles against its affiliates doing so. Thus in 1910 Lena Morrow Lewis was able to report to the Socialist Party convention:

> When it came in Illinois to the point where the association had a chance to come out and perhaps get a limited suffrage, the state president for Illinois said: "No; we stand for the unlimited suffrage. . . . We want all that we stand for, and shall fight until we get it."
>
> In Oklahoma the Democratic party said to the suffrage association: "You can have this measure go through provided you will stand with us on the grandfather clause." . . . That virtually disfranchises the entire colored race. The suffrage association [representative] . . . said to the women there: "I don't know where you stand, but if you stand for this grandfather clause I quit the state of Oklahoma; the National Association will withdraw its support and we shall have nothing to do with you." And the women of the Woman's Suffrage Association of Oklahoma every last one of them stood against that grandfather clause.

Suffrage and the Labor Movement

Some suffrage leaders had strong middle-class prejudices against working people and did not support labor unions. In the 1870s, for example, Elizabeth Cady Stanton wrote in *The*

Revolution—the organ of what most historians term the more radical wing of the suffrage movement—that "the worst enemies of Woman's Suffrage will ever be the laboring class of men."

Stanton was wrong, however, and by the turn of the century many suffragists had reconsidered their antilabor views in the light of facts demonstrating that working people represented a powerful ally of the women's movement.

In Colorado, for instance, the only difference between the 1877 vote, where suffrage lost, and the 1893 vote, where it won, was that the second campaign, according to Alan Grimes in *The Puritan Ethic and Woman Suffrage* (Oxford University Press, 1967), "had the support of the labor organizations," which it had lacked in 1877.

In 1896 Susan B. Anthony and Ida Husted Harper examined the defeat of suffrage in California and concluded it could not be attributed to the "lower classes" and the foreign-born. In *The History of Woman Suffrage* they noted that in San Francisco, "a larger percentage of the opposition" came from "the district containing the so-called best people." In 1906 Anna Howard Shaw was impressed that, though woman suffrage was defeated in Oregon, it received the most votes in the hours when working men went to the polls.

Thus Kraditor and Grimes (who makes the strongest argument for the association of woman suffrage with reactionary causes) are wrong to imply that there was any connection between conservatism and victory.

In a number of states, gains for woman suffrage were closely connected with the work of the Socialist Party. In Nevada, Kansas, and New York especially, the SP threw itself into the suffrage battle. The *Rochester Herald* complained on November 7, 1917, "Wherever the Socialist . . . propaganda made headway . . . the suffrage vote was automatically increased."

In New York, it was the vote of immigrant workers that won the woman suffrage bill in the election of 1917.

Kraditor is correct—despite her oversimplified periodization—to see a racist and conservative period replacing the early alliance between abolitionism and women's rights. She fails, however, to note a third stage, beginning around the turn of the century, when the suffrage movement increasingly turned its attention to working-class and immigrant voters and adopted a more radical stance both in theory and in practice.

By 1900, concessions to racism and conservatism had certainly not ended, but there was clearly a new thrust to suffrage work. Suffrage leaders had begun to see what most recent historians have missed: racist, nativist, and elitist "concessions" won nothing for the woman suffrage struggle. Woman suffrage was won *in spite of* such concessions.

The decisive factor in winning woman suffrage was not the movement's concessions to racism or conservatism but the massive education and action campaign led by women's organizations. These succeeded in mobilizing tens of thousands of women in direct action to win the vote. It was the cumulative impact of two decades of mass mobilizations that changed the consciousness of the American people on the question and forced the government onto the defensive, setting the stage for the victory of woman suffrage in 1920.

The emphasis on mass action increased markedly after 1900. The Boston Equal Suffrage Association, founded in 1901, began to experiment with new kinds of campaigning. Its members went door to door in immigrant and working-class neighborhoods and held outdoor soapbox rallies and street meetings.

In 1907 Harriot Stanton Blatch organized the Women's Political Union, an association of factory and professional women, and began to hold mass parades for suffrage.

The following account gives an idea of the impact of these mass actions. It is a description by Jesse Williams of a suffrage march that he watched from the window of a men's club on New York's Fifth Avenue.

It was Saturday afternoon and the members had crowded behind the windows to witness the show. They were laughing and exchanging the kind of jokes you would expect. When the head of the procession came opposite them, they burst into laughing and as the procession swept past, laughed long and loud. But the women continued to pour by. The laughter began to weaken, became spasmodic. The parade went on and on. Finally there was only the occasional sound of the clink of ice in the glasses. Hours passed. Then someone broke the silence. "Well boys," he said, "I guess they mean it!"

In 1913 Alice Paul and Lucy Burns established the Congressional Union. It played a key role in conceiving and spearheading the mass activity that brought the suffrage issue to the fore in this period. The CU began as part of the NAWSA, but soon broke with the parent organization over tactics.

The CU favored militant, dramatic actions and demonstrations, and wanted to make the amendment a national political issue. The NAWSA favored a lower-key, state-by-state approach. The CU oriented particularly toward working women, organizing public meetings and deputations of working women to Congress, and participating in labor demonstrations with suffrage banners and leaflets.

The Congressional Union merged with Blatch's WPU to form the Woman's Party.

Though the Woman's Party had only 50,000 members, compared with the NAWSA's 2 million, and could not have won suffrage on its own, it did provide the impetus for the final push, and its politics deserve more serious examination than they have been given by historians. Where historians have taken note of the CU and the WP, they have emphasized their militant tactics, ignoring the political approach that underlay them.

This is evident in historians' treatment of two main issues that divided the women's movement in its final period—the question of subordination of the movement to Democratic or Republican party politics, and the attitude to be taken toward World War I.

The CU and its successor, the Woman's Party, took a position that the suffrage movement should not directly support any candidate, but should actively oppose candidates who refused to support suffrage or who belonged to a party in office that refused to implement woman suffrage.

Of course, such a "protest vote" in practice amounted to voting for the other of the two parties of big business, neither of which represented the interests of the masses of women or of working people. But the CU position reflected an attempt by women to find a way of keeping suffrage alive as a political issue during the election campaign.

The NAWSA's alternative—to support the individual campaign of anyone who voted for woman suffrage—proved itself to be a dead end. NAWSA members bartered away their potential to force the Democratic and Republican parties to endorse suffrage. Since the NAWSA bound itself to support any individuals who endorsed suffrage, the Democrats and Republicans could run prosuffrage candidates in strong suffrage districts and antisuffrage candidates everywhere else. Prosuffrage candidates felt no need to win their party to support of suffrage, since they knew they would get the suffrage vote anyway.

In the presidential election of 1916 the suffragists of the WP put the Democrats so much on the defensive that for the first time there was a major discussion of suffrage at the national convention. On Wilson's inauguration day the WP organized a demonstration of 1,000.

By 1916 the Woman's Party had brought the federal suffrage amendment back to life and put so much pressure on the NAWSA that its convention adopted a plan that was unabashedly drawn from Alice Paul's national strategy. Known as Carrie Catt's "Winning Plan," this for the first time committed the NAWSA to a national campaign on the federal amendment. Previously the NAWSA had been for campaigning only in certain states.

World War I

A second area where historians have generally misinterpreted the effects of suffragists' actions is in relation to the war. The outbreak of World War I was greeted differently by the Woman's Party and the NAWSA. Although the NAWSA did not suspend its suffrage work entirely, it subordinated that work to the war effort. The WP refused to do that. It picketed the White House daily, and continued even after picketing was made illegal.

Alice Paul built a "watchfire" in an urn outside the White House gates. Every time Wilson made a speech abroad that referred to freedom, Paul and her supporters burned a copy of the speech in the watchfire.

The NAWSA refused to support the demonstrations and even refused to go on record against the brutal treatment that Woman's Party members received in jail. Carrie Catt was so convinced that she was winning Wilson over that she was able to justify spying on the WP for him—letting Wilson know in advance when they had made plans that might embarrass him.

Flexner calls the NAWSA's actions "realistic" and O'Neill goes so far as to claim that the "principal contribution [of the WP's pickets] was to seriously embarrass an administration that had already been won over to woman suffrage by the patient, skillful efforts of Carrie Chapman Catt and the NAWSA."

But there is no evidence that at the time of the WP demonstrations Wilson had any intention of implementing woman suffrage. His tentative wooing of the suffrage movement during his reelection campaign, for example, had come to an abrupt end with his victory. There *is* considerable evidence that he was highly embarrassed, especially in his international dealings, by the WP actions, and that he very much wanted them stopped. At one point, after a well-publicized watchfire incident, he cabled two senators asking them to support the suffrage amendment.

Certainly the WP could not have won woman suffrage on its own, but it did revitalize the movement and pull the NAWSA into the kind of mass action that tipped the scales and won the vote.

Again and again, though, historians of the woman suffrage movement have downgraded the role of mass action in the final victory. Thus Gail Parker, in her introduction to Elizabeth Cady Stanton's autobiography, *Eighty Years and More,* says rather approvingly: "Mrs. Catt and her closest co-workers were realists, not romantic heroines; tacticians, not radical ideologues." They differed "from the pioneers at Seneca Falls . . . in the political tactfulness of their elitism" (Schocken, 1971).

What Parker calls "romantic heroines" and "radical ideologues" play an important role in history, not as individuals but to the extent that they win the movement to mobilizing the only kind of force that can effectively confront the ruling-class monopoly of wealth and political power—mass agitation and action independent of the ruling class. That is what the radicals of the Congressional Union, the Woman's Party, and the other uncompromising activists and fighters for woman suffrage did, and without them, women like "General Catt"—as so many historians describe the NAWSA leader—would not even have had a cause, much less an army.

The only way to explain why woman suffrage won when and as it did is to throw out any idea that history is made by friendly persuasion, brilliant deals, reliance on individual politicians, or accommodation to threats of "backlash." Women won the vote first by forcing discussion of a demand that most people considered too "extreme" and then by organizing themselves as an independent force, whose demands—not appeals or concessions—were backed up by mass mobilizations.

The suffrage movement not only won concrete gains so that the present feminist movement could start from a higher stage, but it left us a set of lessons on how to organize in the future. It proved that women can organize in their own interests, gain mass support, and win victories even against the determined opposition of the capitalist power structure.

It indicates the futility of any strategy based on counterposing women's rights to the rights of Blacks and other working people, who are potentially powerful allies of the women's liberation struggle. Despite all the opportunist concessions and compromises that mar its history, woman suffrage was won only after women mobilized in direct, independent action around the principled demand of suffrage for all. This is a particularly important lesson in the present economic crisis, when the ruling class is once more stepping up its attempts to divide the working class along race and sex lines as one way of frustrating struggles for social justice.

About the Authors

STEPHANIE COONTZ, one of the pioneers of the Berkeley student movement, played a leading role in organizing the nationwide demonstrations against the Vietnam War. She currently teaches American history at The Evergreen State College in Olympia, Washington.

DIANNE FEELEY is active in the New York chapter of the National Organization for Women, speaking and debating on behalf of the Equal Rights Amendment and organizing classes on women's history. She is also a member of the Socialist Workers Party.

HARRY FRANKEL is a socialist writer, editor, and publisher. He is the author of *Sam Adams and the American Revolution* (Pathfinder, 1971).

DERRICK MORRISON is a longtime activist in the Black movement and a contributor to *Black Liberation and Socialism* (Pathfinder, 1974). As a reporter for the *Militant* he covered such events as the Attica rebellion and the first National Black Political Convention.

GEORGE NOVACK is a leading writer and lecturer on Marxist philosophy and history. He has also been involved for many years in the defense of civil liberties.

JEAN Y. TUSSEY, a leader of the Socialist Workers Party, is active in the International Typographical Union and helped found the Cleveland Coalition of Labor Union Women. She also edited *Eugene V. Debs Speaks* (Pathfinder, 1970).

DEBBY WOODROOFE is a feminist writer, speaker, and organizer. She has also worked in the Vietnam antiwar movement and in defense of Latin American political prisoners. Her article in this collection also appeared as a pamphlet under the title *Sisters in Struggle*.

JOHN G. WRIGHT was the principal translator of Leon Trotsky's works into English until his death in 1956. He also wrote on Soviet affairs and questions of Marxist theory.

Index

FURTHER READING

American Labor Struggles, 1877-1934
by Samuel Yellen $4.45*

Blacks in America's Wars
by Robert W. Mullen $1.45*

Democracy and Revolution
by George Novack $2.95

Eugene V. Debs Speaks
Edited by Jean Y. Tussey $2.95

The First Ten Years of American Communism
by James P. Cannon $3.45

Labor's Giant Step: Twenty Years of the CIO
by Art Preis $3.95

The Origins of American Marxism
by David Herreshoff $2.75*

Racism, Revolution, Reaction, 1861-1877
by Peter Camejo $3.45*

Understanding History
by George Novack $2.45

PATHFINDER PRESS, INC.
410 West Street, New York, N.Y. 10014

* A Monad Press book distributed exclusively
by Pathfinder Press